PORTLAND

HOLLYANNA McCOLLOM

Contents

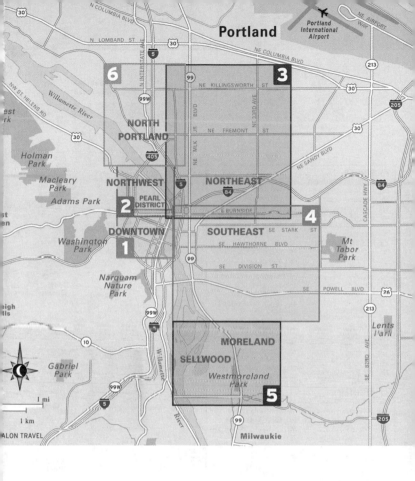

Maps

SEE MAP 2

SIGHTS
10	ZOOBOMB MONUMENT	79	SALMON STREET SPRINGS
24	NORTH PARK BLOCKS	89	PORTLANDIA
40	ANKENY PLAZA	91	THE OLD CHURCH
62	CENTRAL LIBRARY	92	SOUTH PARK BLOCKS
66	PIONEER COURTHOUSE SQUARE	94	IRA KELLER FOUNTAIN
78	MILL ENDS PARK		

RESTAURANTS
6	BLUE STAR DOUGHNUTS	46	PAZZO RISTORANTE
7	MASU SUSHI	47	MOTHER'S BISTRO & BAR
9	CACAO	48	MAMA MIA TRATTORIA
11	JAKE'S FAMOUS CRAWFISH	49	TASTY N ALDER
18	KENNY AND ZUKES	52	RISTORANTE ROMA
19	STUMPTOWN COFFEE ROASTERS	58	RED STAR TAVERN & ROAST HOUSE
23	COURIER COFFEE	61	BLUEPLATE LUNCH COUNTER & SODA FOUNTAIN
25	SAUCEBOX	69	URBAN FARMER
28	EL GAUCHO	80	SOUTHPARK SEAFOOD GRILL & WINE BAR
29	LITTLE BIRD	81	PICNIC HOUSE
31	PORTLAND CITY GRILL	88	HIGGINS
33	VOODOO DOUGHNUT	90	VERITABLE QUANDARY
44	IMPERIAL		

NIGHTLIFE
4	CRYSTAL BALLROOM	34	SHANGHAI TUNNEL
13	SCANDALS	37	KELLS IRISH PUB
14	THE ROXY	59	KELLY'S OLYMPIAN
22	PEPE LE MOKO	60	JACK LONDON BAR
26	BAILEY'S TAPROOM	75	LUC LAC VIETNAMESE KITCHEN
32	DANTE'S		

ARTS AND CULTURE
2	ARTISTS REPERTORY THEATRE	85	PORTLAND CENTER FOR THE PERFORMING ARTS
42	OREGON MARITIME CENTER AND MUSEUM	86	PORTLAND ART MUSEUM
74	AUGEN GALLERY	87	OREGON HISTORICAL SOCIETY
84	OREGON SYMPHONY	95	OREGON BALLET THEATRE

SPORTS AND ACTIVITIES
1	PORTLAND TIMBERS	71	SECRETS OF PORTLANDIA TOUR
36	PEDAL BIKE TOURS	73	GLOWING GREENS
38	HAUNTED PUB	76	WATERFRONT PARK
41	WATERFRONT BICYCLE	77	WATERFRONT BIKE LOOP
67	BEST OF PORTLAND WALKING TOUR	98	PORTLAND BY SEGWAY TOUR
68	EPICUREAN EXCURSION		

SHOPS
5	TANNER GOODS	55	UNDER U4 MEN
8	ODESSA	56	MAGPIE
15	DANNER	63	CRAFTY WONDERLAND
16	UNION WAY	64	REAL MOTHER GOOSE
21	FRANCES MAY	65	MARIO'S
39	PORTLAND SATURDAY MARKET	72	PIONEER PLACE MALL
50	KNIT/PURL	82	JOHN HELMER HABERDASHERY
51	CANOE	97	PORTLAND FARMERS MARKET AT PORTLAND STATE UNIVERSITY
54	FINNEGAN'S TOYS & GIFTS		

HOTELS

3	HOTEL DELUXE	43	HOTEL LUCIA
12	CRYSTAL HOTEL	45	HOTEL VINTAGE PORTLAND
17	THE MARK SPENCER HOTEL	53	THE SENTINEL
20	ACE HOTEL	57	HOTEL MONACO
27	THE BENSON HOTEL	70	THE NINES
30	COURTYARD BY MARRIOTT PORTLAND CITY CENTER	83	HEATHMAN HOTEL
		93	HOTEL MODERA
35	EMBASSY SUITES PORTLAND DOWNTOWN	96	THE RIVERPLACE HOTEL

0   100 yds
0   100 m
DISTANCE ACROSS MAP
Approximate: 0.9 mi or 1.5 km

© AVALON TRAVEL

MAP 2

SEE MAP 6

**NORTHWEST
INDUSTRIAL**

PACIFIC PWY

NW VAUGHN ST

NW TERMINAL ST

NW UPSHUR ST

1
To R, H 2

NW VAUGHN ST

To 3 R

30

NW THURMAN ST

NW THURMAN ST
4 R S 5

NW SAVIER ST

NW RALEIGH ST

NW QUIMBY ST

NORTHWEST

NW PETTYGROVE ST

NW 19TH AVE

405

NW OVERTON ST

NW 14TH
& Northrup

**NW Northrup
& 22nd**

7 R
8 H

Streetcar

**NW 18th
& Northrup**

NW NORTHRUP ST

R 6

NW 23RD AVE

**NW 23rd
& Marshall**

✚

**NW Northrup
& 21st**

NW MARSHALL ST

Legacy Good
Samaritan
Hospital

**NW Lovejoy
& 21st**

✚

**Physicians and
Surgeons Hospital**

Streetcar

NW 16TH AVE

11

NW LOVEJOY ST

NW Lovejoy
& 22nd

R 9

**NW Lovejoy
& 18th**

NW KEARNEY ST

C 10

NW KEARNEY ST

14 R 12,13
S

35 S

15 S 16
S 17
S 18

23
S

NW JOHNSON ST

NW 20TH AVE

19
S 20

NW IRVING ST

NW 22ND AVE

NW 21ST AVE

NW HOYT ST

Couch Park

NW 19TH AVE

NW 18TH AVE

NW 7TH AVE

22 R 21
S

24 N

25 N

NW GLISAN ST

C 32

44 C

26 N
29 H 27 N
28 R

NW FLANDERS ST

405

NW EVERETT ST

NW 23RD PL

30 S

NW KING AVE

NW 20TH PL

NW 20TH AVE

0   100 yds

0   100 m

DISTANCE ACROSS MAP
Approximate: 0.9 mi or 1.5 km

31 R
W BURNSIDE ST

© AVALON TRAVEL

SEE MAP 1

☺ SIGHTS

38 JAMISON SQUARE
41 JEAN VOLLUM NATURAL CAPITAL CENTER
60 THE BREWERY BLOCKS
61 THE ARMORY
65 POWELL'S CITY OF BOOKS
68 UNION STATION
70 PORTLAND VINTAGE TROLLEYS
73 LAN SU CHINESE GARDEN
83 CHINATOWN GATE

☺ RESTAURANTS

1 INDUSTRIAL CAFE AND SALOON
3 ST. HONORÉ BOULANGERIE
4 OLYMPIA PROVISIONS
6 RED ONION
7 PALEY'S PLACE
9 LAUGHING PLANET
11 LE HAPPY
12 BAMBOO SUSHI
13 SALT & STRAW
21 MOONSTRUCK CHOCOLATE CAFÉ
28 SMOKEHOUSE 21
31 COFFEEHOUSE NORTHWEST
33 THE DAILY CAFÉ
37 IRVING STREET KITCHEN
43 ¡OBA!
45 ANDINA
46 BYWAYS CAFÉ
53 ISABEL PEARL
53 CUPCAKE JONES
55 THE PARISH
58 PRASAD
63 LITTLE BIG BURGER
74 HOUSE OF LOUIE
82 MI MERO MOLE

☺ NIGHTLIFE

24 VOICEBOX
25 POPE HOUSE BOURBON LOUNGE
26 BARTINI
27 M BAR
44 10 BARREL
54 TEARDROP COCKTAIL LOUNGE
56 JIMMY MAK'S
57 DESCHUTES BREWERY AND PUBLIC HOUSE
59 FAT HEAD'S
69 WILF'S RESTAURANT AND BAR
71 REMEDY
75 DARCELLE XV SHOWCLUB
78 EMBERS
79 GROUND KONTROL
87 HOBO'S
88 BOILER ROOM

☺ ARTS AND CULTURE

10 COMEDYSPORTZ
32 MISSION THEATER
47 BULLSEYE GALLERY
50 ELIZABETH LEACH GALLERY
62 PORTLAND CENTER STAGE
66 WATERSTONE GALLERY
72 SEQUENTIAL ART GALLERY + STUDIO
76 MUSEUM OF CONTEMPORARY CRAFT
77 BLUE SKY GALLERY
80 BRODY THEATER
84 OREGON JEWISH MUSEUM

☺ SPORTS AND ACTIVITIES

39 JAMISON SQUARE
42 FIREBRAND SPORTS
85 UNDERGROUND PORTLAND
86 CYCLE PORTLAND

☺ SHOPS

5 SMITH TEAMAKERS
14 3 MONKEYS
15 NW 23RD AVENUE
16 OH BABY!
17 GILT
18 KIEHL'S
19 LUSH COSMETICS
20 ZELDA'S SHOE BAR
22 BLUSH BEAUTY BAR
23 NW 21ST AVENUE
30 ELEPHANTS DELICATESSEN
34 PEARL SPECIALTY MARKET & SPIRITS
35 REI
36 LIZARD LOUNGE
40 MABEL & ZORA
48 MOULE
49 LEXIDOG BOUTIQUE AND SOCIAL CLUB
51 HANNA ANDERSSON
64 LUCY ACTIVEWEAR
67 URBAN FAUNA
81 UPPER PLAYGROUND

☺ HOTELS

2 SILVER CLOUD INN
8 INN AT NORTHRUP STATION
29 PORTLAND INTERNATIONAL GUESTHOUSE

SEE MAP 1

SEE MAP 2

SEE MAP 4

© AVALON TRAVEL

S SHOPS

1	IN OTHER WORDS
2	TURN! TURN! TURN!
10	GREEN BEAN BOOKS
13	GRASSHOPPER
17	THE PENCIL TEST
18	ALBERTA ARTS DISTRICT
30	POPINA SWIMWEAR
34	AMENITY SHOES
36	TITLE WAVE BOOKSTORE
41	FOSTER & DOBBS
48	FUREVER PETS
50	WELL SUITED
51	BELLA STELLA
52	THINGS FROM ANOTHER WORLD
62	LLOYD CENTER
63	REDUX
71	POLLIWOG

H HOTELS

6	CARAVAN: A TINY HOUSE HOTEL
29	KENNEDY SCHOOL
46	LION AND THE ROSE VICTORIAN BED & BREAKFAST INN
49	PORTLAND'S WHITE HOUSE
59	HOTEL EASTLUND
61	DOUBLETREE BY HILTON HOTEL PORTLAND
68	EVERETT STREET GUESTHOUSE

DISTANCE ACROSS MAP
Approximate: 2.7 mi or 4.3 km

0 500 m
0 500 yds

SIGHTS
- 42 BEVERLY CLEARY CHILDREN'S SCULPTURE GARDEN
- 55 HOLLYWOOD THEATRE

RESTAURANTS
- 5 THE GRILLED CHEESE GRILL
- 7 SWISS HIBISCUS
- 9 HELSER'S ON ALBERTA
- 11 AVIARY
- 12 ZILLA SAKE HOUSE
- 14 PETITE PROVENCE
- 15 CIAO VITO
- 16 THE CHEESE PLATE
- 20 LA BONITA
- 23 D.O.C.
- 24 AUTENTICA
- 25 BEAST
- 26 YAKUZA
- 27 THE COURTYARD RESTAURANT
- 33 NED LUDD
- 35 SMALLWARES
- 36 TORO BRAVO
- 44 THE RHINELANDER
- 45 MILO'S CITY CAFÉ
- 47 CADILLAC CAFÉ
- 53 SWEET BASIL
- 54 CHAMELEON RESTAURANT & BAR
- 66 RETROLICIOUS
- 69 PIX PATISSERIE
- 70 SCREEN DOOR
- 72 TABLA
- 75 NAVARRE
- 76 LAURELHURST MARKET

NIGHTLIFE
- 8 EVERY DAY WINE
- 21 CORK A BOTTLE SHOP
- 31 SPARE ROOM
- 37 SECRET SOCIETY LOUNGE
- 39 WONDER BALLROOM
- 40 BILLY RAY'S NEIGHBORHOOD BAR
- 64 NOBLE ROT
- 67 PAIRINGS
- 74 ANGEL FACE

ARTS AND CULTURE
- 3 CURIOUS COMEDY
- 19 ANTLER GALLERY
- 22 GUARDINO GALLERY
- 28 KENNEDY SCHOOL
- 32 PORTLAND PLAYHOUSE
- 56 HOLLYWOOD THEATRE
- 73 THE LAURELHURST

SPORTS AND ACTIVITIES
- 4 EVERYBODY'S BIKES
- 43 GRANT PARK
- 57 PORTLAND WINTERHAWKS
- 58 PORTLAND TRAIL BLAZERS
- 60 THE PORTLAND BREW BUS
- 65 PORTLAND ROCK GYM

SEE MAP 3

KERNS

SEE MAP 2

St. Francis Park

Lone Fir Cemetery

BUCKMAN

Colonel Summers Park

Ladd Circle Gardens

Ladd Circle Park & Rose Gardens

Rose Gardens

HOSFORD-ABERNETHY

Willamette River

SEE MAP 1

Ross Island Bridge

Ross Island　SEE MAP 5

⭐ SIGHTS

19 VERA KATZ EASTBANK ESPLANADE
28 LONE FIR CEMETERY
61 LADD CIRCLE PARK & ROSE GARDENS

Ⓡ RESTAURANTS

1 LE PIGEON
10 KEN'S ARTISAN PIZZA
14 LE BISTRO MONTAGE
18 CLARKLEWIS
29 WILD ABANDON
32 SLAPPY CAKES
33 VIKING SOUL FOOD
34 EUROTRASH
40 POTATO CHAMPION
41 CAFÉ CASTAGNA
46 FRIED EGG I'M IN LOVE
59 APIZZA SCHOLLS
69 DOT'S CAFÉ
71 BRODER
73 CLAY'S SMOKEHOUSE
75 LAURETTA JEAN'S
79 SCOOP
80 WY'EAST PIZZA
82 YOKO'S JAPANESE RESTAURANT

Ⓝ NIGHTLIFE

4 DOUG FIR
5 EASTBURN
7 LOVECRAFT BAR
11 THE GOODFOOT
13 SLOW BAR
15 LE BISTRO MONTAGE
23 RUM CLUB
24 HOLOCENE
26 CRUSH BAR
35 HORSE BRASS PUB
36 LUCKY LABRADOR BREW PUB
60 SAPPHIRE HOTEL
64 ALADDIN THEATER
66 BAR AVIGNON
67 NIGHT LIGHT LOUNGE
68 REEL 'M INN
70 DOTS
77 VICTORY BAR
81 HOPWORKS URBAN BREWERY

Ⓒ ARTS AND CULTURE

2 THIRD RAIL REPERTORY THEATRE
8 MIRACLE THEATRE GROUP
21 OREGON MUSEUM OF SCIENCE AND INDUSTRY
25 REVOLUTION HALL
38 HELIUM COMEDY
39 NEWSPACE CENTER FOR PHOTOGRAPHY
52 DO JUMP!
54 BAGDAD THEATER & PUB
72 CLINTON STREET THEATER

SEE MAP 3

DISTANCE ACROSS MAP
Approximate: 3.2 mi or 5.1 km

LAURELHURST

Laurelhurst Park

SUNNYSIDE

SOUTHEAST

RICHMOND

Sewallcrest Park

SEE MAP 5

ⓐ SPORTS AND ACTIVITIES

12	LAURELHURST PARK	27	COLONEL SUMMERS PARK
20	VERA KATZ EASTBANK ESPLANADE	37	CLEVER CYCLES
22	WILLAMETTE JETBOAT EXCURSIONS	62	PEDALOUNGE

ⓢ SHOPS

6	MUSIC MILLENNIUM	49	KIDS AT HEART
9	FOOD FIGHT	50	JACKPOT RECORDS
16	CARGO	51	PRESENTS OF MIND
17	GUARDIAN GAMES	53	BUFFALO EXCHANGE
30	NOUN: A PERSON'S PLACE FOR THINGS	55	MEMENTO
31	BELMONT STREET	56	PASTAWORKS
42	EXCALIBUR BOOKS AND COMICS	57	POWELL'S HOME AND GARDEN
43	HAWTHORNE BOULEVARD	58	MUSE ART & DESIGN
45	CROSSROADS MUSIC	63	DUCHESS CLOTHIER
47	HOUSE OF VINTAGE	65	EDELWEISS
48	IMELDA'S AND LOUIE'S SHOES	74	COFFEE KIDS

© AVALON TRAVEL

ⓗ HOTELS

3	JUPITER HOTEL
44	HAWTHORNE HOSTEL
76	BLUEBIRD GUESTHOUSE
78	EVERMORE GUESTHOUSE

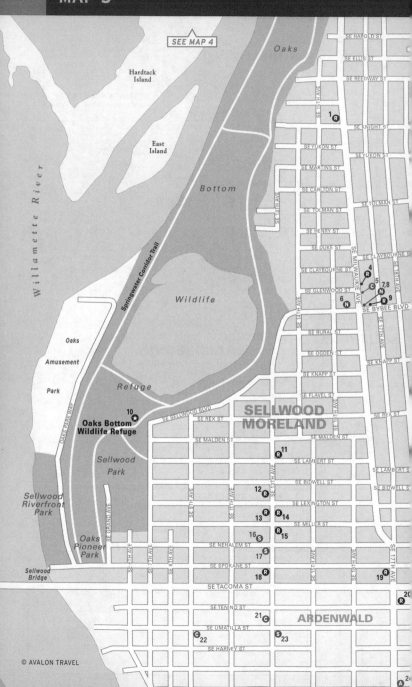

SEE MAP 4

Willamette River

Hardtack Island

East Island

Oaks

Bottom

Wildlife

Springwater Corridor Trail

Refuge

Oaks Amusement Park

Oaks Park Way

Sellwood Riverfront Park

Oaks Pioneer Park

Sellwood Bridge

Sellwood Park

10 ★
Oaks Bottom Wildlife Refuge

SE HAROLD ST
SE ELLIS ST
SE REEDWAY ST

1 R

SE KNIGHT ST
SE YUKON ST
SE YUKON ST
SE MARTINS ST
SE CARLTON ST
SE TOLMAN ST
SE TOLMAN ST
SE HENRY ST
SE DUKE ST

SE CLAYBOURNE S
4 R
SE CLAYBOURNE ST
5 C **7,8** N
SE GLENWOOD ST
6 N
9 R
SE BYBEE BLVD

SE RURAL ST
SE OGDEN ST
SE KNAPP ST
SE KNAPP ST
SE FLAVEL ST
SE REX ST

SELLWOOD MORELAND

SE SELLWOOD BLVD
SE REX ST
SE MALDEN ST
SE MALDEN ST

11 R

SE LAMBERT ST
SE BIDWELL ST
SE LAMBERT S
SE BIDWELL S

12 R
SE LEXINGTON ST
13 R **14** R
SE MILLER ST
16 S
15 R
SE NEHALEM ST
17 S
SE SPOKANE ST
18 R
19 R

SE TACOMA ST
20 R
SE TENINO ST
21 C
ARDENWALD
SE UMATILLA ST
22 C
23 S
SE HARNEY ST

SE 13TH AVE
SE MILWAUKIE AVE
SE 18TH AVE
SE 17TH AVE
SE 13TH AVE
SE 9TH AVE
SE 11TH AVE
SE GRAND AVE
SE 17TH AVE

© AVALON TRAVEL

A

SEE MAP 4

Crystal Springs Pond

Reed College

Crystal Springs Rhododendron Garden

Crystal Springs Lake

Eastmoreland Golf Course

SE WOODSTOCK BLVD

Westmoreland Park

SE TACOMA ST

SIGHTS
- 2 CRYSTAL SPRINGS RHODODENDRON GARDEN
- 10 OAKS BOTTOM WILDLIFE REFUGE

RESTAURANTS
- 1 PAPA HAYDN
- 4 FAT ALBERT'S
- 9 SABURO'S
- 11 A CENA RISTORANTE
- 12 CHOWDAH
- 13 ZENBU
- 14 JADE TEAHOUSE & PATISSERIE
- 15 MEKONG VIETNAMESE GRILL
- 18 GINO'S
- 19 BERTIE LOU'S
- 20 MIKE'S DRIVE-IN

NIGHTLIFE
- 6 OAKS BOTTOM PUBLIC HOUSE
- 7 CORKSCREW
- 8 MUDDY RUDDER

ARTS AND CULTURE
- 5 MORELAND
- 21 12X16 GALLERY
- 22 PING PONG PUPPET MUSEUM

SPORTS AND ACTIVITIES
- 3 EASTMORELAND GOLF COURSE AND DRIVING RANGE
- 24 BIKE COMMUTER
- 25 SPRINGWATER CORRIDOR

SHOPS
- 16 CAMAMU
- 17 SOCK DREAMS
- 23 WELLS AND VERNE

0 — 300 yds
0 — 300 m

DISTANCE ACROSS MAP
Approximate: 2.2 mi or 3.5 km

NORTHWEST

Willamette River

OVERLOOK

NW NICOLAI ST
NW REED ST
© AVALON TRAVEL
NW 21ST AVE
30
NW SHERLOCK AVE
NW BALBOA AVE
NW FRONT AVE

N RIVER ST
N PORT CENTER WAY

DISTANCE ACROSS MAP
Approximate: 1.9 mi or 3.1 km
0
0
300 yds
300 m

Overlook Park

N GREELEY AVE
N OVERLOOK BLVD
N FAILING ST
N SHAVER ST

N MASON ST
N CONCORD AV
N COLONIAL AV
N LONGVIEW AV

Overlook Park

N OVERLOOK BLVD
N MASSACHUSETTS AVE
N INTERSTATE AVE
99W
5

SEE MAP 2

Overlook Park
N MONTANA AVE

7
6

405
99W

N MISSISSIPPI AVE
30
31
32
Albina/
Mississippi

N RUSSELL ST
N KNOTT ST
N GRAHAM ST

N MISSOURI AVE
N MICHIGAN AVE
13
14
15
16
17
18
19
20
12
10
11

Mississippi Avenue

8
9
5

N ALBINA AVE
N BORTHWICK AVE
N KERBY AVE

23
22
21

N BEECH ST
N FAILING ST

ROSIE

Unthank Park

N COMMERCIAL AVE
N SHAVER ST
N MASON ST

N PAGE ST
N ROSS AVE

N BORTHWICK AVE
N KERBY AVE

N IVY ST
N FREMONT ST

N HAIGHT AVE
N GANTENBEIN AVE
N VANCOUVER AVE

Lillis Albina Park

ELIOT
N PAGE ST

Hospital
Emanuel
Legacy

N GRAHAM ST
NE STANTON ST
N GANTENBEIN AVE

Dawson Park

N MORRIS ST
NE MONROE ST
NE COOK ST
NE IVY ST
NE KNOTT ST

SEE MAP 3

26
25
24
27
28
29

N WILLIAMS AVE
NE CLEVELAND AVE

SIGHTS
1 PENINSULA PARK & ROSE GARDEN
15 MISSISSIPPI AVENUE

RESTAURANTS
4 THE FISH AND CHIP SHOP
5 FIRE ON THE MOUNTAIN
9 THE BIG EGG
10 FRESH POT
13 GRAVY
17 LAUGHING PLANET
22 ¿POR QUE NO?
23 FLAVOUR SPOT
27 EAT AN OYSTER BAR
30 WIDMER GASTHAUS

NIGHTLIFE
3 THE OLD GOLD
6 THE ALIBI
8 PROSTI
14 MISSISSIPPI STUDIOS
21 MISSISSIPPI PIZZA
24 TESOAFIA
25 BOX SOCIAL
26 5TH QUADRANT
32 MINT/820

SPORTS AND ACTIVITIES
2 PENINSULA PARK
28 YOGA SHALA

SHOPS
11 ANIMAL TRAFFIC
12 BLACK WAGON
16 MISSISSIPPI AVENUE
18 THE MEADOW
19 BRIDGE CITY COMICS
20 CD GAME EXCHANGE
29 SPIELWERK TCY'S

HOTELS
7 PALMS MOTOR HOTEL
31 WHITE EAGLE MOTEL

DISTANCE ACROSS MAP
Approximate: 12.5 mi or 20.1 km

1 mi
1 km

40
217
PACIFIC HWY W.
5
Raleigh Hills
26

Gabriel Park
35
36
33
34
R
37
R
38
R
32
R
31
R
10
99W
5
99W
405
Portland State University
Washington Park
Oregon Zoo
26
27
28
29
26
Council Crest Park
Narquam Nature Park
Oregon Health Sciences
SOUTHWEST

Tryon Creek State Natural Area
41
Lewis & Clark College
43
Lake Oswego
43

42
Elk Rock Garden
99

Willamette River
SE McLOUGHLIN BLVD
Oaks Bottom Wildlife Refuge
Hardtack Island
Ross Island
30
99
26
SOUTHEAST
SE HAWTHORNE BLVD
SE DIVISION ST
Mt. Tabor Park
13
14
Mt. Tabor Park

SELLWOOD
Westmoreland Park
MORELAND
Reed College
SE 28TH AVE
SE 39TH AVE
SE STEELE ST
16
WOODSTOCK
17
R
15
R
SE 45TH AVE
SE 52ND AVE
SE POWELL BLVD

99
Milwaukie
224
SE KING RD

Linwood
224
213
SE 82ND AVE
213
SE FOSTER RD
26
Lents Park
205
205
SE HAROLD ST
To 18
©AVALON TRAVEL

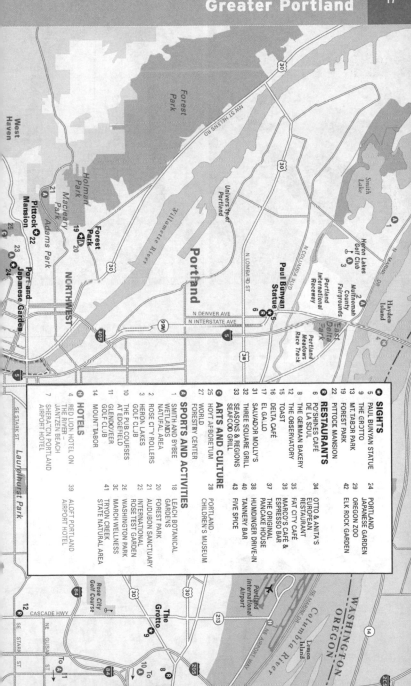

The rain may fall and the skies may be gray, but still they come to Portland. Visitors arrive in droves to see the green forests, snowcapped mountains, and winding trails. Food lovers come to sample the flavors of the Pacific Northwest and the flair of the creative chefs and mixologists who are finding their way onto the pages of the *New York Times*, *Travel + Leisure*, and *Bon Appétit*. Artists and musicians come to Portland to collaborate and learn. Every day the city swells in numbers thanks to the influx of people seeking to answer to the question, "Why is everyone so in love with Portland?"

The truth is, Portland is full of passionate and creative people because it is so contagious. People flock here to immerse themselves in the arts scene. Artists, playwrights, actors, and musicians have made this city a bohemian playground, rich with color, opulence, and inspiration. The collaborative energy and unbridled creativity make for happier living and generate an overarching artistic ecosystem.

Visitors are drawn to Portland for its unique personality and hospitable style. Thanks in part to its pioneering ancestors, Portland has all the stimulation and excitement of a big city and all the charm of a small town. It's hard not to feel like a local when you visit P-Town.

Whether you call it Portland, P-Town, Bridge City, or Stumptown, the city is what you make it. From the urban delights of the downtown Cultural District to the unspoiled wilderness of Forest Park, each corner of this DIY-centric city is bursting with that distinctive Portland energy. From the coffee shops and thrift stores of Hawthorne to the lounges and boutiques of the Pearl District, each neighborhood possesses its own unique voice, all of which lend themselves to the whimsical carnival choir of this dynamic city.

Clockwise from top left: fall foliage; an arch on St. Johns Bridge; water fountain, downtown; iconic Portland sign.

the Chinese New Year celebration at Lan Su Chinese Garden

Planning Your Trip

Where to Go

Downtown

Many of Portland's galleries and performing arts venues are in the heart of downtown, in an area known as the **Cultural District.** To the south is Portland's oldest neighborhood, **Old Town,** home to a number of great nightclubs and restaurants, as well as **Chinatown** and the beautiful **Lan Su Chinese Garden.**

Northwest and the Pearl District

Whether you're in the Pearl District or strolling NW 23rd, the northwest side of Portland is a **shopper's paradise** and the city's most fashionable spot for **galleries, restaurants, boutiques,** and urban living. Farther north, you'll find the area interchangeably known as **Nob Hill** or the **Alphabet District,** an immensely walkable area that is home to a number of Portland's most chic boutiques and **trendy restaurants.**

Northeast

In the midst of modern condos snuggled nicely with historic Victorian homes is the **Alberta Arts District,** where there are blocks of art galleries, studios, and restaurants. The **Irvington District** is where you'll find the Rose Garden Arena, Lloyd Center, and the Oregon Convention Center. To the north is the **Hollywood District,** with an iconic Byzantine-style movie theater, several burger shops, and international restaurants.

Southeast

The southeast is a vibrant and **wildly diverse** sector. **Hawthorne**

Boulevard and its sister, **Belmont Street,** are chock-full of restaurants and shops that are off the beaten path; **Clinton Street,** a six-block section of Southeast Portland, also houses a remarkably large number of locally favored stops.

Sellwood and Moreland

Rounding out the farthest edges of Southeast Portland and extending up to the area known as Woodstock, Sellwood and Moreland are two smaller areas collectively known as **Antique Row,** thanks to the large concentration of **vintage and antiques shops** that inhabit them. There are some lovely walking areas through the neighborhoods of **swank houses,** and you can easily spend a day strolling down some of the main streets—like **13th Avenue**—visiting **quaint shops** and nibbling on food from **homey cafés** and casual but chic eateries.

North Portland

The newest P-Town darling, NoPo is the affordable, **eclectic** home to many of Portland's imaginative newcomers. The influx of artistic energy has made for some remarkable transformations in the area, bringing **fun brew-pubs,** unique dining options, and several **popular bars.** Young and artsy **Mississippi Avenue** is one of Portland's best-kept secrets, with shops and cute cafés galore.

Greater Portland

The city of Portland spans **five quadrants,** but the greater Portland metro area includes a number of suburbs, neighborhoods, and outright cities that are as easy to get to as the other side of town. The hills of Southwest Portland house a number of drive-worthy **restaurants, parks, and natural retreats;** and a little jaunt down the freeway in any direction from the city proper can take you to some stops that perhaps even a few seasoned locals may not have discovered yet.

When to Go

Contrary to popular belief, it is not always raining in Portland. In fact, the metro area experiences less average rainfall per year than Atlanta, Birmingham, Houston, Indianapolis, or Seattle. If you want to avoid the **rainy season,** skip Portland in November, December, and January. If you don't mind getting a little wet, those months are great times to secure cheap hotel rates and catch seasonal attractions like ZooLights and the festival of new theater works, Fertile Ground Festival.

The best time for you to visit depends largely on what you plan to do when you are here. **Ski season** is often at its height between January and March, while **summer** (June through September) is a great time to come experience the city's open-air markets, gardens, and festivals, as temperatures tend to top out at 80-100°F (27-38°C) and days are often clear and dry.

The Three-Day Best of Portland

Portland has a lot to offer, and it can be hard to pack all of the city's charms into a weekend. Stick to one area a day and you can save money by skipping a rental car—you can access most of these places using public transportation or your own two feet.

Day 1

▶ Start your day with a hearty brunch at **Tasty n Alder** to prepare yourself for some walking. Fill up on French toast, charcuterie, and Bloody Marys and don't forget to try the chocolate potato doughnuts.

▶ When you've had your fill, head to Pioneer Courthouse Square, where you can meet up with the **Best of Portland Walking Tour.** Then continue your education at the **Oregon Historical Society,** where you can see the very penny that decided the fate of Portland's name.

▶ Pop over to the **Portland Art Museum,** which is just steps away and the home of more than 240,000 square feet of art.

▶ For a quick lunch, head over to the **food cart "pod" at SW Alder Street between 9th and 10th Avenues,** where there is a variety of delicious options.

▶ If you are hungry for some more culture, pick up theater tickets from the **Portland Center Stage** box office in the Brewery Blocks.

Little Bird is a modern American bistro with a French twist.

detail of Skidmore Fountain

Portland is filled with works of art, from its galleries to its shops to its streets. There are more than 1,000 pieces of public art on display for everyone to see. You can even down load an app (Public Art PDX) that will tell you all about each piece and where to find it.

Allow Me: This guy has been in more selfies than the average teenage girl. Also known as *Umbrella Man,* this bronze sculpture features a man with an umbrella with one hand raised as if hailing a cab. Because of his visibility in Pioneer Courthouse Square, he is often used as a meeting spot.

Animals in Pools: This series of fountains and bronze sculptures that line the blocks of Yamill and Morrison Streets between 5th and 6th Avenue are another popular photography spot, particularly with children. They feature bears, salmon, seals, beavers, deer, ducks, and otters. In 2014, the otters acquired their very own sweaters, knitted for them by "yarn bombers."

Kvinneakt: Better known as the "Expose Yourself to Art" lady, this life-size sculpture of a wind-swept nude was once featured in a poster with soon-to-be mayor Bud Clark, who held his raincoat open away from the camera, flashing the bronze lady in return.

Nepethes: These giant glass sculptures are some of the newest art pieces in Port land, and they have been receiving mixed reviews since they were erected in 2013 along Northwest Davis Street in Old Town. The bulbous pieces represent tropical carnivorous plants of the same name. At night, the statues are fully illuminated thanks to photovoltaic cells.

Portlandia: Arguably the city's most famous and not famous piece of art. She could have been our Statue of Liberty, but her image is fiercely protected by the artist who created her. So, you will never see her on a keychain.

Skidmore Fountain: On the other end of the spectrum from Nepethes is Skidmore Fountain, Portland's oldest piece of public art. It was designed after the fountains in Versailles that its namesake Stephen Skidmore saw over the course of his travels. He wished to have a gathering place that men, horses, and dogs could all drink from.

The People's Bike Library: Otherwise known as the *Zoobomb Pile,* this sculpture is a lot more than just art. It is also a bike rack, a bike lending library, and a visible testimony to the offbeat history of Portland. The piece was created in 2009 in honor of the Zoobombers, a group that meets weekly to ride down the west hills on child-size bicycles at unbelievable speeds.

Where to Spend a Rainy Day

Having fun on a rainy day is no problem in a town that is used to about 36 inches of rainfall per year. When things get wet, Portlanders usually just go on doing what they were doing. But even if you are not used to the rain, there are plenty of things to do during those long months of wet and gray.

If it is sprinkling:

- Take a hike in **Forest Park.** When it is damp, the park comes alive with smells of the trees. Many of the paths are paved, so it is pretty easy to avoid getting muddy.

- If nature is not your thing, do some exploring on **Mississippi Avenue.** The shops, coffeehouses and restaurants in close proximity make it easy to duck in and out while still enjoying the city.

At the Oregon Zoo, you can get up close and personal with the wildlife.

- For post-show late-night eats, walk a few blocks to **Andina** for Peruvian small plates and Latin-themed cocktails.

Day 2

- Skip the hubbub of Voodoo Doughnut and head to **Blue Star Doughnuts,** where you can pick up a blueberry bourbon basil doughnut or the best buttermilk old-fashioned you will ever have.

- Stop in at Portland's own "City of Books," **Powell's,** where you can easily lose an afternoon (and a family member) while perusing the one million books they have on-site.

- Rainy days are also a good day to take in the **Portland Saturday Market.** The crowds tend to shy away when the weather gets wet, so it is easier to see what the merchants have to offer.

If it is raining:

- Visit **Lan Su Chinese Garden.** The urban garden features many covered walkways, so it is easy to dodge the raindrops. Plus sipping a cup of hot tea and nibbling on a bowl of steaming hot dumplings are a special treat when the rain is falling.

- The **Japanese Garden** is also a special experience when it's rainy. Raindrops reflect like jewels off the trees and create beautiful ripples in the koi pond.

- If you are traveling with kids, or you just plain love animals, rainy days are perfect days to visit the **Oregon Zoo.** There are fewer crowds and, for some reason, the rain just seems to bring the animals more out in the open. It is a great day to catch a hippo at play.

If it is absolutely pouring:

- Grab some friends (or make some) at **Guardian Games,** where you can use any number of the games they have on hand and play for hours while you ride out the storm. Or, if table top gaming isn't your thing, head to **Ground Kontrol** and pass the time with classic arcade games like Galaga

- You can also take in a little history at **Pittock Mansion.** The French Renaissance-style home offers expansive views of the city, and at 16,000 square feet, it will keep you out of the rain for a while.

- Whether you are big or small, **Oregon Museum of Science and Industry** is also a fun way to stay dry. There are a number of hands-on exhibits, touring showcases, a planetarium, and the enormous Omnimax theater that shows beautiful documentaries and the occasional first-run blockbuster.

> For lunch, head to **Little Burger** and enjoy custom cheeseburgers and truffle fries.

> Once you are fortified, head deeper into the **Pearl District** where you can shop and check out some galleries like **Bullseye Gallery,** where you can even get some hands-on experience, or **Sequential Art Gallery + Studio,** where you can experience the artistry and design of comic book arts.

> When the sun goes down, head to **Little Bird,** and tuck into some fresh oysters, a delightful duck confit, or their infamous Little Bird Burger. But, maybe save some room for some crème brûlée.

▶ Top the night off with karaoke at **Voicebox,** where you and your friends can belt out songs in your own private room, complete with cocktail and food service.

Day 3

▶ Start your day with a hearty breakfast from **Bertie Lou's,** where the scrambles come with a side of sass.

▶ Head across the river and get in a morning hike through **Oaks Bottom Wildlife Refuge,** where you can spot an egret, a heron, or a beaver.

▶ After your brush with nature, get over to the **Hawthorne District** where you can shop and maybe catch some lunch at ¿Por Que No? taquería. If you can't bear the line, go down to **Bagdad Theater** where you can grab lunch and sip a beer while watching a cheap flick.

▶ Take a self-guided tour through **Distillery Row,** and learn all about Portland's craft spirit makers and then book a seat on the **Pedalounge,** where you and a baker's dozen of friends or strangers can pedal your own party bus on a pub crawl through southeast Portland.

▶ For dinner, enjoy hand-tossed, wood-fired pizzas at **Ken's Artisan Pizza.**

▶ Catch a show at **Revolution Hall,** a renovated high school auditorium that is the regular home of Live Wire! Radio and often books headliner comics and big musical acts.

The quirky Hawthorne neighborhood is a popular place for shopping, dining, and people-watching.

Sights

Look for ★ to find recommended sights.

Highlights

★ **Best Place to Find a Zen Moment:** Right in the middle of Old Town, the **Lan Su Chinese Garden** is an oasis of quiet beauty. The walled garden occupies approximately 40,000 square feet and was influenced by the famous classical gardens in Suzhou, China (page 38).

★ **Best Place to Get Lost:** If heaven were a library, it would look a lot like **Powell's City of Books,** the independent bookstore that occupies an entire city block, with more than one million new, used, and rare books under one roof (page 38).

★ **Best Place to Commune with the Dead:** More park than graveyard, **Lone Fir Cemetery** is a quiet, ethereal spot where more than 25,000 of Portland's dead have been laid to rest (page 41).

★ **Best Place to Spot a Blue Heron:** Hawks, ducks, woodpeckers, and kestrels are just some of the wildlife that inhabit **Oaks Bottom Wildlife Refuge,** a 140-acre floodplain wetland (page 44).

★ **Best Place to Hug a Tree:** Check out **Forest Park,** which stretches across 5,100 acres of hills, trails, streams, and spots of old-growth forest, much of which overlooks the beautiful Willamette River (page 46).

★ **Best Place to Develop House Envy:** The beautiful and stately **Pittock Mansion** is an amazing French Renaissance chateau in the west hills of the city (page 49).

the Lan Su Chinese Garden

Mother Nature spoils us rotten in these parts. Native Portlanders are accustomed to a life alongside the lush and colorful backdrop of trees, flowers, and rolling rivers. However, that is not to say that we take it for granted. Most residents will tell you that one of the reasons they love this city so much is for its proximity to some of the nation's most beautiful scenery.

If you are a nature lover, you are in luck. Portland is home to a number of peaceful wildlife areas like Oaks Bottom Wildlife Refuge and Forest Park. Cultural gardens provide tranquility amid the sort of art that can't be found in a gallery, and botanical retreats allow respite from the bustling city. These little pockets of nature are only part of what makes Portland so unique. It is a key facet of the city's sparkle, in fact, for life in Portland to be defined not by what people do, but by what they create. Ask someone what he or she does for a living and they are more likely to say "I am a fire dancer" than they are to say "I am an accountant." And since inspiration reigns supreme, it makes sense that art springs out of the gray city blocks in unexpected places like the Vera Katz Eastbank Esplanade, Pioneer Courthouse Square, or the facade of a restaurant. When creativity is king, it makes sense that the historical mingles with the avant-garde and that one of the nation's largest urban forests is mere moments outside of downtown. Just take a look at the Zoobomb Monument, with its precariously stacked bikes. What was once an oddity (and to some an eyesore) has been reinvented into art.

Of course, the star of the show in P-Town is the originality. The instinct to create something out of nothing is a feeling that dates back to

Previous: downtown sculptures by Georgia Gerber; autumn maple tree in the Portland Japanese Garden.

the founders of the city, who valued imagination over the idea of building something on the backs of those who had come before them. Still today, Portlanders are known for their scrappy, do-it-yourself creative culture, and that instinct is reflected through all quadrants of the city in the form of art, nature, architecture, and urban planning. The Vera Katz Esplanade grew out of a need to beautify and utilize the east waterfront area. The Park Blocks happened because early planners felt the city needed a "cathedral of trees with a simple floor of grass." From the beginning, there has been an overarching understanding that art, nature, and history are essential fuels for the creative fire. From the chilling beauty of Lone Fir Cemetery to the glittering opulence of the Pearl District and the wooded hills of Forest Park, Portland has a number of must-see sights to spark that flame.

Downtown

Map 1

ANKENY PLAZA

Before Pioneer Courthouse Square became "Portland's living room," Ankeny Plaza was considered the heart of Portland commerce. Built by Captain Alexander Ankeny after an 1872 fire devastated the region, Ankeny Plaza (also known as Ankeny Square) has housed a number of retail businesses, public marketplaces, and performance spaces over the years. When first opened, it was known as the New Market Theater. The area is a popular spot for photographers hoping to capture some of Portland's most historic facades, thanks to its ornate pilasters, pediments, and cornices. In fact, the Victorian Italianate masonry and grand cast-iron columns that surround the equally iconic Skidmore Fountain are considered to be largest and best-preserved group of such architecture in the American West.

MAP 1: SW Ankeny St. and SW Naito Pkwy., 503/823-2223, www.portlandonline.com/parks; 24 hours daily; free

CENTRAL LIBRARY

This Georgian Revival landmark was built in 1903 by A. E. Doyle and bears the names of famous historians, philosophers, scientists, and artists etched along its outer walls and benches, and the interior is no less impressive. Renovated in the mid-1990s, the library boasts a number of awe-inspiring elements, such as lofty, arched ceilings and windows and the grand, intricately etched black granite staircase. The Beverly Cleary Children's Library, named for the author who wrote her beloved Ramona books about growing up on Portland's Klickitat Street, houses a 14-foot bronze *Tree of Knowledge* sculpture by artists Dana Lynn Lewis and Barbara Eiswerth. Its trunk is a menagerie of toys, animals, storybook characters, and musical instruments that both children and adults love to explore while enjoying a little structured (or unstructured) story time. Climb the sweeping staircase to the third floor and you'll find the Collins Gallery, which hosts regular

recitals, poetry readings, community events, and frequent educational and
artistic exhibits.

True to its Oregonian style, however, the library is not only committed to preserving history, but also to protecting the environment. In 2008, the Central Library also became the first library in Oregon to construct an "eco-roof," in response to the growing need for green spaces amid urban growth. Besides extending the overall life of the roof and providing a habitat for wildlife, the eco-roof reduces rain runoff by 70 percent.

MAP 1: 801 SW 10th Ave., 503/988-5123, www.multcolib.org; Tues.-Wed. 10am-8pm, Thurs.-Sat. 10am-5pm, Sun. noon-5pm; free

IRA KELLER FOUNTAIN

Just outside the Civic Auditorium is an enormous fountain built in honor of Ira C. Keller, a Portland civic leader and the first chairperson of the Portland Development Commission (PDC), who is credited with pushing through much of the urban renewal work that happened during his time on the PDC. The grand two-level fountain is designed to mimic the falls and cataracts of the Cascade Range and provide a peaceful white noise to diminish the sounds of the city. It's a popular spot for afternoon business traffic, where people go to unwind or just cool off.

MAP 1: Keller Fountain Park, SW 3rd Ave. and SW Clay St.; daily 5am-9pm; free

MILL ENDS PARK

There are more than 9,000 acres of park space in the Portland metropolitan area—and some areas are so big you can forget that you are in the city. Mill Ends Park could be that kind of escape—providing you're the size of an ant. Noted in the *Guinness Book of World Records* as the world's smallest park, Mill Ends occupies only 452 square inches (yes, inches) and measures just two feet across. As the story goes, Dick Fagan, a columnist for the now-defunct *Oregon Journal,* spotted a leprechaun from his window, which overlooked what is now Naito Parkway. He raced out to capture the creature and, upon doing so, wished for a park of his own. The clever leprechaun granted the wish, but since Fagan had been unspecific as to the size of park he wanted, he was given the small patch of dirt upon which the capture had taken place.

Fairy tales aside, Mill Ends Park was named an official park on St. Patrick's Day in 1971. Over the years, a number of curious "contributions" have shown up, such as a tiny swimming pool (complete with diving board), a Ferris wheel, and several miniature statues.

MAP 1: SW Naito Pkwy. and SW Taylor St., www.portlandonline.com/parks; daily 24 hours; free

THE OLD CHURCH

The Calvary Presbyterian Church was erected in 1883, thanks to the help of architect Warren H. Williams, who donated his designs for the Victorian-style Carpenter Gothic building. It cost a total of $36,000 to build and included a number of elegant touches, like the ornate window traceries, archways, chimneys, buttresses, and spires. Key features are the "wedding ring," which is nestled on the bell tower, and the recently rebuilt porte cochere at the Clay Street entrance. Nowadays, the building is referred to simply as the Old Church, and serves as a secular place for meetings, weddings, concerts, and events. The building is open weekdays for self-guided tours, and each Wednesday there's a free lunchtime concert, which is a great time to check out the cast-iron Corinthian columns, hand-carved fir pews, and elaborate stained-glass windows.

MAP 1: 1422 SW 11th Ave., 503/222-2031, www.theoldchurch.org; Mon.-Fri. 11am-3pm; free

NORTH AND SOUTH PARK BLOCKS

In the midst of Portland's downtown Cultural District are the 18 collective blocks that make up the North and South Park Blocks. The area is sprinkled with some of Portland's most interesting pieces of public art, like the 12-foot-tall father-and-son elephant statue that honors a piece from the late Shang Dynasty (circa 1200-1100 BC) and the 18-foot-tall representation of Rough Rider Teddy Roosevelt.

The land to the south was donated to the public in 1852 by Daniel H. Lownsdale, who hoped that it would become a promenade, a "cathedral of trees with a simple grass floor." Nowadays, the area is a popular gathering place for Portland State University students or the downtown workers who wish to eat their lunch under the 100-plus Lombardy poplars and elms. It is also the home of one of the city's popular farmers markets on Saturday.

To the north, you'll find six blocks lined with big leaf maples, black locusts, and American elms. A popular place for both rest and recreation, the North Park Blocks contain a playground, basketball court, and bocce ball area, as well as a popular fountain, the *Portland Dog Bowl,* designed by famed weimaraner photographer William Wegman.

MAP 1: SW Park Ave. from SW Salmon St. to SW Jackson St., and NW Park Ave. from SW Ankeny St. to NW Glisan St., www.portlandonline.com/parks; daily 5am-9pm; free

PIONEER COURTHOUSE SQUARE

The true heart of Portland is the area affectionately known as "Portland's living room." Occupying 40,000 square feet of the downtown Cultural District, Pioneer Square is the nucleus of performance and function. It's a fashionable spot for locals on lunch breaks, who can grab a bite from the popular food carts, do some people-watching, or just unwind with a book.

The square is home to art pieces like the iconic P-Town statue *Allow Me,* featuring a well-dressed gentleman extending his hand to you while holding an umbrella, and the *Weather Machine,* which opens each day at noon to announce the weather amid trumpet fanfare and flashing lights.

Chess games often crop up on the three bronze chessboards atop what appear to be fallen columns on the Morrison corner built in 2003 by Soderstrom Architects. In the summer, chess clubs and game enthusiasts

Top: Ankeny Plaza. **Bottom:** aerial view of Pioneer Courthouse Square.

meet here (instead of at pubs and coffeehouses) for alfresco matches. It's not uncommon for crowds to gather as they wait for the nearby MAX train.

Whether you're catching a concert, attending a festival, or just hanging out with locals at play, be sure to check out one of the lesser-known novelties here: the **echo chamber** on the western side facing Morrison. In this tiny circular amphitheater if you stand on the small center circle (the Sweet Spot) and speak, your voice will reverberate back to you as if amplified to a massive stadium. Remarkably, the sound of your voice remains unchanged to anyone except you.

MAP 1: City block bounded by SW Morrison St., SW 6th Ave., SW Yamhill St., and SW Broadway, 503/223-1613, www.thesquarepdx.org; daily 5am-midnight; free

PORTLANDIA

Like a sentinel over the city, *Portlandia* sits as inconspicuously as a 35-foot-tall woman can. Based on the city seal of Portland, which bears a woman as a representation of commerce, *Portlandia* was designed by sculptor Raymond Kaskey and is thought to be the second-largest repoussé statue in the United States (after the Statue of Liberty). *Portlandia* can seem both menacing and welcoming in different light, and although she is an iconic figure for the city, her image belongs to the sculptor (which is why you will not see keychains and miniatures of her as you will of Lady Liberty). A plaque at the base of *Portlandia* bears a poem written by Portlander Ronald Talney.

MAP 1: 1120 SW 5th Ave.; daily 24 hours; free

SALMON STREET SPRINGS

This Waterfront Park centerpiece cycles through an impressive 4,924 gallons of water per minute at full capacity, pushing (recycled) water through as many as 137 jets at one time. It is regulated by an underground computer, which switches between the three phases of the fountain. In the first setting, a light mist covers the center of the fountain, as if luring unsuspecting kids into the fray and thus setting them up for disaster. The second setting involves three circles of water, shooting up to resemble a wedding cake. The final setting is by far the most amusing and most dangerous, as water jets around the perimeter of the fountain activate and shoot inwards, creating a huge shower of water in the middle. It's this setting that tends to catch passersby and parents with cameras off guard, soaking them and knocking children to the ground.

MAP 1: SW Naito Pkwy. at SW Salmon St., Waterfront Park; daily 6am-10pm; free

ZOOBOMB MONUMENT

Zoobomb is a weekly bicycling event that has become an integral part of Portland's culture. Every Sunday, cyclists meet up and take a wild ride down the city's west hills. It bears mentioning that most of these riders are not riding mountain bikes. No, the preference for most Zoobombers is a mini bike or child's bike. It's a wild bunch, but they're also some of the nicest and most city-conscious people you'll meet.

It used to be that bombers would chain a pile of these child-sized bikes (mostly spare bikes to use as loaners) to a bike rack outside of Powell's, but back in 2009, the Zoobombers were given their own official sculpture upon which to perch their bikes. Once you spot the giant pile of bikes, look up and gaze at the golden bike, an homage to the city's lively Zoobombers.

MAP 1: SW 13th Ave. and SW Stark St.; daily 24 hours; free

Northwest and the Pearl District

Map 2

THE ARMORY

Built in 1891 to house the Oregon National Guard, the First Regiment Armory Annex (otherwise known as the Portland Armory) served as a home to soldiers during the Spanish-American War and World War I. It was opened to the public in the early 1900s, when the castle-like Romanesque Revival structure played host to operas, circuses, roller derbies, dances, boxing matches, and concerts. The building was one of only a few that could accommodate large crowds, as the truss system within the cavernous fortress allowed for unimpeded sight lines and free movement. Therefore, it served as the gathering spot where citizens heard speeches from the likes of Teddy Roosevelt, William Taft, and Woodrow Wilson.

In 2000, the Armory began a remarkable transformation when it was renovated (to the tune of $36.1 million) into an arts center that is now the permanent home of Portland Center Stage. Besides having two stages, a sprawling multilevel lobby, offices, work areas, and rehearsal spaces, the venue was the first on the National Register to receive platinum-level LEED certification for its sustainable design.

MAP 2: 128 NW 11th Ave., 503/445-3700, www.pcs.org; tours first and third Sat. of each month, noon-1pm; free

THE BREWERY BLOCKS

One of Portland's many nicknames is Beervana, thanks in part to Henry Weinhard, who established his iconic brewery here in the mid-1850s. For years, the Blitz-Weinhard Brewery served as the cornerstone of this former industrial area; although it has been more than a decade since the sale of the brewery's property in 1999 ignited the development of Portland's glittering arts district, the Pearl, the beer giant's influence still shines through. The five blocks and 1.7 million square feet of gritty industrial space is now a mixed-use area sprinkled with luxury apartments, hip boutiques, a Starbucks, some galleries, and some of the city's favorite restaurants.

MAP 2: Between NW 10th Ave., NW 13th Ave., W. Burnside St., and NW Davis St., www.breweryblocks.com; merchant hours vary; free

Top: Chinatown Gate. **Bottom:** Lan Su Chinese Garden.

With its multiple roofs, 78 dragons, 58 mythical characters, and two huge lions, the Chinatown Gate represents more than 135 years of Chinese history in Oregon and marks the official entrance to Chinatown. It's a popular place for photographs in an area that isn't always guidebook-presentable. The lions—Yin on the left side and Yang on the right—signify protection of the young and of the nation. The gate is both a beautiful landmark and a reminder of the era when Portland had the second-largest Chinese community in the United States. These days, Chinatown is compressed into just a few blocks, and with the exception of the gate, a few restaurants, shops, and grocery stores, much of the vibrancy the neighborhood saw in the 1890s is gone.

MAP 2: NW 4th Ave. and W. Burnside St.; daily 24 hours; free

JAMISON SQUARE

When developers were planning the Pearl District in the early 1990s, they wanted to create open gathering spaces within the urban sprawl. Located on the full city block between NW Johnson and NW Kearney, Jamison's real gem is the interactive fountain and tidal pool. It's a popular spot for families in the heat of the summer. Children splash in the low pools and chase the ever-changing flow of water while their parents take advantage of the free Wi-Fi or chat with others. The park is on the streetcar line and adjacent to a number of coffee shops, pizza joints, and other restaurants, so it's a great spot to grab a bite and do some people-watching—providing you like children, of course, since this park is a haven for shrieking, but happy, tykes.

MAP 2: 810 NW 11th Ave., 503/823-7529, www.portlandonline.com/parks; daily 5am-midnight; free; daily 5am-midnight; free

JEAN VOLLUM NATURAL CAPITAL CENTER

The Jean Vollum Natural Capital Center (also called the Ecotrust Building) was the first historic redevelopment in the United States to receive gold-level LEED certification from the U.S. Green Building Council. Originally constructed in 1895, this mixed-use building was redeveloped with a revolutionary focus on ecofriendly practices, materials, and design. Restoration of this beautiful space was done with environmentally friendly materials like recycled paint, wheatboard cabinets, and rubber flooring made from recycled tires. Inside, you will find Patagonia, a clothing company that adheres to a strong environmental ethic, and other like-minded businesses. It's a really pretty space and an innovative idea that has received a lot of attention. The public is welcome to wander through the atrium, mezzanine, and other public areas, and visitors can also inquire about event space or ask about tours.

MAP 2: 721 NW 9th Ave., 503/227-6225, www.ecotrust.org/ncc; merchant hours vary; free

★ **LAN SU CHINESE GARDEN**

Envisioned in 1988 when Portland and Suzhou, China, became sister cities, this Ming Dynasty scholar's garden opened in September 2000 and has since become an oasis for tranquility right in the heart of Old Town/Chinatown. A sanctuary devoted to the "five elements" (rock, water, flora, architecture, and words), the garden is an extraordinary landscape of blossoms, sculpture, and poetry that seems worlds away from the city. The majority of plants and materials contained within the garden's stone walls originated in China, including indigenous plants, limestone rocks from Lake Tai in Suzhou, and many types of fir, gingko, and China pine. The garden offers twice-daily guided tours at no extra cost, and guests are encouraged to visit the Teahouse to experience Chinese tea presentations along with traditional snacks and sweets.

MAP 2: NW 3rd Ave. and NW Everett St., 503/228-8131, www.lansugarden.org; Apr.-Oct. daily 10am-6pm, Nov.-Mar. daily 10am-5pm; $9.50 adults, $8.50 seniors, $7 students, free for children under 6

PORTLAND VINTAGE TROLLEYS

If you would like to see the city for free, hop onto one of Portland's vintage trolleys on select Sundays. A 30-minute round-trip will take you from Union Station to Portland State University, hitting all the MAX stops along the way. The cars are newly constructed replicas of the streetcar that the J. G. Brill Company supplied to Portland in 1904 and feature comfortable rattan seats with reversible backrests, carved oak interiors, brass handrails, and pull-down window shades. You can pick up the trolley at its 5th and Glisan stop, or at Portland State on SW 6th and Morrison.

MAP 2: NW Glisan and NW 5th Ave., 503/323-7363, www.vintagetrolleys.com; select Sun. 10:23am-5:17pm; free, donations accepted

★ POWELL'S CITY OF BOOKS

They don't call it a city of books for nothing. Occupying a full city block, Powell's is the largest independently owned new and used bookstore in the world. Within the walls of this bibliophile's dream, you can find a million new, used, rare, and out-of-print books. Grab a map as you enter or ask an employee to help you navigate the labyrinth of color-coded rooms. Grab a couple of locally produced zines or small-press books and head to the on-site café for a cup of coffee. Whatever your preference, it is easy to lose hours exploring the shelves, listening to guest authors speak in the Pearl Room, or simply people-watching. Since Powell's buys over 3,000 used books every day, they are almost guaranteed to have everything you are looking for and several things you didn't even know you wanted. The rare book room is especially inviting, with its soft lighting, antique furniture, and dark wood shelves housing thousands of first editions, odd volumes, and books far older than Portland itself—some dating as far back as the 1400s.

MAP 2: 1005 W. Burnside St., 503/228-4651, www.powells.com; daily 9am-11pm; free

Top: Union Station. Bottom: Powell's City of Books.

UNION STATION

In the early days of P-Town, Union Station served as a hub for import, export, and transportation, thus supporting the movement of livestock, timber, produce, and most importantly, people. New arrivals came to Portland and marveled at the beautiful Romanesque and Queen Anne-style station with its elegant brick, stucco, and sandstone—and the iconic 150-foot clock tower that now urges passersby to "Go by Train."

Union Station still serves as the depot for all Amtrak and Greyhound service to and from Portland, and is worth a visit, especially for history buffs and train lovers. Look out for the markers that will guide you through a walking tour beginning on Broadway and Hoyt. As you walk up the Broadway Bridge, check out the yards and the expansive views of the Portland skyline before you descend the steps to Naito Parkway and continue on across the east station esplanade through the yards. Climb the stairs to the Yards Plaza and cross the footbridge, where you'll get an up-close overhead look at the station platform.

MAP 2: 800 NW 6th Ave., 503/273-4865, www.amtrak.com; daily 7:15am-9pm; free

Northeast

Map 3

BEVERLY CLEARY CHILDREN'S SCULPTURE GARDEN

If you loved reading about the misadventures of the plucky but not always well-behaved Ramona Quimby, from the unforgettable children's series by Beverly Cleary, you'll want to visit Grant Park, where Ramona, Henry Huggins, and Henry's dog Ribsy are immortalized in bronze. Off the street in a patch of trees there is a fountain where the statues were placed to honor the author who made some of Northeast Portland famous. Cleary grew up in the neighborhood, and a number of her favorite childhood spots are remembered in the stories of Ramona and her sister, Beezus. You can download a map from the Multnomah County website and take a self-guided walking tour of Ramona's neighborhood. You can see the homes where the author grew up or stroll down Klickitat Street (yes, it's real and it's just four blocks from the park).

MAP 3: Grant Park, NE 33rd Ave. between Knott St. and NE Broadway, www.multcolib. org/parents/cleary; daily 5am-midnight; free

HOLLYWOOD THEATRE

A stroll through the Hollywood District wouldn't be complete without a look at the majestic Hollywood Theatre, which has one of the most ornate theater fronts in the Pacific Northwest. The Hollywood opened as a vaudeville house in the 1920s; back then, admission was only a quarter, and the films, which did not have sound yet, were accompanied by an eight-piece orchestra and an organ. The building might have fallen into disrepair if not for the volunteer group Film Action Oregon, which embarked on an aggressive campaign to renovate and save this old Portland landmark. Battling complications with water damage, asbestos, and general deterioration, the nonprofit organization managed to save the structure and savor a little nostalgia, thanks to the help of donations, grants, and the unending passion of its volunteers. In addition to showing regular independent films, the building has also returned to its vaudeville roots to welcome the occasional live theatrical performance or concert.

MAP 3: 4122 NE Sandy Blvd., 503/281-4215, www.hollywoodtheatre.org; open for film screenings and events; prices vary

Southeast

Map 4

LADD CIRCLE PARK & ROSE GARDENS

Though his name may be cursed by drivers trying to navigate through the mystery that is Ladd's Addition, William Sargent Ladd was actually quite clever. He came west during the California Gold Rush and settled in Portland in 1851. The productive businessman and one-time mayor of Portland owned a 126-acre farm on Portland's east side, which he decided to subdivide in a manner similar to Pierre L'Enfant's plan for Washington, D.C. Ladd's design is based on a diagonal street system surrounding a central park and four rose gardens located on the points of a compass. It was a radical departure from the common grid pattern of the expanding city and one that still confuses drivers, who get stuck in a seemingly endless maze.

The central park was designed in 1909 by Park Superintendent Emanuel Mische, who planted camellias, perennials, and a lawn area, as well as numerous rosebushes with the intention of creating a stained-glass effect. The garden is still quite lovely, with over 3,000 roses of 60 varieties.

MAP 4: SE 16th Ave. and SE Harrison St., www.portlandonline.com/parks; daily 5am-midnight; free

★ LONE FIR CEMETERY

Lone Fir Cemetery is a sometimes chilling but always moving representation of Portland's mottled past. Buried among the some 25,000 known and 10,000 unknown souls are many of the city's founders, including Asa Lovejoy, Socrates H. Tryon, J. C. Hawthorne, and Portland's first axe murderess, Charity Lamb. There's a lot of history here (not all of it flattering), and a stroll around this 30-acre arboretum will expose the tales of Chinese immigrants, pioneers, politicians, and soldiers. It was discovered in 2004 that several hundred patients from the Oregon Hospital for the Insane (which Hawthorne founded) are buried here in unmarked graves.

The grounds are well kept, and were it not for the gravestones, it would make a lovely park, speckled as it is with gingko trees, oaks, birches, firs, and dogwoods. If you visit in the summer months, you won't want to miss the Pioneer Rose Garden, where you'll find roses that were carried west

Top: Beverly Cleary Children's Sculpture Garden. **Bottom:** Lone Fir Cemetery.

with the pioneer women who made Portland their home. However, the memorials and grave markers are themselves worth the visit. Many date back to the mid-19th century and are surprisingly evocative of Portland's past.

MAP 4: SE Morrison St. and SE 20th Ave., 503/797-1709, www.friendsoflonefircemetery. org; daily sunrise-sunset; free

VERA KATZ EASTBANK ESPLANADE

One of Portland's numerous nicknames is Bridgetown, and if you head down to the waterfront, it's easy to see why. For years, the land on the east side of the Willamette River was an undeveloped industrial mess. In the late 1980s, developers and city planners began to envision a walkway that would extend north from the Hawthorne Bridge, past the Morrison and Burnside Bridges, to the Steel Bridge, where it would then link across the river to the already popular Waterfront Park on the west side. The finished esplanade contains markers that enumerate some of the area's vibrant history—all artistically lit to make them visible even at night.

While the area is a hotbed of activity—with Portlanders strolling, biking, skating, or simply exploring the underbellies of the city's many bridges—it is also a carefully planned habitat for fish and wildlife. Beavers and herons swim near boat docks as they try to nab salmon and steelhead, while pigeons and ducks nest on the rocks.

Take a quiet stroll down the walk and check out some of the public art installations, such as the ethereal Echo Gate and the bronze statue that commemorates the former mayor for whom the esplanade was named. Climb the steps and cross to the west side or head down to the lengthy floating walkway and feel the ebb and flow of the Willamette beneath your feet.

MAP 4: SE Water Ave. and SE Hawthorne Blvd., 503/823-2223, www.portlandonline.com/ parks; daily 5am-midnight; free

Sellwood and Moreland   Map 5

CRYSTAL SPRINGS RHODODENDRON GARDEN

It began as a "rhody" test garden in 1950, but now this 9.4-acre spot in the middle of Southeast Portland is a botanical oasis devoted to the flowering shrub that thrives better here than anywhere else. The cool, rainy Northwest climate is perfect for growing rhododendrons, but even when they are not in bloom, the garden is still a lush, romantic retreat. Packed with trails, waterfalls, ponds, shaded nooks, and benches, it's a beautiful spot to take a stroll, have a picnic, or capture some great photos of flora and fauna. Mind the geese and ducks, though. They more or less run the ponds and have been known to be a bit temperamental.

When the rhododendrons are in full bloom (usually late spring), Crystal Springs is an explosion of color. The garden houses a remarkable variety of blooms, some of which you can take home if you visit during the annual plant sale held during Mother's Day weekend in May.

MAP 5: SE Woodstock Blvd. and SE 28th Ave., 503/771-8386, www.portlandonline.com/parks; Apr.-Sept. daily 6am-10pm, Oct.-Mar. daily 6am-6pm; day after Labor Day-Feb. free; Thurs.-Mon. Mar.-Labor Day $3 adults, free for children under 12

★ OAKS BOTTOM WILDLIFE REFUGE

Oaks Bottom Wildlife Refuge is a 140-acre floodplain wetland on the east bank of the Willamette River that includes hiking and biking trails. The area is a favorite spot for bird-watchers, as more than 100 varieties of migratory birds manage to find their way to the refuge. You can hop on the trail at the SE Milwaukie Street entrance and head south along the edge of the pond, or opt for the paved Springwater Trail, which eventually connects to the south end of the Vera Katz Eastbank Esplanade.

In 1969, the city blocked development of this area into an industrial park because it was one of the few remaining marshlands around. Now the area is maintained by a volunteer organization that not only cares for the land but also works to restore the natural habitat of creatures such as wrens, raccoons, quails, kestrels, frogs, ducks, and the iconic blue heron.

MAP 5: SE Sellwood Blvd. and SE 7th Ave., 503/797-1709, www.portlandonline.com/parks; daily 5am-midnight; free

North Portland

Map 6

MISSISSIPPI AVENUE

Arguably one of the most walkable streets in Portland, Mississippi is still being quietly referred to as "one of the best-kept secrets in Portland," but it's not likely to stay hush-hush for long. What was once a haven for drug deals and debauchery is now a harbor for both shoppers and foodies, thanks to a recent (and much-needed) shot in the arm from the influx of creative souls looking to establish themselves in the Rose City. Unable to settle into the expensive Pearl lofts and unable to find space in the hotbed of the Alberta Arts District, artists and young entrepreneurs began to build their own neighborhood here, injecting into it their own ethos and style.

Mississippi Avenue is packed with some of the city's most creative restaurants, stylish bars, and quaint boutiques, but it's also a testament to Portland's commitment to sustainability. Near North Fremont Avenue stands the ornate Dada-esque facade of **The ReBuilding Center** (3625 N. Mississippi Ave., 503/331-1877), which hides a labyrinth of doors, windows, fixtures, and wood salvaged from homes all over the region and resold to locals who want to add unique touches to their home without creating a bigger carbon footprint.

MAP 6: N. Mississippi Ave., between N. Fremont St. and N. Skidmore St.; merchant hours vary; free

Top: Crystal Springs Rhododendron Garden. Bottom: Oaks Bottom Wildlife Refuge.

PENINSULA PARK & ROSE GARDEN

Designed in the early 1900s as part of the City Beautiful movement, this park is equal parts elegant formal garden and community gathering space. Enter the sunken rose garden on Albina Avenue and stroll among the 6,500 rose plantings, which include more than 65 fragrant varieties. The heart of this garden, which is bedecked with lantern-style lights and stone pillars, is where you'll find a historic fountain; it's been the centerpiece of the park for nearly 100 years, and it is here that Portland's official city rose, Mme. Caroline Testout, was first cultivated and is maintained to this day.

Just past the formal garden, you'll find a grand octagonal gazebo, built in 1913 and preserved as a historic landmark, the last of its kind. Today, it is a popular spot for weddings and concerts. Beyond that are baseball fields, tennis courts, playgrounds, and a whimsical wading pool complete with a giant frog and flower sprinkler. At this end of the 16-acre park is also where you'll find Portland's first and oldest community center. The center, an Italian villa-style structure, has a 33-yard outdoor swimming pool that is a popular retreat for locals—and once served as the home for a number of Humboldt penguins awaiting transport to Washington Park Zoo.

MAP 6: 700 N. Rosa Parks Way, 503/823-2525, www.portlandonline.com/parks; daily 5am-midnight; free; daily 5am-midnight; free

Greater Portland   Map 7

ELK ROCK GARDEN

The Garden of the Bishop's Close, known as Elk Rock, was created to show a collection of rare and native plants, magnificent trees, and remarkable views of the Willamette River and Mount Hood. It is a private garden and the home of the Episcopal Bishop of Oregon. The family bequeathed the home to the church, leaving with it an endowment for the care and maintenance of the garden, and a requirement that it be left open to the public. It's a lovely, contemplative spot to visit, so long as you respect the rules. Dogs must be leashed; visitors may not bring picnics; and there is a prohibition against "frolicking," but nonetheless, it is a peaceful place to visit. You won't find any signage on Highway 43 indicating the garden is there, which makes it all the more of a treasure hunt, the reward of which is winding paths through magnolia trees, rhododendrons, giant sequoias, golden rain trees, gingkos, witch hazel, and burning bushes.

MAP 7: 11800 SW Military Ln., 503/636-5613, www.elkrockgarden.com; daily 8am-5pm; free

★ FOREST PARK

If you really want to get away from it all, go no farther than Forest Park, the 5,100-acre urban forest that sits just outside of downtown Portland in the Tualatin Hills. Featuring 70 miles of trails for hikers, bikers, bird-watchers, and horseback riders, the park provides a never-ending abundance of flora and fauna. The massive canopy of trees offers a safe and prosperous habitat for the 112 species of birds and 62 species of mammals that call the park home. Extending along the east ridge above the Willamette River, Forest Park is bounded by West Burnside Street on the south, and its juxtaposition to the Alphabet District in Northwest Portland makes it a popular retreat for those who seek peace and solitude without having to travel far.

At the southeastern end of the park, the popular Wildwood Trail passes Pittock Mansion and offers breathtaking panoramic views of Mounts Hood, St. Helens, Rainier, Adams, and Jefferson.

MAP 7: NW 29th Ave. and NW Upshur St.; daily 5am-10pm; free

THE GROTTO

The National Sanctuary of Our Sorrowful Mother, or The Grotto, as it is more commonly called, is a 62-acre botanical garden and Catholic shrine that is a sight to see, for anyone, be they Christians, agnostics, or followers of the Flying Spaghetti Monster. Towering fir trees and imposing basalt cliffs bend to the careful artwork of peace and tranquility. A highlight of the visit is Our Lady's Grotto, a shrine to Mary that was carved out of the black cliffs in 1925 and features a marble replica of Michelangelo's famed work, the *Pietà*. Take a tour (call ahead to schedule) or stroll through on your own and explore the statuary hidden among the trees, streams, and passageways. Buy a token from the gift shop for $3.50 and ride the elevator to the upper level, which sits atop a 130-foot sheer rock cliff and offers unequalled views of the Columbia River and Mount St. Helens.

In the wintertime, The Grotto is home to one of Portland's most popular holiday events, the Festival of Lights. Volunteers spend months installing over half a million lights, animated displays, and fiber-optic representations of the holiday spirit. It is the only time of year when an admission fee is required, but tickets ($9 adults, $4 children, free for children under 3) include concerts in the cathedral-like 500-seat chapel, petting zoos, and theatrical performances.

MAP 7: 8840 NE Skidmore St., 503/254-7371, www.thegrotto.org; Jan. daily 9am-5pm, Feb.-early Mar. daily 9am-5:30pm, early Mar.-day before Mother's Day daily 9am-6:30pm, Mother's Day-Labor Day daily 9am-8:30pm, day after Labor Day-Oct. daily 9am-6:30pm, Nov.-day before Thanksgiving daily 9am-5:30pm, day after Thanksgiving-Dec. daily 9am-4pm; free, except evenings Thanksgiving Day-Dec.

MT. TABOR PARK

This 196-acre park in Southeast Portland is the home of an extinct volcanic cinder cone, one of only two urban volcanoes in North America. The park has several miles of walking trails and is a popular place for cycling. In the summer, you will find many a Portlander picnicking or sunning themselves on the grassy hillsides. There are basketball hoops and an outdoor amphitheater near the peak of Mount Tabor, as well as off-leash dog areas, playground equipment, tennis courts, volleyball courts, and horseshoe pits

Top: Forest Park. **Bottom:** a shrine in The Grotto.

scattered around the rest of the park. Mt. Tabor Park is also the home of the annual Adult Soapbox Derby, a riotous event in which grown men and women race each other down the hill in their home-built nonmotorized cars at breakneck speeds.

MAP 7: SE 60th Ave. and Salmon St., www.portlandonline.com/parks; daily 5am-midnight; free

OREGON ZOO

The Oregon Zoo has a lot of great animal exhibits, like the Red Ape Reserve, where you will find orangutans and gibbons, and the Africa Savanna, where you will see giraffes, hippos, and rhinos. The polar bears, penguins, sea lions, otters, and the African rainforest are always big winners, the latter with underwater viewing tanks that contain slender-snouted crocodiles. Over at the Asian elephant exhibit, you can learn about Packy the pachyderm and find out why he is Portland's sweetheart, or visit the zoo's exciting Predators of the Serengeti exhibit, which features lions, cheetahs, African wild dogs, African rock pythons, and caracals.

MAP 7: 4001 SW Canyon Rd., 503/226-1561, www.oregonzoo.org; Jan.-Feb. daily 10am-4pm, Mar.-late May daily 9am-4pm, late May-early Sept. daily 9am-6pm, early Sept.-Dec. daily 9am-4pm; $10.50 adults, $9 seniors, $7.50 children ages 3-11, free for children under 3

PAUL BUNYAN STATUE

Originally built to greet visitors to the Centennial Exposition for Portland's 100th anniversary on February 14, 1959, this big guy still looms tall over NoPo, as if watching over the adjacent Dancin' Bear, a famous local strip club. The legendary lumberjack of lore stands 31 feet tall and was recently added to the National Register of Historic Places.

Composed mostly of steel, plaster, concrete, and paint, Paul is remarkably well constructed for his age (especially considering the fact that he was only intended to last six months). Thankfully, Paul has been lovingly cared for over the years by neighbors who saw him as a symbol of both the lumberjacks of Portland's past and the working class of today.

MAP 7: N. Interstate Ave. and N. Denver Ave.; daily 24 hours; free

★ PITTOCK MANSION

One thousand feet above the city stands a monument to some of Portland's most fundamental qualities: natural beauty, progress, civic enthusiasm, and historical preservation. The Pittock Mansion was built in 1914 by Henry and Georgiana Pittock, both active contributors to progressive mid-19th-century Portland. Henry (a newspaperman who developed what is now *The Oregonian*) made his way to Oregon at the age of 19, penniless but driven. He and Georgiana married in 1860 and began a life of hard work, committing countless hours to community service, all the while building an empire from their real estate, banking, railroad, ranching, and mining investments. The Pittocks had six children and 19 grandchildren, many

P-Town for the Pint-Sized

Portlanders are known for keeping their kids in tow instead of opting for nannies or babysitters. It's no surprise then that the city offers numerous places that appeal both to the young and the young-at-heart.

Young and old alike will find themselves wanting to touch, twirl, poke, and examine things around every corner of the **Oregon Museum of Science and Industry** (1945 SE Water Ave., 800/955-6674, www.omsi.edu). You can ride the motion simulator, check out a flick in the incredible IMAX theater, tour a real U.S. Navy submarine, or visit the latest traveling exhibition. You can also find fun for all ages at **Oaks Amusement Park** (7805 SE Oaks Park Way, 503/233-5777, www.oakspark.com). Ride the Scream-n-Eagle, take a spin around the old-school skating rink, or have a picnic along the banks of the Willamette River. The rink is open most days, and rides are operational on Saturday and Sunday noon-7pm and during special events.

Of course, the **Oregon Zoo** (4001 SW Canyon Rd., www.oregonzoo.org) is a big draw for families, with its Asian elephants, adorable penguins, majestic polar bears, fascinating fruit bats, and a plethora of animals from all corners of the world. In fact, on any given day, there are 2,200 specimens representing 260 species of birds, mammals, reptiles, amphibians, and invertebrates. You can check out the daily keeper talks or ride the zoo train, which takes you around the zoo and shows off some of the pretty forested areas of Washington Park. Wintertime visitors can also check out **ZooLights,** when the zoo is transformed into a colorful wintry wonderland and hours are extended past dark.

A great day trip with the kids is the 20-minute drive out to **Sauvie Island** (www.sauvieisland.org), where there are U-pick farms and wildlife areas to explore. A favorite in the fall is the **Pumpkin Patch** (503/621-3874, www.thepumpkinpatch.com), where kids can hop on a hayride out to the pumpkin patch. If you pick a pumpkin, you pay according to the size and weight, but otherwise, it's free. The produce market is full of fresh fruits and vegetables (as well as pumpkin-carving kits, fall decor, and other goodies), and you can pick up some hot buttered corn and homemade cider at the concession stands. While you're out there, visit the **Maize** (www.portlandmaze.com), a truly mind-boggling five-acre corn maze; and after dark, in October, the truly brave-hearted can traipse through the Haunted Field of Screams.

Portland Saturday Market (48 Naito Pkwy., 503/241-4188, www.portlandsaturdaymarket.com) has long been a favorite for kids, especially since it's the place where elephant ears were invented. Portland's Elephant Ears is one of many carts in the market's food court, but this one is a particular favorite among the small set. The smell of those ginormous fried dough treats is hard to resist, especially when you can douse them in marionberries, apple butter,

of whom were raised on the 46-acre estate—which was purchased by the city of Portland (and thereby saved from demolition) for a mere $225,000.

The home was designed by Edward Foulks (who also designed the Tribune Tower in Oakland, California) in the French Renaissance style and boasts remarkably innovative features for its time, such as a central vacuum system, an intercom system, a walk-in freezer, and a Turkish smoking room. About 80,000 visitors tour the house each year (you can take a self-guided or docent-led tour) and then wander through the lush park-like

elephant at the Oregon Zoo

cinnamon and sugar, or whatever you like. Kids are also pretty fond of touring the merchant booths, as there are a number of vendors with things to touch, test-drive, or try on.

There are great stops for the little reader in your life. **Powell's City of Books** (1005 W. Burnside, 503/228-4651, www.powells.com) has a truly jaw-dropping kids' room. In fact, it has been dubbed the "largest children's book section on the West Coast." There are tables and chairs for impromptu story-time, and a staff person is on hand to help you or your child find exactly what you are looking for. Plus, it has a fun merchandise section with irresistible craft items, T-shirts, and cool educational toys. On the east side of the river, you'll find **Green Bean Books** (1600 NE Alberta St., 503/954-2354, www.greenbean-bookspdx.com), which has a fantastic collection of books for young readers and soon-to-be-bibliophiles. It also has an amusing collection of old vending machines that now distribute things like fake mustaches, finger puppets, and little fuzzy friends.

Many Portland hotels feature kid-focused packages. **Hotel Monaco** (506 SW Washington, 888/207-2201, www.monaco-portland.com), for instance, offers a "Mini DaVinci" deal with passes to the Portland Children's Museum, milk and cookies, and even paint sets and canvasses for you to keep.

gardens that blossom with rhododendrons and flowering cherries. There are also trails through **Pittock Acres Park** (daily 5am-9pm), which connect with the adjacent Forest Park and are popular with hikers and joggers for their verdant landscapes and spectacular views.

MAP 7: 3229 NW Pittock Dr., 503/823-3623, www.pittockmansion.org;
Sept.-Dec. and Feb.-June daily 11am-4pm, July-Aug. daily 10am-5pm; closed Jan.,
Thanksgiving Day, Christmas Day; $9.50 adults, $8.50 seniors, $6.50 children ages 6-18,
free for children under 6

Top: Pittock Mansion. **Bottom:** Portland Japanese Garden.

If the urban sprawl has you itching to find a much-needed moment of peace and tranquility, seek it among the winding stone steps, wooden bridges, waterfalls, and koi ponds of the beautifully landscaped Japanese Garden. High above the city, the garden is encircled by stately Douglas fir and western red cedar trees and the rolling green hills of Washington Park. Inside, the garden is divided into five spaces: the Sand and Stone Garden; the Natural Garden; the Flat Garden; the Tea Garden; and the Strolling Pond Garden, with its exquisite Heavenly Falls and five-tiered pagoda lantern. It has taken years of cultivation to bring such serenity and authenticity to the gardens, but the efforts have certainly paid off. In 1998, Kunihiko Saito, the Japanese ambassador to the United States, declared this "the most authentic Japanese garden, including those in Japan."

The Portland Japanese Garden offers several guided tours daily between April and October and once daily on weekends between November and March. Reservations aren't necessary for these tours, but you can also call ahead to set up a private group tour.

MAP 7: 611 SW Kingston Ave., 503/223-5055, www.japanesegarden.com; Apr.-Sept. Mon. noon-7pm, Tues.-Sun. 10am-7pm; Oct.-Mar. Mon. noon-4pm, Tues.-Sun. 10am-4pm; $9.50 adults, $7.75 seniors and students, $6.75 children ages 6-17, free for children under 6

Restaurants

PRICE KEY

$ Entrées less than $10
$$ Entrées $10–20
$$$ Entrées more than $20

Pick up a copy of the *New York Times, Bon Appétit,* or *Food & Wine* and you are likely to see Portland featured within its pages. Food and travel editors are in love with the city's energy and creativity. Celebrity chefs are made here, and their influence is being seen in cookbooks, on televisions, and in kitchens across the country. In Portland, it's not really about having a clever conceit or quirky angle; it's about finding better ways to use the ingredients you have, often by embracing old or forgotten ways of cooking, grilling, or crafting cocktails.

Furthermore, Portland chefs, mixologists, and restaurateurs are creating a buzz for the way they utilize the bounties of the Pacific Northwest. In Portland, there is a joke that the "six degrees of separation" rule does not apply. Here we have only three degrees, and the same can be said for our food. Greens come from neighborhood gardens, beef from local farms, and it's likely that the mushrooms were picked by the chef. The coffee is fair trade and roasted by "that guy down the block." The wines are biodynamic and made from grapes grown in a vineyard you can drive to in less than an hour.

Chefs have flocked to Portland over the last 10 years, much in the same way the artists did 10 years before that, bringing with them a passion and energy that has moved the city's culinary status from the underground. Every quadrant of this town is positively bursting with restaurants, food

Previous: Blue Star Doughnuts; food carts.

Look for ★ to find
recommended restaurants.

Highlights

★ **Best Place to Ruin Your Lunch:** Breakfast is so good at **Tasty n Alder,** you may wonder if you could ever top it. Ambitious small plates and hearty favorites keep this place on the top of the brunch list (page 62).

★ **Best Place to Find Locals Getting Doughnuts:** The sophisticated flavors and perfectly balanced textures at **Blue Star Doughnuts** have Portlanders singing a different tune than you might have heard. But get in line early (page 62).

★ **Best Place to Indulge a Chocolate Craving:** If you have never tried drinking chocolate, get yourself to **Cacao.** This is not the hot chocolate of your youth. This is rich, thick, intense chocolate that will forever change what you think hot chocolate should be (page 62).

★ **Best Place to Suck the Marrow Out of Life:** A charming French-inspired bistro, **Little Bird** serves up rich, indulgent dishes like Foie Gras au torchon and roasted marrow bones (page 65).

★ **Best Place Impress a Date:** No one knows how to make you feel like a VIP quite like **El Gaucho,** where the attention to detail borders on obsessive (page 67).

★ **Best Place to Indulge Your Inner Carnivore: Olympia Provisions** makes excellent hand-crafted meats and charcuterie. Sip some wine while savoring wild boar sausage, succulent rotisserie chicken, or salami with pickled vegetables (page 70).

★ **Best Ecofriendly Eats: Bamboo Sushi** is a sustainable sushi restaurant that would do well even if it didn't employ all-green practices. The fish used in their rolls, soups, and specialties meets strict guidelines, so everything is about as fresh as if you plucked it from the sea yourself (page 72).

★ **Best Place to Find a Sweet Surprise:** The cupcake craze is unlikely to end any time soon and **Cupcake Jones** has always been ahead of the curve. This sweet spot is a favorite among locals for their moist, dense, cream-filled cupcakes and for their magnanimous support of the city and the LGBT community (page 75).

★ **Best Six-Course Extravaganza:** Chef Naomi Pomeroy has been recognized in a number of national cooking magazines. **Beast** is her baby, offering six-course dinners with such starters as a charcuterie plate that includes foie gras bonbons (page 83).

★ **Best Place to Sample a Little of Everything:** Spanish-inspired **Toro Bravo** is always bustling, but it runs a tight ship. Plates come out hot and loaded with such treasures as squid ink pasta, oxtail croquettes, and bacon-wrapped dates (page 88).

★ **Best Place to Get a Piece of Pie:** Forget ice cream, this pie doesn't need it. **Lauretta Jean's** unbeatable crust is the key, but fillings like salted honey, blueberry streusel, or banana chocolate cream don't hurt (page 90).

shops, quirky food carts, and pretty lounges, all devoted to the idea that fresh is best, local is key, and uniformity is passé.

Downtown

Map 1

Downtown Portland, occasionally referred to as the Cultural District, has the fortune of being a hub for vacationers, theater-goers, and business travelers. Hotel bars abut late-night coffeehouses, and everywhere there is a buzz of energy. No one is in a hurry, but they are not about to waste a moment on anything subpar. Because of this, the culinary scene is about as diverse as it gets. On one corner, a crowd of food carts can offer quick, tasty bites, while one block away, a five-star chef garnishes a dry aged steak before sending it out.

AMERICAN

BLUEPLATE LUNCH COUNTER & SODA FOUNTAIN $

This tiny lunch spot fills up quickly around noontime, as it's a top choice among locals who want to grab a bite to eat on their break. Blueplate is only open for a few hours on weekdays, and the service is often a bit hurried, particularly before 3pm. But somehow, the cozy comfort food and down-home diner atmosphere make it all worthwhile. Blueplate has only a handful of regular entrées (all quite reliable) and a rotation of favorites like house-made meatloaf and slow-cooked brisket pot roast, but if you look around, you'll see that the real star of the show is a good old-fashioned bowl of tomato soup paired with a grilled cheese sandwich. This place is also famous for its 1950s-style soda fountain, featuring house-made cane sugar sodas and incredible milk shakes. In fact, the chocolate peanut butter shake is so decadent, it's like reliving your childhood in a glass.

MAP 1: 308 SW Washington St., 503/295-2583, www.eatatblueplate.com; Mon.-Fri. 11am-4pm

IMPERIAL $$

If anyone could open a hotel restaurant and bar that does not suffer from being stodgy and overpriced, it is James Beard Award-winning Vitaly Paley (also owner of Paley's Place). Imperial is bold and unabashed with upscale decor that is gritty and masculine like exposed brick, stone pillars, and bike chain chandeliers. The food is rich and portions large, often served on boards and in cast-iron pans. You can't go wrong with tails and trotters, or rib eye from their wood-fire grill, but make sure you get some Parker House rolls and duck meatballs for the table.

MAP 1: 410 SW Broadway, 503/228-7222, www.imperialpdx.com; Mon.-Thurs. 6:30am-2pm and 5pm-11pm, Fri. 6:30am-2pm and 5pm-midnight, Sat. 8am-2pm and 5pm-midnight, Sun. 8am-2pm and 5pm-11pm

KENNY AND ZUKES $$

Kenny and Zukes was born out of a desire for more authentic Jewish deli food in Portland—more specifically, for good pastrami. Owner Ken Gordon went to work creating just that: a pastrami to serve as the backbone for a number of the dishes in this popular delicatessen. Waits can be long and prices can be steep, but the sandwiches are delicious and huge. You can get a traditional Reuben or pastrami sandwich or mix it up with coleslaw and chopped liver. If you really want to get crazy, try the pastrami burger. The best deal on the menu is the lunch special, a half sandwich served with a cup of soup (try the Hungarian mushroom) or a green salad. If you can't make lunch, happy hour is also a less expensive option.

MAP 1: 1038 SW Stark St., 503/222-3354, www.kennyandzukes.com; Mon.-Thurs. 7am-8pm, Fri.-Sat. 7am-9pm, Sun. 8am-8pm

PICNIC HOUSE $$

This cute American and French-style bistro is bright and open. When the owners of Picnic House pulled up the years of carpeting and paint to reveal the original dark wood and black and white tile, the rustic Prohibition-style Heathman Hotel setting immediately took shape. The menu is simple, with a few entrées and small plates featuring soups, salads, and sandwiches as well as charcuterie and desserts. You can even rent a fully-loaded picnic basket house-made treats and wine and eat it in the adjacent Park Blocks.

MAP 1: 723 SW Salmon St., 503/227-0705, www.picnichousepdx.com,; Mon.-Sat. 11am-3pm, 5pm-10pm

RED STAR TAVERN & ROAST HOUSE $$$

The best place to settle in at Red Star is one of the elevated booths in the bar. From there, you have a fantastic view of the restaurant and the enormous wall of booze that features one of the city's best collections of bourbon. The menu tends to focus on classic American cuisine, with rotisserie meats as the main attraction. Chef Tom Dunklin likes to use organic and local products whenever possible, so the menu changes often but always provides a healthy balance of vegetarian and carnivore-friendly dishes.

MAP 1: 503 SW Alder St., 503/222-0005, www.redstartavern.com; Mon.-Thurs. 6:30am-10:30am, 11:30am-2:30pm, and 5pm-9pm, Fri. 6:30am-10:30am, 11:30am-2:30pm, and 5pm-11pm, Sat. 8am-3pm and 5pm-11pm, Sun. 8am-3pm and 5pm-9pm

VERITABLE QUANDARY $$$

Tucked into the trees and high-rises of downtown is this tiny Portland classic that the locals tend to call "The VQ." This establishment has been around since 1971 and has since been a favorite for the lunchtime business crowd, post-theater-goers, and foodies alike. The menu changes almost daily and often includes such must-have delights as bacon-wrapped dates, wild mushroom salad, and osso bucco. The chocolate souffle is also

Top: Imperial. **Bottom:** Red Star Tavern & Roast House.

delightful, but order it at the beginning of your meal. It takes 40 minutes to prepare!

MAP 1: 1220 SW 1st Ave., 503/227-7342, www.veritablequandary.com; Mon.-Fri. 11:30am-3pm, 5pm-10pm, Sat.-Sun. 9:30am-3pm, 5pm-10pm

ASIAN

MASU SUSHI $$$

Masu is to sushi what Bob Fosse is to choreography—sexy and surprising, but still introspective. The feel is all at once fluid and angular. During the daytime, Masu is open and bright, lit by the huge windows and white curtains that adorn this second-story space. At night, the space heats up with an amber glow that is perfect for intimate dining. It would appear that the specialty rolls are the real stars here—and they are worth their price, but since Masu is really more about the fish, not the sauce, the *nigiri* is not to be ignored. If that's not your thing, try the burger: this Kobe beef patty with kimchi mayo and caramelized onions is surprisingly delicious.

MAP 1: 406 SW 13th Ave., 503/221-6278, www.masusushi.com; Mon.-Thurs. 11:30am-11pm, Fri. 11:30am-midnight, Sat. 4pm-midnight, Sun. 4pm-10pm

SAUCEBOX $$

Since 1995, the folks at Saucebox have attempted to bring together fantastic food, perfectly crafted cocktails, exceptional music, and inspired decor to create an approachable chic nightlife atmosphere. In short, they have spent a long time cultivating a "place to be seen" cocktail lounge. Saucebox's dinner menu features sushi and simple but cautiously creative pan-Asian dishes that put this place shoulder-to-shoulder with many of Portland's fine dining destinations. Plates arrive with the beautiful presentation, but the use of fresh local and regional ingredients saves it from being too pretentious. You can order dim sum-style dishes like pot stickers, chicken dumplings, and salad rolls, or dig into a full-size entrée such as Korean ribs or grilled duck.

MAP 1: 214 SW Broadway, 503/241-3393, www.saucebox.com; Tues.-Fri. 4:30pm-midnight, Sat. 5pm-2am

BREAKFAST AND BRUNCH

MOTHER'S BISTRO & BAR $$

With a name like Mother's, you can probably guess what sort of food owner Lisa Schroeder is famous for serving up. Comfort is key here, and while you stare at the ample plates full of such belly-rich dishes as the near-infamous crunchy French toast, you can almost hear your mother whisper, "Eat! You look skinny!" The sun-drenched dining room is a fine place to start your day, but make sure you come back and hunker down in the richly appointed Velvet Lounge, where Mom's Meatloaf & Gravy is served well into the night.

MAP 1: 212 SW Stark St., 503/464-1122, www.mothersbistro.com; Tues.-Thurs. 7am-2:30pm, 5:30pm-9pm, Fri. 7am-2:30pm, 5pm-10pm, Sat. 8am-2:30pm and 5pm-10pm, Sun. 8am-2:30pm

Top: Voodoo Doughnut. Bottom: Mother's Bistro & Bar.

★ TASTY N ALDER $$

John Gorham is a bit of a legend in the Portland culinary scene—responsible for Tasty n Alder and its big brother **Tasty n Sons** (3803 N. Williams St., www.tastynsons.com) and their big daddy, Toro Bravo. You will find the occasional customer-favorite items on all of the menus, like the bacon-wrapped dates or the chocolate potato doughnuts with crème anglaise. But, for the most part, each restaurant has its own, expertly crafted menu. There are few places in Portland where it is truly worth the potentially long brunch line, and this is one of them.

MAP 1: 580 SW 12th Ave., 503/621-9251, www.tastynalder.com; Mon.-Thurs. and Sun. 9am-10pm, Fri.-Sat. 9am-11pm, 5pm-10pm

VOODOO DOUGHNUT $

After the bartenders announce last call and the waitstaff swipe the empty glasses from all the tables of Portland's downtown bars, one late-night eatery is still going strong. Voodoo Doughnut in the Old Town neighborhood has been a haven for creatures of the night since its opening in 2003. Owners Tres Shannon and Kenneth Pogson reject conformity by offering such doughnuts as the Dirt Doughnut, covered in vanilla glaze and crushed Oreos, and the Maple Blazer Blunt, a cinnamon doughnut rolled to look like an oversized joint with a red sprinkled tip. Still, the real draw here is the peculiar atmosphere. The offerings are quirky, queer, and not a bit serious. You can even get legally hitched under the giant Cruller Chandelier of Life. Voodoo is a cash-only establishment.

MAP 1: 22 SW 3rd Ave., 503/241-4704, www.voodoodoughnut.com; daily 24 hours

COFFEE AND DESSERTS

★ BLUE STAR DOUGHNUTS $

Blue Star opened their first location in December of 2012. Now, they have four locations around town and still often close their doors by 3pm because the last doughnut is already gone. The difference is in the dough. Owner Micah Camden decided to go with a brioche-style dough, which is labor-intensive, but results in a chewier, more pillow-like doughnut. The flavors are sophisticated as well with favorites such as Blueberry Bourbon Basil, Passion Fruit and Cocoa Nib, and Contreau Crème Brulee. Small children might be turned off by the more complex flavors, but they are likely to appreciate the Old Fashioned Buttermilk, which is just about the best thing you will ever put in your mouth.

MAP 1: 1237 SW Washington St., 503/265-8410, www.bluestardoughnuts.com; daily 8am-sold out

★ CACAO $

There's nothing like a cup of hot chocolate to fight off the rain and cold, unless of course you have had a cup of drinking chocolate. What's the difference? Hot chocolate is made from cocoa powder containing only a small amount of cocoa butter, and the drinking chocolate is made with whole chocolate, which naturally contains more than 50 percent cocoa butter. The flavor is rich and intense. It is all at once soothing and invigorating. If you are used to hitting a cup of coffee first thing in the morning, give Cacao a try. A small, thick cup of drinking chocolate might bring you quite surprising results.

MAP 1: 414 SW 13th Ave., 503/241-0656, www.cacaodrinkchocolate.com; Mon.-Thurs. 10am-8pm, Fri.-Sat. 10am-10pm, Sun. 11am-6pm

COURIER COFFEE [$]

While other coffee shops attempt to turn their spaces into high-tech living rooms as a draw, Courier is much more laid-back about its approach. Coming to Courier is like visiting a really cool friend—only that friend makes really great coffee. On a hot summer day they are likely to offer you a mason jar of water while you wait for your coffee to go. Meanwhile, they make every cup of drip coffee individually; reduce their own vanilla syrup; hand-write menus, business cards, and bag logos; and bake up some truly amazing treats. The most famous of these treats is the *canelé*, a bundt-shaped French pastry with a soft, tender custard center and a dark, thick caramelized crust.

MAP 1: 923 SW Oak St., 503/545-6444, www.couriercoffeeroasters.com; Mon.-Fri. 7am-6pm, Sat. 9am-5pm

STUMPTOWN COFFEE ROASTERS [$]

Portlanders take their coffee pretty seriously (in a reusable or recyclable cup, thank you), and Stumptown is at the top of the list for most java hounds. The beans at Stumptown are meticulously selected, sorted, roasted, and brewed so that you get the distinct flavor, sweetness, and complexity of the bean, not the scorched bean flavor that so many of us have become accustomed to. This particular hamlet of the Stumptown universe is near the ground floor of the all-too-hip Ace Hotel, and you are welcome to take your coffee and enjoy it in the comfy lobby of the hotel. Just don't forget to pick up a bag of beans to take home. You are going to want them later.

MAP 1: 1026 SW Stark St., 503/224-9060, www.stumptowncoffee.com; Mon.-Fri. 6am-7pm, Sat.-Sun. 7am-7pm

FRENCH

HIGGINS [$][$][$]

Higgins is classic Portland-style dining meets French countryside, with its comfortable and classy dining room, attentive but not intrusive service, and robust, locally harvested menu. Higgins was doing vegetarian long before it caught on, and while it still does it right, the real specialty is meat. House-cured charcuterie plates always satisfy. The seasonally prepared duck is a favorite among critics, and the Whole Pig Plate (a dish heaped with such things as roast loin, kielbasa, braised belly, and ribs) frequently shows up on lists of the top must-have dishes in Portland. Higgins is a popular pre-show

Top: Blue Star Doughnuts. **Bottom:** Stumptown Coffee Roasters.

spot, given its proximity to many of the downtown concert halls and theaters, so it is best to make a reservation.

MAP 1: 1239 SW Broadway, 503/222-9070, www.higginsportland.com; Mon.-Fri. 11:30am-midnight, Sat.-Sun. 4pm-midnight

★ LITTLE BIRD $$

Sophisticated little sister to the award-winning east-side Portland favorite Le Pigeon, Little Bird opened in late 2011 to much acclaim. Little Bird features audacious French-inspired dishes but with a slightly simpler, more traditional palate. Reviews of the place border on salacious, with critics turning out lustful phrases about roasted marrow bones and charcuterie plates. There are many blush-worthy items on the menu, but don't overlook the Le Pigeon burger. It's pricey but well worth it. If you can manage to snag an upstairs table, do it. You will be treated to a slightly more intimate and quieter perch for people-watching.

MAP 1: 219 SW 6th Ave., 503/688-5952, www.littlebirdbistro.com; Mon.-Fri. 11:30am-midnight, Sat.-Sun. 5pm-midnight

ITALIAN

MAMA MIA TRATTORIA $$

Mama Mia Trattoria is not the place to find traditional Italian, but if you are looking for comfort, this is the spot. Owner Lisa Schroeder is famous for her pillow-soft gnocchi and her Sunday gravy, a sauce she simmers all day and serves with penne, sausage, pork, and a meatball the size of your fist.

It's in an elite class for Portland, which otherwise lacks for true Italian-American soul food. The food here seems like it was snatched from the kitchen of someone's *nonna,* yet surprisingly, Mama Mia's has vegetarian options and will make many of the dishes vegan-friendly upon request. If you have room for dessert (or even if you don't), grab some out-of-this-world *zeppole* (fried dough balls sprinkled with powdered sugar) and a glass of moscato before you go.

MAP 1: 439 SW 2nd Ave., 503/295-6464, www.mamamiatrattoria.com; Mon.-Thurs. 4pm-9pm, Fri. 4pm-10pm, Sat. 10am-10pm, Sun. 10am-9pm

PAZZO RISTORANTE $$$

Pazzo has been serving up classic, reliably satisfying Italian dishes with a Pacific Northwest influence since 1991. It's a popular place for lunchtime and dinnertime business traffic. Pazzo does the simplest things best, like a butternut squash ravioli in an unfussy brown butter sauce, or a salad of young greens with berries and balsamic vinaigrette. The adjacent bakery, Pazzoria, supplies all of the bread and baked goods, and if you're looking for a quick bite—a salad, sandwich, slice of pizza, or pastry—rather than a rich meal, that's where you will want to go.

MAP 1: 627 SW Washington St., 503/228-1515, www.pazzo.com; Mon.-Thurs. 7am-10:30am, 11:30am-2:30pm, and 5pm-9:30pm; Fri. 7am-10:30am, 11:30am-2:30pm, and 5pm-11pm; Sat. 8am-2pm and 4:30pm-11pm; Sun. 8am-2pm and 4pm-9pm

How to Hack the Line

It is a long running joke that Portlanders' favorite pastime is waiting in line, and a quick look around will make that seem very plausible. Lines for ice cream stretch around the block. Brunch lines groan out onto the sidewalks. Fortunately, there are a few tricks to help you avoid losing valuable time standing around.

Salt & Straw (three locations, www.saltandstraw.com) is getting national attention for their amazing small batch artisanal ice cream. Even on drizzly, wet days, you will see a line of people waiting to sample a little Honey Lavender or Stumptown Coffee and Burnside Bourbon. Is it worth it? Yeah, it is—especially since you can have an opportunity to sample as many flavors as you like before choosing. However, if you have an inkling of what you would like, simply walk in and grab a pint from the prepacked freezer. There's no need to wait in line to pay.

If beer is more your thing, but you can't stand the idea of wading through the throngs of people at the nearest pub, check out one of Portland's many bottle shops or growler stations. **Belmont Station** (4500 SE Stark St., 503/232-8538, www.belmont-station.com) has long been a destination for beer lovers, and with its proximity to so many popular pubs and bars, it is often a stop for folks looking to get out of the scene and settle in with a good beer. The same can be said for **The Hop and Vine** (191 N. Killingsworth St., 503/954-3322, www.the-hopandvine.com) and **The Cheese Bar** (6031 SE Belmont St., 503/222-6014, www.cheese-bar.com). While both spots are great little hangouts in their own right, they are also solid spots to grab some treats and a bottle of your favorite brew or vintage and head to the hills (or a hotel).

Many pubs and markets also offer growler filling. You simply bring a glass jug (or buy one from the venue) and they will fill it and send you on your way. **Fat Head's Brewery** (131 NW 13th St., www.fatheads.com) in the Pearl District is happy to pour you a jug of their Headhunter IPA, or whatever else you fancy. And **Fire on the Mountain** (three locations, www.portlandwings.com), despite being known for their wings, has their own brewery and offers both 32-ounce and 64-ounce growlers of their ale.

Feel peckish before the blues band you are about to see? If you are waiting for a show at **Aladdin Theater** (3017 SE Milwaukie Ave., 503/234-9694, www.aladdin-theater.com), pop into the Lamp next door and order some dinner. They will give you a wristband to bypass the line when the doors open.

RISTORANTE ROMA $$

If you are looking for a quaint dining atmosphere and authentic Italian food, Ristorante Roma is a pretty safe bet with simple, elegant nods to the old-world recipes that employ all of the best resources Italy has to offer, including the sea. Try the cold sea salad with salmon, calamari, octopus, and shrimp or the near perfect gnocchi—but save room for the house-made *panna cotta*. The tiny place gets quite crowded around dinnertime, but it does take reservations.

MAP 1: 622 SW 12th Ave., 503/241-2692, www.ristoranteromaportland.com; Mon.-Thurs. 11:30am-2pm and 5:30pm-9pm, Fri.-Sat. 5pm-9:30pm

Salt & Straw

Sometimes, the key to getting want you want is to stake out the other locations of a Portland hot spot. Tourist favorite **Voodoo Doughnut** (www.voodoodoughnut.com) has a second and much larger location on the east side of the river. **Cupcake Jones** (www.cupcakejones.net) opened a shop on northeast Alberta Street that is much less cramped than their Pearl District location.

Finally, with some places, you just have to know when to go. With touristy spots, you will have a better chance when the weather turns for the worse. Dinner in Portland is a bit of an affair and people take their time getting to it. Skip the happy hour and head straight to dinner. Most restaurants start seating at about 4pm or 5pm, and it is much easier to get a table. At **Toro Bravo** (120 NE Russell St., 503/281-4464, www.torobravopdx.com) the dinner crowd gets thick around 7pm, so it is best to show up at 5pm. Don't eschew an opportunity to sit at the bar. You will get seated faster, and your service will be much more focused.

STEAK AND SEAFOOD

★ EL GAUCHO $$$

El Gaucho is an anomaly among Portland restaurants. While most thrive on a balance of quality food with a laid-back setting, the tuxedo-clad servers at El Gaucho will come just short of cutting your 28-day dry-aged Porterhouse for you. In fact, if you asked them to do it, they probably would. A meal will run you a pretty penny, but the steaks are some of the best. Skip the sides and focus on the collection of stellar appetizers, like the amazing (albeit ostentatious) seafood tower and the Caesar salad, prepared tableside. If you still have room, order the bananas Foster, also prepared tableside over an open flame.

MAP 1: 319 SW Broadway, 503/227-8794, www.elgaucho.com; Mon.-Thurs. 4:30pm-11pm, Fri.-Sat. 5pm-midnight, Sun. 4:30pm-10pm

JAKE'S FAMOUS CRAWFISH $$

Jake's is a Portland legend that has been a city landmark for more than 100 years. Inside, the deep burnished wood booths and rich decor lend a touch of masculine luxury and class to the place. The menu at Jake's is printed daily (and occasionally reprinted) to incorporate freshly caught fish and in-season specialties. While the seafood here is some of the best in the Northwest (and eventually launched an entire chain of restaurants for owners Bill McCormick and Doug Schmick), Portlanders love Jake's for its affordable and extensive happy hour—with nosh like the Jake's burger or shrimp ceviche for only $1.95. For that reason, it's a popular spot for locals to gather for post-work cocktails, Kobe beef sliders, and plate after plate of peel 'n' eat shrimp.

MAP 1: 401 SW 12th Ave., 503/226-1419, www.mccormickandschmicks.com; Mon.-Thurs. 11:30am-10pm, Fri.-Sat. 11:30am-11pm, Sun. 3pm-10pm

PORTLAND CITY GRILL $$$

If you would like to get a greater perspective on the city of Portland, look no further than Portland City Grill. Resting 30 floors above the city in the "Big Pink" U.S. Bankcorp Tower, the restaurant provides not only spectacular views of town and the Cascades, but also a classy atmosphere perfect for special occasions. This place is all about making an impression, so if you can, make a reservation and secure a table by the window. The menu at City Grill is a mix of traditional steakhouse and high-end sushi joint. But whether you opt for a rib eye or some wild Northwest salmon, make sure you order some of the infamous Kung Pao calamari.

MAP 1: 111 SW 5th Ave., 503/450-0030, www.portlandcitygrill.com; Mon.-Thurs. 11am-midnight, Fri. 11am-1am, Sat. 4pm-1am, Sun. noon-11pm

SOUTHPARK SEAFOOD GRILL & WINE BAR $$$

Riding the edge between the downtown core and the South Park Blocks, the exterior of Southpark Seafood Grill is deceptively unassuming. With little more of note than a statue of a bronze salmon bursting through the brick facade, the restaurant and wine bar seems like an innocuously quaint bistro. Inside, however, Southpark is a rock-solid example of Northwest cuisine, with an impeccable wine list and a staff knowledgeable enough to back it up. Of course, seafood is the forte, with fresh-caught crab, prawns, scallops, and fish starring on the menu. Daily specials are often fresh-from-the-sea, simple, and creative. Reservations are recommended, but if you don't have one or if you arrive early, you can visit the adjacent wine bar (open daily until midnight), sample some superb Northwest wines, and choose from a respectable selection of favorites from the full Southpark menu.

MAP 1: 901 SW Salmon St., 503/326-1300, www.southparkseafood.com; Mon.-Thurs. 11:30am-3pm and 5pm-10pm, Fri.-Sat. 11:30am-3pm and 5pm-11pm

Top: Little Bird. **Bottom:** Pazzo Ristorante.

URBAN FARMER $$$

A new kid on the upscale block is Urban Farmer, a modern-style American steakhouse on the eighth floor of the Nines Hotel. Without any discernible walls, the restaurant seems to shrink into the vast open space of the overhead four-story atrium. While the scene evokes an elegant rooftop bar, the vibe is decidedly chill and the clientele characteristically eclectic. The menu is beef-centric, and there are plenty of choices to suit your taste, whether you prefer pasture-fed, corn-fed, or the oh-so-buttery Wagyu beef. After you order, your server will present you with a wooden box, from which you may choose your own knife, and a tin can filled with a tasty loaf of pumpkin bread (a signature recipe). Wash it all down with one of the classic cocktails, many made with locally distilled spirits.

MAP 1: 525 SW Morrison St., inside the Nines Hotel, 503/222-4900, http://urbanfarmerrestaurant.com; Sun.-Thurs. 6am-3pm, 5pm-10pm, Fri.-Sat. 6:30am-11pm

Northwest and the Pearl District

Map 2

From the industrial swank of the Pearl District to the bustling energy of the Alphabet District and Nob Hill, Northwest Portland is a wonderfully walkable area with a dizzying array of culinary options. Stroll the Pearl for some of the newest darlings on the scene, for tapas bars, posh cafés, and elegant eateries. Or venture onto NW 23rd (also known as "Trendy Third"), where some of Portland's best restaurants have dwelled for years.

AMERICAN

INDUSTRIAL CAFE AND SALOON $$

Outfitted in rustic wood and industrial metalwork, this café is both trendy and laid-back. It offers traditional American fare for lunch and dinner, such as hamburgers, steaks, macaroni and cheese, and salads. Brunch-time diners will find breakfast highlights like biscuits and gravy (with industrial cog-shaped biscuits), apple French toast, omelets, and chipped beef on toast. Industrial has a respectable beer and wine menu as well as a cocktail menu that befits its theme. There's nothing fancy here, just simple, hearty food and a diverse enough menu to satisfy most appetites.

MAP 2: 2572 NW Vaughn St., 503/227-7002; Mon.-Fri. 8am-9pm, Sat.-Sun. 8am-3pm

★ OLYMPIA PROVISIONS $$

Opened in 2009, Olympia Provisions is Oregon's first USDA-approved *salumeria* (cured-meat shop), and it operates out of two locations in Portland: the original **Southeast Portland location** (107 SE Washington St., 503/954-3663) and this one, tucked in a warehouse space under the Morrison Bridge. At the back of this 30-seat house is a 4,000-square-foot all-purpose meat-curing facility, where award-winning salumist Elias Cairo

Top: Olympia Provisions. Bottom: ¡Oba!.

crafts some of the finest charcuterie meats around. The menu is simple: a smattering of rustic European-inspired fares and Northwest favorites. And if cured meats really are king here, the queen is perhaps the signature roasted chicken, cooked to perfection on a vintage rotisserie and then crisped in a pan. You can order the famous Sunday Chicken Dinner (complete with salad and seasonal sides) to dine on there or take with you for a high-class picnic. But no visit to Olympia Provisions is complete without sampling the charcuterie. At the least stop at the counter and purchase some to take with you.

MAP 2: 1632 NW Thurman St., 503/894-8136, www.olympiaprovisions.com; Mon. 11am-3pm, Tues.-Fri. 11am-10pm, Sat. 10am-10pm, Sun. 10am-9pm

SMOKEHOUSE 21 $$

Authentic barbecue is tough to find on this coast, but many agree that Smokehouse 21 is on the right track. It has all the requisite menu items that define a good barbecue joint: brisket, ribs, pulled pork, braised greens, cornbread, potato salad, and macaroni and cheese. Both the brisket and the pulled pork are moist, rich, and smoky, and all the meats are served with a choice of four sauces. The sides are good enough to stand alone, especially the mac and cheese and the baked beans, both in a ramekin and topped with a breadcrumb crust and bits of meat. To top it all off, Smokehouse 21 has a small selection of wines and an impressive selection of canned beers (which are quite appropriately served nestled in a house-branded beer koozie).

MAP 2: 413 NW 21st Ave., 971/373-8990, www.smokehouse21.com; Sun.-Thurs. 11:30am-10pm, Fri.-Sat. 11:30am-midnight

ASIAN

★ BAMBOO SUSHI $$$

There are a number of really great sushi restaurants in Portland, but Bamboo Sushi made waves when it opened in 2008, not just because the sushi was top-notch, but also because this was the first certified sustainable sushi restaurant in the world. The NW 23rd location is the second and newest outpost to their immensely popular **Southeast Portland location** (310 SE 28th Ave., 503/232-5255), but it doesn't mean the lines will be shorter, so make reservations whenever possible. There are fun specialty rolls, like the Green Machine with tempura asparagus, avocado, green onion, and cilantro sweet chili aioli, or the Highway 35 (a critic favorite), which has red crab, spicy sesame aioli, avocado, cucumber, and asparagus topped with sake-poached pears and eel sauce. Sample the sashimi and *nigiri* rolls, but don't overlook the Kobe burger. It is, arguably, one of the best in the city.

MAP 2: 836 NW 23rd Ave., 971/229-1925, www.bamboosushi.com; daily 4:30pm-10pm

HOUSE OF LOUIE $

If you're a fan of dim sum, House of Louie will have you singing for your brunch, because here, the dim sum carts run daily. One of the most popular items is *nor my gai* (pronounced "normy guy"), a gooey, sticky rice wrapped in lotus leaves and stuffed with little treasures like shrimp, Chinese sausages, chicken, and barbecued pork. Diners also love Louie's garlicky Chinese broccoli and the sautéed bok choy. For the kiddies—or the kiddies at heart—Louie's will swing around a cart that is toppling with Jello-filled parfait dishes adorned with colorful flags. It may seem daunting, but the best choice is the creamy, white coconut gelatin. It's not too sweet and the smooth texture is a nice finish to the meal. If you miss the dim sum hours (10am-3pm) or if you can't bear to wait for an item to come around, you can order most of the dishes directly from the menu.

MAP 2: 331 NW Davis St., 503/228-9898; daily 10am-10pm

RED ONION ❶❸

Portlanders love Thai food, and Red Onion is a cut above. Former owner of two other local restaurants, chef Dang Boonyakamol has made a name for himself by creating authentic northern Thai dishes—both traditional and unexpected. If you are a fan of heat, you will appreciate that they can actually bring it here without sacrificing the flavor. If you must, stick with the standards such as *pad kee mao* or chicken curry, but if you are feeling adventurous, try one of the more distinctive specialties, like a crisp-skinned catfish or rolls filled with Chinese sausage, shrimp, egg, and cucumber and topped with Dungeness crab.

MAP 2: 1123 NW 23rd Ave., 503/208-2634, www.redonionportland.com; Mon.-Fri. 11am-3pm and 5pm-9:30pm, Sat. noon-9:30pm, Sun. noon-9pm

BREAKFAST AND BRUNCH
BYWAYS CAFÉ ❸

Byways has received a healthy helping of fame since the Food Network paid a visit, but locals have been flocking here for years to sample the omelets, scrambles, and corned beef hash. Byways is also famous for its blue corn pancakes, made with ground blue corn and served with honey pecan butter. The corn cakes are good, but nothing compares to the amaretto French toast.

The weekend wait can be long here, as at many Portland breakfast joints. To make it more bearable, arrive early, bring something to read, and pick up something caffeinated on the way. Byways doesn't offer free sidewalk coffee, but servers will take your drink order if you ask.

MAP 2: 1212 NW Glisan St., 503/221-0011, www.bywayscafe.com; Mon.-Fri. 7am-3pm, Sat.-Sun. 7:30am-2pm

THE DAILY CAFÉ ❶❸

Sundays at the Daily Café are prix-fixe brunch days, and the seats fill up fast. It's not much of a surprise when you consider the fact that the Daily has one of the cheapest (albeit quality) brunches in town. For about $14, you get your choice of appetizer and entrée as well as a basket of freshly baked goodies for the table. Have a bowl of Josie's "soon-to-be-famous"

fruit and nut granola with a savory frittata, or nibble on some mascarpone rice pudding while you wait for your cornmeal-crusted trout and eggs. If you really do love the granola, you can take a bag home with you; just ask.
MAP 2: 902 NW 13th Ave., 503/242-1916, www.dailycafeinthepearl.com; Mon.-Fri. 7am-5pm, Sat. 8am-3pm, Sun. 9am-2pm

ST. HONORÉ BOULANGERIE $

If your idea of a good breakfast is a smooth latte and a buttery pastry, St. Honoré is a great place to start your day. Named for the patron saint of bakers, St. Honoré takes its influences from the bakery ovens of Normandy. The traditional clay brick oven was imported brick by kaolin clay brick to Portland—where the earthen sides retain moisture and provide for more even baking (in other words, perfectly flaky croissants and custard-rich *canalets*). If you don't have much of a sweet tooth, ask for a slice of freshly made quiche or the astounding *croque monsieur* sandwich (grilled brioche with Black Forest ham, Emmentaler cheese, béchamel sauce, and Dijon mustard) and grab a seat at one of the sidewalk tables.
MAP 2: 2335 NW Thurman St., 503/445-4342, www.sainthonorebakery.com; daily 7am-8pm

BURGERS

LITTLE BIG BURGER $

Little Big Burger may have only six items on the menu (cheeseburger, hamburger, veggie burger, fries, soda, and floats), but each is well-executed and unfussy. Cheeseburgers come with a choice of Tillamook cheddar, Swiss, chèvre, or blue cheese. Fries are cooked in white truffle oil and sprinkled with sea salt. If you have a hearty appetite, you will probably want to order two burgers. LBB uses quarter-pound patties of Cascade beef on a brioche bun, so it is basically the size of a large slider. Make sure you try some of the Camden's Catsup created by LBB owner Micah Camden. It's a mix of tomato paste, champagne vinegar, hemp seed, and spices, with honey and just a touch of Sriracha sauce for a kick.
MAP 2: 122 NW 10th Ave., 503/274-9008, www.littlebigburger.com; daily 11am-10pm

COFFEE AND DESSERTS

COFFEEHOUSE NORTHWEST $

Don't let the generic name fool you; Coffeehouse Northwest has been a longtime favorite in the Nob Hill area. They take the coffee-making process so seriously they would frankly rather you stay for a while and sip your cappuccino out of a real cup, not a paper to-go cup. The menu is simple and pared down to just a few basics—coffee, cappuccino, latte, espresso, and mocha—but each beverage is made with the utmost care. There are a couple of larger tables for gathering, but mostly, the place is lined with small tables and outlets for plugging in laptops. The exposed brick walls always have art adorning them, but with Edison lamps and woodwork all over, the place is a work of art on its own.

MAP 2: 1951 W. Burnside St., 503/248-2133; Mon.-Fri. 6:30am-6pm, Sat.-Sun. 8am-5pm

★ CUPCAKE JONES $

It doesn't take a thinking man to figure out why cupcakes have become so popular. They're sweet, portable, and provide infinite possibilities for creative flavor combinations. Cupcake Jones knows a thing or two about the business. Owners Peter and Lisa are adamant about using locally sourced ingredients and giving everything they can back to the community. At the tiny Pearl District bakery (second location at 1405 NE Alberta St.) it's not uncommon to see a line out the door of people waiting to get their hands on one of the daily specials. They have almost a dozen standard flavors available every day (among them Lemoncello, red velvet, carrot and Boston cream), and a handful of seasonal offerings each day as well. Cupcakes can be ordered in miniature bite-size treats or jumbo-size filled cakes that are roughly the size of a softball. They have vegan and gluten-free options in some flavors and even special cupcakes for dogs.

MAP 2: 307 NW 10th Ave., 503/222-4404, www.cupcakejones.net; Mon.-Sat. 10am-8pm, Sun. noon-6pm

MOONSTRUCK CHOCOLATE CAFÉ $$

Moonstruck has three café locations in Portland—and some of the best coffee drinks around. A Mexican mocha is less of a morning pick me-up and more of a decadent treat, especially since you get a free coin of dark chocolate to nibble on with your drink. The cafés have all manner of hot drinks throughout the year, and when summer comes around, they break out some pretty unbelievable ice cream shakes. While the coffee, hot chocolate, and truffles—did I mention the truffles?!—are enough to send any chocoholic into cardiac arrest, various cakes will also satisfy that sweet tooth. The other two Portland locations are **downtown** (608 SW Alder St., 503/241-0955; 700 SW 5th Ave., 503/219-9118).

MAP 2: 526 NW 23rd Ave., 503/542-3400, www.moonstruckchocolate.com; Mon.-Thurs. 8am-10pm, Fri.-Sat. 8am 11pm, Sun. 9am-9pm

SALT & STRAW $

In a city like Portland, where you'll find an abundance of food carts and restaurants dedicated to very specific food passions, it makes sense that there would be an ice cream shop that specializes in small-batch innovative concoctions. Owners Tyler and Kim Malek have collaborated with a number of Portland chefs to create a roster of flavors ranging from sea salt with a caramel ribbon and honey lavender to pear with blue cheese and arbequina olive oil. And while their ice cream continues to receive national acclaim, their Northwest Portland location includes a bakery where they

Top: Cupcake Jones. **Bottom:** pints available at Salt & Straw.

are serving up other goodies, like Stumptown Coffee, hand pies, dough-nuts, and freshly baked scones, muffins, and cookies.

MAP 2: 836 NW 23rd Ave., 971/271-8168, www.saltandstraw.com; daily 7am-11pm

FRENCH
LE HAPPY $

In one of the lesser-traveled areas of Northwest Portland is a tiny little café that specializes in the French equivalent of comfort food: the crêpe. Trust me now, these are nothing like your average pancake-chain crêpes. Besides being tasty and filling, the darn things are pretty versatile, too. You can order them savory or sweet in styles that range from elegant (such as the Saumon Fumé, with smoked salmon and white wine) to the downright trashy (Le Trash Blanc, with bacon and cheddar, and an optional can of Pabst Blue Ribbon on the side). On the sweeter side of the menu, some local favorites are the simple clover honey and lemon crêpe and the delectable Spectac, made with Grand Marnier, Nutella, and banana flambé.

MAP 2: 1011 NW 16th Ave., 503/226-1258, www.lehappy.com; Mon.-Thurs. 5pm-midnight, Fri.-Sat. 5pm-1:30am

PALEY'S PLACE $$$

Chef-owners Vitaly and Kimberly Paley are renowned in kitchens across the nation, having worked in some of the most illustrious restaurants on the map. Thankfully, the couple settled in Portland in the early 1990s for the blessed bounty of ingredients. Years after opening their intimate 50-seat restaurant, the Paleys are still receiving national acclaim for their French-influenced dishes, such as seasonal risottos, crispy sweetbreads, and hearty cassoulets. After dinner, switch things up a bit and ask for a cheese course instead of dessert. Pair it with a glass of local wine for a perfectly rounded meal.

MAP 2: 1204 NW 21st Ave., 503/243-2403, www.paleysplace.net; Mon.-Thurs. 5:30pm-10pm, Fri.-Sat. 5:30pm-11pm, Sun. 5:30pm-10pm

LATIN
ANDINA $$$

One of Portland's best restaurants, this Pearl District Peruvian tapas place has one of the most inspired and extensive small plates menus in town. You can order traditional entrées—like pork tenderloin or Pisco-brined Cornish hen—but a better bet is to order two or three *pequeño* (small) plates each and share. The empanadas, filled with slow-cooked beef, raisins, and olives, are a must—as is the yucca root stuffed with cheese.

Both floors of Andina get packed nearly every night, so expect a wait or book ahead online. Once seated, order a Sacsayhuamán cocktail (just say, "sexy woman") and soak in the atmosphere.

MAP 2: 1314 NW Glisan St., 503/228-9535, www.andinarestaurant.com; Sun.-Thurs. 11:30am-2:30pm and 5pm-9:30pm, Fri.-Sat. 11:30am-2:30pm and 5pm-10:30pm

ISABEL PEARL 💲💲

Isabel Cruz, the California-based chef and owner of this smallish Pearl District fusion café, draws influence from Puerto Rican, Cuban, Mexican, Japanese, and Thai cooking. While lettuce wraps and edamame alongside carnitas may seem strange, Cruz manages to make it work. Her food is akin to spa food—elegant, colorful, and oftentimes quite good for you. Order Cruz's signature Crispy Dragon Potatoes as a breakfast entrée with eggs and bacon or as an appetizer. For dinner, the Big Bowls are always reliable. The menu also includes a decent happy hour, but the breakfast and lunch offerings are still more extensive.

MAP 2: 330 NW 10th Ave., 503/222-4333, www.isabelscantina.com; daily 8am-3pm and 5pm-9pm

¡OBA! 💲💲

Show up around happy hour at ¡Oba! and you'll see where many of the pretty Pearl District denizens hang out, sipping exotic cocktails and nibbling at equally pretty plates of ceviche. While the happy hour is popular for its affordability and see-and-be-seen buzz, you should skip that and splurge on the full dinner experience. The staff is usually very attentive and informed, and the dining room is warm and inviting, with a conversation-friendly layout. It's a wonderful spot to linger and enjoy a long meal. Try the *queso fundido*, a traditional Mexican cheese dip that is served warm with tortilla chips. Follow it up with grilled ahi tuna, served with coconut rice and fresh mango salsa.

MAP 2: 555 NW 12th Ave., 503/228-6161, www.obarestaurant.com; Mon.-Thurs. 4pm-10pm, Fri.-Sat. 4pm-midnight, Sun. 4pm-10pm

SEAFOOD

IRVING STREET KITCHEN 💲💲💲

Irving Street Kitchen is upscale without being snobby—so great for dates and business dinners. It's a touch high-concept, but the Southern-influenced New American cuisine feels both sophisticated and satisfying, with dishes like grilled octopus and frisee salad with a bacon vinaigrette, Dungeness crab stuffed with dirty rice, and maple-smoked brook trout. Don't leave without trying the Angels on Horseback (bacon-wrapped oysters in remoulade sauce), a somewhat silly name for a delight you will be thinking about for days. The menu is not, of course, limited to seafood and includes reliably delicious beef and chicken dishes as well as a pretty good dessert array. If you run out of room, order one of the butterscotch puddings with caramel sauce to go. Served in a reusable glass jar, it's a nice treat once your stomach is less full.

MAP 2: 701 NW 13th St., 503/343-9440, www.irvingstreetkitchen.com; Mon.-Thurs. 4:30pm-10pm, Fri. 4:30pm-11pm, Sat. 10am-2:30pm and 4:30pm-11pm, Sun. 10am-2:30pm and 4:30pm-10pm

THE PARISH $$$

The Parish, which opened in 2012, is the sister restaurant to North Portland's EaT: An Oyster Bar. And, like EaT, it features some of the freshest bivalves available. Oysters are served up raw, baked, and grilled along with a number of their seafaring friends and a bevy of Southern staples like gumbo, étouffée, and jambalaya. A large chalkboard tells you what the freshest catch is, but there's no need to know the difference between a blue pool and a Kumamoto. The staff is knowledgeable and perfectly willing to steer even the most inexperienced eater toward the bivalve that will suit him or her best. Furthermore, if you don't feel like dining at the restaurant, you can walk right up and order some of the day's special oysters and a bottle of wine to go.

MAP 2: 231 NW 11th Ave., 503/227-2421, www.theparishpdx.com; Sun.-Thurs. 11:30am-10pm, Fri.-Sat. 11:30am-11pm

VEGETARIAN

LAUGHING PLANET $

Laughing Planet is a great option if you have meat eaters and vegetarians in tow. The generously sized burritos and bowls will satisfy herbivores and carnivores alike. At this quick-service café (and its six other Portland locations), you will find traditional offerings like a simple grilled chicken burrito with beans, organic brown rice, and Tillamook cheese, but you will also find some more exotic options, like the Che Guevara, with beans, plantains, sweet potatoes, rice, pico, and spicy barbecue sauce. The bowls make for a filling meal as well, with nods to Thai, Moroccan, Indian, and Latin American cuisine. If you don't finish your bowl, you can take it home and throw it into a tortilla later for an all-new twist on your meal.

MAP 2: 922 NW 21st Ave., 503/445-1319, www.laughingplanetcafe.com; daily 11am-9pm

MI MERO MOLE $

For as much as the average Portlander would walk a mile in the rain for a good taco, it is pretty hard to find good, authentic Mexican food. It is even harder if you are a vegetarian. Enter Mi Mero Mole. With two locations in town (the original is at 5026 SE Division), taco lovers on both sides of the river can now get delicious tacos and authentic guisados (comfort food) just like you might score from street vendors in Mexico City. They have some great meaty dishes here, but their vegan and vegetarian dishes are hearty and satisfying and involve ingredients like cactus, squash, mushrooms, or seeds and nuts.

MAP 2: 32 NW 5th Ave., 971/266-8575, www.mmmtacospdx.com; Mon.-Thurs. 11am-9pm, Fri. 11am-10pm, Sat. noon-10pm

PRASAD $

In the Yoga Pearl healing arts center, Prasad stands out as one of Portland's favorite vegetarian cafés. Owner Karen Pride offers up remarkably varied dishes made from locally grown, organically farmed vegetables delivered each day by bicycle. It's a fine fit with the adjacent yoga studio, and although you are asked to keep it quiet out of respect for those meditating, raw foods, salads, pastas, and smoothies they offer are touted to have you leaving feeling better than you did when you came in. Order the Chili Bowl—rice or quinoa, roasted garlic chilies, scallions, and avocado topped with green chili and garlic tahini sauce—and follow it up with a smoothie, a green tea *matcha* latte, or an invigorating shot of wheatgrass.

MAP 2: 925 NW Davis St., 503/224-3993, www.prasadcuisine.com; Mon.-Fri. 7:30am-8pm, Sat.-Sun. 9am-8pm

Northeast
Map 3

The Northeast section of town is easily the most diverse of all the Portland quadrants. From the vibrancy of Martin Luther King Jr. Boulevard to the stately elegance of Irvington and the historic Hollywood District, the cuisine here is just as diverse as the residents who call this area home. The quadrant's high residential base and unpretentious attitude make it a popular destination for families and those who prefer a mom-and-pop-style dining experience.

AMERICAN

CHAMELEON RESTAURANT & BAR $$$

Don't let the unassuming exterior fool you. This place tends to disappear into the backdrop of the Hollywood District, but inside it's a real gem. Cool green drapes adorn the patio, which is lovely in the warmer months. Inside the dining room, white linens and soft amber lighting create a cozy and intimate ambience. The menu changes regularly, reflecting the eclectic tastes of chef-owner Pat Jeung. The seafood dishes and Asian-inspired entrées are especially reliable, but Jeung's butternut squash ravioli, grilled rack of lamb with merlot sauce, and *tom yum* soup are favorites among the regulars.

MAP 3: 2000 NE 40th Ave., 503/460-2682, www.chameleonpdx.com; Wed.-Sat. 5:30pm-10pm

THE COURTYARD RESTAURANT $$

The McMenamin brothers, who own more than 55 pubs, hotels, and theaters around the Northwest, saved this old elementary school from almost certain destruction when they decided to convert it into a hotel and restaurant. The old cafeteria is now The Courtyard Restaurant, where slimy spinach and overcooked beans-and-weenies are no longer on the menu. Instead, they offer hearty salads, freshly baked pizzas and calzones, and generous burgers served alongside thin, shoestring fries. Grab a pint of stellar McMenamins Terminator Stout and check out the specials while you nibble on a basket of tater tots.

MAP 3: 5736 NE 33rd Ave., 503/249-3983, www.mcmenamins.com/797-courtyard-restaurant; daily 7am-1am

LAURELHURST MARKET $$$

Laurelhurst Market is equal parts American brasserie, butcher counter, lunchtime sandwich shop, and neighborhood diner. While a lot of places go overboard showing off the talents of a chef, Laurelhurst seems to revel in the simple touches, like a rib eye finished with blue cheese butter and garnished with fried Walla Walla sweet onions, or the expertly prepared mussels topped with steak frites, Dijon mustard, and crème fraîche. If you want to sample the wares but don't feel like shelling out the cash for dinner, stop by the sandwich counter and try one of the six daily special sandwiches, all constructed with Laurelhurst's own house-made deli meats.

MAP 3: 3155 E. Burnside St., 503/206-3097, www.laurelhurstmarket.com; dinner daily 5pm-10pm, butcher shop and sandwich counter 10am-10pm

NED LUDD $$

The rustic elegance of this Northeast Portland spot is immediately warm and inviting. With stacks of apple and pear wood tucked into corners, dishes piled high on every flat surface, and an open kitchen spilling over with market-fresh produce, this feels just like home—assuming you live in a beautiful cabin and know how to cook. Owners Benjamin Meyer and Jason French have done something really special with their house-made charcuterie and pickle plates, but it's that enormous brick hearth in the middle of the kitchen that makes this place so different.

Named after the same guy that tech-hating Luddites are, Ned Ludd eschews fancy technology in favor of a good old-fashioned wood-fire oven. That means homey wood-fired meat pies, cherry-glazed game hens, and oven-roasted s'mores, all infused with the essence of fruitwood. Monday nights are "Pizza Mondays" when the music gets cranked up and they have special pizza offerings, often from celebrity chefs and well-known pizzaiolos.

MAP 3: 3925 NE Martin Luther King Jr. Blvd., 503/228-6900, www.nedluddpdx.com; Mon.-Fri. 5pm-10pm, Sat.-Sun. 10am-2pm and 5pm-10pm

BREAKFAST AND BRUNCH

CADILLAC CAFÉ $$

Cadillac Café is a breakfast standard, but not in the gritty, greasy spoon way. This is not a venue for nursing your Friday night hangover; rather, it's the sort of place where you might take your mom on Mother's Day. Cadillac is bright and clean with a sprightly sort of attitude that makes you think the servers were nipping into the coffee long before the doors opened. If you have a sweet tooth, you won't want to miss the hazelnut-crusted French toast; otherwise, sink your fork into filet mignon and eggs or one of the hearty scrambles. Oh, and in case you were wondering, there is indeed a Cadillac in the Cadillac Café. A full-size 1961 Caddy in perfect condition is showcased in the center of the restaurant.

MAP 3: 1801 NE Broadway, 503/287-4750, www.cadillaccafepdx.com; Mon.-Fri. 6am-2:30pm, Sat.-Sun. 7am-3pm

RESTAURANTS NORTHEAST

HELSER'S ON ALBERTA $$

If you go to Helser's for any reason, go for the German pancake (also known as a Dutch baby, but that seems a little macabre). The eggy puffed pancake is baked until golden brown and approximately the size of a bowler hat. One is enough to feed the entire table, especially if you order Scotch eggs on the side (hard-boiled eggs wrapped in bratwurst, breaded and fried). If that's not your cup of tea, try the brioche French toast or the smoked salmon hash topped with poached eggs and hollandaise. Order a mimosa made with fresh orange juice and you are well on your way to a food coma.

MAP 3: 1538 NE Alberta St., 503/281-1477, www.helsersonalberta.com; daily 7am-3pm

MILO'S CITY CAFÉ $$

When you visit Milo's, you might have the distinct feeling that you've been there before, not because it's familiar, but because everyone seems to treat you like a regular. The scrambles and omelets are superb, and if you like a good Benedict, there are six to choose from. The crab cake Benedict with fresh Dungeness crab and béarnaise sauce is a neighborhood favorite—as is the Marianne, with cooked-to-order petite tenderloin. Make sure you arrive before 10:30am if you plan to have breakfast. The café switches to lunch at 11, and with the average wait time on the weekends exceeding half an hour, you may not get a chance to order before they stop serving.

MAP 3: 1325 NE Broadway, 503/288-6456, www.miloscitycafe.com; Mon.-Fri. 6:30am-2:30pm and 4:30pm-9:30pm, Sat.-Sun. 7:30am-2:30pm and 4:30pm-9:30pm

COFFEE AND DESSERTS
PIX PATISSERIE $$

Pix is a dessert place in the strictest sense of the word, and it's all about indulgence. Beautiful cakes and tarts looking like they belong on a wall in a gallery instead of on a cake plate sit in ordered, anticipatory silence. Colorful macarons in flavors such as raspberry, rose, and passion fruit beckon to be touched and tasted. A signature dish here is the Amelie, an orange-vanilla crème brûlée atop a glazed chocolate mousse with caramelized hazelnuts, praline crisp, and Cointreau génoise. Check out the website for upcoming dim sum nights, when you may choose from over 20 different desserts as they make their rounds through the restaurant. Each dessert is $3 or less, and you can sample beers for $1 and dessert wines for $3.

MAP 3: 2225 E. Burnside St., www.pixpatisserie.com; Mon.-Fri. 4pm-midnight, Sat.-Sun. 2pm-midnight

FOOD CARTS
THE CHEESE PLATE $

While many of the food carts around Portland are deep-frying their wares, The Cheese Plate is taking a classier approach to indulgence by catering to the frugal gourmet. Take, for example, the namesake dish, which consists of three Oregon cheeses, the cart's own *fromage fort,* three chèvre truffles, a seasonal jam, and cart-made crackers for $8. You can also build your own picnic platter (and consume it at the nearby picnic tables) with items like soft-boiled eggs with truffle oil and seaweed caviar, mushroom and kale pâté, and freshly made pickles. There is always a seasonal cheese-focused sandwich option on the menu and usually something heavier like macaroni and cheese. The cart also sells house-made spreads and crackers to take home.

MAP 3: 2231 NE Alberta St., www.thecheeseplatepdx.com; Wed.-Thurs. 11am-8pm, Fri.-Sat. 11am-9pm, Sun. 11am-6pm

THE GRILLED CHEESE GRILL $

Could anything be more inspired than a restaurant solely devoted to that childhood favorite, the grilled cheese sandwich? This place has Portland written all over it. Owner and grilled cheese enthusiast Matt Breslow turned an old Airstream trailer into a kitchen and set up picnic tables where hungry patrons can devour the cheesy delights. Somehow, even the most reticent adults get giddy as schoolchildren when they see the colorful school bus redesigned into a cozy seating area. You can go for something basic, like a classic cheddar-on-white-bread sandwich (with or without crusts), or get a little crazy with bacon, apples, blue cheese, and Swiss. If you're feeling particularly kinky, try the Cheesus Burger, a patty melt nestled between two grilled cheese sandwiches and garnished with lettuce, tomato, and grilled onion.

MAP 3: 1027 NE Alberta St., 503/206-8959, www.grilledcheesegrill.com; Wed.-Thurs. 11:30am-8pm, Fri. Sat. 11am-9pm, Sun. 11am-6pm

RETROLICIOUS $

Retrolicious delivers a made-from-scratch menu evoking picket fences, cozy casseroles, and cupcakes in the oven. The menu changes weekly but often includes things like chicken and waffles, macaroni and cheese (made with pimento loaf), meatloaf, lemon bars, and red velvet cupcakes. You will find Retrolicious in the Green Castle food pod on NE 20th and NE Everett, and with its hot pink and silver cart, it is hard to miss. After you get your chicken, or your butter-basted burger or Cuban sandwich, sit back and enjoy it in one of the colorful chairs while you hang out with the yard flamingos.

MAP 3: 1930 NE Everett St., 503/539-3808, http://eatretrolicious.com; Mon.-Fri. 11am-2pm

FRENCH

★ BEAST $$$

Chef-owner Naomi Pomeroy is a legend in the Portland food scene, named one of the Best New Chefs of 2009 by *Food & Wine* and featured in *Bon Appétit* within months of opening. Pomeroy has drawn eyes thanks to her unabashed approach to "French grandma-style" cooking.

The prix-fixe dinner is $60 per person for six courses, and it changes each week. Each meal usually begins with a delicate soup followed by a charcuterie plate stocked with such nibbles as foie gras bonbons, chicken liver mousse, and pickled seasonal vegetables. For the main course, you might find stuffed rabbit, braised duck, or pork cheeks (if you're lucky). As long as you are splurging, opt for wine pairings in addition to the meal ($35 for six small glasses).

MAP 3: 5425 NE 30th Ave., 503/841-6968, www.beastpdx.com; Wed.-Sat. dinner seatings at 6pm and 8:45pm, Sun. brunch seatings at 10am and noon, dinner seating at 7pm

PETITE PROVENCE ⓢ

Whether you stop by Petite Provence for breakfast or lunch, make sure you take away one of the buttery pastries in a bag for later. If you can get past the cream puffs, caramel tarts, and opera cakes, take a gander at the full menu, stocked with French egg dishes, grilled sandwiches, and country-style salads. The Colette omelet is a neighborhood favorite, with its combination of basil and eggs topped with artichoke hearts, tomatoes, and mozzarella and then placed under the broiler until it's bubbly. For lunch, salads are a good bet. The goat cheese salad is simple enough, with medallions of cheese tossed with greens, onions, red peppers, roasted walnuts, and a light vinaigrette dressing. It's satisfying and refreshing, but still leaves room for a bowl of French onion soup and an almond croissant.

MAP 3: 1824 NE Alberta St., 503/284-6564, www.provence-portland.com; Sun.-Thurs. 7am-9pm, Fri.-Sat. 7am-10pm

TABLA ⓢⓢⓢ

Tabla calls itself a Mediterranean bistro, but its menu takes a big lesson from the French. The $24 three-course tasting menu allows you to choose three items from the regular menu; wine pairings are available with each course for just a bit more. Start off with a chilled vichyssoise or a warm haricot vert salad and move on to the tagliatelle with spicy pork *sugo*. Hopefully, you'll still have room for the fresh pan-seared salmon or halibut cheeks.

Tabla has long been one of the best restaurants in the area. Nowadays, there's a lot more competition, but it is still a reliable, chic choice in a comfortable, relaxed, and airy atmosphere. It can get a bit pricey, but you can save money by bringing your own bottle of wine and paying a $15 corkage fee.

MAP 3: 200 NE 28th Ave., 503/238-3777, www.tabla-restaurant.com; Tues.-Sun. 5pm-10pm

GERMAN

THE RHINELANDER ⓢⓢ

The Rhinelander is an experience all on its own, kitschy and fun and sometimes downright silly. There's a wandering accordion player during dinner, and it's not uncommon for the staff to belt out good old-fashioned German folk songs. At the start of your meal, you will get complimentary fondue (there's a charge for it on the bar side), but go easy. The meals are rich and hearty. Make sure you add a cup of the lentil soup; it's to die for. If you are dining with a group, The Rhinelander offers affordable sampler feasts served family style, so you can try out a number of rich meats like sauerbraten, cordon bleu, schnitzel, rotisserie pork loin, bier sausage, and other such things.

MAP 3: 5035 NE Sandy Blvd., 503/288-5503, www.rhinelander.com; Tues.-Sun. 5pm-9pm

SWISS HIBISCUS $$

Though the Hawaiian-inspired decor may tell a different story, this little hole-in-the-wall family establishment is all about Switzerland. The owner and chef of the café can thank her Swiss father and Hawaiian-born mother for that. The menu speaks to her heritage, with Swiss comfort foods served with a side of aloha spirit. You will find Wiener schnitzel, gravlax, goulash, and bratwurst heaped with caramelized onions. House salads are served with the restaurant's famous Swiss dressing (available for purchase), or get a sampler plate of all the salads with a superb bowl of Swiss onion soup. To wet your whistle, they have bottled beers and a small selection of wine in addition to canned sodas and water.

MAP 3: 4950 NE 14th Ave., 503/477-9224, www.swisshibiscuss.com; Tues.-Thurs. 5pm-9:30pm, Fri. 5pm-10pm, Sat. 11:30am-2:30pm and 5pm-10pm

ITALIAN
CIAO VITO $$$

Ciao Vito is a diamond in the rough in the otherwise artsy, granola-crunching Alberta Arts District. The menu is a bit pricey but includes simple, elegant, well-prepared dishes like pork *sugo* with crispy fried polenta, Bolognese *ragu* with fettuccini, and arguably the best beet salad in Portland. Start with the calamari and antipasti plate, served with bread from Ken's Artisan Bakery and spicy olive oil. When your entrée comes, don't be afraid to nibble at it and save room for dessert. Many of the heartier dishes here reheat well as leftovers, and Ciao Vito's *panna cotta* with amarena cherry and caramel sauce is not to be missed.

MAP 3: 2203 NE Alberta St., 503/282-5522, www.ciaovito.net; Wed.-Sat. 4:30pm-10pm, Sun. 4:30pm-10pm

D.O.C. $$$

If you think you've seen an open kitchen, you have never seen one like D.O.C.'s (Denominazione di Origine Controllata, the Italian food and wine control). Walk through the front door of this tiny establishment, just past the windows with red-checkered curtains and mason jars stacked in the sills, and you will find yourself smack-dab in the middle of the kitchen. It can be a bit disconcerting at first, but soon you will find yourself mesmerized by the tidiness and efficiency with which things are run. The restaurant opened in June 2008 and still receives accolades for providing polished and chic, yet intimate, dining. Chef Greg Perrault's cuisine nears perfection with dishes like tagliatelle, beef cheeks, and risotto. Order in courses or opt for the chef's tasting menu ($50), which gives you five courses, including dessert.

MAP 3: 5519 NE 30th Ave., 503/946-8592, www.docpdx.com; Tues.-Sat. 6pm-10pm

JAPANESE

YAKUZA [$][$]

A sushi restaurant named after the Japanese mafia? Well, not exactly. The original meaning of the word *yakuza* was meant to describe people who aren't easily categorized. So it's a surprisingly good fit for this Japanese joint, which takes what it likes from both Japanese culture and the Pacific Northwest influence of owner Micah Camden. The dining room is sexy and sleek, with whimsical murals adorning the walls and large garage door windows. The menu is a good mix between traditional sushi and Asian-inspired hot dishes. Plan to order about three or four plates per person, as most items are served family-style and you'll want to sample a number of things. Panko-fried goat cheese is a must, as is the carpaccio and the spicy tuna roll. Be sure to try one of the signature cocktails as well. The Whiskey #1 is particularly tasty, with Maker's Mark, brandied apricots, and a dash of nutmeg.

MAP 3: 5411 NE 30th Ave., 503/450-0893, www.yakuzalounge.com; Wed.-Sun. 5pm-11pm

ZILLA SAKÉ HOUSE [$][$]

Zilla Saké House is pleasant, dark, and cozy, with high-backed booths and rain-colored walls adorned with funky decor. The staff is knowledgeable and helpful without a hint of pretentiousness. For that reason, and thanks to the sheer volume of options, it is a great place to become a burgeoning sake drinker and sushi eater. If you like to nibble slowly, order the edamame, seasoned with ginger in addition to the traditional sea salt and pepper. The spicy *ika* (dried squid jerky) is a surprisingly delightful choice, especially with wasabi mayo on the side. The sashimi, particularly the *hamachi,* is all quite good and served with real wasabi (which looks more like pesto than green paste).

MAP 3: 1806 NE Alberta St., 503/288-8372, www.zillasakehouse.com; Mon.-Fri. 5pm-10pm, Sat.-Sun. 3pm-10pm

MEXICAN

AUTENTICA [$][$]

As you can probably guess, Autentica is Spanish for authentic, and at this Concordia neighborhood restaurant, they mean it. The dishes hail from the Guerrero region of Mexico, which is as diverse in horticulture as the Pacific Northwest. There are the beaches (think Acapulco) that bring an abundance of seafood, but there are also plains and mountains and tropical regions that offer other more exotic flavors. Don't expect to get bowls of chips and salsa. Instead, you will find fresh ceviche, creamy soups, moist and flavorful pork tacos, and sensational tamales. On Thursday night, don't miss the pozole, a tasty, traditional Mexican stew steeped in tradition.

MAP 3: 5507 NE 30th Ave., 503/287-7555, www.autenticaportland.com; Tues.-Fri. 5pm-10pm, Sat.-Sun. 10am-2pm and 5pm-10pm

LA BONITA $

This little taquería may not look like much from the outside, but the food is quick, inexpensive, and delicious—and the walls display the work of local artists. La Bonita is family-owned and claims to be "as authentic as Mexican gets." They come darn close with their *al pastor* tacos and unbelievably good carne asada. The burritos are enormous and run about $6 each. If you stop in a little early or want to plan ahead for tomorrow, grab a breakfast burrito, filled with eggs, chorizo, and hash browns.

MAP 3: 2839 NE Alberta St., 503/281-3662; daily 10am-10pm

SOUTHERN AND CREOLE

SCREEN DOOR $$

One of the most secretly celebrated restaurants in Portland, Screen Door never takes itself too seriously. This is where you're likely to find off-shift chefs and bartenders, and it's no coincidence. The menu spits in the face of the hoity-toity low-carb or raw food mentality, but still manages to use some of the best local ingredients in its soul-quenching dishes. This is food the way it was meant to be eaten. Crispy fried oysters dripping with *gribiche* sauce (an egg sauce) or fried green tomatoes with remoulade, followed by some of the best fried chicken in the city, will have you singing the praises of this quaint little Burnside joint. Will you wait for a table? Yes, probably. Will you clutch your belly in gluttonous joy as you roll yourself out the door? It's quite likely. Will it be worth every sticky, drippy, carb-laden bite? Absolutely.

This is another one of Portland's popular brunch spots. If you manage to get a table, don't walk away without sampling Screen Door's infamous praline bacon and equally notorious Bloody Mary.

MAP 3: 2337 E. Burnside St., 503/542-0880, www.screendoorrestaurant.com; Mon. 5:30pm-9pm, Tues.-Fri. 5:30pm-10pm, Sat. 9am-2:30pm and 5:30pm-10pm, Sun. 9am-2:30pm and 5:30pm-9pm

TAPAS

AVIARY $$$

Smack dab in the heart of Portland's Alberta Arts District, Aviary is a pretty and minimalistic site. But if they spared a little flourish in the decor, they certainly spent it on the menu. Everything is delivered in such an artful way, you almost hate to eat it. The three co-chefs have a fine résumé of experience in both New York City and Portland, and it shows in their touch of molecular with a nod to Asian cuisine. Occasional stand-out dishes include the oxtail croquettes, fresh oysters, and spiced duck leg, but the menu changes with available meat and produce. Aviary is different, for sure, but the dishes are original without being overly theatrical.

MAP 3: 1733 NE Alberta St., 503/287-2400, www.aviarypdx.com; Mon.-Thurs. 5pm-10pm, Fri.-Sat. 5pm-11pm

NAVARRE $$

The food at Navarre is like improv; you never quite know what you're going to get, but the off-the-cuff brilliance is impressive. Chef John Taboada builds his menu daily around the ingredients he gets from a nearby CSA. If parsnips are in season, they might just get tossed into a warm crab salad. Fresh greens may be tucked under foie gras. Cauliflower is transformed into gratin. Green tomatoes are breaded and fried. Whatever you choose, make sure you order some bread (from Ken's Artisan Bakery down the street) to soak up all the bits of sauce and dressing from the other plates. Since it's technically a wine bar, Navarre has more than 50 different wines by the glass, so it's easy to pair a vintage with the eclectic array of plates on the table. Ask your server for recommendations if you get overwhelmed.

MAP 3: 10 NE 28th Ave., 503/232-3555, www.navarreportland.blogspot.com; Mon.-Thurs. 4:30pm-10:30pm, Fri. 4:30pm-11:30pm, Sat. 9:30am-11:30pm, Sun. 9:30am-10:30pm

SMALLWARES $$$

A wholly different take on the tapas concept, Smallwares serves up what they call "inauthentic" Asian dishes with an artful flair. Timid diners should prepare to throw caution to the wind, because there are some truly plum pickings for those willing to be daring. Order several plates to share, like the fried kale with mint, fish sauce, and candied bacon; the chicken lollipops with Sriracha aioli; or the *somen* noodles, dressed in chili paste and sesame and topped with fried egg and black *hijiki* seaweed. In an attached bar called Barwares, the drinks are casually named after the liquor they're made with: The Whiskey, The Scotch, The Vodka, The Gin, etc. They also have a pretty good list of sakes, beers, and wines that accompany the flavor profile of the menu.

MAP 3: 4605 NE Fremont St., 971/229-0995, www.smallwarespdx.com; Mon.-Fri. 5pm-1am, Sat.-Sun. 11am-3pm and 5pm-1am

★ TORO BRAVO $$

Toro Bravo set Portland on its ear when it opened in 2007. Dinner here is an event, a whirlwind of noise and activity, a mish-mash of fast-moving plates and eager conversation. The general excitement is palpable because everyone is waiting for their next little morsel to arrive. The tapas are expertly crafted, right down to the last loving detail. Must-try dishes include the bacon-wrapped dates in warm honey, oxtail croquettes, and delectable olive oil cake with caramel. The wait for a table can be agonizingly long, so be prepared. Don't come when you are ravenous. Reservations aren't offered for parties with fewer than seven people on weekdays and not at all for Friday and Saturday. Come early, put your name on the list, and head upstairs to the Secret Society Lounge, where you can imbibe cocktails and snack while you wait.

MAP 3: 120 NE Russell St., 503/281-4464, www.torobravopdx.com; Sun.-Thurs. 5pm-10pm, Fri.-Sat. 5pm-11pm

THAI
SWEET BASIL ⓢⓢ

Sweet Basil resides in an old Portland home that has three cozy rooms and a large patio out back that's open in warmer months. They lean toward the traditional, with delicate touches that make dishes unexpectedly exciting. Start with a few appetizers while you wait for your entrées, or make a meal of appetizers, like the aptly named "O My God," a mix of crab, basil, and cream cheese wrapped in a tortilla, fried golden, and served with house-made plum sauce.

You must be accurate about how spicy you want things. If you say you want it at level 10, they will kick it up with small Thai chilies, making your meal truly fiery. Thank goodness a side of black jasmine and white jasmine rice (charmingly, in the shape of a star and a moon) is served alongside the entrées.

MAP 3: 3135 NE Broadway, 503/281-8337, www.sweetbasilor.com; Mon.-Thurs. 11:30am-2:30pm and 5pm-9pm, Fri. 11:30am-2:30pm and 5pm-10pm, Sat. 5pm-10pm, Sun. 5pm-9pm

Southeast   Map 4

Southeast Portland is fast becoming a home for great food, sassy presentation, and an adherence to artistic creativity—and less about the ever-popular but ironic dive bar. Since Southeast is home to the burgeoning area known as Distillery Row, where craft distillers such as House Spirits, New Deal, and Integrity have set up shop, the area has been imbued with a passion for flavor, comfort, and delight. In other words, moderation isn't really part of the vocabulary here.

BREAKFAST AND BRUNCH
BRODER ⓢⓢ

Broder manages to not be just like all the other breakfast spots in town by being the only place in Portland to serve up authentic Swedish favorites. No, really, and it goes way beyond meatballs. Here you will find fluffy *aebleskiver* with lemon curd or lingonberry jam, apple fritters with baked eggs and sausage, and *lefse* filled with the daily special ingredients. If you have heroic battles to endure over the course of your day, perhaps you should try the Swedish Breakfast Bord—brown bread and rye crisp, cured meat, smoked trout, hard cheese, seasonal citrus, yogurt with fruit and granola, and daily salad. Pair that with a little nip of aquavit and you should be able to accomplish anything.

MAP 4: 2508 SE Clinton St., 503/736-3333, www.broderpdx.com; daily 8am-3pm

SLAPPY CAKES $$

It was Tessie Tura from the musical *Gypsy* who said, "You gotta get a gimmick," and Slappy Cakes was listening. This breakfast spot is bustling on weekends thanks to pancake griddles they have so cleverly built into their dining tables. Instead of ordering a boring old stack of round pancakes, you order a bottle of batter (there are four types) and a side of add-ins like chocolate chips, berries, or bacon. It's a lot of fun to create your own shapes, and the process is surprisingly idiot-proof. If you don't feel like cooking, the staff at Slappy Cakes are happy to do it for you. Plus, they have a number of other great items on the menu, like pork belly Benedict and chicken-fried bacon. Yes, you read that right: chicken-fried bacon.

MAP 4: 4246 SE Belmont St., 503/477-4805, www.slappycakes.com; Mon.-Fri. 8am-2pm, Sat.-Sun. 8am-3pm

COFFEE AND DESSERTS

★ LAURETTA JEAN'S $

So, you are out on Division Street, craving something sweet and, of course, the line at Salt & Straw is halfway down the block. Never fear, just head up the street to Lauretta Jean's. This little bakery is, first and foremost, a pie shop, and they have, hands down, some of the best pies in town. It all comes down to the amazing crust, which has just the right balance of tenderness and flakiness. You can pick up a slice or a whole pie, or just sit and eat your wedge of salted honey pie while enjoying a cocktail from the 1950s-inspired menu.

MAP 4: 3402 SE Division St., 503/235-3119, www.laurettajeans.com; Mon.-Thurs. 8am-10pm, Fri.-Sat. 8am-11pm, Sun. 8am-10pm

FOOD CARTS

EUROTRASH $

If you are under the impression that foie gras and escargot only come from fancy restaurants, then you have never visited this food cart. Curried prawns with a curried coconut slaw on a baguette? Foie gras grilled and served atop freshly made chips? Escargot drowning in garlic butter? Yes, please. One of the cart's most famous items is "Fishy Chips," which eliminates the excess by turning the fish (in this case Spanish sardines) into the chips. The little guys are breaded, deep fried, and served with a lemon and garlic aioli. If you can't make it to Southeast, don't worry. There's another EuroTrash **downtown** (SW 10th Ave. and SW Washington St.).

MAP 4: 4298 SE Belmont St., www.eurotrashcart.com; Mon. 10am-8pm, Tues.-Sat. 7am-8pm, Sun. 7am-1pm

FRIED EGG I'M IN LOVE $

Fried Egg is a music-themed cart that is silly in name but serious in delivering a tasty breakfast. The menu consists of a series of sandwiches, all served on lightly toasted sourdough bread, and all but a couple are built around the eggs. The signature dish is the Yolko Ono—a fried egg with "magic egg dust," a hand-pressed seasoned sausage patty, and a layer of pesto and parmesan cheese. Vegetarians can order the PB Jammin' (peanut butter and jelly) or the Back in Black, a mix of black beans, veggies, and spices served with avocado and green onion. Recently, some vegan and gluten-free bread options have been added to the menu.

MAP 4: 3217 SE Hawthorne Blvd, www.friedegglove.com; Wed.-Fri. 8am-3pm, Sat.-Sun. 9am-3pm

POTATO CHAMPION $

In the midst of Cartopia, one of Portland's favorite pods of late-night carts, you will find Potato Champion, a colorful cart that serves up fries in small or large paper cones. These are not the greasy, soggy mess from some state fair; the fries at Potato Champion are hot, salty, and crispy on the outside, while still being soft and warm on the inside. They're good on their own, but just for kicks, PC offers an array of dips like rosemary ketchup, sweet hot mustard, tarragon anchovy mayonnaise, and remoulade. If you're feeling really indulgent, try the *poutine*, a Canadian treat that involves smothering fries with cheese grits and gravy

MAP 4: 1207 SE Hawthorne Blvd., 503/683-3797, www.potatochampion.tumblr.com; Tues.-Sun. noon-3am

SCOOP $

Scoop has nearly 20 ice cream flavors available year-round—the best of which is salted caramel—and five or six seasonal flavors at any given time. They specialize in organic, hand-made concoctions that utilize local ingredients. You can buy it by the scoop in a cone or dish, splurge for a sundae, or opt for a float, smoothie, milk shake, or vegan sorbet. When the season is right, the ice cream can also be sampled and purchased at many of the local farmers markets (an updated list is on the website).

MAP 4: 4926 SE Division St., 503/928-2796, www.scooppdx.com; Tues.-Sat. noon-8pm, Sun. 1pm-5pm

VIKING SOUL FOOD $

It's the only Norwegian cart in the city, with a menu that focuses on *lefse* (pronounced "lef-suh") in true Scandinavian style. The thin potato flatbread is warmed up on the griddle and topped with any number of ingredients, from sweet (like lingonberries and cream cheese) to savory (Norse meatballs, *gjetost* cheese sauce, and pickled cabbage). One of the best might be the aquavit-cured smoked salmon rolled with dill crème fraîche, lightly pickled shallots, and watercress. Make sure you get at least one of those.

Cart O' My Cart

Portland has a little culinary secret that might come as a great surprise. Some of the best food in the city doesn't come from fancy kitchens; it comes from food carts.

When you think about it, this makes sense. With such a strong focus on self-reliance and self-expression, the city is entirely welcoming of businesses that toss out the notion that a restaurant needs a brick-and-mortar building to be considered good and instead set out to make the best waffle, taco, or french fries in town. There's even a website devoted to the phenomenon, Food Cart Portland (www.foodcartsportland.com), which provides details on locations, menus, prices, and hours. Across the city, countless Twitter pages and Facebook updates discuss the mobile culinary culture with an excitement otherwise reserved for major music festivals and show openings. The result is such that over a few short months of business, certain carts develop a cult-like following. While in some places, grabbing lunch or a late-night snack from a food cart might seem like slumming, in Portland, it's an indulgence and an adventure.

For one thing, the carts in P-Town have fixed locations and are usually clustered together, like miniature food courts. Downtown, there are a few clusters in areas such as Tom McCall Waterfront Park, Portland State University, and Pioneer Courthouse Square.

One major hub of carts is at SW 5th Avenue and Oak Street. Here you'll find Jarochita (503/421-9838), a Mexican food cart that serves standard burritos, tacos, and quesadillas. However, Jarochita makes the list of must-try carts because of its banana leaf-wrapped enchiladas (about $1.50 each) and *huaraches,* made with an oblong, fried masa base and stuffed with a cornucopia of toppings. Also in this area is Tabor (503/997-5467, www.schnitzelwich.com), home of the Schnitzelwich—a gorgeous sandwich made with breaded, fried pork loin on a ciabatta roll with sautéed onion, horseradish, and paprika-spiced pepper spread. It's authentic Czech cuisine, with treasures like goulash, wild mushroom soup, and spaetzle on the menu. Another standout is Brunchbox (503/477-3286), where the name just doesn't do the place justice. Yes, there are fantastic breakfast items, like egg sandwiches made with homemade English muffins, but it's the Black and Blue Burger that puts Brunchbox on the map. Arguably one of the best burgers in town, this beast of a sandwich has blackened Angus beef and creamy blue cheese crumbles. Brunchbox also has a fun kids' menu with items like dino-shaped cheese or PB&J sandwiches for $1.50.

Another big gathering of carts can be found at SW 10th Avenue and Alder Street at the Alder Street Food Cart Pod, where Sawasdee Thai (503/330-2037) offers delicious pumpkin and green curries. All of the dishes there are well proportioned and balanced between veggies, meat, and sauce. Or, if it's a blustery day, head over to Savor Soup House (503/750-5634, www.savor-souphouse.com), where the star of the show is (naturally) hearty, belly-warming

Food carts are a way of life in Portland. You will find large pods of them in all five quadrants of the city.

soup—like curried cauliflower and red lentil, broccoli and cheddar, or New England clam chowder topped with bacon. Also on this block, you will find **Nong's Kaho Man Gai**, a cart where the namesake dish, chicken and rice, is far from boring. Cart owner Nong Poonsukwattana is a former cook for the hugely popular restaurant Pok Pok, and her skills are unmatched. The signature dish includes tender strips of poached chicken atop rice that cooked in a delicious mix of chicken stock and Thai herbs. It is served with crisp cucumber slices, cilantro and the incomparable Khao Man Gai sauce (fermented soybean, ginger, garlic, chili, Thai vinegar and soy sauce).

In North Portland, you'll find the drool-inspiring **Flavour Spot** (2310 N. Lombard St., 503/289-9866, www.flavourspot.com) and **Son of Flavour Spot** (N. Mississippi Ave. and N. Fremont), a pair of waffle carts that are reinventing breakfast one gooey Black-Forest-ham-and-Gouda-stuffed waffle at a time. Lines form on the weekends as people hover, waiting for their hangover remedy of coffee and waffles stuffed with Nutella and jam, or sausage and maple butter. Also in this neck of the woods is **Mississippi Marketplace** (4233 N. Mississippi Ave., 503/358-7873, www.mississippimarketplace.com), a hub of carts next to the German pub, Prost. This collection of carts includes seating, covered areas, and popular carts like KOI Fusion, Native Bowl, Miss Kate's Southern Kitchen, and Homegrown Smoker Vegan BBQ.

While the taste may be fit for a Viking, the portions are not. Order more than one if you plan to make a meal out of it.

MAP 4: 4262 SE Belmont St., 503/704-5481, www.vikingsoulfood.com; Tues.-Thurs. noon-8pm, Fri.-Sat. noon-9pm

WY'EAST PIZZA $$

Pizza from a trailer? Yup, especially when it's one of these 12-inch, made-to-order beauties. An outdoor trailer with an 800-degree oven in the middle of Southeast Portland is an oddity at best, but the service and quality of food squash any questions about whether the owners know what they're doing. Wy'east (the Multnomah name for Mount Hood) always has a handful of pizzas to choose from, like the Zig-Zag Glacier, a delicious white pie with kalamata olives, arugula, and copious amounts of garlic. They take phone orders as early as 4pm. If you bike or walk there, you'll get a $1 discount, but no matter what, bring cash.

MAP 4: 3131 SE 50th Ave., 503/701-5149, www.wyeastpizza.com; Wed.-Sat. 4:30pm-9:30pm, Sun. 4:30pm-8:30pm

FRENCH

CAFÉ CASTAGNA $$

While the atmosphere at Café Castagna is a bit stark—with concrete floors and simple tables—the food is like a great big hug. Café Castagna can only loosely be categorized as French, but the coq au vin is phenomenal—it's not uncommon for the restaurant to run out of it—and so is the *tarte aux pommes* with gruyère, which is available on occasion. The real star, however, is the burger. While on the pricier side at around $11, it is as close to perfection as you can get. It's made with PaintedHills ground sirloin and cooked to your liking, and the pickles—which are sweet and seasoned with coriander, cumin, cloves, and cinnamon—merit almost as much attention.

MAP 4: 1758 SE Hawthorne Blvd., 503/231-9959, www.castagnarestaurant.com; Tues.-Sat. 5pm-10pm, Sun. 10am-2pm and 5pm-10pm

LE PIGEON $$$

Portland has its fair share of vegan and vegetarian joints, but Le Pigeon ain't one of them. This place is all about indulgence, particularly the carnivorous kind. Chef Gabriel Rucker has achieved celebrity status for his use of classic French techniques with a modern twist. How about a pork belly salad or a foie gras jelly doughnut? The menu changes according to the chef's whim (and what's available at the local markets), but if you get a chance to try the beef cheeks, do not pass it up. The meat absolutely melts in your mouth. This is a great spot if you're feeling adventurous, because it's not uncommon to find pig's tail, sweetbreads, and, yes, even pigeon.

MAP 4: 738 E. Burnside St., 503/546-8796, www.lepigeon.com; daily 5pm-10pm

Top: monkeybread at Le Pigeon. **Bottom:** Lauretta Jean's.

JAPANESE

YOKO'S JAPANESE RESTAURANT $$

Word to the wise: The wait at Yoko's is always long. Arrive mere moments after the doors open and it's still likely be an hour. To make things easier, leave your cell phone number on the sign-up sheet and head next door to C Bar, where the bartenders are happy to serve you a cocktail and offer you a sympathetic sigh.

Once inside the tiny sushi shack, peruse the extensive sake menu and order some rolls to share family-style. Yoko's is known for creative, artful creations, and that is where it really excels. If you just stick to the things you know, , you might be disappointed. Try the rainbow roll or the popular Batman Roll, made with eel and cream cheese. Whatever you do, don't skip the Taka tuna, a local favorite.

MAP 4: 2878 SE Gladstone St., 503/736-9228; daily 5pm-9pm

PACIFIC NORTHWEST

CLARKLEWIS $$$

Deep in the gritty industrial area of Portland's inner southeast is an old loading dock that has been transformed into one of the city's swankiest restaurants. With small, elegant tables set into a cement and steel backdrop, the place is romantic without an overdose of femininity. In the cooler months, when they can't open the great garage-style doors to let in light, the dinner hour can get downright dark. It's often so dark, in fact, that your server will bring you a tiny flashlight to read your menu by.

Your best bet is to chuck the menu and go for the Chef's Choice, a prix-fixe four-course meal ($55 per person). For an additional $55, wine pairings will accompany each course. Be sure to tell them if you have any allergies, and then sit back and eat like an expert epicurean.

MAP 4: 1001 SE Water Ave., 503/235-2294, www.clarklewispdx.com; Mon.-Thurs. 11:30am-2pm and 4:30pm-9pm, Fri. 11:30am-2pm and 4:30pm-10pm, Sat. 4:30pm-10pm

WILD ABANDON $$

Wild Abandon is well known for its brunch scrambles, Benedicts, and omelets for both vegetarians and omnivores. The brunch is good—so good, in fact, that it often overshadows the cozy, romantic dinner. The small venue does not lend itself well to large groups, but the bohemian decor and low lighting make it a great place to canoodle over a chocolate truffle torte. While the menu changes often, it is not uncommon to find pan-fried oysters, grilled rib eyes made from locally raised beef, or market-fresh Pacific fish among the entrées. Ask your server what the manicotti and risotto specials are; they change regularly and are often superb.

MAP 4: 2411 SE Belmont St., 503/232-4458, www.wildabandonrestaurant.com; Mon. and Wed.-Thurs. 4:30pm-9pm, Fri. 4:30pm-10pm, Sat. 9am-2pm and 5:30pm-10pm, Sun. 9am-2pm and 5:30pm-9pm

PIZZA

APIZZA SCHOLLS [$$]

When was the last time you waited an hour for a table to get a pizza? While it might seem crazy, Portlanders do it almost every night at Apizza Scholls. It's not uncommon for folks to be lined up outside the place when the doors are unlocked. That's because Apizza has achieved that terrific balance that is required to make really good pizza. The crust is tantamount to pizza's success, and this one is crispy on the outside, soft on the inside, and still maintains a flavor of its own that does not compete with the toppings.

MAP 4: 4741 SE Hawthorne Blvd., 503/233-1286, www.apizzascholls.com; Mon.-Fri. 5pm-9:30pm, Sat.-Sun. 11:30am-2:30pm and 5pm-9pm

KEN'S ARTISAN PIZZA [$$]

Ken's Artisan Pizza formed out of necessity when the bakery of the same name was flooded by requests for its hand-tossed, wood-fired pizzas—much like what you would find in Italy. The wait is long here. Reservations aren't accepted, and they won't seat a group larger than 10. To-go pizzas are occasionally done at the discretion of the staff (according to how busy they are) and are limited in number. Pizzas come in one size, which is perfect for one or two people, and there are appetizers (try the lamb and pita) and salads to round out the meal.

MAP 4: 304 SE 28th Ave., 503/517-9951, www.kensartisan.com/pizza.html; Mon.-Sat. 5pm-10pm, Sun. 4pm-9pm

SOUTHERN AND CREOLE

CLAY'S SMOKEHOUSE [$$]

Portland has a number of barbecue spots, each with its own signature. At Clay's, you can smell the meat cooking for a three-block radius. All the meat is smoked on the premises—including the juicy brisket, chicken, and catfish—forming a carnivorous cloud around this quaint little block of Division Street. The meats are all fine, but oddly enough, Clay's also has remarkable salads. The spinach salad (with alder-smoked salmon, hazelnuts, pears, and white cheddar) is out of this world, and the grilled pork loin salad (with bleu cheese, spicy pecans, pepperoncini, tomatoes, croutons, and balsamic vinaigrette) is a delight for those who want their greens but just can't pass up a healthy portion of pig.

MAP 4: 2932 SE Division St., 503/235-4755, www.clayssmokehouse.ypguides.net; Wed.-Sun. 11am-10pm

DOT'S CAFÉ [$]

Dot's Café has become a part of the Portland iconography. This is partly due to its location in the heart of the Clinton Street District, one of the smallest but most beloved (by locals) neighborhoods around—but it's also because Dot's serves fantastically gut-busting fare until the wee hours of the morning. Dot's is like a 1950s diner, except you're more likely to hear Radiohead than Chubby Checker blasting through the sound system, and you can't help but wonder if someone forgot to turn on the lights. While the velvet wallpaper and kitschy diner vibe lend to its charm, Dot's really wins with its menu, chock-full of things like chili cheese fries, Swiss and mushroom patty melts, burgers, and tuna melts. What's more, Dot's has vegetarian options, like garden burgers, falafel wraps, vegan burritos, and hummus platters. Cash only.

MAP 4: 2521 SE Clinton St., 503/235-0203; Mon.-Fri. noon-2:30am, Sat.-Sun. 10am-2:30am

LE BISTRO MONTAGE $$

Visiting Le Bistro Montage is almost a rite of passage for Portlanders. The service can be abrupt, abrasive, or almost absent, but the various "Macs" are cheap, filling, and worth any abuse you might suffer. It's tempting to try the oddities on the menu, like frog legs and alligator linguini, but you're better off sticking with the Montage classics. The original macaroni and cheese recipe, Old Mac, was featured on the Food Network, and is a simple garlic, parmesan, and heavy cream delight. Another staple is the jambalaya, hearty and spicy with Cajun gravy and your choice of chicken, catfish, rock shrimp, crawfish, scallops, oysters, andouille sausage, or, yes, even alligator.

There are no boring doggie bags here. Instead, leftovers are wrapped in foil and sculpted into a veritable cornucopia of shapes, like snails, flowers, swords, and cats.

MAP 4: 301 SE Morrison St., 503/234-1324, www.montageportland.com; Sun.-Thurs. 5pm-2am, Fri.-Sat. 5pm-4am

Sellwood and Moreland Map 5

Deep in Southeast Portland, you'll find the quaint neighborhood of Sellwood, which is bordered by Westmoreland to the north, Eastmoreland to the east, and the city of Milwaukie to the south. The area has a small-town feel and was once, in fact, its own city. Nowadays, Sellwood is home to a fine collection of friendly small businesses, mom-and-pop bars, and neighborly restaurants.

Moreland is split into distinctive halves. To the east, you will find Eastmoreland, the home of Reed College, Crystal Springs Rhododendron Garden, and a number of chi-chi independently owned boutiques. And while it is difficult to tell when you have crossed into Westmoreland, the neighborhood is known for its manicured yards, stately homes, and impressive mansions.

AMERICAN

MIKE'S DRIVE-IN $

A throwback to the days of old is Sellwood's Mike's Drive-In, where the shakes are often made with fresh, local ingredients like strawberries, marionberries, and peaches; seasonal choices like pumpkin and eggnog; and a bevy of whimsical choices like marshmallow, orange Creamsicle, and Skor chocolate bars. But the list of options at Mike's does not end there. Like any good drive-in worth its salt, Mike's has an extensive menu filled with things that are fried, grilled, or covered with cheese, including a pretty good list of burgers, foot-long hot dogs, Reubens, and sandwiches made on soft pretzel buns.

MAP 5: 1707 SE Tenino St., 503/236-4537; Mon.-Thurs. 10am-10pm, Fri.-Sat. 10am-11pm, Sun. 11am-10pm

PAPA HAYDN $$

This chic but slightly more understated sister to the Papa Haydn in **Northwest Portland** (701 NW 23rd Ave., 503/228-7317) is a fine place for desserts, but the elegant, airy atmosphere also makes it a nice stop for a meal or Sunday brunch. If you go for dinner, start with the gorgonzola and fontina fondue, order some entrées to share, and then see if you have room for fresh berry cobbler or peanut butter mousse cake. Go early for quick seating; at both Papa Haydn outposts, the dining room fills up later in the evening when people come for dessert.

MAP 5: 5829 SE Milwaukie Ave., 503/232-9440, www.papahaydn.com; Mon.-Thurs. 11:30am-10pm, Fri.-Sat. 11:30am-midnight, Sun. 10am-9pm

ASIAN

JADE TEAHOUSE & PATISSERIE $$

Do not be deceived into thinking that Jade Teahouse is a bustling fast-food place, despite the counter service. This calm, peaceful restaurant invites lingering, and with countless excellent teas, free Wi-Fi, and some of the best Vietnamese food in town, it's easy to do so. The salad rolls are fresh and spicy, with a great balance of texture and flavors, and the french fries with truffle oil alone are worth the trip.

MAP 5: 7912 SE 13th Ave., 503/477-8985, www.jadeteahouse.com; Tues.-Sat. 11am-9pm

MEKONG VIETNAMESE GRILL $

This simple yet spacious Vietnamese restaurant was named for the Mekong Delta, an area abundant with rice, vegetables, and fruit. The Sellwood neighborhood has long hungered for good Asian cuisine, particularly a good *pho*. Thankfully, this spot serves good takeout or dine-in fare that is both quick and healthy. The menu has a handful of grilled items, like salads and skewers of chicken, beef, pork, or tofu, as well as egg rolls and salad rolls, and rice and noodle entrées. Be sure to check out the daily specials, which often feature *pho*.

MAP 5: 7952 SE 13th Ave., 503/808-9092, www.mekonggrill.com; daily 11:30am-9pm

BREAKFAST AND BRUNCH

BERTIE LOU'S $

Bertie Lou's is the Estelle Getty of the breakfast world in PDX. She's tiny, colorful, and a bit rough around the edges, but oh boy, does she pack a punch. Bertie's offers a truly extensive collection of standard breakfast offerings like biscuits and gravy, Benedicts, scrambles, and omelets with witty descriptions like, "if you're a little hungover . . . this one's for you" and "the things I do for money." Bike riders get a 10 percent discount, but breakfast will only run you about $6-10 anyway, so it's affordable even if you arrive in a gas-guzzler.

MAP 5: 8051 SE 17th Ave., 503/239-1177; Mon.-Fri. 7am-2pm, Sat.-Sun. 8am-2:30pm

FAT ALBERT'S $

You won't really want to linger at Fat Albert's. For one thing, there is a sign that discourages you from "camping." For another thing, there's probably going to be a horde of hungry people eyeing your table and drooling over every plate of home-style potatoes that goes by. It's not the sort of place that will fuss over you, so don't expect anyone to spread jelly on your toast or cut up your chicken-fried steak for you. This place is all about no-nonsense, good food. The portions are generous and the food is great, which is really all that matters. Bring cash.

MAP 5: 6668 SE Milwaukie Ave., 503/872-9822; Mon.-Fri. 7am-2pm, Sat.-Sun. 7am-3pm

FOOD CARTS
CHOWDAH $

Chowdah is easy to miss if you aren't looking for it, but tucked behind the Pine Tree Mini Mart you will find some of the best chowder in the city. Owner Chris Langley grew up just north of Boston, so we guarantee you won't find that tomato-based Manhattan-style chowder on the menu. Instead, Langley serves up award-winning, perfectly hot, creamy chowder, filled with hearty pieces of clams, potatoes, and bacon. Chowdah has a mean Philly cheesesteak and a "Killah" grilled cheese sandwich option, wherein you choose your cheese and bread and then add things like tomato, avocado, bacon, or ham.

MAP 5: 7875 SE 13th Ave., 503/867-2475; Mon.-Wed. 11:30am-7pm, Thurs.-Fri. 11:30am-8pm

ZENBU $

While ordering sushi from an Airstream trailer in a parking lot may seem sketchy, the atmosphere at Zenbu will set your mind at ease. The menu is extensive and includes a number of *nigiri* and hand-rolled sushi options, as well as Asian-inspired entrées like panko-crusted ginger chicken, Szechuan green beans, or pork and kimchi *gyoza*. They have regularly changing specials that always prove adventurous, like the Spyder Burger, a tempura soft shell crab tucked into a bun with spicy garlic aioli, greens, tomatoes, and avocado. Or, if you are really feeling bold, order the *omakase* (chef's choice, about $15) for a substantial variety of things like tempura fish tacos, sushi rolls, broiled mussels, seared ahi, or smoked salmon (only available when business is slow). Outdoor seating next to the trailer includes a covered area to keep you cool in the summer and dry when the weather turns fickle.

MAP 5: 7909 SE 13th Ave., 971/227-7610, http://zenbupdx.com; Tues.-Sat. 11:30am-7pm

ITALIAN

A CENA RISTORANTE $$$

A Cena (pronounced "a-CHAY-na") focuses on seasonal, locally grown produce for a contemporary yet modern take on simple Italian cuisine. The extensive wine list features regional Italian wines and several local selections, and the two rustic dining rooms offer an intimate experience that lends itself well to the meaning of the name—"come to supper." But it is the hand-made breads, pastas, and cheeses and freshly cured meats that have made this casual Italian restaurant a popular place to grab lunch or brunch with friends or family. If it's on the menu, don't miss the lobster *agnolotti*. If it's not, ask for recommendations. The seasonal specials are usually quite good, and the servers happy to give suggestions as to what will best suit your palate.

MAP 5: 7742 SE 13th Ave., 503/206-3291, www.acenapdx.com; Mon. 5pm-9pm, Tues.-Thurs. and Sun. 11:30am-2:30pm and 5pm-9pm, Fri.-Sat. 11:30am-2:30pm and 5pm-10pm

GINO'S $$

Gino's is a great place to find traditional Italian soul food: good old-fashioned cioppino; hearty ravioli tossed with seasonal sauces; chicken marsala; and a simmered-on-the-stove-all-day tomato, pork rib, and beef sauce tossed over penne. If you're on a budget, skip the expensive steaks, which are good but not exceptional. Instead, opt for the hearty pastas and a family-size Caesar salad. If you're dining on the bar side, there is also a very small, inexpensive bar menu that occasionally includes some specialty dishes.

MAP 5: 8051 SE 13th Ave., 503/233-4613, www.ginossellwood.com; Sun.-Thurs. 4pm-10pm, Fri.-Sat. 4pm-11pm

JAPANESE

SABURO'S $$

There are some who would question why people line up outside this Sellwood spot for hours waiting for spicy tuna rolls or salmon belly *nigiri*. For those folks, Saburo's will toss a cell phone-size sushi roll on their plate and say, "What do you think of that?" The fish here is always quite fresh and artfully prepared, but the real killer is the portion control (or lack thereof).

Yes, the wait is long and the staff can be a bit brusque, but it's worth the wait. Order everything you think you might want at once, including dessert, because you will not be allowed to order again. Frankly, you would be hard pressed to leave here hungry.

MAP 5: 1667 SE Bybee Blvd., 503/236-4237, www.saburos.com; Mon.-Thurs. 5pm-9:30pm, Fri. 5pm-10:30pm, Sat. 4:30pm-10pm, Sun. 4:30pm-9pm

Portland's newest little darling, NoPo (North Portland), started out as an inexpensive place for the city's creative class to set up shop. With their artistic influence, the area has developed into a veritable melting pot of ideas and tastes. This spirit is reflected in the cuisine as well. Local, homey neighborhood spots reign supreme. On this side of the river, everyone takes their time and food is more of an art form than a means of sustenance.

AMERICAN

FIRE ON THE MOUNTAIN $

If you are hankering for wings, most Portlanders will send you to Fire on the Mountain for some of the freshest wings around, with over 10 different homemade sauces to slather them in. You have the option of standard wings (made with all-natural, free-range chicken, of course), boneless wings, or vegan nuggets, or burgers, sandwiches, or salads if wings are not your thing. The smallest order is six wings (served with celery and dressing), and you may want to save room for dessert. If you have never had a deep-fried Twinkie or Oreo, this is the place to try one. There are **two other locations** (1708 E. Burnside, 503/230-9464; 3443 NE 57th Ave., 503/894-8973).

MAP 6: 4225 N. Interstate Ave., 503/280-9464, www.portlandwings.com; Mon.-Thurs. 11am-11pm, Fri.-Sat. 11am-midnight, Sun. 11am-10pm

BREAKFAST AND BRUNCH

GRAVY $$

A great spot for a good old American greasy spoon breakfast, Gravy is a testament to the joys of gluttony. Biscuits and gravy get a lot of attention here and deservedly so. The biscuit is the size of a plate and smothered with a decidedly un-Atkins-approved portion of gravy. A single order is enough to share between two people. The weekday lunch menu leans to the Southern side: You can get a salad, but why would you when there are fried egg sandwiches, tuna melts, and gravy-soaked fries?

Word to the wise: The wait can be long on weekends, as for any Portland breakfast joint. Come prepared with a cup of coffee from one of the many nearby coffeehouses.

MAP 6: 3957 N. Mississippi Ave., 503/287-8800; daily 7:30am-3pm

COFFEE AND DESSERTS

FRESH POT $

Fresh Pot is a cute little café housed in the historic Rexell Drug Building, and it is a truly charming place with all the atmosphere one might expect from an old-time coffee shop. In fact, it was the set of the 2007 film *Feast of Love,* which captured the coffee shop's inherently welcoming vibe. Fresh Pot serves local favorite Stumptown Coffee, as well as pastries from Bittersweet, Pearl, and Black Sheep Bakeries; and it has free Wi-Fi, so you are welcome to plug in, sip some coffee, and feel transported to a place that's just a little more relaxed.

MAP 6: 4001 N. Mississippi Ave., 503/284-8928, www.thefreshpot.com; Mon.-Fri. 6:30am-6pm, Sat.-Sun. 7am-6pm

FOOD CARTS

THE BIG EGG $

Expect a big wait—sometimes as long as 30 minutes—for a sandwich, and you will be rewarded with one of the best breakfast treats around. Soft, sunny, herb-scented eggs nest inside slices of local bakery Grand Central's soft brioche bread. Thick strips of bacon taste just like your nose has been expecting them to. The Big Egg's take on the Monte Cristo (when available) is nothing short of amazing, and the breakfast wraps are so popular, they frequently sell out long before closing time.

MAP 6: 4233 N. Mississippi Ave., http://thebigegg.com; Wed.-Fri. 8am-2pm, Sat.-Sun. 9am-2pm

FLAVOUR SPOT $

At this long-time Portland institution, you can get a made-to-order waffle sandwich stuffed with things like Black Forest ham and smoked gouda cheese, Nutella and raspberry jam, or sausage with real maple syrup. It is an irresistible delight and quite a filling way to start your day. They're called Dutch tacos, and they put Flavour Spot on the map as one of the first food carts to garner attention outside the city. If you are tempted to try more than one, opt for one savory and one sweet. If you can't finish them both, the savory ones reheat surprisingly well and don't get as soggy as their sugary counterparts.

MAP 6: 810 N. Fremont St., 503/282-9866, www.flavourspot.com; Mon.-Fri. 8am-7pm, Sat. 9am-7pm, Sun. 9am-3pm

GERMAN

WIDMER GASTHAUS $$

Sehr gut! The Widmer Gasthaus has great beer, of course, since it's brewed right across the street. The company is famous for its brews, not the least of which is its Hefeweizen—the first made in the United States. The menu is a fabulous assortment of German-inspired dishes, from the crispy and delicious chicken or pork schnitzel to the slow-roasted beef sauerbraten. It's all about comfort food. It's hard to hold back when there are bread chunks to be dipped in fondue and plates of sausage to be sampled.

MAP 6: 929 N. Russell St., 503/281-3333, www.widmer.com; Mon.-Thurs. 11am-10:30pm, Fri.-Sat. 11am-11:30pm, Sun. 11am-10:30pm

MEXICAN

LAUGHING PLANET $

At Laughing Planet, the idea seems simple. Take great organic and local ingredients, then wrap them in a tortilla or put them in a bowl, and make it all really cheap. The burritos at Laughing Planet are big and hearty, but they are also remarkably healthy. Opt for a traditional-style wrap with beans, grilled chicken, Tillamook cheese, and brown rice, or try something with an international spin, like the Che Guevara, which comes with plantains, sweet potatoes, and spicy barbecue sauce.

Laughing Planet serves beer and wine, in addition to freshly squeezed organic juices (in varieties from apple to beet) and some pretty fantastic smoothies—like the PB&J with strawberries, bananas, organic peanut butter, and apple juice.

MAP 6: 3765 N. Mississippi Ave., 503/467-4146, www.laughingplanetcafe.com; daily 11am-9pm

¿POR QUE NO? $

If you're looking for cheap and sublime tacos, this is the place. Try the delicious and juicy carnitas with braised local pork in handmade tortillas, or wild shrimp, sautéed and served with a dollop of *crema*. The ceviche (line-caught snapper and wild shrimp marinated in seasoned lime) is superb, and it's served with house-made tortilla chips. If you're thirsty (and you should be after that), try a pomegranate margarita, which tastes like summer. Or order a glass of *horchata*, which is creamy, sweet, and delicious, especially when spiked with rum. There is a **second location** (4635 SE Hawthorne St.), and both almost always have a line so bring a friend to chat with.

MAP 6: 3524 N. Mississippi Ave., 503/467-4149, www.porquenotacos.com; Mon.-Sat. 11am-10pm, Sun. 11am-9:30pm

SEAFOOD
EAT: AN OYSTER BAR $$

Owners Ethan Powell and Tobias Hogan (the E and T of the restaurant's name) get shipments each week from different oyster farms, making their bivalves just about the freshest in town. A chalkboard on the wall announces the most recent arrivals from Oregon, Washington, and the East Coast. If you're new to eating oysters, ask your knowledgeable server for guidance. The freshness of the raw oysters, served on the half shell, really speaks for itself, but EaT also makes a mean oysters Rockefeller. Baked and topped with a puree of watercress, garlic, and spinach, and then finished with a touch of absinthe, they are remarkably rich and earthy.

MAP 6: 3808 N. Williams Ave., Ste. 122, 503/281-1222, www.eatoysterbar.com; Mon.-Thurs. 11:30am-10pm, Fri.-Sat. 11:30am-midnight, Sun. 10am-10pm

THE FISH AND CHIP SHOP $$

If your idea of fish-and-chips normally involves a heavily breaded and dry piece of fish, the Brit-born owner of this sparsely decorated but charming hole-in-the-wall shop wants to show you what you've been missing. You can choose from cod, red snapper, Dover sole, haddock, and halibut, or whatever else is fresh. The fish here is cut when you order it, so be prepared to wait as long as 30 minutes for your food. In true British style, Scotch eggs, pasties, sausage rolls, mushy peas, and Heinz curry beans are also on offer.

If you aren't already stuffed from that, they will fry you up some dessert as well. The banana and pineapple fritters are delightful, but it's the sinfully fabulous deep-fried Mars bar that really tips things over the edge.

MAP 6: 1218 N. Killingsworth St., 503/232-3344, www.thefishandchipshop.com; Mon.-Thurs. 11am-3pm and 5pm-9pm, Fri.-Sat. noon-midnight, Sun. noon-8pm

Greater Portland

Map 7

A few places outside the core of the city are worth a gander. If you're heading out to Bridgeport Village to do some shopping, you have options that don't involve consuming food served on a stick. Also, traveling up into the deep western hills of Portland can be a pretty drive, but the weather doesn't always cooperate enough to allow picnicking. Fortunately, the outskirts of the city are populated with eclectic and interesting places to dine.

AMERICAN

HUMDINGER DRIVE-IN $

Thick and delicious ice-cream milk shakes and fat burgers dominate the menu at Humdinger, which is on Barbur Boulevard near Lewis and Clark College. If you like a good balance between meat, cheese, and bread, order a double (or more) and eat as much as you can—or split it. You will be happier with the overall flavor than if you get two single burgers. Side dishes—like crinkle-cut fries, deep-fried mushrooms, onion rings, and the very popular tater tots—are also stellar. Bring cash.

MAP 7: 8250 SW Barbur Blvd., 503/246-8132; Mon.-Sat. 10am-9pm

TANNERY BAR $$

In this small neighborhood restaurant, you'll find an open kitchen serving an ever-changing menu of Pacific Northwest small plates. The focus here is comforting, from-scratch dishes that rotate as ingredients become available. Hearty stews and rich sandwiches like the Monte Cristo are go-to choices, but the majority of the food is reliably fresh, interesting, and tasty. Seating is limited and not entirely intimate, comprised of 2 family-style tables and 10 bar seats, but the place manages to stay welcoming in a hip, basement bar kind of way. The lamp-lit space is cozy despite the cold, industrial look. There is even a "DJ Zone" with turntables and records for impromptu music moods.

MAP 7: 5425 E. Burnside St., 503/236-3610, www.tannerybarpdx.com; Mon.-Fri. 4pm-1am, Sat. 9am-2pm and 4pm-1am, Sun. 9am-2pm

THREE SQUARE GRILL $$

Why come to Three Square Grill? Deep-fried pickles. Also, there's an adorable kids' menu—clearly designed by finicky kids—and a menu that was clearly designed for discerning adults. Delta-style crab cakes with lemon remoulade, smoked salmon hash, and roast chicken with chanterelle mushrooms are just a few of the popular dishes, but it's the sampler of fried pickles, okra, and hush puppies that makes this worth the drive out to the hills of Southwest Portland.

MAP 7: 6320 SW Capitol Hwy., 503/244-4467, www.threesquare.com; Tues.-Sat. 5pm-9pm, Sun. 9am-2pm and 5pm-9pm

BREAKFAST AND BRUNCH

FAT CITY CAFÉ Ⓢ

Fat City Café has numerous awards for its quirky style and delicious food; for many locals, it's the perfect place to enjoy classic diner favorites in generous proportions. Cinnamon rolls the size of a baby's head are the big star at this neighborhood café; the recipe hasn't changed since 1974. Breakfast is the specialty here, served all day, but there's also a terrific lunch menu full of burgers, sandwiches, and other such things.

MAP 7: 7820 SW Capitol Hwy., 503/245-5457; daily 6:30am-3pm

MARCO'S CAFÉ & ESPRESSO BAR ⓈⓈ

This quaint Multnomah Village café is a neighborhood favorite, which is why you don't hear much about it in the city. With friendly service and reliably good breakfasts, this charmer is a well-guarded secret. The extensive menu has a heavy emphasis on scrambles, omelets, and Benedicts; everything is organic and fresh. If you're not a fan of egg-heavy breakfasts, opt for a hearty veggie breakfast burrito filled with brown rice, black bean chili, corn, tomato, avocado, and pepperjack cheese, or try the superb tofu scramble with mixed veggies in a tandoori or Korean barbecue marinade.

MAP 7: 7910 SW 35th Ave., 503/245-0199, www.marcoscafe.com; Mon.-Fri. 7am-9pm, Sat.-Sun. 8am-9pm

THE ORIGINAL PANCAKE HOUSE ⓈⓈ

The Original Pancake House has locations around the country, but this is the original Original—and it is not to be confused with the "International" chain we are all so familiar with. OPH has simple but fantastic breakfasts that include all the usuals, like waffles, corned beef hash, omelets, and of course, pancakes. It's all very classic and simple, with the exception of the Dutch baby and the German pancake. Both dinner plate-size treats are oven-baked, enormous, puffy, and delicious. You'll wait a little longer to get one, but if you have a sweet tooth, it's worth the wait.

MAP 7: 8601 SW 24th Ave., 503/246-9007, www.originalpancakehouse.com; Wed.-Sun. 7am-3pm

TOAST ⓈⓈ

Toast is a cozy and casual neighborhood restaurant that makes a point of using local and seasonal products. It bakes fresh breads and pastries and grinds meats for its sausages and burgers in house. Brunch diners will be treated with complimentary fresh scones upon arrival, a nice gesture considering the wait for a table can be kind of long. Try the Dismal Times, a tasty dish of ground hanger steak, white cheddar, seasonal greens, and fried eggs with a potato *rosti* on the side. If you are unfamiliar with potato *rosti*, you are in for a treat. The Swiss dish is similar to hash browns but cooked in a circular mold for a crispy outside and a soft, creamy inside.

MAP 7: 5222 SE 52nd Ave., 503/774-1020, www.toastpdx.com; Sat.-Tues. 8am-2pm, Wed.-Fri. 8am-2pm and 5pm-9pm

CARIBBEAN

SALVADOR MOLLY'S $$

Salvador Molly's is just plain fun. They call it "pirate cookin'" because they have stolen cuisine concepts from all over the Seven Seas. You'll find Caribbean jerk chicken, Baja fish tacos, Hawaiian kalua pork, and Creole jambalaya—and that's just a smattering of the eclectic entrées. Some starters you won't want to miss, like the unforgettable Cheesy Poofs, fried mashed potato fritters with a touch of cheese and chipotle chiles. But if you really want an adventure, order the Great Balls of Fire. If you can manage to eat all five habanero cheese fritters with the sauce, you'll get your picture on the Wall of Flame.

MAP 7: 1523 SW Sunset Blvd., 503/293-1790, www.salvadormollys.com; Mon.-Tues. 11:30am-9pm, Wed.-Thurs. 11:30am-10pm, Fri.-Sat. 11:30am-11pm

EUROPEAN

OTTO & ANITA'S EUROPEAN RESTAURANT $$

At this quaint underground Bavarian restaurant, everyone is talking about dill pickle soup. Invented by Otto himself, it is both terrifyingly green and remarkably delicious. The decor is casual and kitschy, and the rest of the menu is rounded out with a variety of schnitzels and sausages. The *zigeunerschnitzel* (two pieces of pork loin in a red wine paprika sauce with vegetables and spaetzle) is phenomenal, and so is the *maultaschen*, a Swabian dish of noodles filled with spiced pork and served in a beefy onion broth. Save room for dessert (or take some to go), because this is Anita's specialty. Black Forest cake, coconut cream cake, and a rum-soaked chocolate cake are just a few that top the list.

MAP 7: 3025 SW Canby St., 503/425-1411, www.ottoandanitas.com; Tues.-Fri. 11am-2pm and 5pm-9pm, Sat. 5pm-9pm

FOOD CARTS

EL GALLO $

This little Woodstock-area food cart has rustic, made-from-scratch street tacos that are so popular, the cart sometimes has to close up early. At $2 a pop, it's tempting to try one each of the four varieties of meat (in addition to fish and vegetarian), but three is probably enough for most. There are also hefty burritos and seasonal specials, but the Nevada Tostada at El Gallo is like nothing you've ever had before: an eight-inch circle of fry bread topped with your choice of meat, beans, cabbage, pickled onions, and—the best part—citrus sour cream. It is unapologetically messy and delicious.

MAP 7: 4804 SE Woodstock Blvd., 503/481-7537; Tues.-Sat. 10am-7pm

GERMAN
THE GERMAN BAKERY ⊙

As unassuming as the name of this establishment—equal parts bakery, deli, café, and grocery—is, most lovers of German cuisine know what you are talking about when you say, "The German Bakery." Here, you'll find everything from schnitzel to spaetzle, from streusel to kuchen. There is a fine selection of imported goods and cases of imported beers, along with a deli counter showcasing classic wursts, sausages, and deli meats. Come early and snag a *salzbretzelen* (soft pretzel roll) or drool over the dessert cases filled with poppy-seed strudels, Black Forest cakes, fat eclairs, chocolate-covered "pig ears," linzers, and so much more.

MAP 7: 10534 NE Sandy Blvd., 503/252-1881, www.the-german-bakery.com; Tues.-Sat. 8am-6pm

PACIFIC NORTHWEST
THE OBSERVATORY ⊙⊙

The Observatory may seem unassuming, but that's because it gets so many things right. The venue lighting is a perfect balance between practical and serene. The menu is both elegant and approachable. The drink menu is populated with champagne cocktails, negronis, manhattans, and old-fashioneds. The beer and wine list gives nods to famous locals and familiar imports. For starters, try the oregano fry bread (served with basil crème fraîche and tomato puree) or the apple and beet salad. Move on to the catch of the day special, the pulled pork sandwich, or the lamb burger with feta, balsamic tomatoes, *tzatziki* sauce, and marinated onions.

MAP 7: 8115 SE Stark St., 503/445-6284, www.theobservatorypdx.com, Sun.-Mon. 11am-11pm, Tues.-Sat. 11am-midnight

SEAFOOD
FIVE SPICE ⊙⊙⊙

Five Spice in the nearby city of Lake Oswego has fantastic lake views and Pacific Northwest cuisine with an Asian flair that arrives looking so pretty that it almost rivals the landscape. The wine selection is excellent, with a number of French, Californian, and Northwest favorites, as well as a respectable collection of ports and dessert wines. Seafood is terrific, with Pacific treats like halibut with saffron potatoes or sturgeon with black rice risotto and *shimeji* mushrooms. Given its location in a bustling part of Lake O, this place gets crowded, so it's best to make a reservation by phone or email at least a day in advance.

MAP 7: 315 1st Ave., Ste. 201, Lake Oswego, 503/697-8889, www.fivespicerestaurant.com; Mon.-Sat. 11:30am-10pm, Sun. 11:30am-9pm

SEASONS & REGIONS SEAFOOD GRILL $$

This homey little seafood restaurant in Portland's Multnomah Village is known for serving fresh clams, salmon, crab, and various other fresh finds from the sea, but the menu is surprisingly well-rounded. In fact, there's a full menu with appetizers, entrées, salads, and desserts for vegetarian diners and for those with gluten allergies (just ask). If you get there before they run out, try the salmon cakes. The specials change regularly, but you will always see some Pacific Northwest favorites like chinook salmon or red snapper. Everything tends to reflect what is fresh and in season. In fact, Seasons & Regions has its own 13-acre farm just outside of Estacada, where they grow their own heirloom fruits, vegetables, herbs, and flowers. Parking is tight, but there is overflow parking across the street.

MAP 7: 6660 SW Capitol Hwy., 503/244-6400, www.seasonsandregions.com; Mon.-Thurs. 11:30am-9:30pm, Fri. 11:30am-10pm, Sun. 9am-9:30pm

SOUTHERN AND CREOLE

DELTA CAFÉ $$

In the heart of the Woodstock neighborhood, Delta Café is a favorite haunt for nearby Reed College students on a carbohydrate binge and families who know kids love nothing more than ooey-gooey mac and cheese. If you can get past the appetizer menu—with its hush puppies, cornbread, sweet potato fries, and catfish bites—settle into a plate of fried chicken or a bowl of crawfish étouffée. Or simply order a sampler platter. Delta also has a fantastic cocktail menu that utilizes a variety of house-infused vodka, tequila, rum, and whiskey.

MAP 7: 4607 SE Woodstock Blvd., 503/771-3101, www.deltacafepdx.com; Mon. 4pm-11pm, Tues.-Fri. 4pm-1am, Sat. 9am-2pm and 5pm-1am, Sun. 9am-2pm and 5pm-11pm

PO'SHINES CAFÉ DE LA SOUL $

Po'Shines is worth a visit. Not just because it serves up some of the best Southern soul food in town, and not just because the hush puppies that accompany most baskets and platters are deep-fried gems. You may not even notice it as you scarf down ribs, smoky brisket, and fried okra, but this restaurant is a nonprofit organization helping train people in the community for work in restaurants. In fact, most employees, from the server to the chef, volunteer their time to the cause of strengthening the community.

MAP 7: 8131 N. Denver St., 503/978-9000, www.poshines.com; Mon. 7am-3pm, Tues.-Thurs. 7am-8pm, Fri. 7am-10pm, Sat. 8am-10pm

Nightlife

Thanks in part to Portland's DIY youth culture, the city has a lot of spirit. When people in Portland go out, they like to talk, share, imbibe, and indulge. You won't find many dance clubs pumping out top 40 hits, and if you do, it is not the locals who are crowding the floor. As a rule, Portlanders do not like theme bars or splashy concepts. Those venues are shunned in favor of more eclectic spots with interesting back stories, great cocktails, and comfortable gathering spaces. The music found at most popular venues is as varied as the personalities of the city itself. While some flock to hear the latest indic label band at the Crystal Ballroom, others will be sipping a martini and listening to some of today's hottest jazz at Jimmy Mak's.

The Pacific Northwest has long been considered a key player in the independent music scene. But long before bands like the Decemberists, Pink Martini, Modest Mouse, the Dandy Warhols, or the Shins called Portland home, it was still a favorite stop for many jazz, blues, and bluegrass players. These days, the music that first put Portland on the map is still an active part of its fabric, with annual festivals that draw thousands to see the likes of Etta James, B. B. King, Mel Brown, and Bobby Torres.

If the music scene isn't your bag, you're still in luck. Portland is fast becoming a destination spot for the burgeoning "cocktail renaissance," with local bistros, taphouses, lounges, and watering holes being featured on television, in magazines, and in blogs across the country. Like legendary chefs in decades past, hometown mixologists are reaching cult star status, recognized for their particular tastes and their ability to encapsulate the perfect experience in a glass.

Previous: Doug Fir; Kelly's Olympian.

Look for ★ to find
recommended nightlife.

Highlights

★ **Best Place to Walk on Air:** For 90 years, music lovers have flocked to the **Crystal Ballroom** to dance on the legendary "floating" dance floor (page 114).

★ **Best Spot to Fall in Love With Amaretto Sours Again:** At **Pepe Le Moko**'s one of the best bartenders in the world is reclaiming some much maligned cocktails, by digging into the past. The results are spectacular (page 116).

★ **Best Place to Beat Your High Score:** Part bar, part well-appointed arcade, **Ground Kontrol** will make the kid in you squeal with delight (page 116).

★ **Best Place to Meet Marvelous Dames:** After 40 years, **Darcelle XV**

Showclub is more than just a drag show. It's a Portland rite of passage (page 117).

★ **Best Place to Dig That Crazy Beat:** Rated as one of the top 100 jazz clubs in the world, **Jimmy Mak's** draws some of the best acts around (page 120).

★ **Best Place to Kiss Over a Cocktail:** The cocktails are pretty and the lighting is low. **Slow Bar** is just the place for a clandestine moment (page 126).

★ **Best Place to Grab a Pint:** With arguably one of the best selections of drafts from around the globe, **Horse Brass Pub** is one of the most recognized British pubs (outside of Britain, of course) (page 126).

Crystal Ballroom

BARS

JACK LONDON BAR

In the basement of the Rialto Poolroom, Jack London Bar is nothing like its upstairs neighbor. A little dark with a slight speakeasy resemblance, it hosts history lectures, open mics, art shows, author readings, and even tap dance lessons. This bar is for literature nuts, history buffs, and bookish cool cats. It was named not for the legendary author, but after the hotel atop the space, at the time, called the Jack London Hotel.

MAP 1: 529 SW 4th Ave., 503/228-7605, www.rialtopoolroom.com; hours vary, usually closed Wed. and Sun.; free

KELLS IRISH PUB

If you're out roving for a pint, Kells Irish should be where you point your feet. With a fantastic collection of beers on tap and a fine collection of whiskey, Kells can be a lot of fun with live Irish music many nights. It's also a fine place to chat or watch soccer. Hand your server a dollar and a couple of quarters and ask to see "the dollar trick." You'll lose the money, but it's for a good cause.

MAP 1: 112 SW 2nd Ave., 503/227-4057, www.kellsirish.com; Mon.-Wed. 11:30am-midnight, Thurs. 11:30am-1am, Fri. 11:30am-2:30am, Sat. 8am-2:30am, Sun. 8am-midnight; free most nights

SHANGHAI TUNNEL

Learn a little about Portland's history and you'll understand why Shanghai says it's to "bars what Bruce Campbell is to horror films." The dark, seedy journey into the bowels of Old Town is part of the novelty, but it's also a pretty good bar. Skip straight to the narrow staircase to the basement, where the cocktails are stellar and pool is $0.50 a pop. Shanghai isn't classy, but that's okay because it never means to be.

MAP 1: 211 SW Ankeny St., 503/220-4001, www.shanghaitunnel.com; daily 4pm-2:30am; free

BREWPUBS AND TAPHOUSES

BAILEY'S TAPROOM

Bailey's Taproom is like a library for beers. The selection is extensive and constantly changing. It even sends out tweets and posts of what's new. While it doesn't serve food, Bailey's allows you to bring in anything you like—or you can order from the Mexican joint next door and have the food delivered to your table. Keep an eye on the digital menu that displays real-time keg levels on each of the taps.

MAP 1: 213 SW Broadway, 503/295-1004, www.baileystaproom.com; Mon.-Fri. 2pm-midnight, Sat. 4pm-midnight, Sun. 2-10pm; free

NIGHTLIFE
DOWNTOWN

GAY AND LESBIAN
SCANDALS

Scandals launched on the scene about 30 years ago now as the first gay bar in the area. Nowadays it's a favorite haunt for pretty boys and sassy girls who like cheap, strong drinks, and a more laid-back, hospitable crowd than many of the popular meat markets nearby. Scandals is a great spot to sit and linger before heading off to dance or see a show, and it's also a perfect place to decompress afterward.

MAP 1: 1125 SW Stark St., 503/227-5887, www.scandalspdx.com; daily noon-2:30am; free most nights

LATE-NIGHT BARS
LUC LAC VIETNAMESE KITCHEN

When the theater lets out or the concert ends, the night is not over. If you are hoping for a pretty cocktail, some stir-fry or pho, you're in luck. Luc Lac comfortably fills the great void that is the downtown late-night food scene. Here, you order at the front and wait to be seated. During peak hours, the wait for a table can be long, but food usually arrives within moments of sitting down.

MAP 1: 835 SW 2nd Ave., 503/222-0047; Mon.-Thurs. 11am-2:30pm, 4pm-midnight, Fri. 11am-2:30pm, 4pm-4am, Sat. 4pm-4am, Sun. 11am-2:30pm, 4pm—midnight; free

THE ROXY

A few things in life are constant. Around here, we take comfort in knowing the rain will always return and The Roxy will always offer sweet, fantastic French toast and bacon at 2am (unless it's Monday). The food is good here, especially after a night sweating to 1980s pop. Check out the decidedly irreverent T-shirt collection and tip your server well (who else will bring you chili cheese fries at that hour?).

MAP 1: 1121 SW Stark St., 503/223-9160; Tues.-Sat. 24 hours; free

LIVE MUSIC
★ CRYSTAL BALLROOM

The McMenamin brothers have made a name for themselves in the Pacific Northwest for breathing life into some pretty remarkable historic venues. The Crystal Ballroom is no exception, having seen a lot of action in its 90 years: dance revivals, police raids, fabled rock concerts, and even near-demolition. It is rumored that Little Richard once fired Jimi Hendrix mid-concert on the Crystal's stage. But what people can't seem to stop talking about is the floor. One of only a few like it in the country, it moves on ball bearings, giving a whole new meaning to "dance on air."

MAP 1: 1332 W. Burnside St., 503/225-0047, www.mcmenamins.com/venues; box office daily 11:30am-6pm, later for shows; price varies

Top: Crystal Ballroom. **Bottom:** Ground Kontrol.

Spend an evening at Dante's and you can practically hear "In-a-Gadda-Da-Vida" seeping through the walls. Dante's has a long and sordid history, having been a brothel, flop house, punk club, and gambling hall. These days, it's the home of two must-see weekly events: Sinferno Cabaret, a weekly mash-up of fire dancing, burlesque, and debauchery; and Karaoke from Hell, where wannabe rock stars can sing with a live band.

MAP 1: 1 SW 3rd Ave., 503/226-6630, www.danteslive.com; daily 11am-2:30am; price varies

KELLY'S OLYMPIAN

If Portland has a biker bar, this is it. Kelly's looks a kitschy downtown diner by day, chock-full of motorcycle memorabilia and fully-restored bikes, but when night falls, it becomes a hot venue for local punk, indie, and underground rock shows. You won't see many hipsters here, rather a lot of post-work bartenders and servers, actors, and retail denizens. Besides the great music, Kelly's has all the good dive bar elements: stiff drinks, hot bartenders, and fried late-night nosh.

MAP 1: 426 SW Washington St., 503/228-3669, www.kellysolympian.com; daily 10am-2am; free-$7

LOUNGES

★ PEPE LE MOKO

This little crown jewel—named for a 1937 French film about a gangster hiding out in the Casbah—is a smarter, more sophisticated baby sister to popular Clyde Common around the corner. From the 10th Street entrance, it looks the size of a one-chair barbershop. But this 36-seat subterranean bar is not to be missed. At first glance, the cocktail menu looks like a collection of bad ideas. The Blue Hawaii, the Amaretto Sour, the Long Island Ice Tea all sound like drinks for a college sports bar, not a lush, intimate lounge. But in the hands of cocktail genius Jeffery Morgenthaler, these old concoctions are reclaimed.

MAP 1: 407 SW 10th Ave., 503/546-8537; daily 4pm-2am; free

Northwest and the Pearl District

Map 2

BARS

★ GROUND KONTROL

What could be more appealing than an arcade full of classic games from Galaga to Street Fighter that also serves cocktails and hosts regular Dance Dance Revolution and Rock Band tournaments? Thought so. Ground Kontrol is a time warp into the days of Atari, Pumas, and Apple Iie . . . but with beer. It's basically a hands-on museum to the bleep, bleep, whirr digital past, but also a really fun way to spend a date or an evening out with friends when you tire of playing pool for the umpteenth time.

MAP 2: 511 NW Couch St., 503/796-9364, www.groundkontrol.com; daily noon-2:30am; free

BREWPUBS AND TAPHOUSES

DESCHUTES BREWERY AND PUBLIC HOUSE

For more than 20 years, Deschutes Brewery has been hand-crafting ales that are popular all over the world, like Mirror Pond Pale Ale and Black Butte Porter. The Portland pub (sister to the flagship in Bend, Oregon) has become a favorite spot for folks to grab a pint before they hit the theater or galleries. Order a sampler tray and try six brews for just slightly more than the price of a single pint.

MAP 2: 210 NW 11th Ave., 503/296-4906, www.deschutesbrewery.com; Mon.-Tues. 11am-10pm, Wed.-Thurs. 11am-11pm, Fri.-Sat. 11am-midnight, Sun. 11am-10pm; free

FAT HEAD'S

This Ohio-based brewery opened shop in the Pearl District in November of 2013, and while they may not fit the neighborhood as well as, say, a swanky cocktail lounge, they do beer and big food well. They keep several house beers on tap, and are known for hoppy IPAs, particularly their West Coast-style Head Hunter IPA. They also have about two dozen rotating guest beers on tap including sours, radlers, seasonal ales and ciders.

MAP 2: 131 NW 13th Ave., 503/820-7721, www.fatheadsportland.com; Mon.-Thurs. 11:30am-11pm, Fri.-Sat. 11:30am-midnight, Sun. 11:30am-10pm; free

10 BARREL

When Bend, Oregon-based darling 10 Barrel announced they were selling to Anheuser-Busch, beer lovers were crushed. But the company promised that nothing would change with the beer the fiercely loyal fans had come to expect. The sale did allow them to upgrade and expand and the brewpub in the Pearl District. Check out their brew board for what's on tap, like the specially made Pearl IPA, with a strong hoppy punch, but smooth finish.

MAP 2: 1411 NW Flanders St., 503/224-1700, www.10barrel.com; Mon.-Thurs. 11am-11pm, Fri.-Sat. 11am-midnight, Sun. 11am-11pm; free

GAY AND LESBIAN

★ DARCELLE XV SHOWCLUB

"That's no lady, that's Darcelle!" She's an icon in Portland and has been for more than 40 years. The girls at Darcelle's perform weekly shows that are full of bawdiness, humor, and sparkle. Make reservations before you go and catch the late Saturday show if you can. It's followed by a stripped-down and sexy performance by The Men of Darcelle at no additional charge.

MAP 2: 208 NW 3rd. Ave., 503/222-5338, www.darcellexv.com; Wed.-Thurs. 6pm-11pm, Fri.-Sat. 6pm-2:30am; $15 most shows

Yeast Meets West: Brewpubs A-Z

With more than 70 microbreweries in and around Portland, there are plenty of pints to sip, sample, and savor. Here are a few favorites.

- **Alameda Brewhouse** (4765 NE Fremont St., 503/460-9025, www.alamedabrewhouse.com) has won a number of awards, particularly for its Black Bear XX Stout. The Klickitat Pale Ale—which shares a name with the real street made famous by Beverly Cleary's Ramona Quimby books—is another great beer with bold hops and a caramel finish.

- **Base Camp Brewing** (930 SE Oak St., 503/477-7479, www.basecampbrewingco.com) is a favorite among backpackers and adventurous sorts—not only because they happen to package their beer in backpack-friendly aluminum bottles, but also because the beer inside them is exceptional. Try the S'more Stout. It is served with a toasted marshmallow.

- A longtime award-winner and staple in the local microbrew scene, **Bridgeport** (1313 NW Marshall St., 503/241-3612, www.bridgeportbrew.com) has a terrific ale called Blue Heron released in 1987 as a special tribute to the Audubon Society. The pale ale is round and soft on the palate, but finishes crisply. Of course, Bridgeport is probably better known for its IPA, a consistent Gold Medal winner in the World Beer Championship.

- It has taken a few years for **Burnside Brewing Company** (701 E. Burnside St., 503/946-8151, www.burnsidebrewco.com) to hit its stride, but it surely has now. Popular for their dependable Burnside IPA and Sweet Heat (made with heaps of apricots and imported Jamaican Scotch Bonnet peppers), they also have some seasonal ales that keep people excited with anticipation all year, such as the winter ale, Permafrost.

- Brewed in Bend, Oregon, **Deschutes** (210 NW 11th Ave., 503/296-4906, www.deschutesbrewery.com) has a number of beers that are recognized well beyond the Pacific Northwest: Black Butte Porter, Nitro Obsidian Stout, and Mirror Pond Pale Ale, just to name a few. The Portland pub also features a 100 percent gluten-free Golden Ale, which is derived from sorghum, brown rice, and roasted chestnuts.

- **Hopworks Urban Brewery** (2944 SE Powell Blvd., 503/232-4677, www.hopworksbeer.com) burst onto the scene in 2008 with Christian Ettinger

EMBERS

It's practically a Portland icon, with its dual-purpose venue housing a stage on one side and a small, vibrant dance floor on the other. The music is loud and fast—mostly combos of house music, 1980s songs, and top 40 hits—but the spirit of the place gets you dancing. It's just so darn joyful. Plus, the opportunity to do a little cage dancing or take a spin on the catwalk is hard to resist.

MAP 2: 110 NW Broadway, 503/222-3082, www.theembersavenue.com; daily 11am-2am; free-$6

at its helm. From the very start, Hopworks' beers were winning awards and turning the heads of beer snobs everywhere. Hopworks was also the first "eco-brewpub" to offer all organic hand-crafted beers. Nowadays, the 20-barrel brewery produces about 11,000 barrels of beer each year.

- **Laurelwood Brewing Co.** (5115 NE Sandy Blvd., 503/282-0622, www. laurelwoodbrewpub.com), a locally owned, certified-organic brewery and collection of pubs, is popular with many locals thanks to the stellar Tree Hugger Porter, Free Range Red, and especially the Workhorse IPA, which bears a larger-than-life hop flavor and a 7.5 percent alcohol-by-volume kick.

- At the Southeast location of **Lucky Labrador Brew Pub** (915 SE Hawthorne Blvd., 503/236-3555, www.luckylab.com), you can bring your own four-legged friend and sip some fantastic craft brews, like Black Lab Stout, Hawthorne's Best Bitter, Königs Kölsch, Reggie's Red, Stumptown Porter, and Dog Day IPA. Even better, try your favorite brew from the nitro tap for a smoother, creamier experience.

- This Portland darling has a number of locations, but the original is known as **The New Old Lompoc** (1616 NW 23rd Ave., 503/225-1855, www.newoldlompoc.com). The beers are almost all terrific, but it's LSD (Lompoc Strong Draft), with its smoked malt and generous hop flavor, that's won most beer lovers' hearts.

- There's a pirate in every bunch, and **Rogue Ales** (1339 NW Flanders St., 503/222-5910, www.rogue.com) is Portland's resident scallywag. Rogue has a truly impressive lineup of beers, but it does dark best. In particular, the Shakespeare Stout is rich, chocolatey, and earthy. Another popular one is the Dead Guy Ale, which is done in the German maibock style—and you'll be sold on the packaging before you even taste it.

- **Widmer Brothers Brewery** (929 N. Russell St., 503/281-2437, www. widmer.com) is probably the most widely recognizable Northwest brewer, thanks to its wildly successful Hefeweizen. Operating since 1984, the Widmer brothers have been doing it right for some time now. Sample the Hefeweizen, but move on to some of the other notable beers, like Drop Top Amber Ale and Broken Halo IPA.

HOBO'S

Had Old Blue Eyes and the rest of the Rat Pack been gay, this is where they would have hung out. Dark and comfortable, each table feels a little bit private, and with the addition of flickering candlelight and the soft piano, it's downright romantic. The Hobo's staff is friendly and attentive, and it's an elegant choice for anyone seeking clandestine conversation over cocktails and delectable entrées.

MAP 2: 120 NW 3rd Ave., 503/224-3285, www.hobospdx.com; daily 4pm-2:30am; free

KARAOKE
BOILER ROOM

Every night beginning at 9pm, the Boiler Room rolls out the karaoke. There's no stage, so singers have the pleasure of being surrounded by dancers as they rock the mic. It can get crowded, so get here early and place your songs. While you wait, play some pool or belly up to the bar. Drinks here are both strong and reasonably priced, which goes a long way toward making you sound like Joan Jett.

MAP 2: 228 NW Davis St., 503/227-5441, www.boilerroomportland.com; Sun.-Mon. 8pm-2am, Tues.-Wed. 7pm-2am, Thurs.-Sat. 7pm-2:30am; free

VOICEBOX

If you love belting out some karaoke, but hate listening to strangers, you will love Voicebox. Guests get private rooms, each slightly different but comfortably fitting 6-30 people. The song selection is decent and controlled with a remote, so no cheesy KJ banter either. Table service comes to the rooms, and there is a selection of sake, sake cocktails, beer, and wine as well as an assortment of appetizers, sandwiches, and silly things like a plate of gummy worms.

MAP 2: 2112 NW Hoyt St., 503/303-8220, www.voiceboxpdx.com; Tues.-Thurs. 4pm-midnight, Fri. 4pm-2am, Sat. 2pm-2am, Sun. 2pm-midnight; $4 and up

LIVE MUSIC
★ JIMMY MAK'S

This place is slick; you walk in and just *feel* cooler. There's not a bad seat in the house, and while the drinks are reliably strong, the music is hands down the reason to go. *Down Beat* magazine named Jimmy Mak's one of the top 100 places in the world to hear jazz, and they weren't kidding around. The venue draws some of the biggest names in the business, who love its dark intimacy and nostalgic air.

MAP 2: 221 NW 10th Ave., 503/295-6542, www.jimmymaks.com; Mon.-Thurs. 5pm-midnight, Fri.-Sat. 5pm-1am; free-$15

WILF'S RESTAURANT AND BAR

If you picture a piano bar (the elegant kind, not the cheesy kind), you'll get an idea of an evening at Wilf's. High-backed red chairs and the dark, deep-colored surroundings make for a swank affair. In fact, Wilf's somehow manages to feel an awful lot like an affair: secretive, romantic, and unpredictable. The talent is reliably great, and it is not uncommon to feel as though you have stumbled into *A Star Is Born*.

MAP 2: 800 NW 6th Ave., 503/223-0070, www.wilfsrestaurant.com; Mon. 11:30am-6pm, Tues.-Thurs. 11:30am-10:30pm, Fri. and Sun. 11:30am-midnight, Sat. 5pm-midnight; $5 cover

LOUNGES

BARTINI

The name of the game here is creative, colorful cocktails with giggle-worthy names like Snickertini, a concoction of vanilla-infused vodka, crème de cacao, and Frangelico shaken with cream and topped with caramel. This is a particularly popular spot with the ladies because there is a veritable fruit basket of cocktails to sample, like the hot-sweet spicy mango martini and the blueberry smash, with rum, blueberries, and mint.

MAP 2: 2108 NW Glisan St., 503/224-7919, www.urbanfondue.com; Mon.-Thurs. 5pm-10pm, Fri.-Sat. 4pm-11pm, Sun. 4pm-9pm; free

POPE HOUSE BOURBON LOUNGE

This little Southern-themed lounge and restaurant in an old Victorian serves up an extensive array of whiskey and bourbon, everything from the bottom-shelf Old Crow to the hidden-somewhere-safe 23-year Pappy Van Winkle. Order some hush puppies and ask your bartenders for recommendations. They know their stuff. And if you really, really love bourbon, join the Pope House Bourbon Derby: sample 50 or more types of bourbon and be immortalized on a horseshoe on the wall.

MAP 2: 2075 NW Glisan St., 503/222-1056; daily 4pm-midnight; free

TEARDROP COCKTAIL LOUNGE

This is the spot for classic cocktails with a DIY Portland twist. The owners infuse booze, make their own bitters, and stock some stuff you can't possibly find in the liquor store. The menu changes regularly to reflect the season and what ingredients are locally available. If you need proof that these guys know what they are doing, just look around at the clientele; chances are, most of them are bartenders themselves.

MAP 2: 1015 NW Everett St., 503/445-8109, www.teardroplounge.com; Mon.-Thurs. 4pm-12:30am, Fri.-Sat. 4pm-2am; free

WINE BARS

M BAR

Arguably one of the smallest bars in Portland (think big closet, but with wine, beer, and sake), M Bar packs a lot of charm into its tiny space. The selection is simple, and the happy hour prices (which last until 8pm) are laughably low. There are no fussy menus here; a chalkboard mounted above the bar declares the choices for the day.

MAP 2: 417 NW 21st Ave., 503/228-6614; daily 6pm-2:30am; free

REMEDY

Remedy Wine Bar has the cure for what ails you. It was once home to a druggist supplying supposed cure-all mixtures and body-purifying tonics. These days, they are running on the idea that a good glass of wine and some delicious nibbles will do the trick. In this cozy, urban living room-like bar, find a focus on smaller brands and family-run wineries and a rotating selection of small plates using season produce and homemade charcuterie.

MAP 2: 733 NW Everett St., 503/222-1449, www.remedywinebar.com; Tues.-Wed. 4pm-9pm, Thurs.-Sat. 4pm-10pm; free

Northeast

Map 3

BARS
BILLY RAY'S NEIGHBORHOOD BAR

Billy Ray's is as unassuming as it gets. It's the sort of bar you drive by for months and never think twice about, which may be part of its charm, or like that accidentally hot, soft-spoken friend you've had for years who suddenly grows on you. Nothing outside claims it as "Billy Ray's" or announces that *Playboy* named it one of the top dive bars in America or *Portlandia* filmed an episode there; they are just too cool to make a fuss.

MAP 3: 2216 NE Martin Luther King Jr. Blvd., 503/287-7254; daily noon-2am; free

KARAOKE
SPARE ROOM

The book lover in me hopes this bar is named after Lucy's home beyond the wardrobe in the "The Chronicles of Narnia," but even if it isn't, it has a magical sort of quality about it. Karaoke happens Monday-Wednesday and if you are lucky, you can catch Karaoke From Hell providing a live band backup instead of canned tunes (don't worry, they still give you the lyrics). Adding to the charm, you can order a "Mystery Shot" for only $2.50. A dice roll decides what you get. Spoilers: It's not always pretty.

MAP 3: 4830 NE 42nd Ave., 503/287-5800, www.thespareroompdx.com; daily 7am-2:30am; free for karaoke, show prices vary

LIVE MUSIC
WONDER BALLROOM

Easily one of the top venues for big acts, the Wonder has recently become an active part of the live music scene. The 1914 ballroom, beautifully restored in 2005, now hosts big-name bands, fashion shows, and raucous charity events. There's a fairly spacious dance floor, and the balcony (if open) is a fine place to escape with a drink while you rest your feet. Make sure you check out the Under Wonder Lounge downstairs with delicious food under $10.

MAP 3: 128 NE Russell St., 503/284-8686, www.wonderballroom.com; show nights 5pm-midnight (for Under Wonder Lounge); price varies

LOUNGES
ANGEL FACE

This bar is about as precious as it gets. The limited food menu has things like almonds with lavender, oysters and cheese boards. There is no cocktail menu, but rather a stellar selection of top-shelf spirits, and they are experts at designing a cocktail to complement your small plates. The fun part is the surprise. You tell them you like, for instance, vodka, but don't care for sweet things, and let them do the rest. The wallpaper of this place is meticulously hand-painted.

MAP 3: 14 NE 28th St., 503/239-3804, www.angelfaceportland.com; Mon.-Thurs. 5pm-midnight, Fri.-Sat. 5pm-1am, Sun. 5pm-midnight; free

SECRET SOCIETY LOUNGE

With its rich decor, low lighting, and classic cocktail menu, the Secret Society Lounge makes you feel hipper than you are. Try the corpse reviver (Aviation gin, Lillet, lemon juice, and absinthe), a lounge favorite. The Moscow mule and the Chrysanthemum cocktail are also lovely. If you're a woman, check out the bathroom, as the "ladies lounge" is almost cooler than the bar.

MAP 3: 116 NE Russell St., 503/493-3600, www.secretsociety.net; Sun.-Thurs. 5pm-midnight, Fri.-Sat. 5pm-1am; free

WINE BARS

CORK: A BOTTLE SHOP

This wine bar has more than 100 bottles for $20 or less. It's also sells Alma Chocolates and DePaula Confections. Cork is the only all-solar-powered wine shop in Portland, and it takes its ecofriendly approach to a further degree by offering wines from the nation's first Carbon-Neutral Challenge, wherein wineries created vintages using only solar panels, lighting retrofits, and tank insulation as well as goats and sheep instead of lawn-mowers and pesticides to complete the process. If wine is not your thing, there's a rotating selection of 100 beers both local and from around the world organized by region and the shopkeepers are happy to make suggestions.

MAP 3: 2901 NE Alberta St., 503/281-2695, www.corkwineshop.com; Tues.-Sat. 11am-7pm, Sun. 11am-6pm; free

EVERY DAY WINE

Every Day Wine is as laid-back as it gets for a wine bar. There's no wine list; simply choose a bottle and it will be popped open for you. Drink it by the glass or share the whole bottle with friends. Food isn't served, but you're welcome to bring your own—there are plenty of restaurants nearby to choose from. Ask about the Friday Night Flights, where you can sample several wines for just $12.

MAP 3: 1520 NE Alberta St., 503/331-7119, www.everydaywine.com; Tues.-Sun. 2pm-10pm; free

NOBLE ROT

If your wallet is a little light but you still want to sip some great wines, Noble Rot is your new best friend. The bottle markup here is only $7 above retail. The selection of flights changes almost nightly—as does the extensive tapas-style menu, which includes items accented by greens grown on the rooftop garden. The 3,000-square-foot garden (which you can tour if you ask) is just one example of The Rot's ecofriendly focus.

MAP 3: 1111 E. Burnside St., 503/233-1999, www.noblerotpdx.com; Mon.-Thurs. 5pm-10pm, Fri.-Sat. 5pm-11pm, Sun. 5pm-9pm; free

PAIRINGS

Wondering what kind of wine pairs with the news of the day? Or perhaps with your outfit? Or what kind of wine goes with Harry Potter? (It's an Oratorie St. Martin "Les Douyes" Cairanne '12, by the way.) Jeff Weissler can tell you. His fun with pairings is what makes the experience at this wine bar so lighthearted and enjoyable. There is no food, but they encourage you to bring food in with you.

MAP 3: 455 NE 24th Ave., 541/531-7653, www.pairingsportland.com; Tues.-Wed. noon-8pm, Thurs. noon-9pm, Fri.-Sat. noon-10pm; free

Southeast

Map 4

BARS
EASTBURN

When it comes to hangout spots for Portlanders, EastBurn is at the top of the list. Is it the skee-ball? The year-round closed-in patio with mosaic fire tables, outdoor heaters, and chair swings? The fact that they call their happy hour "recess"? It's probably all that, plus the great selection of locally produced beer and wine as well as a menu with favorites such as the Grover's Mackin' Cheese. EastBurn's laid-back, sports-bar style makes it a great place to watch a game or catch a drink and some great conversation.

MAP 4: 1800 E. Burnside St., 503/236-2876, www.theeastburn.com; Mon.-Fri. 4pm-2am, Sat.-Sun. 10am-2am; free

NIGHT LIGHT LOUNGE

At the edge of the Clinton Street neighborhood favored by the DIY youth culture sits an outpost for Portland's artistic scene. Writers, musicians, artists, and the like flock to the Night Light, crowd into the dark booths or huddle into the couches, and sip on PBRs while engaging in the (only partially) accidental task of seeing and being seen. The Night Light makes great cocktails, and the food menu is both elegant and affordable. It's all very upscale, but in a laid-back atmosphere with prices that do not offend.

MAP 4: 2100 SE Clinton St., 503/731-6500, www.nightlightlounge.net; Mon.-Fri. 2pm-2:30am, Sat.-Sun. 10am-2:30am; free

REEL 'M INN

This Clinton-area dive bar has cheap stiff drinks, brassy bartenders, and a constant stream of regulars along with free pool, an online jukebox, and poker machines. So what sets this dive apart? It has the best fried chicken

Top: Hopworks Urban Brewery. **Bottom:** Lucky Labrador Brew Pub.

in town, that's what. They go through about 800 pounds of chicken each week. It's simple, cheap, and served with enormous jojo potatoes and a six-pack of dipping sauces.

MAP 4: 2430 SE Division St., 503/231-3880; Mon.-Sat. 10am-2:30am, Sun. 10am-1am; free

★ SLOW BAR

This bar is sexy—like it was built for secret meetings and intimate affairs. Dim, slightly reddish lighting, high-backed curved booths, and cozy corners only add to the ambience. Just sip on your Dark and Stormy in secluded comfort and hide from the world. When you get hungry, order a Slowburger, a consistent winner of the "who has the best burger in Portland" argument and that has even spawned a mini-restaurant.

MAP 4: 533 SE Grand Ave., 503/230-7767, www.slowbar.net; daily 11:30am-2:30am; free

BREWPUBS AND TAPHOUSES

HOPWORKS URBAN BREWERY

Portland's first eco-brewpub, Hopworks Urban Brewery (HUB) makes organic brews from locally grown ingredients on-site in its sustainability-focused facility. This is where the beer snobs of Portland debate the use of adjuncts (like raspberry, peach, or chocolate) in the brewing process. Try the boozy Hopworks float made with vanilla ice cream and the signature Organic Survival "Seven Grain" Stout.

MAP 4: 2944 SE Powell Blvd., 503/232-4677, www.hopworksbeer.com; Sun.-Thurs. 11am-11pm, Fri.-Sat. 11am-midnight; free

★ HORSE BRASS PUB

Named one of the best bars in America by *Esquire,* this is a public house in the true sense of the term. The sprawling interior is welcoming and warm with wood paneling and decor that belie its Pacific Northwest location. Inside it's easy to believe you've hopped the pond. There are more than 50 beers on tap (and some of the best from around the world, at that), but the menu really hollers for a good nip of Scotch to wash down the delicious fish-and-chips or Scotch eggs. With brewpubs popping up all over, Horse Brass is still the best spot to toss a few darts or sip an IPA.

MAP 4: 4534 SE Belmont St., 503/232-2022, www.horsebrass.com; daily 11am-2:30am; free

LUCKY LABRADOR BREW PUB

There are few things Portlanders love more than their beer and their dogs—and at Lucky Lab, you can sip a pint with your pup at your side. Absolutely unpretentious and packed with some of the most laid-back native Portlanders, it's a great place to linger on the patio, munch on hand-tossed barley flour pizza, and enjoy a glass of Stumptown Porter.

MAP 4: 915 SE Hawthorne Blvd., 503/236-3555, www.luckylab.com; Mon.-Wed. 11am-11pm, Thurs.-Sat. 11am-midnight, Sun. noon-10pm; free

THE GOODFOOT

The Goodfoot is like the Odd Couple subletting a bar together. Upstairs, there's the tidy and bright Felix with his art and carefully arranged pool tables; in the basement it's Oscar, with his windowless, squat space filled with duct-taped benches and odd-tiled floors. Surprisingly, both atmospheres are ideal for their purpose. The music downstairs is some of the best and least predictable in town, particularly the Soul Stew spins on Friday nights with DJ Aquaman.

MAP 4: 2845 SE Stark St., 503/239-9292, www.thegoodfoot.com; daily 4pm-2:30am; free upstairs, $1-15 downstairs

HOLOCENE

Holocene has a stark industrial feel, and while it seems spacious at the outset, the open spaces fill up quickly some nights. They play some great music here with some of the city's most fashionable DJs spinning every week. One popular events is Double Down, a hot and sweaty queer-friendly dance party the last Saturday of each month. Holocene gets big props for the sunken projection-lit dance floor, which looks like a living room in the midst of a gritty industrialized loft.

MAP 4: 1001 SE Morrison St., 503/239-7639, www.holocene.org; Wed.-Thurs. and Sat. 8:30pm-2:30am, Fri. 5pm-2:30am, open select Sun.-Tues. for shows; price varies

LOVECRAFT BAR

This horror-themed goth bar named for the granddaddy of the genre H. P. Lovecraft, is creepy, but in the cutest way possible. Black lights illuminate animal skulls and random bones on walls and shelves. Painted tentacles adorn the walls. Near the bathrooms is a shrine of old movie posters and dead horror legends. The Gate of the Necronomicon is painted on the ceiling. This is the place to catch some great industrial, goth, and metal nights, as well as belly dancing, burlesque, art classes, and movie nights.

MAP 4: 421 NE Grand Ave., 971/270-7760, www.thelovecraftbar.com; Mon.-Thurs. 8pm-2am, Fri.-Sun. 3pm-2am; free-$6

GAY AND LESBIAN

CRUSH BAR

A favorite queer-friendly bar, Crush also happens to be a favorite hangout for performers, bartenders, and servers. There are burlesque shows several times a month, movie nights, and DJ dance parties. They even host a monthly Dr. Sketchy's event where models pose in various themed costumes (and occasionally states of undress) for life drawing. The vibe here is welcoming to all. They even implemented one of the city's first all-gender bathrooms; only the stalls are private.

MAP 4: 1400 SE Morrison St., 503/235-8150, www.crushbar.com; Mon.-Sat. noon-2am, Sun. noon-1am; free most nights, show prices vary

Liquid Chemistry

Sure, we've done our share of bellying up to the bar with a crumpled wad of bills in our hand. We've been the customer who asks the bartender for a pitcher of the cheapest beer on tap. But there are occasions when even the most frugal among us want to indulge our swankier side. Fortunately, in a city whose culinary culture is exploding with promise, the cocktail scene isn't far behind. Some might even argue that it's ahead of its time.

In the heart of the Pearl District, the owners of the **Teardrop Cocktail Lounge** (1015 NW Everett St., 503/445-8109, www.teardroplounge.com) have been hard at work conjuring their own custom bitters, tinctures, specialty liqueurs, and tonic. While some area lounges offer a few house-infused spirits, these guys are attempting to set the bar a bit higher, acting as catalysts for nothing short of a modern-day cocktail renaissance. The rotating cocktail menu features house specialties and highlights seasonal ingredients and historical events, such as the repeal of Prohibition. Utilizing a wide range of both local and international top-shelf spirits, Teardrop has a truly awe-inspiring menu that most second-rate bartenders could only hope to pronounce, let alone prepare.

At **Multnomah Whiskey Library** (1124 SW Alder St., 503/954-1381, www.multnomahwhiskeylibrary.com), cocktails never tip over into the silly or sweet category. This is a serious bar with one of the most impressive collections of Scotch and whiskey in the states. The atmosphere is that of an exclusive club with oak paneling, chandeliers, library ladders, and walls of gleaming bottles. The wait is long (unless you fork over the considerable amount of cash it takes to become a member), but it is worth it. Their Old Fashioned, made with Henry Mckenna single barrel bourbon, is so well crafted, it will ruin you for all other wannabes.

Alternatively, if rum is more your thing, visit the mixologists at **Rum Club** (720 SE Sandy Blvd., 503/265-8807, www.rumclubpdx.com). At this eclectic bar, rum finds a happy friend with a whole cadre of interesting underused spirits and tinctures. You can go for a classic daiquiri or something unique like the

LATE-NIGHT BARS

DOTS

The Clinton Street district (all six blocks of it) has so much charm. Much of this comes from the high concentration of youthful artists frequenting the bars along this stretch—and finding their way to Dots come midnight for chili cheese fries or hearty helpings of comfort food before committing themselves to bed. The food here is great and the drinks (especially the lime rickey) are delightful, but the real star is the late-night people-watching.
MAP 4: 2521 SE Clinton St., 503/235-0203; daily 2pm-2:30am; free

DOUG FIR

With a fascinating collection of nocturnals and a menu that spans from gut-busting breakfast to the cheeky Fir Burger, Doug Fir is the perfect salve after an evening of heavy dancing. Because the plucked-from-the-'50s diner is connected to the Jupiter Hotel and guests often spill into the outdoor fire

Fino Countdown, a mix of sherry, blackstrap and Jamaican rum, fresh lemon, bitters, and spices.

Another Portland cocktail superstar, Lucy Brennen, owner of **Mint/820** (816 N. Russell St., 503/284-5518, www.mintrestaurant.com), has been recognized in *Food & Drink* magazine as one of the nation's top five mixologists, and her influence shows in 820's creative cocktail menu. Brennen's signature drink is the avocado daiquiri, a blend of light and gold rums with slices of avocado, cream, lemon, lime juice, and sugar. It sounds odd, but it's remarkably delicious. Brennen understands that balance is key when blending spirits, a skill that is also evident in her take on classic drinks that are often overlooked by less passionate mix-masters.

Just off of northeast Burnside, **Angel Face** (14 NE 28th Ave., 503/239-3804, www.angelfaceportland.com) is a quiet little sister next door to the bustling Navarre, which is owned by the same people. At Angel Face, there is no house cocktail menu, so if you know what sort of cocktail you like to drink, it is a great place to discover a new twist. If you don't have a go-to cocktail, the bartenders can craft something specific to your taste. That is part of the fun. It is a concept that could come off as snooty and impersonal, but instead feels special, hospitable, and consciously crafted.

Finally, at **Pepe Le Moko** (407 SW 10th Ave. 503/546-8537, www.pepelemokopdx.com), it is all about reclaiming what has been lost— the art of the cocktail. This is not a place for fussy garnishes and state-of-the-art smokes and ices. This tiny cocktail lounge, which abuts Clyde Common at the Ace Hotel, does not reinvent the daiquiri but instead brings it back to its heyday. A Blue Hawaiian is no longer a college bar Tuesday Tea special, but instead the balanced tropical delight it was meant to be. Think you know an Amaretto Sour? In the hands of bar manager Jeffery Morganthaler, the sickly sweet drink we often disdain becomes a delight with balanced overproof bourbon, lemon, and egg white.

pits and smoking lounges, the party at Doug Fir has been known to rage on late. Its also a popular live music venue.

MAP 4: 830 E. Burnside St., 503/231-9663, www.dougfirlounge.com; daily 7am-2:30am; free

LE BISTRO MONTAGE

For natives, sitting here in the wee hours of the morning consuming large bowls of garlicky Old Mac is just a part of being a Stumptown inhabitant. The service is decidedly coarse and the ambience has all the intimacy and gentleness of unexpected cannon fire, and yet, there's nothing like the crowd come 1am, buzzed with enthusiasm, indifferent to mistreatment, and desperate for hot bowls of jambalaya and alligator linguine.

MAP 4: 301 SE Morrison St., 503/234-1324, www.montageportland.com; Mon. 6pm-2am, Tues.-Thurs. 11:30am-2pm and 6pm-2am, Fri. 11:30am-2pm and 6pm-4am, Sat. 10am-2pm and 6pm-4am, Sun. 10am-2pm and 6pm-2am; free

LIVE MUSIC

ALADDIN THEATER

Since its days as a vaudeville house, the Aladdin has hosted some of the greatest performers of our time, particularly for blues, jazz, bluegrass, soul, and pop. The 600-plus-seat house lends intimacy to the experience, whether it's a quiet sit-down show, a screaming punk show, or the occasional music festival. Arrive early and grab some food and a pint at The Lamp (get it?) next door if you have your tickets already. When it comes time for entry, they will give you a wristband to jump the line, which often snakes around the block.

MAP 4: 3017 SE Milwaukie Ave., 503/234-9694, www.aladdin-theater.com; box office Mon.-Sat. 11am-6pm; price varies

LOUNGES

RUM CLUB

Where do the practiced Portland bartenders go to get a drink when they are not working? The Rum Club with one of the most extensive collections of rum in the city also makes many of its syrups, tonics, and bitters in-house. Everything in here, from the cocktail menu to the decor is a nod to Earnest Hemingway (whether intentional or not)—a perfect balance of rugged and romantic. Try the daiquiri. No really. It will forever ruin you for all other daiquiris.

MAP 4: 720 SE Sandy Blvd., 503/265-8807, www.rumclubpdx.com; daily 4pm-2am; free

SAPPHIRE HOTEL

There's something about the soft, red ambience of The Sapphire that makes everyone feel a bit more romantic and beautiful. The space was once the lobby of a rather questionable motel. These days, the hotel is gone, but the lobby continues to be a gathering place. The cocktail menu is full of tongue-in-cheek references to the bar's sordid past, like Going Up?, made with serrano pepper-infused tequila muddled with cilantro, lime juice, and sweet and sour.

MAP 4: 5008 SE Hawthorne Blvd., 503/232-6333, www.thesapphirehotel.com; Mon.-Sat. 4pm-2am, Sun. 4pm-midnight; free

VICTORY BAR

If you're not that familiar with Belgian beer, the options here can be a bit intimidating. Still, *Imbibe* magazine rated Victory as one of the best places in the United States to have a beer. That is reason enough to go, but the dark, cozy, ambient environment helps—as does the impressive cocktail list, with such classics as the corpse reviver, old-fashioned, and French 77. The bar is not shy about saying that it's a "bartender's bar," and it has a following of industry leaders to prove it.

MAP 4: 3652 SE Division St., 503/236-8755, www.thevictorybar.com; Mon.-Sat. 5pm-1am, Sun. 5pm-midnight; free

BAR AVIGNON

In this sleek, simply appointed bar, the focus is all about imbibing. Owners Randy Goodman and Nancy Hunt have a long history in the Portland restaurant business, and they seem to have hit it out of the park here. Bar Avignon is a perfect spot for a slow evening conversation over dessert with a gently sparkling glass of moscato or a cheese board served with a soft French red.

MAP 4: 2138 SE Division St., 503/517-0808, www.baravignon.com; Mon.-Thurs. 5pm-10pm, Fri.-Sat. 5pm-midnight, Sun. 5pm-9pm; free

Sellwood and Moreland   Map 5

BREWPUBS AND TAPHOUSES

OAKS BOTTOM PUBLIC HOUSE

This addition to the Lompoc family was named for the Oaks Bottom Wildlife Refuge, just west of the pub. It's everything a neighborhood pub is supposed to be: cozy, welcoming, and blessed with good beer. The expected Lompoc brews are available, but you can also find some very unique guest beers on tap. Regular patrons sing the praises of the limited but pleasing menu, which includes "totchos," an unholy mash-up of tater tots and nachos.

MAP 5: 1621 SE Bybee Blvd., 503/232-1728, www.newoldlompoc.com; Mon.-Sat. 11:30am-midnight, Sun. 11:30am-10pm; free

LIVE MUSIC

MUDDY RUDDER

This neighborhood pub in a converted home has cozy, rustic decor and a laid-back homey feel. They have a full bar, beer, and live music gravitating toward bluegrass, blues, acoustic, and Irish. The pizzas are homemade with local organic flour and produce. It's not large and finding a place to see when music is playing can be difficult, but if you just want to listen, you can hear just fine. A dog-friendly patio is out back.

MAP 5: 1665 SE Bybee Blvd., 503/239-9463; Mon.-Wed. 4pm-10:30pm, Thurs. 4pm-11:30pm, Fri.-Sat. noon-11:30pm, Sun. noon-10:30pm; free

WINE BARS

CORKSCREW

It's a little like drinking inside a wine barrel, what with all the reclaimed wood and vaulted ceilings, but Corkscrew is cozy. The wines rotate regularly, and there are small-plate options to accompany your vintage, like artisan cheese, charcuterie, and bread with olive oil. The bottles are organized by flavor profiles, and bartenders are happy to suggest pairings or flights. Patrons frequently wander in while waiting for a table at nearby Saburo's and are often treated with live music or open mic entertainment.

MAP 5: 1665 SE Bybee Blvd., 503/239-9463; Mon.-Thurs. 5pm-11pm, Fri.-Sun. 4pm-midnight; free

North Portland   Map 6

BARS
THE OLD GOLD

The Old Gold is a whiskey and bourbon bar—just the sort of watering hole North Portland needed. This bustling bar lives somewhere between cozy, neighborhood dive and cocktail lounge. On the wall, hangs a handmade wooden sign that's a nod to the famous White Stag sign over downtown and reads "Drink in Oregon." Check the board for the rotating booze selections as well as the ever changing local taps. If you are feeling really fancy, you can push the "Champagne Button" and your server will appear with champagne. No, really.

MAP 6: 2105 N. Killingsworth St., 503/894-8937, www.theoldgoldpdx.com; Mon.-Tues. 4pm-midnight, Wed.-Thurs. 4pm-1am, Fri.-Sat. 4pm-2am, Sun. noon-midnight; free

BREWPUBS AND TAPHOUSES
5TH QUADRANT

The 5th Quadrant is part of the Lompoc family of brewpubs, favored by locals who appreciate fine, locally made beer. Sip on a glass of LSD (Lompoc Strong Draught) or sink into a hoppy C-Note Imperial Pale. If you don't know what you'd like, the servers here are more than happy to direct you. Happy hour (daily 4pm-6pm) is a pretty good time to check it out, but if your budget is tight, head here on Tightwad Tuesdays for $2.50 pints.

MAP 6: 3901 N. Williams Ave., 503/228-3996, www.newoldlompoc.com; daily 11am-1am; free

PROST!

This German-themed pub anchors the north end of Mississippi Avenue serving European ales in traditional glassware. Belgian ales get a tulip, scotch ales get the thistle, wheat beers get the skinny-on-the-bottom, wide-on-top Weizen glass. And then there is The Boot, a 2-liter beer served in a shaped glass and meant to be shared and passed without letting it touch the table. Prost has a sizable beer garden with outdoor heaters and access to a pod of food carts. They also have a full kitchen with traditional German wares.

MAP 6: 4237 N. Mississippi Ave., 503/954-2674, www.prostportland.com; Mon.-Fri. 3pm-2:30am, Sat.-Sun. 11am-2:30am; free

Don't Just Drink, Do Something

Drinking can be fun. Especially with all the great beer, wine, and craft cocktails to be found in this fair city. But Portlanders don't tend to sit still for very often, so it makes sense that there would be a number of events catering to the idea of drinking and doing something a little bit different.

If you fancy yourself a history buff, check out **History Pub Mondays** (www.mcmenamins.com) at the **McMenamins' Kennedy School** (5736 NE 33rd St.). You can enjoy a pint of McMenamins ale or sip a glass of wine while listening to exciting presentations about local and regional history from the Oregon Historical Society and the Holy Names Heritage Society. Or, check out **Stumptown Stories** (www.stumptownstories. org) at the **Jack London Bar** (529 SW 4th Ave., 503/228-7605) in the basement of The Rialto on the second Tuesday of every month. You will hear history experts and Portland scholars tell crazy, weird, and wild stories about the history of the city while you sip a cocktail.

Got a nose for science instead? You can check out **Science Pub** (www. omsi.edu), a twice monthly lecture (with booze!) about such subjects as engineering, earth science, volcanology, forensics, and nanotechnology. The lectures are held at places like the historic Hollywood Theatre or Mission Theater, both of which offer local beers, ciders, wine, and pizza. There is also **Science on Tap** (www. viaproductions.org) at the **Clinton Street Theater** (2522 SE Clinton St., 503/238-5538) which offers a laid-back, but informative lecture once a month.

You can also explore the **Oregon Museum of Science and Industry** (www.omsi.edu) without the crowds of small children at the popular **OMSI After Dark.** You can taste the difference between grain and potato alcohol, try on some "beer goggles" which simulate different levels of impairment, or test your stability in the earthquake simulation house.

Artistic types can engage their muse at **Dr. Sketchy's Anti-Art School** (www.drsketchy.com), which meets on the last Sunday of every month at **Crush Bar** (1400 SW Morrison St., 503/235-8150). Themes come in all shapes and sizes with a focus on dynamic characters like pirates, burlesque stars, comic book heroes, and H.P. Lovecraft creations. Costumed models pose for small and long stretches of time and artists can sketch, share their work with other artists, or simply draw in silence.

At **Bottle and Bottega** (1406 SW Broadway St., 971/205-5070, www. bottleandbottega.com), you can learn how to paint while imbibing some wine or beer. The studio offers reasonably priced classes every day which include materials, instruction, and a take-home canvas of your very own work. They have Tap It Tuesdays (with specials on beer), Wine Down Wednesdays (with wine specials), Thirsty Thursdays, and the Mimosa Mornings class, which offers daytime weekend lessons complete with bubbly.

Finally, if you are looking for a team-building activity, there are a number of bars that offer weekly pub trivia, a very popular activity for locals. The Wednesday night **Quizissippi** at **Mississippi Pizza** (3552 N. Mississippi Ave., 503/288-3231, www.mississippi.com/geeks) is frequently voted most popular, as is **Geeks Who Drink** (www.geekswhodrink.com), a rotating group that holds trivia events and multiple places around the city on multiple nights.

NIGHTLIFE
NORTH PORTLAND

KARAOKE

THE ALIBI

Comfortable as an old sweater—complete with holes—and as friendly and helpful as a Smurf, The Alibi tops many a local's list for after-work drinks, happy hour, and karaoke. It's a bit kitschy, but maybe that's why we like it. After a full day, what we need is a drink—and $2.50 chicken strips—served up with a "Hey, how are ya?" There is the added charm of feeling like you're drinking in the Tiki Room at Disneyland.

MAP 6: 4024 N. Interstate Ave., 503/287-5335; daily 11am-2:30am; free

LIVE MUSIC

MISSISSIPPI PIZZA

Mississippi Pizza and the siren-themed Atlantis Lounge in the back are a popular spot any night of the week. Tuesday is for the popular Baby Ketten Karaoke, and Wednesday crowds pack in for the Quizzissippi pub trivia. The rest of the week features live music of all walks from a Romanian and Balkan band to Zydeco or a comedy folk band. On the weekends, they often have live music for little ones and occasionally even a pub trivia geared just toward the 12 and under set.

MAP 6: 3552 N. Mississippi Ave., 503/288-3231, www.mississippipizza.com; Mon., Wed-Thurs., and Sun 11am-midnight, Tues. and Sat. 11am-1am; free most nights

MISSISSIPPI STUDIOS

This former Baptist church turned music venue is in the heart of the artistic Mississippi Avenue neighborhood. The intimate venue is known for having great acoustics and offering up nearly 500 local, regional, national, and international acts each year. All shows are general admission (cash only), and if the on-site bar is too crowded, your ticket allows you access to Bar Bar, the attached bar with two large outdoor patios and a garden in the back. Seating is limited to the balcony and is first-come, first-served, but still quite close to the stage. In summer months, watch for the "Summer Sessions" series—free concerts by local artists on the outdoor patio.

MAP 6: 3939 N. Mississippi Ave., 503/288-3895, www.mississippistudios.com; daily noon-2am; free-$20

LOUNGES

BOX SOCIAL

Box Social is a self-proclaimed "cocktail parlor," and while that may seem a bit self-serving, it's pretty accurate. Everything here is made to order with precision and care. Ice is hand crushed, fresh citrus is squeezed, and "smoked" cocktails require matches. The atmosphere is dark and romantic, and the service is attentive, but not fussy. Try the Beatnik, made with bourbon, Amaro CioCiaro (a bitter orange digestif), tawny port, and burnt lemon peel.

MAP 6: 3971 N. Williams St., 503/288-1111, www.bxsocial.com; daily 4pm-2am; free

There's a reason why Mint/820 has been around for so long and continues to be such a great place to imbibe. Cool, swanky, and casually intimate, it's the perfect spot for a date or anyone you want to impress. The drink list is smashing, and the avocado daiquiri is to die for. It's no wonder that the drink is owner and mix-goddess Lucy Brennan's signature cocktail.

MAP 6: 820 N. Russell St., 503/284-5518, www.mintand820.com; Tues.-Sat. 5pm-10pm; free

WINE BARS

TESOARIA

TeSoAria is a Roseburg-based winery that tends to focus on Italian grapes, like primitivo, vermentino, and dolcetto. A younger winery with a lot of awards under their belt, TeSoAria's flagship is a Hungarian-style wine with a tradition dating back to the 16th century. Bull's Blood is a full-bodied, earthy offering made from the dark-skinned kadarka grape, of which they have the only U.S. planting. The tasting room and wine bar is warm and welcoming, and they offer small plates of treats like truffled potato chips.

MAP 6: 4003 N. Williams St., 971/229-0050, www.tesoaria.com; Mon.-Thurs. 1pm-9pm, Fri.-Sat. 11am-10pm, Sun. 11am-9pm; free

Arts and Culture

Like the flowers that bloom each spring, Portland is a city that is vibrant with renewal. It is a renaissance city, a "jack-of-all-arts," if you will, deeply rooted in the past and reaching out into the future. Even for a local, the city is full of surprises because the landscape—both literal and figurative—is always changing. The arts scene in Portland is vibrant and filled with groups and individuals who are taking risks and challenging traditional notions. Cello players collaborate with fire dancers, and drummers lend their rhythm to a new play, performed without words. Many people travel to Portland because they hear it's quirky and fun, but people stay because of the intoxicatingly imaginative spirit that comes from all of the artists, performers, writers, and patrons who are eager to do more and share more.

You might think the weather would be prohibitive. Sure, it rains a lot, but the locals seem to take it in stride. It is the price one must pay to live in a state so rich with trees, trails, and rivers, a state just begging to be biked, hiked, climbed, fished, and explored. Just look around and you can see that maybe it is worth all those months spent bundled up and indoors. Besides, it gives us all the more time to work on that painting or write that novel.

It is often said that Portland has the best of both worlds; and that's pretty true across the board. It is the diversity of our surroundings that makes the area so entertaining. You can ski or you can surf. You can watch Shakespeare in the park or see a world premiere play. You can listen to some soulful blues in a club or a comedy folk duo in a park pavilion. Take in an afternoon at the art museum looking at Van Gogh and Monet or hit the galleries on Last Thursday and meet an artist who makes encaustic art. The

Previous: the World Forestry Center; members of the Portland Cello Project.

Look for ★ to find
recommended arts and culture.

Highlights

★ **Best Place to Find Art with a Story:** Explore the amazing art that comes to life in the pages of comic books at **Sequential Art Gallery + Studio** (page 146).

★ **Best Theater Performance:** Portland's biggest theater company, **Portland Center Stage** balances its season between daring new works and classic plays (page 148).

★ **Most Unique and New Theater:** Housed in an old church, **Portland Playhouse** puts on surprising and innovative productions and thoughtful plays (page 151).

★ **Best Cheap Flick in Classic Style:** The Colonial Revival architecture of the **Bagdad Theater & Pub** makes it a Portland landmark; it's also a great cheap date (page 152).

★ **Best Place to Fall in Love with Science:** Where else but the **Oregon Museum of Science and Industry** can you experience an earthquake, visit the Milky Way, climb aboard a submarine, and trip out in the Omnimax theater all in one day (page 154)?

★ **Best Place to Take a Toddler: Portland Children's Museum** is fun for all ages, but especially the very little ones who will love the water room, the pet hospital, play grocery store and theater complete with costume closet (page 157).

★ **Best Way to Merge the New with the Old:** The talented musicians of **Portland Cello Project** perform the music of artists not normally associated with the cello, like Kanye West or Britney Spears, giving the tunes a vibrant old-world twist (page 158).

the Oregon Museum of Science and Industry

city of Portland thrives because it wants to welcome all ideas and desires. Where else can you find such a celebration of self-expression? Where else can you attend a gay pride festival, plunder with pirates, and ride your bike naked through the streets all in one day? Where else can you hike through a forest on your way to work? Portlanders want to do it all, and if "it" doesn't exist yet, "it" is created. Maybe that's why so many artists, writers, master chefs, and performers flock here. In this town, there is an assumed license to reinvent, redefine, or completely obliterate the boundaries of normalcy. It's terribly comforting and exhilarating all at the same time.

With all its natural beauty, and its emphasis on self-expression and independent thinking, it's no wonder that Portland is a destination spot for creatives. The energy of young artists, playwrights, poets, and musicians injects the city with vibrancy and color. One of the most compelling things about the arts scene in Portland is the expectation that whatever you are is exactly what you should be, so long as it brings you inspiration and pleasure. Artists in Portland tend to thrive on a mutual respect, rather than competition. There is pretty much room for everyone. No one is any more or less weird than anyone else, and all of it—the theater, visual arts, dance, music—comes together to create a rich environment for imagination to thrive.

Downtown   Map 1

GALLERIES
AUGEN GALLERY

The building housing Augen Gallery was erected in 1894 and stands in the Yamhill Historic District three blocks from the center of the business district and two blocks from the Willamette River. The gallery now occupies 10,000 square feet on two floors and showcases contemporary prints and works on paper by well-known and emerging artists. There's a second gallery in the Desoto Building arts complex, which houses four galleries and the Museum of Contemporary Craft. Both are worth a visit, especially if you can make it out for expanded First Thursday hours (until 8:30pm).

MAP 1: 817 SW 2nd Ave., 503/224-8182, www.augengallery.com; by appointment only

MUSEUMS
OREGON HISTORICAL SOCIETY

The Oregon Historical Society (OHS), founded in 1898, is Oregon's premier history museum. OHS is home to the permanent exhibit "Oregon My Oregon" occupying 7,000 square feet. There are two theaters, interactive displays, and several re-created environments, such as a Hudson Bay Company ship hull, a 19th-century explorer's tent, and a store stocked with 1940s-era merchandise from the Hood River Yasui Brothers Mercantile.

OHS also presents major traveling exhibitions on a variety of themes from the history of Claymation to Northwest traditions.

MAP 1: 1200 SW Park Ave., 503/222-1741, www.ohs.org; Mon.-Sat. 10am-5pm, Sun. noon-5pm; $11 adults, $9 seniors and students (with ID), $5 children 6-18, free for children under 6

OREGON MARITIME CENTER AND MUSEUM

To get a real understanding of the significance Portland played in maritime travel and commerce in years past, you'll want to visit this intriguing museum. Housed on the steam-powered *Portland* moored at Tom McCall Waterfront Park, the floating museum's exhibits feature navigation instruments, model ships, photographs, memorabilia, and artifacts from vessels of the region's maritime past. Other attractions include "Mom's Boat," a fishing boat from the late 1920s, and the barge *Russell*. Lectures and educational programs are often offered, and there is a gift shop on-site.

MAP 1: 115 SW Pine St. in Waterfront Park, 503/224-7724, www.oregonmaritimemuseum. org; Wed. and Fri.-Sat. 11am-4pm, Sun. 12:30-4:30pm; $7 adults, $5 seniors, $4 students, $3 children ages 6-12, free for children under 6

PORTLAND ART MUSEUM

The Portland Art Museum (PAM) was founded in 1892, which happens to make it the oldest art museum on the West Coast and seventh oldest in the United States. At 240,000 square feet, it is also one of the 25 largest art museums in the United States. Galleries begin with European Impressionism and transition to more current pieces, in addition to whichever major traveling exhibit is here. The permanent collection display is constantly changing and showcases more than 42,000 works of art, with a center for Northwest art, Native American art, Asian art, African art, and contemporary art, sculpture, and photography. PAM is also home to the Northwest Film Center.

MAP 1: 1219 SW Park Ave., 503/226-2811, www.pam.org; Tues.-Wed. 10am-5pm, Thurs.-Fri. 10am-8pm, Sat. 10am-5pm, Sun. noon-5pm; $15 adults, $12 seniors and students (with ID), free for children under 18

MUSIC

OREGON SYMPHONY

The Oregon Symphony has a long history in Portland, stretching back to 1896, when it was known as the Portland Symphony Society. These days, the orchestra entertains some 225,000 people per season with classical concerts, pops concerts, shows geared specifically for children, and special guest performances. Arrive one hour early for any of the classical series concerts and hear 30-minute conversations between the music director, conductor, and symphony musicians as they chat live on the radio about the music, the composers, and the history of the piece that will be performed.

MAP 1: Arlene Schnitzer Concert Hall, 1037 SW Broadway, 503/228-1353, www. orsymphony.org; price varies

Top: the Oregon Historical Society. Bottom: the Oregon Maritime Center and Museum.

THEATER AND DANCE

ARTISTS REPERTORY THEATRE

Formed in 1982, Artists Repertory Theatre (ART) is Portland's oldest continuously run theater company. In the early days, ART (which is always pronounced spelled out "A-R-T") performed in a 110-seat venue in a YWCA. The company has come a long way and now has its own two-stage venue (which has been renovated to allow easier access between the two stages). ART has survived as long as it has in part because it has committed since its inception to performing new, innovative works and taking dramatically different approaches to classics.

MAP 1: 1515 SW Morrison St., 503/241-1278, www.artistsrep.org; box office Tues.-Sun. noon-6pm; price varies

OREGON BALLET THEATRE

Oregon's premier classical dance company, Oregon Ballet Theatre (OBT) was the product of a 1989 merger of Ballet Oregon and Pacific Ballet Theater. Under artistic director James Canfield, a former dancer with the Joffrey Ballet, the company repertoire grew to comprise over 80 ballets, from evening-length works to contemporary pieces. Every holiday season, the company performs the West Coast production of George Balanchine's *The Nutcracker*, which includes OBT's full company and nearly 100 students from the OBT School.

MAP 1: Keller Auditorium, 222 SW Clay St., 503/227-0977, www.obt.org

PORTLAND CENTER FOR THE PERFORMING ARTS

The Portland Center for the Performing Arts (PCPA) is actually three separate buildings: the Keller Auditorium, the Arlene Schnitzer Concert Hall, and Antoinette Hatfield Hall (formerly the New Theatre Building), which houses the Newmark and Dolores Winningstad Theatres and Brunish Hall. Portland Center Stage used to occupy much of the calendar in Hatfield Hall, but now that it has its very own venue, PCPA has an even wider array of performances almost any night of the week. In fact, there are 21 resident companies calling PCPA home, among them Portland Opera, Oregon Ballet Theatre, Oregon Symphony Orchestra, Oregon Children's Theatre, White Bird Dance Company, and Broadway in Portland.

MAP 1: 1111 SW Broadway, 503/248-4335, www.pcpa.com; box office Mon.-Sat. 10am-5pm

Top: Artists Repertory Theatre production of *Exiles*. **Bottom:** the Portland Center Stage production of *Dreamgirls*.

Northwest and the Pearl District

Map 2

COMEDY

BRODY THEATER

This downtown theater hosts open mic comedy twice a week, usually on Monday and Wednesday, and improv shows, tournaments, and stand-up other nights of the week. There is a full bar inside the theater that also serves bagels, wraps, and paninis. Open mic nights are free with the purchase of one item (which doesn't have to be booze).

MAP 2: 16 NW Broadway, 503/224-2227, www.brodytheater.com; Mon, Wed. 9:30pm; free with drink purchase

COMEDYSPORTZ

If you are familiar with shows like *Whose Line Is It Anyway?* then you'll get ComedySportz. The troupe of sketch comedians has been performing fast-paced, hilarious (but clean) comedy in Portland since early 1993 and is still going strong. Two teams of comedians take turns making up scenes, playing games, and singing songs. There's a lot of audience participation, and at the end the audience decides which team did better. On select Sundays, the group performs a ComedySportz 4 Kids show, focusing on games and suggestions from the 12-and-under crowd; they even give a bunch of the audience members a chance to be in the spotlight.

MAP 2: 1963 NW Kearney St., 503/236-8888, www.portlandcomedy.com; Fri.-Sat. 8pm; $15

GALLERIES

BLUE SKY GALLERY

Blue Sky Gallery, also known as the Oregon Center for the Photographic Arts, is a nonprofit space focused on educating the public about photography. You may not already know the work of local, national, and international artists on display at Blue Sky, but you will soon. Blue Sky has been credited with the best record for discovering new photographers of any artists' space in the country. As a nonprofit, Blue Sky is largely supported by grants and its membership program, which costs as little as $40 and comes with a gaggle of incentives and gifts.

MAP 2: 122 NW 8th Ave., 503/225-0210, www.blueskygallery.org; Tues.-Sun. noon-5pm

BULLSEYE GALLERY

Bullseye Glass Company has been a maker of colored glass for art and architecture since 1974 and was the first company in the world to formulate and manufacture glass that is factory-tested for fusing compatibility. Chances are, if you know an artist who works with glass, some of his or her materials come from Bullseye. The company has also supported individual artists and art-school programs by developing new materials technologies

Winter Schminter:
10 Things to Do in the Cold

- **Chinese New Year at Lan Su Chinese Garden:** This urban garden comes alive each year with a two-week celebration involving lion dances, lanterns, cultural activities, and demonstrations.

- **Coastal Storm-Watching:** Whether you head to the Columbia River Gorge or the Oregon coast, you're not far from some pretty spectacular storm-watching. Come January and February, there's nothing like holing up behind a grand picture window by a warm fire while Mother Nature puts on a show.

- **Fertile Ground Festival:** This annual festival of new works, which is held in January, is a fine example of why Portland is becoming a launch pad for creative and exciting new plays.

- **The Grotto:** More than half a million lights illuminate the National Sanctuary of Our Sorrowful Mother, a Catholic sanctuary that is more commonly called The Grotto. It's a breathtaking sight that you don't have to be Catholic (or celebrate Christmas) to enjoy.

- **Holiday Ale Festival:** Toast the dark, cold month of December at the only beer festival in the Northwest to be held outdoors in Pioneer Courthouse Square. There are usually 30-40 beers on tap, all of which are special edition winter ales.

- **New Year's Eve with the Portland Winterhawks:** At the turn of every year, Portland's hockey team hosts the Seattle Thunderbirds in what can easily be categorized as a civil war. The game starts at 8pm and makes a good way to ring in the new year with the family.

- *The Nutcracker:* Every year, Portlanders know that the holiday season has begun when the Oregon Ballet Theatre begins dancing *The Nutcracker*. This is a holiday tradition that families flock to every year and the only West Coast production of George Balanchine's version of the famous ballet.

- **Portland Jazz Festival:** The city of Portland has a long and vibrant jazz history. This annual multi-venue festival features headlining talent such as Wayne Shorter, McCoy Tyner, Dianne Reeves, Regina Carter, Tom Grant, and Eddie Palmieri, along with a number of free showcase performances highlighting regional talent.

- **Ski Season:** Oregon has the longest ski season in North America thanks to all that precipitation. Putting up with a little rainfall in the city means an opportunity to carve some serious powder on the slopes of Mount Hood.

- **ZooLights Festival:** This annual holiday event is a delight. Each winter, the Oregon Zoo comes alive with thousands of lights, hundreds of musical groups, and the brightly lit Zoo Train. Stroll through after dark and see how active the animals get in the chilly night air.

that have helped change the field of kiln-formed glass artistry. Its Bullseye Gallery works with a group of international artists in the field of kiln-formed glass and showcases some of the most dynamic creators through exhibitions and projects.

MAP 2: 300 NW 13th Ave., 503/227-0222, www.bullseyegallery.com; Tues.-Sat. 10am-5pm, or by appointment

ELIZABETH LEACH GALLERY

Established in 1981 and considered the second-oldest gallery in Portland, the Elizabeth Leach Gallery offers a comprehensive selection of contemporary fine art. It is definitely a high-caliber place, with excellent work on display that will particularly delight serious collectors. The gallery occupies a 4,000-square-foot space in the Pearl District, and it features a video and light installation *Light on the Horizon* by Portland light artist Hap Tivey, who has long been active on the local arts community boards.

MAP 2: 417 NW 9th Ave., 503/224-0521, www.elizabethleach.com; Tues.-Sat. 10:30am-5:30pm, or by appointment

★ SEQUENTIAL ART GALLERY + STUDIO

Sequential Art is a gallery that loves a good story. As the name implies, it focuses on works carrying a sequential narrative. It often showcases paintings, photography, mixed media, fabric, and other forms of art in a single panel or whole collections that are part of a larger story. Here you will find the work of comic book legend Matthew Clark, known for his work on *The Amazing Spiderman, Punisher,* and *Ghost Rider.* The gallery also features rising stars and works to foster the idea that comic books and comic art deserve a place in the company of other fine art. While you are there, be sure to say hello and give some scritches to Mochi Manju, the gallery cat.

MAP 2: 328 NW Broadway, 503/916-9293, www.sequentialartgallery.com; Thurs. 3-7pm, Sat. 11am-5pm, or by appointment

WATERSTONE GALLERY

Waterstone Gallery was founded in 1992 by four established artists who believed that an artist-run gallery would provide uniquely intimate interaction with their clientele. Today, Waterstone still offers clients the opportunity to have direct contact with the artists who own and operate the space—though it has grown to include 14 nationally and internationally known artists. You will always find creative, contemporary, original art that is carefully crafted and beautifully presented.

MAP 2: 124 NW 9th Ave., 503/226-6196, www.waterstonegallery.com; Wed.-Sat. noon-6pm, Sun. noon-4pm

HISTORIC MOVIE HOUSES
MISSION THEATER

Probably the most varied past of the McMenamin brothers' kingdom belongs to Mission Theater. Built in 1912, the site once housed the Portland

Art Walks

Last Thursday on Alberta is an art walk with a side of circus.

First Thursday in the Pearl (www.firstthursdayportland.com) is one of the most popular and well-attended art walks. Most of the galleries launch new exhibits on this day, hosting receptions with free wine and goodies, where you can meet the artist in person and listen to live music. Generally, the hours are 6pm-9pm, but some parties can last well into the night. Stroll through the streets and stop at whichever gallery, shop, or restaurant calls to you.

The next day, you can head over to the **Central Eastside Arts District First Friday Art Walk** (www.firstfridayart.com). The event is less of a walk than an opportunity to check out the launch of some new exhibits, as it is scattered as far north as NE Broadway and as far south as Sellwood. A good area to hit is East Burnside Street, where you will find a few galleries and a number of restaurants to relax in. There's a lot to see, but with it being spread out across much of the city's inner core, it can be a bit of a scavenger hunt. The website provides a map of galleries, shops, restaurants, and bars that are participating.

Third Thursday in Kenton (www.kentonbusiness.org) is the first art walk for the north side of town. The Kenton neighborhood (home to the giant Paul Bunyan statue) has seen a significant influx of new restaurants and shops along North Denver Avenue, but it still maintains a homey, small-town feel. The monthly art walk is a great chance to explore boutiques, cafés, and galleries that are new on the scene.

Finally, **Last Thursday on Alberta** (www.artonalberta.org) is the splashy, wild child in the bunch. Year-round, the crowds on Last Thursday are thick with people searching for affordable art, a little nip of wine, or just a good time. Officials close down about 15 blocks of NE Alberta Street between 10th and 30th Avenues, which alleviates some of the crowding. It's a good thing, because the real focus is the street vendors who set up their art on sidewalks, tables, trees, patches of dirt, or chain-link fences. Be sure to hit the streets for some unparalleled people-watching. It is not uncommon to see an impromptu parade, a live band on someone's porch, or a stilt walker strolling by.

Swedish Mission Covenant congregation, very focused on mission work which took them all over the world. By 1954, however, the community had outgrown the space in a neighborhood becoming much more commercial. When the gentle Swedes moved out, dockworkers moved in, and the venue became a hiring hall for longshoremen. The McMenamins opened the Mission Theater and Pub in 1987, the first of what would become a long list of pub-based theaters. The success of the cheap movie concept was staggering, and the Mission still stands as a community-based gathering place, hosting concerts and TV showings in addition to second-run movies.

MAP 2: 1624 NW Glisan St., 503/223-4527, www.mcmenamins.com; Mon.-Fri. 5pm-close, Sat.-Sun. 2pm-close

MUSEUMS
MUSEUM OF CONTEMPORARY CRAFT

Founded in 1937, the Museum of Contemporary Craft has long been dedicated to celebrating and showcasing excellence and innovation in craft from the early 20th century to the present in a 4,500-square-foot exhibition space spanning two levels. The museum takes a more active approach to its subject than a traditional gallery often does, pointing out that "craft is engaged as a verb as well as a noun." There is an emphasis on the re-imagination of the place of craft in contemporary society, using physical interaction with objects, dynamic exhibitions, educational programs, and performances. In addition to interesting exhibits, the museum frequently hosts events to bring artists and the community closer together.

MAP 2: 724 NW Davis St., 503/223-2654 or 503/223-2654, www.museumofcontemporarycraft.org; Tues.-Sat. 11am-6pm, first Thurs. 11am-8pm; $4 adults, $3 seniors and students, free for children under 13

OREGON JEWISH MUSEUM

The Oregon Jewish Museum is the only Jewish museum in the Pacific Northwest, and therefore serves as a museum for historical materials from the entire region, not just Oregon. At any time in the museum there is a wide array of Jewish art, cultural pieces, and historical artifacts. It also has a surprisingly extensive collection of organizational records, family papers, photographs, and ephemeral materials dating from 1850 to the present—the largest documented and visual history of Oregon's Jews—which is available to researchers, students, and scholars.

MAP 2: 310 NW Davis St., 503/226-3600, www.ojm.org; Tues.-Thurs. 10:30am-4pm, Fri. 10:30am-3pm, Sat.-Sun. noon-4pm; $6 adults, $4 seniors and students, free for children under 12

THEATER AND DANCE
★ PORTLAND CENTER STAGE

The sparkling (and super-sustainable) renovation of its home, the Gerding Theater at the Armory, would be reason enough to make Portland's second-oldest theater company worth a visit. The circa-1895 Armory became the first historic renovation and the first theater to achieve a LEED platinum certification for green practices. The result? An airy, visually stunning lobby (complete with Wi-Fi and a café) and two state-of-the-art performance spaces. On the 599-seat Main Stage, you'll find hit musicals like *Ain't Misbehavin'* and *Sweeney Todd* mixed with national bestsellers like *A Streetcar Named Desire* and *Othello*, plus world premieres and readings at the theater's annual playwrights festival, JAW. The downstairs studio space, the 200-seat Ellyn Bye Studio, leans toward smart, cutting-edge performances that are scaled for the stage's more intimate advantage.

MAP 2: 128 NW 11th Ave., 503/445-3700, www.pcs.org; box office daily noon-5:30pm, noon-7:30pm on performance days

Northeast   Map 3

COMEDY
CURIOUS COMEDY

Curious Comedy is a nonprofit that hosts a number of shows each week. On Thursday nights, Open Court is a sort of improv open mic. The next evening the popular Curious Comedy Showdown takes the stage for a competitive improv game where only one comic can be victorious. Immediately following is one of several popular late-night events, like Friday Night Fights of improv teams facing off against each other. Sunday night is a stand-up open mic, which is free.

MAP 3: 5225 NE Martin Luther King, Jr Blvd., 503/477-9477, www.curiouscomedy.org; Mon, Wed. 9:30pm; free, with drink purchase

GALLERIES
ANTLER GALLERY

Antler Gallery is so named because owners Susannah Kelly and Neil Perry believe that an antler is the perfect marriage of form and function, both adornment and tool. The natural world is a strong theme at Antler, and the pieces on display are a mixture of contemporary art and innovative craft. There are a few well-curated items for sale, and the owners are very knowledgeable about art and delightful to talk to.

MAP 3: 2728 NE Alberta St., 503/285-6757, www.antlerpdx.com; daily noon-9pm

GUARDINO GALLERY

Guardino Gallery has been doing monthly rotating art shows since 1997, which is a long time for a gallery to last. The building housing Guardino also hosts four other businesses, so there is a lot to see under one roof. The gallery occupies two of the six storefronts and has a reputation for presenting great contemporary works by Northwest artists and select special guests. There is also a retail shop with great selection of contemporary crafts and fine gifts.

MAP 3: 2939 NE Alberta St., 503/281-9048, www.guardinogallery.com; Tues.-Sat. 11am-6pm, Sun 11am-4pm

HISTORIC MOVIE HOUSES
HOLLYWOOD THEATRE

Built as a 1,500-seat vaudeville house in 1926, the Hollywood is one of the most ornate theater fronts in the Northwest, with a beautiful Byzantine rococo tower. The theater is currently split into three venues, each capable of screening films. There is a 468-seat main auditorium, which was the original orchestra level, a 180-seat venue (one-half of the original balcony), and a 190-seat venue (the other half of the original balcony). The theater was purchased in 1997 by the nonprofit Film Action Oregon (FAO), which has been on an aggressive campaign to renovate and save this old Portland landmark. The Hollywood has also returned to its vaudeville roots to welcome live theatrical performances, concerts, and lectures.

MAP 3: 4122 NE Sandy Blvd., 503/281-4215, www.hollywoodtheatre.org; daily 1pm-9pm

KENNEDY SCHOOL

When this elementary school was built in 1915, it was as rural as it got. Most nearby residents lived without electricity, running water, or telephones. After 1975 the building served as a community center, but was then threatened with demolition. With the help of the community and the Portland Development Commission, it was successfully spared, and the McMenamin brothers began putting their signature style on the space in 1997. The school's auditorium now lets you grab a slice and watch great movies from the comfort of some pretty cushy couches. Hey, you might still get an education, but at least you can have a beer while you do it.

MAP 3: 5736 NE 33rd Ave., 503/249-3983, www.mcmenamins.com; Mon.-Fri. 5pm-close, Sat.-Sun. 11am-close

THE LAURELHURST

The owners of the beautiful art deco Laurelhurst Theater, Prescott Allen and Woody Wheeler, had been regulars of the Bagdad Theater on Hawthorne when Allen discovered a run-down old theater that needed new life. The space was built as a single-screen venue in 1923 and was equipped with an orchestra pit and grand organ. In the 1950s, Laurelhurst was adorned with a small retail space and a soda fountain—which is now an additional screening room. The venue now offers four screens that show modern, independent, and classic films. Concessions, most of which are provided by local businesses, include pizza, microbrews, and wine. Despite its classic Hollywood look, this surprisingly environmental gem now runs on wind power.

MAP 3: 2735 E. Burnside St., 503/232-5511, www.laurelhursttheater.com; Mon.-Fri. 4pm-close, Sat.-Sun. 1pm-close; about $3 for screenings

THEATER AND DANCE

★ PORTLAND PLAYHOUSE

When Portland Playhouse came on the scene in 2008, it wasn't exactly a splashy entrance. The original company made use of an old church in the NE King neighborhood, an area quite lacking in exposure to the arts. For their first few performances, attendance was abysmal. But soon the company began to produce the kind of work that spoke to the neighborhood and inspired conversation. After they almost lost their church in 2012 due to city rules about the use of church space, it was the community that stepped in and demanded they be allowed to stay. The request was granted and company has since continued to grow and become one of the most talked-about theater companies in the city for their polished, professional, and evocative performances.

MAP 3: 602 NE Prescott St., 503/281-4215, www.portlandplayhouse.org; Tues.-Fri. 10:30am-4pm (by phone only)

Southeast

Map 4

COMEDY

HELIUM COMEDY

Helium Comedy hosts a number of big headliners and fun comedy events. They also have one of the most popular open mic comedy nights in town on Tuesday when around 20 comedians are allowed three to seven minutes on the mic. Admission for the open mic is free with a two item purchase, and you can order food or beverages. Stick with the well drinks if you decide to get a cocktail. Their specialty cocktails get pretty pricey.

MAP 4: 1510 SE 9th Ave., 503/477-9477, www.heliumcomedy.com; Tues.-Thurs. 5-11pm, Fri.-Sat. 5pm-2am

GALLERIES

NEWSPACE CENTER FOR PHOTOGRAPHY

Newspace Center for Photography is a complete photography resource center offering classes; gallery exhibits; digital lab, darkroom, and lighting studio access; artists' lectures; and portfolio reviews. It also serves as community hub for students, working artists, professional photographers, educators, and photo enthusiasts. The gallery launches 12 exhibits each year featuring one or two artists at a time, with the occasional group show or juried exhibition. While exhibits can be quite varied, the emphasis is on modern, fine art, and documentary photography.

MAP 4: 1632 SE 10th Ave., 503/963-1935, www.newspacephoto.org; Mon.-Thurs. 10am-10:30pm, Fri.-Sat. 10am-6pm

Portland on Film

Oregon is blessed with a beautiful landscape, which filmmakers have long sought because of its versatility. If some of the scenery you encounter looks familiar, don't be surprised. Here's just a sampling of the films that were made in Portland:

- *Body of Evidence:* The movie, which featured Madonna and Willem Dafoe, was largely considered a clunker, but many scenes in this erotic thriller were filmed in Portland, including a number at the Governor Hotel.

- *Come See the Paradise:* This historical drama set before and during World War II is about the treatment and internment of 100,000 Asian Americans. The movie starred Dennis Quaid and was filmed in Astoria, Portland, and the Willamette Valley.

- *Coraline:* Neil Gaiman's creepy-cool story of a plucky young girl who wishes for better parents was painstakingly animated in the Portland stop-animation studio Laika.

- *Drugstore Cowboy:* This film, which was Gus Van Sant's second, starred Matt Dylan and Kelly Lynch. It was filmed in and around areas such as the Nob Hill Pharmacy on NW Glisan and the Irving Apartments near NW 21st and Irving. While the film was set in the 1970s, a number of buildings appear on screen that were not built until the 1980s.

- *Feast of Love:* This film starring Morgan Freeman, Greg Kinnear, Radha Mitchell, and Selma Blair was set at Portland State University but filmed at Western Seminary and Reed College.

- *The Hunted:* Directors of this film starring Benicio del Toro and Tommy Lee Jones picked Portland because they needed a lot of rain for filming. Sadly for them, Portland was visited by an unusually dry spell that lasted several weeks.

- *Into the Wild:* This adaptation of the Jon Krakauer book starred Emile

HISTORIC MOVIE HOUSES
★ BAGDAD THEATER & PUB

One of Portland's most notable historic theaters—immortalized in the 2004 film *What the Bleep Do We Know!?*—the Bagdad Theater & Pub is a McMenamin brothers restoration success story. Built in 1926 with the help of Universal Pictures with the Middle Eastern influences popular at the time, it was intended to be a vaudeville house, but by the early 1930s, vaudeville was dead. The site then became a cinema-only venue divided into a triplex before Mike and Brian McMenamin purchased it in 1991 and began serving beer and pizza alongside film screenings. In February 2006, the brothers converted the unused backstage space into a bar that stretches seven stories up. The space, now appropriately known as the BackStage

Hirsch, Marcia Gay Harden, and William Hurt. The graduation scene was filmed at Reed College.

- *Men of Honor:* The Cuba Gooding Jr. film about the first African American U.S. Navy diver filmed some restaurant exterior shots in Portland.

- *Mr. Holland's Opus:* The Richard Dreyfuss film about a composer who agrees to teach music in order to support his family was filmed in and around Grant High School in Northeast Portland.

- *My Own Private Idaho:* Gus Van Sant's sad film about two young men on a journey of personal discovery was set in Van Sant's hometown and favorite locale, Portland.

- *Paranoid Park:* The Gus Van Sant film about a teenage skateboarder who accidentally kills a security guard was set in and filmed in Portland—in particular, the Burnside Skatepark, the Willamette River, and the Steel Bridge.

- *Short Circuit:* Number 5 came alive in Oregon. The 1986 comedy starring Ally Sheedy and Steve Guttenberg was filmed in Astoria, Portland, the Cascade Locks, and other portions of the Columbia River Gorge.

- *Untraceable:* This thriller starring Diane Lane as an FBI agent on the hunt for a serial killer was filmed in a number of Portland locales, including Oaks Amusement Park and the Broadway Bridge.

- *What the Bleep Do We Know!?:* This documentary-style film about quantum physics and human consciousness was filmed at the Bagdad Theater & Pub on Hawthorne, in the Pearl District, and in the MAX tunnel, which serves as the Washington Park Zoo stop.

- *Wild:* Portland author Cheryl Strayed's harrowing tale of her own journey along the Pacific Crest Trail. Portland shooting locations included Hotel deLuxe, The Driftwood Room, Mississippi Studios, and Casba Mediterranean Café in Northeast Portland.

Bar, was large enough to house a full fly system for the theater's vaudevillian past, but now it houses an enormous mural that depicts the building's theatrical beginnings.

MAP 4: 3702 SE Hawthorne Blvd., 503/249-7474, ext. 1, www.mcmenamins.com/theaters; Mon.-Thurs. 11am-midnight, Fri.-Sat. 11am-1am, Sun. noon-midnight

CLINTON STREET THEATER

Clinton Street Theater was built in the early Craftsman style in 1914, and it is said to be the oldest continuously operating movie house west of the Mississippi. The theater plays host to underground and independent movies and festivals, such as Filmed by Bike, with screenings devoted to bike-themed independent shorts, and the Portland Underground Film Festival

(PUFF). The theater is best known, however, for playing the *Rocky Horror Picture Show* every Saturday night since 1978. Fans of the cult classic line up for the midnight showing in full costume armed with rice, toast, newspapers, and other appropriate props to wield or throw as they scream, sing, and dance along with the movie.

MAP 4: 2522 SE Clinton St., 503/238-8899, www.clintonsttheater.com; doors open 30 minutes before each show

MUSEUMS
★ OREGON MUSEUM OF SCIENCE AND INDUSTRY

Oregon Museum of Science and Industry (OMSI) is one of the top science centers in the world offering a variety of exhibits and activities guaranteed to entertain and engage both children and adults. Take a tour of the USS *Blueback*, the U.S. Navy's last non-nuclear, fast-attack submarine, which appeared in the movie *The Hunt for Red October* (claustrophobics, beware). Watch a film on the five-story domed IMAX projection screen or a laser light show in the Kendall Planetarium, or explore your way through some of the most exciting exhibits that are touring the world today. Admission to the Omnimax theater, planetarium, submarine, and the museum's multisensory motion simulator are not included in admission.

MAP 4: 1945 SE Water Ave., 503/797-4000, www.omsi.edu; Tues.-Sun. 9:30am-7pm; $13.50 adults, $9.75 seniors and children ages 3-13, free for children under 3, parking $5

PERFORMING ARTS
REVOLUTION HALL

Revolution Hall is a state-of-the-art performing arts center that was built in the former auditorium of Washington High School, which was closed in 1981. The historic building was the perfect spot to house the 850-seat venue, which boasts big musical acts and indie bands, and also serves as the home of NPR's Live Wire radio program. There are two on-site bars (accessible during shows).

MAP 4: 1300 SE Stark St., 503/288-3895, www.revolutionhallpdx.com; ticket prices vary

THEATER AND DANCE
DO JUMP!

Do Jump! calls its performers "actorbats." It is a fitting term because their shows are a unique blend of theater, dance, aerial work, acrobatics, dynamic visuals, and live music that defies categorization. The company was established in 1977 as a group of volunteers under the direction of Robin Lane. Today, Do Jump! has progressed into a troupe of salaried players with Lane still at the helm. Many also serve as teachers for Do Jump!'s Movement Theater School, which offers classes in trapeze, acrobatics, and aerial yoga.

MAP 4: The Echo Theatre, 1515 SE 37th Ave., 503/231-1232, www.dojump.org; ticket prices vary

Top: the Bagdad Theater & Pub. **Bottom:** the Oregon Museum of Science and Industry.

Miracle Theatre Group produces a broad array of works focused on celebrating Latino culture and language, sometimes bridging it with American theater traditions. The company is consistently—and delightfully—different, whether presenting a vibrant Día de los Muertos (Day of the Dead) combination of dance, music, and theater or a dark, compelling historical piece. Miracle manages to keep things fresh while holding on to its Latino heritage. The company occasionally performs in Spanish (usually with projected super-titles), but even if you don't understand the language, the performances are full of heart and compelling to watch. Purchase tickets online, by phone, or in person at the box office (425 SE 6th Ave.), or at Milagro Theatre one hour prior to a performance.

MAP 4: Milagro Theatre, 525 SE Stark St., 503/236-7253, www.milagro.org; box office Mon.-Fri. 9am-5pm; $16-25

THIRD RAIL REPERTORY THEATRE

Third Rail Repertory Theatre burst on the scene in 2003 with a core group of actors already known for solid, dynamic performances. As the company began putting together progressively risky and exciting works, everyone kept expecting—but dreading—the moment when it would stumble. In fact, the company managed to remain a darling among the temperamental and often obstinate local theater critics. It performs at the Imago Theater in Southeast Portland, and you can purchase tickets online or by phone.

MAP 4: 17 SE 8th Ave., 503/235-1101, www.thirdrailrep.org; box office Mon.-Fri. 10am-4pm; $25-42.50

Sellwood and Moreland   Map 5

GALLERIES
12X16 GALLERY

This Sellwood gallery is an artist collective producing the art on display either collaboratively or as individuals. There are about a dozen members of the collective at 12x16, and while each has a distinct style and form, there is a through line that pulls them together. So you often find similar themes and styles that play off each other and add to the richness. The gallery changes once a month and occasionally features guest artists from around the Pacific Northwest.

MAP 5: 8235 SE 13th Ave., #5, 503/432-3513, www.12x16gallery.com; Thurs.-Sun. noon-5pm

HISTORIC MOVIE HOUSES
MORELAND

This theater hasn't changed since it first opened its doors in 1926. Back then, it was still called Moreland Theater and showed vaudeville acts along with silent films. Pretty soon, the vaudeville acts went away and the silent films became talkies, but the theater remains largely unchanged. This is both great and terrible. Seats are sometimes uncomfortable, and there is nary a cup holder in sight. What it lacks in comfort it makes up for in charm. The tickets are cheap, and the theater shows first-run films. Oh, and one more thing that hasn't changed: they don't accept any of that new-fangled plastic money, so you better bring cash.

MAP 5: 6712 SE Milwaukie Ave., 503/236-5257, www.morelandtheater.com; doors open 15 minutes before first show; $7.50

MUSEUMS
PING PONG PUPPET MUSEUM

If you have fond memories of watching *The Muppet Show* or *Mr. Rogers*, chances are you will be absolutely charmed by the Puppet Museum. Operated by puppet builders and enthusiasts Steve Overton and Marty Richmond, this space is full of all your favorite characters and clever new ones. The guys have a storied history in the puppetry industry, having built puppets for Walt Disney, Tears of Joy Theater, and Will Vinton. You will often find them in the midst of constructing a new puppet, and they are happy to show you the inner workings. They also give demonstrations of the different forms of puppetry—string, sock, rod, hand, and electronic.

MAP 5: 906 SE Umatilla St., 503/865-8733, www.puppetmuseum.com; Thurs.-Sun. 2pm-8pm; free

Greater Portland   Map 7

MUSEUMS
HOYT ARBORETUM

Part park, part museum of trees, the Hoyt Arboretum has miles of hills and trails showcasing tree life from all over the world. There are hours to be lost exploring all the 10,000 individual trees and shrubs, and sometimes, even with a map (provided outside the visitor's center) it is quite easy to become disoriented. The walk is beautiful and full of lovely secluded places to think, explore, or have a woodland picnic. Mapped-out self-guided tours include one-, two-, and four-mile segments, portions of which have paved and ADA-accessible paths.

MAP 7: 4000 SW Fairview Blvd., 503/865-8733, www.hoytarboretum.org; visitors center Mon.-Fri. 9am-4pm, Sat. 11am-3pm; grounds daily 6am-10pm; free

★ PORTLAND CHILDREN'S MUSEUM

This is a fun museum, especially if you are traveling with very small children. Kids over eight might find it a bit boring, but then again, even adults have been amused here. In Building Bridgetown, kids can panel a wall, connect plumbing fixtures, take measurements, work the "button and latch" board, and build with blocks on the custom-designed building table. It's a lot of fun, especially if you have a block lover in tow. Water Works features a 12-foot-high waterfall, a hand-cranked "conveyor belt" that carries water in little recycled objects, a twirling collection of kitchen mops, and instruments that kids can play by spraying the water cannon. They provide waterproof smocks for this exhibit, which you will most definitely want.

MAP 7: 4015 SW Canyon Rd., 503/223-6500, www.portlandcm.org; daily 9am-5pm; $10.75 adults and children, $9.75 seniors, free for children under 1

WORLD FORESTRY CENTER

This 20,000-square-foot museum has interactive exhibits about the trees here in the Pacific Northwest and all over the world. So why go to a museum to learn about trees when you could just go to a forest? Well, the Forestry Center has a lot to say that those trees won't say themselves, like how to approach forest sustainability and how the intricate systems, structures, and cycles within the forests affect each other and us every day. Plus it's fun, since you can take a simulated ride down Class IV rapids, practice being a smokejumper, and try your hand at logging.

MAP 7: 4033 SW Canyon Rd., 503/228-1367, www.worldforestry.org; daily 10am-5pm; $9 adults, $8 seniors, $6 children ages 3-18, free for children under 3

Various Venues

MUSIC
PORTLAND BAROQUE ORCHESTRA

Presenting mostly 17th- and 18th-century music, the Portland Baroque Orchestra performs baroque and classical music on centuries-old instruments or truly authentic replicas to match when the music was composed. Using the lute, harpsichord, lirone, and other options, they can play the music in a way that modern orchestras can't—and the way it was originally intended. The approach brings a whole new complexity to Beethoven, Handel, Vivaldi, and Bach, and the results are particularly noticeable when you hear something like Handel's *Messiah*.

Various Venues: 503/222-6000, www.pbo.org; ticket prices vary

★ PORTLAND CELLO PROJECT

This "indie cello orchestra" is as hip as it gets, oftentimes collaborating with the likes of the Dandy Warhols, the Builders and the Butchers, Loch Lomond, and 3 Leg Torso or sharing repertoire including everything from Bach and Beethoven to Britney Spears and Led Zeppelin. When the 8-16 cellists get together, they are just as likely to play any of those songs as they are to invent something completely new. With their quirky attitude and undeniable ability to attack any song with the passion and fervor of a moth around a porch light, it's no surprise that they have a rock star following in Portland.

Various Venues: www.portlandcelloproject.com; ticket prices vary

Third Angle turns the traditional concept of chamber music on its ear with modern and inventive expressions of works by 20th- and 21st-century composers. They have presented over 90 programs of contemporary music, commissioned more than 20 new works, and released five recordings to much critical acclaim. The ensemble produces three to five programs each year, interspersed between recording projects and educational outreach projects. The company has garnered a well-deserved reputation for musical excellence and interesting, positively electric performances.

Various Venues: 503/331-0101, www.thirdangle.org; ticket prices vary, free for children under 3

THEATER AND DANCE
PENDULUM AERIAL DANCE THEATRE

Boundaries are tested and then distinctly ignored by Pendulum Aerial Dance Theatre. Using various aerial apparatuses from a trapeze to darn near anything they can suspend themselves from, the multitalented and captivating company puts on quite a show. In some moments, the movements are so smooth and controlled; it is as if they are underwater. At the core of their physically demanding performances is sheer physical prowess and strength, and a whole new concept of dance that is one part circus, one part burlesque, and a whole lot of imagination.

Various Venues: www.pendulumdancetheatre.org; ticket prices vary

WHITE BIRD

White Bird brings established and emerging companies and choreographers to Portland that audiences here wouldn't otherwise see. It has commissioned several new works, developed numerous partnerships, thought up some otherwise unimaginable collaborations, and retained a strong relationship with the local performing arts community. Since 1997, partners Walter Jaffe and Paul King have presented more than 118 companies from all over the world and given Portland a remarkable helping of modern dance. As the audience has grown more sophisticated, so has White Bird, bringing in increasingly more complex and compelling companies and challenging returning companies to perform more innovative works.

Various Venues: 503/245-1600, www.whitebird.org; ticket prices vary

ARTS AND CULTURE
VARIOUS VENUES

Sports and Activities

Around here, we don't always wait for the sun to start shining in order to enjoy a bit of recreation outdoors. We are lucky enough in Portland to have access to more than 290 municipal parks that are perfect spots for walking, jogging, cycling, or simply enjoying a little rest and relaxation. If you are more the active sort, you would be hard pressed to find a city more suited for cycling or hiking than Portland. Portlanders are all about living the two-wheeled or two-legged lifestyle, and the sheer number of bike lanes, trails, and pedestrian bridges in town is a testament to that fact.

There are a lot of ways to experience the city. You can rent a bike and take a do-it-yourself tour or hitch yourself up to one of the many tours offered in town from the traditional walking tour to those delivered on a Segway, pedicab, or trolley. You can hike up a trail and see the city from above or traipse into the marshlands and meet some of the local wildlife. You can scream your lungs out in the stands of the Portland Timbers Army or sniff a historic bloom in one of the many rose gardens. Whatever your preferred adventure, Portland has a little something for everyone.

Look for ★ to find
recommended sports and activities.

Highlights

★ **Best Place to Go with the Glow:** **Glowing Greens** brings a little weirdness to miniature golf, with a pirate-themed, 3-D, glow-in-the-dark course right in the middle of the city (page 163).

★ **Best Portland Crash Course:** In just a few hours, the **Best of Portland Walking Tour** will have you eating and talking like a local (page 164).

★ **Best Place to Drink and Bike:** If you are looking for a party and a way to visit some of Southeast Portland's popular brewpubs, jump aboard **Pedalounge,** a

human-powered bicycle built for 12. And don't worry. Someone else will steer the way (page 172).

★ **Best Place to Hug a Hundred Trees:** Deep in the hills of Northwest Portland, **Forest Park** is one of the country's largest urban parks with more than 5,000 acres of trees, trails, and topography to explore (page 177).

★ **Best Place to See a Real Smackdown:** The roller derby queens of **Rose City Rollers** are tough and seriously entertaining. In this gutsy sport, don't be surprised if you see a little blood (page 179).

the Rose City Rollers

BIKE RENTALS AND TOURS
PEDAL BIKE TOURS

Pedal Bike Tours is a bike rental place and tour guide company rolled into one. Tours range from simple rides around the city to a nine-mile jaunt through the Columbia River Gorge. Tours are themed and include the bike rental, helmet, and all the other equipment you might need. Take a trip through historic downtown and old town, go on an ecotour, or cruise the five-mile Oregon Brewery Tour past several of the area's most popular breweries and take a tour of one. Pedal Bike will custom design a tour for you if you have something special you want to do. Want a tour of coffee shops and roasteries? Just ask.

MAP 1: 133 SW 2nd Ave., 503/243-2453, www.pedalbiketours.com; daily 10am-6pm; tours $49-89 per person, rentals $6-10 per hour

WATERFRONT BICYCLE

If you're looking to rent a cruiser for a little downtown exploration, Waterfront Bicycle has top-notch equipment and service. Hybrid bikes, cruisers, and road bikes all come with a helmet, bike bag, map, and lock. Road bike rentals also come with blow-out bags and a pump for fixing any flats. For kids in tow, they have trailers, trailer bikes, and kid-size rides, or for two, rent a tandem cruiser, which always looks adorable, by the way.

MAP 1: 10 SW Ash St., 503/227-1719, www.waterfrontbikes.com; daily 10am-6pm; $30-65 for 24 hours

BIKE TRAILS
WATERFRONT BIKE LOOP

This 12-mile loop on both sides of the Willamette is a great way to see the city without dodging cars. West side access is found in Tom McCall Waterfront Park, along the seawall and bollards. On the east side, it's best to enter along the Vera Katz Eastbank Esplanade. If you would like to do a shorter route and stick with spectacular downtown views, loop between Hawthorne Bridge and Steel Bridge. If you want the full route going as far south as Sellwood Bridge, download a map from the "Getting Around" section of www.downtownportland.org by clicking on "PDOT Bike Maps." It will show you the exact route, telling you about places where you should be cautious of traffic, children, and narrow passages.

MAP 1: Western access: Waterfront Park; eastern access: Vera Katz Eastbank Esplanade; daily 5am-midnight; free

GOLF
★ GLOWING GREENS

Glowing Greens is a minigolf course like no other. This underground course in the midst of downtown is like a radioactive mash-up of Pirates of the Caribbean meets Alice in Wonderland. Only in Portland would you find an indoor black light 3-D miniature golf course (yes, 3-D). Animated creatures, psychedelic sea scenes, and stimulating sound effects pretty much turns your average Putt-Putt on its butt-butt. Opt for the 3-D glasses, but don't be afraid to take them off. They're trippy and fun, but not exactly helpful when making a shot.

MAP 1: 509 SW Taylor St., 503/222-5554, www.glowinggreens.com; Sun.-Thurs. noon-10pm, Fri.-Sat. noon-midnight; $11 adults, $9 seniors and children

GUIDED TOURS

★ BEST OF PORTLAND WALKING TOUR

Did you know that Clark Gable once worked in the Meier & Frank tie department? Or that the local Elk Lodge boycotted the unveiling of the elk statue in the Plaza Blocks because they considered it an abomination? How about that Portland was named based on a coin toss? The guides that take you on this Portland 101 tour are equipped with all the inside tips, historical snippets, rumors, and realities you need to get to know the real Portland. Reservations are required, but the Best of Portland Tour, like many of the Portland Walking Tours, departs at exactly 10am daily.

MAP 1: Meeting point: Pioneer Courthouse Square, 503/774-4522, www. portlandwalkingtours.com; $20 adults, $17 seniors and children ages 11-17, $9 children ages 5-10, free for children under 5

EPICUREAN EXCURSION

The Epicurean Excursion is a delightful tour through Portland's tastiest places. Guests try any number of treats, like Oregon wine and imported mustards, gelato, sorbet, cheese, pizza, chocolate, and bread. As you sample and savor, you will also learn about how things are made, how sustainable practices work, and what Portland is doing differently that makes everything taste so good. Be sure you don't wear open-toed shoes for this one, because you will be traipsing through some kitchens.

MAP 1: Meeting point: Pioneer Courthouse Square, 503/774-4522, www. portlandwalkingtours.com; $59 all ages

HAUNTED PUB CRAWL

The existence of ghosts may be debatable, but it sure is fun to hear about them. This tour combines two things that Portlanders love: beer and good stories. The one-mile, approximately 2-hour tour winds through Old Town with stops for libations at two pubs along the way (beer is included in the price). Participants are treated to tales of Portland's sordid past with an emphasis on the gangsters and ne'er-do-wells that occupied the barstools and bedrooms of Old Town's historic buildings. The tour also includes a stop by the Merchant Hotel, a spot featured on the Travel Channel's *Ghost Adventures*.

MAP 1: Meeting point at Kell's Irish Pub, 112 SW 2nd Ave., www.beerquestpdx.com; $40

A fun way to do some sightseeing in downtown Portland is to hop aboard the Portland by Segway tour. The guides are equipped with some interesting facts about various landmarks and can answer question along the way. It is a one- to two-hour tour including a tutorial on how to ride the machine (it is easier than it looks once you trust it). This tour is more about taking in the sights than learning about the city and a good alternative for people who have trouble biking or walking very far.

MAP 1: 150 SW Harrison St., www.portlandbysegway.com; $55-65

SECRETS OF PORTLANDIA TOUR

If you have about two hours to kill and enjoy corny jokes, check out the free Secrets of Portlandia tour running seven days a week, rain or shine. The tour meets across the street from Pioneer Courthouse Square and there is no reservation required. Just show up and look for the guy in the bright green shirt. The tour is off-beat, silly, and occasionally inaccurate, but touches on many things like Voodoo Doughnut, *Portlandia* (the statue), the world's smallest park, food cart culture, and some suspected ghosts. The tour is free, but it is customary to tip about $10-20 if you enjoyed it.

MAP 1: Meeting point across from Pioneer Courthouse Square on SW 6th Ave., www.secretsofportlandia.com; free

PARKS AND GARDENS
WATERFRONT PARK

On the west bank of the Willamette River, stretching the length of most of downtown, is Tom McCall Waterfront Park, named for Oregon governor Tom McCall. After a seawall was installed in 1920 to protect the downtown area from rising winter waters, city planners began to reexamine ways to provide access to the riverbanks and green spaces and constructed walkways and open park spaces along the river, which gained particular popularity in the mid-1980s, when McCall was governor.

Between NW Davis and SW Naito Parkway, you'll find the Japanese American Historical Plaza built to honor citizens deported to internment camps during World War II. At the intersection where Salmon Street meets the park, the Salmon Street Springs is a popular fountain for children (of all ages) to cool off in the summer heat. The three cycles of the fountain are called misters, bollards, and wedding cake, and at full capacity, the fountain recycles 4,924 gallons of water per minute, through as many as 137 jets at once.

MAP 1: SW Naito Pkwy. between SW Harrison St. and NW Glisan St.; daily 5am-midnight; free

SPECTATOR SPORTS
PORTLAND TIMBERS

The Timbers are more than just a soccer team, they are practically a way of life. The acronym RCTID (Rose City 'Til I Die) you'll spot on bumper stickers, scarves, and bathroom walls all over the city is not just a mantra in support of Portland, it is a catchphrase for unwavering support of the Portland Timbers. Enthusiastic supporters known as "The Timbers Army" describe themselves as "part carnival, part mosh pit, part revival meeting, part Christmas morning, filled with people from every part of the community and every walk of life." Taking in a soccer game can be a lot of fun, even if you aren't seated in the sea of green and white with the Army. The Timbers are tough competitors and, who knows, you might find yourself moved to join in when the crowd starts singing "You Are My Sunshine" at the 80th minute. It's a tribute to the former mascot Timber Jim.

MAP 1: Providence Park, 1844 SW Morrison St., www.timbers.com

Northwest and the Pearl District

Map 2

BIKE RENTALS AND TOURS
CYCLE PORTLAND

Cycle Portland was one of the first companies in the city to offer tours by bike. Founder Evan Ross was surprised that it wasn't something more bike shops and enthusiasts offered. The tours Ross and his team put together are engaging and educational; You can tell that they really love their city. While the Essential Portland tour, which takes you through the streets of downtown and the Pearl District, is very enlightening, it is more fun to go off book and let the guides run really deep into their Portland nerdery. Recently, Ross put together a Simpsons tour around the long-running popular show and its Portland-based creator Matt Groening.

MAP 2: 117 NW 2nd Ave., 844/739-2453, www.portlandbicycletours.com; tours $39-59 adults, bike rental starting at $5/hour or $20/day

GUIDED TOURS
UNDERGROUND PORTLAND

The Underground Portland Tour, or "Worst of Portland Tour" as it is wont to be called, shines an unflattering light on the prostitution, gambling, racism, and crimping of days gone by. Drunken sailors might find themselves pressed into service, kidnapped, or just plain tricked. Portland was ripe with the sort of people that made a business of the trade called "crimping." One notorious crimper was Mary Boggs, who had a barge parked on the Willamette complete with saloon and bordello. Most of this tour takes place in Old Town and Chinatown, so you will also get a good peek at what life was like for the numerous Asian Americans who lived in Portland at a time when they were facing near constant banishment and ridicule. And no tour about Portland's dirty underbelly would be complete without a few ghost stories, like those of the basement of Old Town Pizza, where ghosts are rumored to walk the halls. This tour is not recommended for children under 11.

MAP 2: Meeting point 226 NW Davis St., 503/774-4522, www.portlandwalkingtours.com; $20 adults, $17 seniors and children ages 11-17

GYMS AND HEALTH CLUBS
FIREBRAND SPORTS

If you are looking for a way to work off all that food cart sampling, drop in and take a one-time introductory class at Firebrand; it will definitely make you sweat. Firebrand is geared toward the integration of cardio and toning, with offerings such as the Bike and Barre class combining spinning with ballet-driven barre work. Their signature workout is Pyrolates, which is like Pilates turned up to 11. The whole 50-minute routine is done on a machine called the "Megaformer" which consists of a moving platform and a series of pulleys and springs. It sounds complicated, but really it is just an intense workout without the stress and strain of a normal cardio push.

MAP 2: 500 NW 14th Ave., 503/715-5513, www.firebrandsports.com; $15 for introductory class

PARKS AND GARDENS
JAMISON SQUARE

In the summer months, you can hear the squeals of children for blocks. This urban park features a fountain and large wading pool very popular with the under-5 set. Unlike some of the other Portland fountains that can sometimes startle and knock down a wee child, the Jamison Square fountain is more laid-back and gentler. The park also features several sculptures, streetcar access on both sides, and a wooden boardwalk that connects it to Tanner Springs Park two blocks away.

MAP 2: 810 NW 11th St., 503/823-7529, www.portlandonline.com/parks; free

Northeast
Map 3

BIKE RENTALS AND TOURS
EVERYBODY'S BIKES

Everybody's Bikes highlights the culture and lifestyle of the Northeast and North Portland neighborhoods. The Beer and Parks tour takes you by a number of great eastside breweries and four area parks. The other tour introduces urban farms and treats you to baked goods, gourmet doughnuts, and sandwiches. Rental is affordable and available by the day or week. Everybody's Bikes has a number of well-maintained vintage bikes in addition to touring bikes and rugged steel-framed road bikes. They will find a bike that suits you and make the necessary adjustments to make it a perfect fit.

MAP 3: 305 NE Wygant St., 503/358-0152, www.portlandbicycletours.com; tours $45 adults, bike rental starting at $25/day

Bike City, USA

Some of the bike lanes in Portland have comedic twists.

Portland has long been a city for cyclists and is frequently bestowed honors for being one of the most bike-friendly cities in the United States (and sometimes the world) by the likes of *Forbes, Cycling Magazine,* and the Travel Channel. Here are a few things to know about kicking up the kickstand in Portland.

- **Bike Lanes:** You will find bicycle lanes painted on most Portland streets (sometimes with whimsical twists). Particularly hazardous lanes are sometimes painted blue to alert cyclists and motorists of added danger. When bike lanes are not present, cyclists are expected to ride with the flow of traffic at a reasonable pace and as close to the edge of the roadway as safely possible.

- **Bike Maps:** There are many bike maps available online from various sites, including Portland's Department of Transportation, where you can download a pdf map or access an interactive map that will tell you the best route to take on your adventure.

- **Bike Share:** The summer of 2016 brings the launch of Portland's long awaited Bike Share Program, a public rental system intended for short trips. Using an app on your phone, you can rent a bike in downtown, Old Town/Chinatown, inner Northwest, Goose Hollow, South Waterfront, West End,

Pearl District, Central Eastside, Rose Quarter, Lloyd District, and inner North Portland. Rental costs are predicted to be as low as $2.50 for 30 minutes.

- **Bridges:** Cycling is allowed on most Portland bridges, and sidewalks are widened to allow cyclists to share the space with pedestrians.

- **Green Bike Boxes:** The City of Portland added these "Advanced Stop Line Boxes" to some difficult intersections to prevent the accidents that occur when a motorist is turning left and a cyclist is continuing forward. As a cyclist, if you come to a green box intersection, simply ride to the front of the box and wait for the light to change. If you are a motorist, stop behind the box and allow cyclists to move to the front.

- **Helmets:** Helmets are mandatory for everyone under the age of 16 unless wearing a helmet "would violate a religious belief or practice of the person." While adults over 16 are not required to wear helmets, it is a pretty good idea to do so anyway.

- **Limited Visibility:** Gray, rainy conditions mean less visibility, which is especially dangerous for cyclists. A front white light that is visible from at least 500 feet is required in these conditions and at night, as is a red rear reflector. But it is a good idea to also attach a flashing light to yourself or your backpack to increase visibility.

- **May:** The month of May is Portland Bike Month and the city is alive with celebrations all over the city as well as workshops and classes geared toward bike safety and advice.

- **Sharing the Road:** Most Portland drivers are accustomed to sharing the road with cyclists, but you should follow the basic rules of safety. Ride with the flow of the traffic, not against it. Wear visible colors and lights, especially on rainy days or in the dark. Obey all traffic signals and maintain control of your bicycle.

- **Parking:** It is often easier to find bike parking than automobile parking. Many businesses have free bike parking on the sidewalk or in small sections of the street. You will need to bring your own lock. Bike Lockers are also available for long-term rental throughout Portland through the Portland Department of Transportation.

- **Transit:** The buses, the streetcar, the aerial tram, and the MAX are all equipped with bike holders, and it does not cost extra to transport your bike.

GUIDED TOURS
THE PORTLAND BREW BUS

Get ready to sample some of Portland's finest as you visit places like Amnesia Brewing, Lucky Labrador, Portland Brewing, and Widmer Brothers Brewery. This tour bus takes you around Portland to three or four breweries, where you can sample different beers, tour several locations, and ask questions of the resident brewers. On this fun, educational tour, you'll learn the history of craft brewing, hear about different styles of beer (ales, lagers, porters, stouts), and find out why Portland is the home of craft brewing.

MAP 3: 1000 NE Multnomah St., 503/647-0021, www.brewbus.com; $45

GYMS AND HEALTH CLUBS
PORTLAND ROCK GYM

Like the idea of climbing but not keen on the idea of doing it on an actual rock? Hit the walls at Portland Rock Gym. This largest rock gym in Oregon hosts a 40-foot lead climb, a second gym devoted to bouldering, a weight room, cardio machines, and yoga classes. The gym offers private and group lessons and daily and monthly passes in addition to annual memberships. The numerous routes on the walls range from beginner to advanced. During the winter, the gym get can pretty crowded, particularly on the lead wall, but the bouldering area is spacious and oftentimes less crowded.

MAP 3: 21 NE 12th Ave., 503/232-8310, www.portlandrockgym.com; Mon., Wed., Fri. 11am-11pm, Tues. and Thurs. 7am-11pm, Sat. 9am-9pm, Sun. 9am-6pm; $17 adults, $12 children

PARKS AND GARDENS
GRANT PARK

Lovers of Beverly Cleary's Ramona books will want to grab a picnic and head to this northeast Portland park. In addition to having tall, shady trees and vast expanses of green grass, it shelters sculptures of Ramona, Henry Higgins, and Henry's dog Ribsy. The neighborhood was once home to Cleary, and many of the streets will look familiar to fans, especially Klickitat Street, the site of Ramona's home. There is a splash pad (which is similar to a fountain, but with little or no standing water), a playground, and an accessible restroom, so it is a great place to spend a sunny afternoon.

MAP 3: NE 33rd St., 503/823-7529, www.portlandonline.com/parks; free

SPECTATOR SPORTS
PORTLAND TRAIL BLAZERS

Love or hate them, the Portland Trail Blazers have been an active part of professional basketball since 1970 and always a Portland team. Portlanders tend to be loyal in their support but fickle in their devotion. Blazer fever kicks in with a vengeance whenever the team is successful, but when it is failing, the same base is rather nonplussed. That was all different in 1976, when Bill Walton led the team to a 49-33 season and the 1977

Championship. Blazer mania peaked again in the early 1990s, shortly after billionaire Paul Allen purchased the team. With team legend and sentimental favorite Clyde "The Glide" Drexler as charismatic forward and a starting lineup including Buck Williams, Jerome Kersey, and Kevin Duckworth, the team was back in its fans' good graces.

What followed a decade later is what most Portlanders refer to as the "Jail Blazers" era. Every day it seemed that another player was facing arrest. Players such as Rod Strickland, Isaiah Rider, Ruben Patterson, and Qyntel Woods seemed to get more press for their off-court behavior than their game skills. Hot-headed Rasheed Wallace was repeatedly ejected from games. Despite the continued wins, fans were giving up on the Blazers in droves. These days, the fans are slowly starting to regain trust in their team. With a number of strong (and well-behaved) players like Damian Lillard, Meyers Leonard, and CJ McCollum, the now very young team is starting to remind Portlanders of the days when the "Rip City Rhapsody" (a team spirit song written for and recorded by the 1990s-era Blazers) was on everybody's brain.

MAP 3: Rose Garden Arena, 1 N. Center Court St., 503/797-9600, www.nba.com/blazers

PORTLAND WINTERHAWKS

The Portland Winterhawks are a major junior ice hockey team in the Western Hockey League based in western Canada and the Pacific Northwest. It is one of three leagues that make up the Canadian Hockey League, the highest level of nonprofessional hockey in the world. Most home games are at the Memorial Coliseum, though typically a few each season go to Rose Garden Arena. A great number of Winterhawks have graduated to play in the National Hockey League, including Mike Vernon, Gary Yaremchuk, Clint Malarchuk, Ray Ferraro, Adam Deadmarsh, Steve Knowalchuk, Glen Wesley, Nolan Pratt, Byron Dafoe, Brendon Morrow, Jozef Balej, and Richie Regeh. The Winterhawks have won the Memorial Cup twice—in 1983 and again in 1998. They are known for doing fundraising events, like the Teddy Bear Toss, wherein fans toss brand-new bears onto the ice—which will then be donated to children's charities by the team. Portland broke the record in 2006 for most bears donated on one night, and then broke it again in 2007 when they collected 20,372 animals in one night. The 2014 record went to the Calgary Hitmen with 26,000 bears.

MAP 3: Memorial Coliseum, 300 N. Winning Way, 503/238-6366, www.winterhawks.com

Southeast   Map 4

BIKE RENTALS AND TOURS
CLEVER CYCLES

Clever Cycles is very clever indeed. In a city positively teeming with bike enthusiasts, they tapped into a market many bike shops had missed. Here it's not about the rising cost of oil or the newest fad in fitness bikes; the bikes are geared (pun intended) toward practical transportation. The company has about 20 bikes to rent out, and during the peak summer months, those are often sold out. The majority are Brompton folding bikes, which are sturdy and comfortable for people of all heights. The beauty of the folding bike is that it is easily carried on mass transit and in vehicles, making it much simpler to decide when you are done with your ride.

MAP 4: 900 SE Hawthorne Blvd., 503/334-1560, www.clevercycles.com; Mon-Fri. 11am-6pm, Sat.-Sun. 11am-5pm; bike rental starting at $30/day

★ PEDALOUNGE

This isn't so much a bike tour as a human-powered trolley trip. Twelve passengers—or "Loungers"—sit along a rail facing each other and pedal (there are also two spots for non-peddling passengers), while a captain steers the way on a 2.5-hour voyage to as many as four breweries, pubs, and dive bars. Loungers can drink at the stops and also choose from a number of designated stops. But the journey is really the best part as the party rolls through the streets of Southeast Portland, ringing bells, singing songs, and waving to passersby.

MAP 4: 1125 SE Division St., 503/285-4844, www.pedalounge.com; pricing varies, about $20

BIKE TRAILS
VERA KATZ EASTBANK ESPLANADE

A leisurely ride along the waterfront is a great way to get a good look at the city, and from the Eastbank Esplanade, you have a choice of heading north and following the route across the Steel Bridge into downtown or south to the Springwater Corridor. There are several urban markers depicting the eastside city grid and interactive panels provide information on the river and the city's history. The esplanade is named for former Portland mayor Vera Katz, and a statue of the lady herself smiling and saving a spot for you on a bench is near the Hawthorne Bridge.

MAP 4: SE Water Ave., 503/823-7529, www.portlandonline.com/parks; free

PARKS AND GARDENS
COLONEL SUMMERS PARK

This park may not seem like much. Other than picnic tables, a basketball court, and an adorable community garden, it is mostly open space. But on weekends and Monday evenings, the area is buzzing with energy as jugglers, hula hoopers, and fire dancers converge to hang out, practice, and collaborate. It has become a sort of unofficial meeting spot for the types of people you might otherwise see busking for dollars on the street. The vibe is relaxed and welcoming, particularly if you want to bring your own tools and join in.

MAP 4: SE 17th and SE Taylor St., 503/823-7529, www.portlandonline.com/parks; free

Top: Vera Katz Eastbank Esplanade. **Bottom:** Waterfront Park in autumn

LAURELHURST PARK

Laurelhurst Park has a little bit of something for everyone. Within its 31 acres, there is a basketball court, soccer field, tennis court, volleyball court, playground, off-leash dog zone, horseshoe pit, picnic tables, a stage, and restrooms. There are also multiple paths winding through and around the park for strolling and observing some flora and fauna. The pond in the center of the park is well-populated with ducks; you are not supposed to feed them, but they are fun to watch anyway.

MAP 4: 3756 SE Oak St., 503/823-7529, www.portlandonline.com/parks; free

WATERSPORTS

WILLAMETTE JETBOAT EXCURSIONS

If you are not the floating and paddling sort, maybe you would rather see the Portland waterfront whiz past you while you enjoy sights, history, and scenic beauty from the seat of a jet boat. This tour shows off giant ships, bridges, elegant riverfront homes, historic Oregon City, and the majestic Willamette Falls. Each boat holds about 50, and there are both one- and two-hour excursions available. Reservations are highly recommended, particularly in the height of summer. Oh, and by the way, do wear sunblock and expect to get a little wet.

MAP 4: 1945 SE Water Ave., 503/231-1532, www.willamettejet.com; $39 adults, $25 children ages 4-11, free for children under 4

Sellwood and Moreland   Map 5

BIKE RENTALS AND TOURS

BIKE COMMUTER

Just one block from the Springwater Corridor, this handy bike shop rents out bikes by Jamis, Breezer, and Redline. They are uncomplicated and easy, even for a less experienced rider. You can rent by the hour, day, or week including lock and helmet. The folks here are happy to give you some pointers and guide you toward the best ride. They also make sure your bike is in working order and a good fit. Check out their lounge where you can relax and sip a pint from one of 10 rotating taps. Don't worry: there's plenty of bike parking.

MAP 5: 8524 SE 17th Ave., 503/505-9200, www.pdxbikecommuter.com; Tues.-Sat. 10am-7pm, Sun. 10am-5pm; bike rental starting at $25/day

GOLF

EASTMORELAND GOLF COURSE AND DRIVING RANGE

Eastmoreland's golf course is a fun, short course, with wide fairways lined by low-limbed trees. A few of the holes require a bit of strategy, as some have significant doglegs, and one plays over a ravine. The lit and covered

driving range has two different levels, with 17 tees on the lower and 17 on
the upper. It's pretty cheap, too: less than $10 for 100 balls.

MAP 5: 2425 SE Bybee Blvd., 503/775-5910, www.eastmorelandgolfcourse.com; daily dawn-8pm; $15-38 per 18 holes

HIKING
SPRINGWATER CORRIDOR

Springwater Corridor is a small segment of a 40-mile loop beginning in Southeast Portland and including Oaks Bottom Wildlife Refuge, Tideman Johnson Nature Park, and Powell Butte Nature Park. The Springwater Trail follows a former railroad route that ceased service in 1989. Most of it is paved and bordered by fields and trees; though the trail does span some busy streets, most are equipped with crossing lights. In the summer of 2006, construction of three new bridges allowed cyclists access to the Eastbank Esplanade. The trail can get crowded on the weekends, particularly near the Esplanade, but the less populous areas are abundant in flora and fauna.

MAP 5: SE Reedway and SE 124th Ave.; daily 24 hours; free

North Portland

Map 6

PARKS AND GARDENS
PENINSULA PARK

This Piedmont neighborhood park was the city's first public rose garden and original site of the Rose Festival. There are more than 5,000 roses in this very walkable garden, and a fountain and gazebo make it look like a Rodgers and Hammerstein musical might spring up at any moment. Be sure to seek out the official rose of Portland, the Madame Caroline Testout, a large rose-pink flower that symbolizes the early days of the city's budding history when 10,000 of them lined the streets.

MAP 6: 700 N. Rosa Parks Way, 503/823-7529, www.portlandonline.com/parks; free

YOGA
YOGA SHALA

Yoga Shala is dedicated to the sacred practice of Hatha yoga in a variety of different styles, so you are sure to find a class to suit you, regardless of experience or ability. It even offers classes for moms-to-be along with moms and babies, as well as anatomy and philosophy classes to better understand the practice. If you really want to dive in, try one of the three- to four-week immersion classes. Advanced study and teacher training are also available.

MAP 6: 3808 N. Williams Ave., 503/963-9642, www.yogashalapdx.com; Mon.-Thurs. 9am-8:30pm, Fri. 9am-5:30pm, Sat.-Sun. 10am-5:30pm; $12 per class

BIKE TRAILS
MOUNT TABOR

Mt. Tabor Park is named for the eponymous dormant volcanic cinder cone that it surrounds. It wasn't until 1912, many years after the neighborhood and the park had been established at its base, that it was discovered that the mountain was actually a volcano (extinct for 3,000 years). The beautiful 195-acre park was designed by the Olmsted brothers and includes basketball courts, picnic areas, play areas, off-leash dog areas, horseshoe pits, a stage, tennis courts, and volleyball courts. It's a popular spot for many reasons, but the numerous paved and unpaved trails make it a great ride for cyclists and dirt bikers alike.

MAP 7: SE 60th Ave. and Salmon St.; daily 5am-midnight; free

GOLF
GLENDOVEER GOLF CLUB

Glendoveer has 36 holes, and when it's in tip-top shape, it's considered by many to be the best public course in the city. Many regular users prefer the East Course because it's hillier and more heavily treed, which presents interesting challenges depending on how the wind picks up over the hills. The West Course is easier for most because it lacks the tight, tree-lined passages and does not have any water hazards. The weekends can get crowded and require more patience while you wait for your opportunity to hit, so book on a weekday or during off-hours if you can. This course also has a jogging trail (open to the public) that circles the greens. With all the huge, old trees and rolling greens, it makes for a really beautiful walk or run, whether or not you golf.

MAP 7: 14015 NE Glisan St., 503/253-7507, www.golfglendoveer.com; daily 6:30am-9pm; $10-35 per 18 holes

HERON LAKES GOLF CLUB

Heron Lakes has two 18-hole, par 72 courses: Greenback and the Great Blue. There's water everywhere, so bringing a handful of extra balls is not a bad idea. The Great Blue is a traditional links-style track where you will find the par 4, 466-yard 8th hole, which has a 90-degree dogleg left and a dangerous slough. Greenback is a better course for beginners but comes with plenty of challenges for more seasoned players as well (like numerous trees that must be avoided). Tee times can be booked online through the website or over the phone.

MAP 7: 3500 N. Victory Blvd., 503/289-1818, www.heronlakesgolf.com; daily 6am-9pm; $13-42 per 18 holes

THE PUB COURSES AT EDGEFIELD

There are many reasons to head out to Edgefield and set of meander through the stately property, and the Pub Courses are at the top of the list.

There are two separate pitch-n-putt courses, including a 20-hole course (West) and a 12-hole course (East). The holes range about 40-80 yards throughout, and there is one mat tees for all hitters. The newest portion, which opened in the spring of 2008, was modeled after Burningbush, the fantasy fairways from Michael Murphy's Golf in the Kingdom, and includes 15 holes. It's a good place to practice your short game or simply entertain yourself while gathering with friends and drinking some of the famous McMenamins beer.

MAP 7: 2126 SW Halsey St., Troutdale, 503/492-5442, www.mcmenamins.com; hours vary seasonally; $12-18

GYMS AND HEALTH CLUBS
MARCH WELLNESS
At the base of the Aerial Tram, you'll find March Wellness, which is housed in the first two floors of the Center for Health and Healing at Oregon Health and Sciences University. The center offers trainers and health coaches, a pool, cooking classes, and yoga. The programs follow a scientific approach designed to improve overall health and healing and promote long-lasting results.

MAP 7: 3303 SW Bond Ave., 503/418-6272, www.marchwellness.com; Mon.-Fri. 5am-10pm, Sat.-Sun. 7am-7pm; day pass free with appointment only

HIKING
AUDUBON SANCTUARY
This 150-acre nature sanctuary, nestled against Forest Park, is only five minutes from downtown, but it feels miles away. Chock-full of native flora and fauna, it has over four miles of forested hiking trails. At various times during the year, you can find over 40 species of birds and 60 species of mammals making their home in this sanctuary. Pick up a trail guide at the Audubon House, which will provide you with a look at all three trails. The Pittock Bird Sanctuary trailhead is most accessible from the parking lot, but try finding the Founders trailhead first (across the street). It offers more exercise and lovely forest scenery as well as a view of Oregon's native plants unfettered by the invasive effects of English ivy and other nonnative plants.

MAP 7: 5151 NW Cornell Rd., www.audubonportland.org; daily dawn-dusk; free

★ FOREST PARK
Whether you're looking for a quick hike without leaving the city or want to lose yourself in midst of the inclines, tall trees, moss, flowers, birds, and quiet, this is your park. There are numerous trails to select, and you can make it as challenging or simple as you like. What is really spectacular is the feeling of escape once you're in the park. As the largest urban park in the world, Forest Park's peaceful surroundings make it hard to imagine that there is a city just outside its perimeter.

If you're feeling ambitious, you can take a 12-mile jog from the Leif Erickson Drive entrance, which is conveniently metered at each quarter-mile with a white pole sign. There are some spectacular views along the way, especially at Mile 3, where you get a great view of the city. Another picturesque trail is the Lower Macleay Trail, which you can find at Macleay Park (near NW Thurman and NW 29th). It's a really pleasant short hike through shady trees and small streams. Stick to the trail and you'll end up at the Audubon Sanctuary, which has its own circuit of beautiful trails.

MAP 7: NW 29th Ave. and Upshur St. to Newberry Rd., www.forestparkconservancy.org; daily 5am-10pm; free

TRYON CREEK STATE NATURAL AREA

Tryon Creek State Natural Area is a 645-acre park that lies between Boones Ferry Road and Terwilliger Boulevard in Southwest Portland. The park includes hiking trails and horse trails, and a paved bicycle path runs along the east edge of the park toward Lake Oswego. The park once belonged to pioneer settler Socrates Hotchkiss Tryon Sr., who left the land to his family when he died. Years later, the land was sold, and the few decades were spent logging the cedar and fir trees, until the infamous Columbus Day Storm blew down most of the remaining trees. In 1969, Multnomah County bought 45 acres in the hopes of establishing a municipal park. Citizens banded together to help and eventually formed the nonprofit Friends of Tryon Creek, which to this day helps raise funds, purchase land, and maintain the beauty and health of the reserve.

These days, the land is beginning to thrive as Douglas firs, western red cedars, and big-leaf maples tower over trilliums and sword ferns. As you stroll, it's not uncommon to see owls, woodpeckers, blue herons, and deer, as well as steelhead trout, Coho salmon, salamanders, banana slugs, and beavers.

MAP 7: 11321 SW Terwilliger Blvd., www.tryonfriends.org; daily dawn-dusk; free

PARKS AND GARDENS

INTERNATIONAL ROSE TEST GARDEN

Portland's famous rose garden in Washington Park is the oldest continuously operated test garden in the United States. While the primary purpose of the garden is to test and protect new rose hybrids (a tradition that began in the midst of World War I when people from around the world sent roses to Portland to keep them safe from bombing), the 4.5 acres of blooms are a shining example of why Portland is known as "The City of Roses." You can picnic in the Shakespearean Garden, where you'll find blooms that are named for characters in the bard's plays scattered among the benches, archways, and graceful trees. As you near the garden's edge and enjoy a panoramic view of the city, amble along the Queen's Walk, where the Rose Festival Queens are remembered with a plaque that bears their names and signatures. Next, stroll past the sprawling outdoor amphitheater (a perfect spot for a picnic), where you just might catch a summertime show or live music showcase.

MAP 7: 400 SW Kingston Ave., 503/823-3636, www.rosegardenstore.org; daily 7:30am-9pm; free

LEACH BOTANICAL GARDENS

If you head deep into Southeast Portland, you'll discover hidden treasure at the Leach Botanical Gardens. Named for Lilla Leach—who is famous for botanical research, her exploration of the Siskiyou and Klamath mountains, and discovering five plant species new to science—and her husband, this combination of forest and garden offers a woody feel. The original Leach residence is still on the property and serves as one of several entries to the garden's nine acres of walkable land. This botanical garden—or living museum—sits next to Johnson Creek and offers 2,300 planted species, a rock garden, physics garden, fern collection, wildflowers, and even a composting demonstration center.

MAP 7: 6704 SE 122nd Ave., 503/823-9503, www.leachgarden.org; Tues.-Sat. 9am-4pm, Sun. 1pm-4pm; free

WASHINGTON PARK

Washington Park is a sprawling public park that is home to the Oregon Zoo, the World Forestry Center, Hoyt Arboretum, the Children's Museum, an outdoor amphitheater, an archery range, tennis courts, and 40 acres of forest, trails, playgrounds, and gardens. Washington Park is also home to the oldest continuously operated public test garden, where more than 550 varieties of roses are cultivated and judged every year at the Portland Rose Festival. Take the MAX out to Washington Park and you will see the deepest transit station in North America, Portland's only underground stop. Despite being 260 feet below ground, the elevators can carry 35 people up to street level in about 20 seconds.

MAP 7: 400 SW Kingston Ave.; daily 5am-10pm; free

SPECTATOR SPORTS

★ ROSE CITY ROLLERS

The Rose City Rollers, a collection of roller derby divas, have been tearing up tracks in Portland since 2004. Sure, they have tongue-in-cheek names like Madame Bumpsalot, Layla Smackdown, and Rocket Mean (their cofounder and executive director), and their costumes often involve fishnet stockings under their knee pads, but once the skates go on, they take their sport pretty seriously. At the derby, teams battle it out for points, with five girls from each team on the track at any given time. While one player fights her way through the crowd, earning one point for every member of the opposite team that she passes, her teammates try to ensure that she can stay on her feet, all the while endeavoring to stop the opposition from passing. Basically, it's a whole lot of elbows, shoulders, and knees, flying about at (literally) breakneck speed. Rose City Rollers events often draw as many as 2,500 spectators, and oftentimes sell out the seats of the Expo Center.

MAP 7: Portland Expo Center, 2060 N. Marine Dr., www.rosecityrollers.com

WATERSPORTS

MILO MCIVER STATE PARK

There are a number of rivers and streams that are fun spots to float, swim, or soak when the weather gets warm. Estacada's Milo McIver State Park on the lower Clackamas River is a great spot for inner tubing or raft floating. Flotation devices can be purchased at most outdoor stores, Fred Meyer stores, or tire shops. There are some mild rapids along the Clackamas, so wearing a life vest is always a good idea—as is avoiding any alcohol until after you're out of the water.

MAP 7: 24101 S. Entrance Rd., Estacada, 503/630-7150, www.oregonstateparks.org/park_142.php; daily 7am-10pm; $5 per day

SMITH AND BYBEE WETLANDS NATURAL AREA

The Smith and Bybee Wetlands Natural Area, consisting of around 2,000 acres of protected wetlands, is the largest of its kind within an American city. Surrounded by industrial areas in North Portland, this fragile ecosystem was developed for waterborne activities such as paddling. There's also a short trail with wildlife-viewing platforms from which you can spot beaver, river otters, and one of the largest western painted turtle populations in the state.

MAP 7: 5300 N. Marine Dr., 503/797-1850; daily 5am-sunset; free

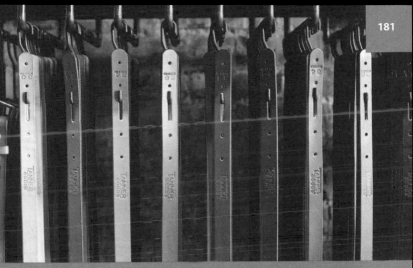

Shops

Look for ★ to find
recommended shops.

Highlights

★ **Best Place to Buy a Unique Gift:**
Every Saturday and Sunday, artists bring their
jewelry, paintings, photographs, clothing,
and sculptures out to **Portland Saturday
Market,** the largest continuously operated
market in the United States (page 185).

★ **Where to Find Your Inner Child:**
Even the most straitlaced adult has a hard
time not squealing for joy at **Finnegan's
Toys & Gifts** (page 185).

★ **Best Local Designer Boutique:**
Find arty designer wares at **Frances May,**
a shop that specializes in clothing and accessories for men and women (page 189).

★ **Best Place to Begin Your I Dos:** At
Gilt you're likely to find an engagement ring
that is one-of-a-kind and has a history that
bears repeating (page 190).

★ **Best Place to Embrace Your Inner
Geek:** A treasure trove of board games,
role-playing games, and video games,
Guardian Games is a must for gamers
(page 206).

★ **Best Place to Dig for Rare Vinyl:**
Independent record retailer **Music
Millennium** has a remarkable selection of
used and new CDs, vinyl, and DVDs, as well as
posters, memorabilia, and T-shirts (page 206).

★ **Best Place to Find Fashion at a
Fraction:** If you are looking for designer jeans, a funky dress or vintage T-shirts,
Buffalo Exchange has an eye for what
is hip; and these downtown and Hawthorne
District resale shops are pretty picky about
their selections. (page 210).

★ **Best Place to Fill a Sock Drawer:**
Socks for Christmas were never much fun
until **Sock Dreams** came along. This internationally beloved company makes boring
black socks seem like an insult to your feet.
(page 211).

tea cup bird feeders at Portland Saturday Market

A mantra for many Portlanders is "Shop Local." While you will find a handful of malls, department stores, and chains scattered about the city, most citizens prefer to purchase everything, from the shoes on their feet to the paint on their walls,

from people in their own backyard. Because of this, P-Town has become known for unique boutiques, stylish designers, and creative concept stores. Over the past several years, the city has earned a reputation as a shopping mecca because of its indisputable style and personal touch. It's not only about buying local for Portlanders; they also want to know the story behind the food they buy and the clothes they wear. For years, NW 23rd Avenue led the pack as the foremost shopping district in town; now other neighborhoods, like Mississippi Avenue and the Alberta Arts District, are developing a distinct flair and presence all their own.

In the past few years, the fashion world has started noticing the many up-and-coming designers that first set their roots down in Portland. There has always been a sense that Portland fashion was built on the back of its DIY roots, and for many locals, the core motivation is the idea that if someone else can make something, it can done better and more green right here in Portland. The garment industry has taken this notion and run with it. Since individuality and creativity reign supreme here, designers have taken it upon themselves to create the kind of fashions that reflect that principle— and the world is paying attention.

The adherence to shopping local and the focus on individuality are not about elitism, but about allowing everyone to express their innermost desires and whimsies. That is why neighborhood boutiques and mom-and-pop stores thrive. There is a little something for everyone. If you don't find it in one shop, just walk two doors down.

Portlanders don't tend to get too fancy when it comes to fashion, but they do tend to have a lot of personality. While suits and jeans commingle in most of the city's restaurants and arts venues, a night out on the town just might call for a vintage statement necklace or a fedora. Fortunately, Portland is a hotbed of jewelry designers, haberdashers, and handbag artists who are all about giving you the icing for your cake.

Downtown

Map 1

ACCESSORIES AND JEWELRY
JOHN HELMER HABERDASHERY

For about 80 years now, the Helmer family has been outfitting the heads of Portland with some pretty distinguished styles. Focusing on menswear, accessories, and tailoring, they are above all a haberdashery. Whether you are the sort to don a leather driving cap or sport an English derby, chances are they have a style that will work. They also have a very small selection of ladies' hats (particularly around the Kentucky Derby season). Shopping at John Helmer is like stepping back into a time when hats, scarves, and sock garters were de rigueur. The staff is still mostly Helmers (second and third generation), and just as knowledgeable and friendly as the originals.

MAP 1: 969 SW Broadway, 503/223-4976, www.johnhelmer.com; Mon.-Fri. 9:30am-6pm, Sat. 9:30am-5:30pm

TANNER GOODS

Step inside Tanner Goods and you are met with the rich, buttery smell of leather. This West Burnside shop features handcrafted belts, wallets, and other accessories that are made to last. The shop has a lot of repeat customers, particularly for their wallets. Opt for a natural, untreated leather, and the piece will soften and develop its own unique character over time. Or pick up some soft deerskin gloves or a custom monogrammed wrist band or luggage tag. The store also sells rugged rucksacks as well as socks and hiking boots.

MAP 1: 1308 W. Burnside St., 503/222-2774; Mon.-Sat. 11am-7pm, Sun. 11am-6pm

ARTS AND CRAFTS
CRAFTY WONDERLAND

Here you will find jewelry, T-shirts, greeting cards, retro aprons, miniature shrines, kitschy barrettes, stuffed robots, handmade candles, and more. Everything has that inexplicable Portland charm so this is a great place to find a gift to commemorate a visit to the city. Crafty Wonderland is basically the Portland Etsy community come to life. In fact, many of the artists featured here have their own Etsy store, and it is fun to see it all in

one place. The store started as a pop-up retail version of the hugely popular
annual bazaar of the same name.

MAP 1: 808 SW 10th Ave., 503/224-9097, www.craftywonderland.com; Mon.-Sat.
10am-6pm, Sun. noon-5pm

KNIT/PURL

The area surrounding Knit/Purl was referred to in *Sunset* magazine as the "Fiber Arts District," thanks to a cluster of shops devoted to fabric crafts. Knit/Purl is an upscale knitting store lined with cubbies positively bursting with skeins of luxurious yarns from all over the world. While the price point may be slightly higher than at some of the other knit shops in town, the selection can't be beat, particularly if you are looking for Koigu and ShiBui sock yarns. Check out the "Knit Nights" on Wednesdays, when they keep the doors open late so folks can gather as they knit, or the drop-in knitting clinics geared toward intermediate knitters looking for support and ideas.

Knit/Pearl is also conveniently right next to Josephine's Dry Goods, a purveyor of beautiful silks, laces, and other high-end fabrics, as well as pretty notions.

MAP 1: 1101 SW Alder St., 503/227-2999, www.knit-pearl.com; Mon.-Sat. 10am-7pm, Sun. noon-5pm

★ PORTLAND SATURDAY MARKET

Portland Saturday Market is the nation's largest open-air craft market. Each Saturday and Sunday, artists haul their paintings, sculptures, lawn art, clothing, and jewelry down to Old Town and assemble one of the best displays in town. Stroll through row after row of handmade items and talk to the artists who contracted them. Visit the iconic Spoonman and see what you would look like with a wrench through your head. The east side of the market is where you will find the best handmade merchandise. Every artist on this side was chosen by a jury. If you are short on time, skip the other side, which is an international import market focused on jewelry, clothing, incense, tapestries, and other such things.

MAP 1: 48 SW Naito Pkwy., 503/241-4188, www.portlandsaturdaymarket.com; Mar.-Dec.
Sat. 10am-5pm, Sun. 11am-4:30pm

CHILDREN'S STORES
★ FINNEGAN'S TOYS & GIFTS

Spacious but stuffed to the rafters with smiling penguins, wind-up birds, colorful trains, and every game under the sun, Finnegan's is truly a gem. Find classic and collectible toys like Raggedy Ann, Playmobil, Curious George, and Radio Flyer, as well as fun newfangled robots and crazy building sets from Zoob, K'Nex, and Lego. There is a train table in one corner to keep little hands busy, and when it's time to leave, there are small, inexpensive trinkets to distract them from that expensive toy they are likely to cling to. Finnegan's is a popular spot for families to stop in and play, thanks to its proximity to the Multnomah County Library and the MAX line.

MAP 1: 820 SW Washington St., 503/221-0306, www.finneganstoys.com; Mon.-Sat. 10am-6pm, Sun. noon-5pm

GIFTS AND HOME

CANOE

Canoe is a pretty little store full of crafts, housewares, gifts, and other such things. They focus on finding unique, hand-crafted pieces that showcase artistry and design. The space is tidy, warm, and welcoming and the staff is friendly, if aloof. It's a great place to shop for gifts or trinkets to spruce up your home. Everything here is modern and beautiful, and while you might not need any of it, you sure will want it.

MAP 1: 1136 SW Alder St., 503/889-8545, www.canoeonline.net; Mon.-Sat. 10am-6pm, Sun. 11am-5pm

REAL MOTHER GOOSE

Part gallery and part retail shop, the Real Mother Goose has been a long-time staple in downtown Portland. Whether you are just beginning to understand that a Gustav Klimt poster tacked to your wall with pushpins does not qualify as decorating or you are a serious collector, Real Mother Goose has pretty, distinctive elements in prices from $15 to several thousands of dollars. Whether it's ceramics, jewelry, wood, furnishings, fine art, blown glass, children's toys, or even wearable art, it's all here.

MAP 1: 901 SW Yamhill St., 503/223-9510, www.therealmothergoose.com; Mon.-Thurs. 10am-5:30pm, Fri.-Sun. 10am-6pm

GOURMET TREATS

PORTLAND FARMERS MARKET AT PORTLAND STATE UNIVERSITY

The biggest of many farmers markets in Portland, this Saturday market fills up the Park Blocks with as many as 250 produce stands, art booths, and food vendors. You can't get fruits, vegetables, and flowers any fresher than this, short of growing them yourself. The market is a great place to grab a bite to eat, listen to some music, or stock up on special handmade treats like freshly smoked salmon from The Smokery or lavender-infused jelly from Sundance Lavender Farm. For a special evening indulgence, pick up some of Rogue Creamery's world-class blue cheese, a bottle of Shy Chenin Blanc from Twist, and a Pearl Bakery baguette.

MAP 1: Portland State University in the South Park Blocks between SW Harrison St. and SW Montgomery St.; Apr.-Oct. Sat. 8:30am-2pm, Nov.-Dec. Sat. 9am-2pm

MEN'S CLOTHING

UNDER U4 MEN

This is a small boutique that offers every kind of men's underwear, sleep-wear, and swimwear that you could hope to find, from basic to exotic.

Underwear comes in a multitude of colors, shapes, material, and support levels, turning this store into a hipper, sportier version of Victoria's Secret—for men. Whether you prefer boxers, briefs, bikinis, no-show bikinis, or thongs, it has them in everything from silk to bamboo.

The items here are comfortable, athletic, and sexy enough to make anyone blush, but don't expect such style to come cheap. You can expect to pay $20-30 for each pair of underwear and considerably more for sleepwear and swimwear.

MAP 1: 800 SW Washington St., 503/274-2555, www.underu4men.com; Mon.-Thurs., Sat. 10am-7pm, Fri. 10am-9pm, Sun. 11am-6pm

SHOES
DANNER

In the early days of Portland, the city was filled with loggers, pioneers, and working men who stomped around in rugged boots. By the early 1930s, a lot of those boots were Danner boots. The company has long been recognized as a maker of durable work boots, but they have recently embraced a more lifestyle-focused approach. The downtown shop in the swanky new Union Way shopping arcade is Danner's first stand-alone retail shop. In it, you can find the sort of rugged boots Danner is known for, but also the Stumptown collection, a line that mixes the modern with the vintage in an homage to the Portland of the past.

MAP 1: 1022 W. Burnside St., 503/262-0331, www.danner.com; Mon.-Sat. 11am-7pm, Sun. 11am-6pm

SHOPPING CENTERS
PIONEER PLACE MALL

Inside downtown's side-by-side shopping towers, Pioneer Place, you will find a fairly walkable mall that houses such upscale retailers as Ann Taylor, Juicy Couture, and Coach, as well as some affordable favorites like Forever 21, Gap, and J. Crew. There is a food court on the bottom floor, and sky bridges over the streets will carry you between the two buildings.

MAP 1: 700 SW 5th Ave., 503/228-5800, www.pioneerplace.com; Mon.-Sat. 10am-8pm, Sun. 11am-6pm

UNION WAY

Upscale boutiques like Tanner Leather Goods, Danner Boots, and Spruce Apothecary are packed into this modern shopping arcade at Portland's West End across from Powell's Books. You can also find special treats and eats from Boxer Ramen, Little T American Bakery, and Quin Candy Shoppe.

MAP 1: 1022 W. Burnside St., 503/922-0056; hours vary via shop

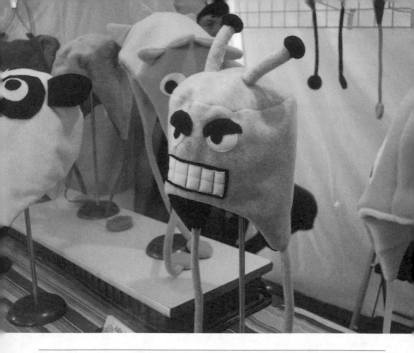

Top: quirky hats at Portland Saturday Market. **Bottom:** sporty swimwear at Under U4 Men.

DOWNTOWN

Shopping in downtown Portland is remarkably accessible, thanks to the proximity of most places and the affordable parking options. There are Smart Park garages located all over downtown where you can park for about $1.50 per hour and ample street parking for shorter trips. It is best to head near SW Yamhill between SW 3rd and SW 4th Avenues, where there are a number of parking options adjacent to the Pioneer Place Mall and other local shops. Hop on the MAX or the streetcar if you want to venture to the west end of downtown where you will find Powell's, the Union Way shopping arcade, and the Brewery Blocks.

MAP 1: Bounded by W. Burnside to the north, I-405 to the east and south, and the Willamette River to the west

VINTAGE AND ANTIQUES

MAGPIE

Near the heart of downtown is a darling little vintage shop where you can find that perfect get-up for a groovy 1960s-themed party, or a lovely *Mad Men*-style sheath dress. For all their style, and given the quality of items, the clothes at Magpie are remarkably affordable. You just might spend less on your dress or hat than you will on the martini you'll drink when you wear it. Magpie has a fantastic collection of vintage baubles, cigarette holders, and hats for the ladies, as well as a terrific collection of men's suits, vests, shoes, and coats. Before you leave, take a look at the jewelry selection up front. It is outstanding and contains new, modern pieces in addition to many beautiful vintage ones for both men and women.

MAP 1: 520 SW 9th Ave., 503/220-0920; Mon.-Sat. noon-7pm

WOMEN'S CLOTHING

★ FRANCES MAY

Owned by a grandmother-granddaughter team, Frances May blends modern-day panache with sweet, old-fashioned whimsy. In addition to having a handful of amazing one-of-a-kind vintage pieces, they carry the latest from hot local designers like Church+State, Emily Katz, and Moth Love. Throughout the season, you can also find vintage-inspired jewelry from Anna Korte and a timeless collection of shoes and belts by Rachel Comey.

Francis May has always been a Portland favorite for fashion-forward women's clothes, and they now carry a slick selection of menswear as well.

MAP 1: 1013 SW Washington St., 503/227-3402, www.francesmay.net; Mon.-Sat. 11am-7pm, Sun. noon-6pm

MARIO'S

Mario's is to a department store like Kobe beef is to an overcooked sirloin. The service is intended to be attentive and hospitable instead of merely advantageous. The first floor of this downtown shrine to excess is devoted to menswear; ladies will find their haven upstairs, where sales associates offer a glass of wine or champagne to sip while you shop.

If you are looking for labels, Mario's has all the drool-worthy ones, like Prada, Pucci, Vera Wang, Dolce & Gabbana, and Christian Louboutin. Yes, the prices are high, but the sales are spectacular.

MAP 1: 833 SW Broadway, 503/227-3477, www.marios.com; Mon.-Sat. 10am-6pm, Sun. noon-5pm

ODESSA

This quaint little boutique packs a powerful punch with designer clothing from the likes of Jeffrey Monteiro, Jill Stuart, AF Vandervorst, Comme des Garçons, and Isabel Marant. The eclectic but sophisticated boutique is a favorite for casual urbanites who don't mind paying a little extra for exquisite apparel. In fact, the stocklist rivals what you'd find in Los Angeles or New York. Established in 1996, Odessa has a loyal following. Truthfully, the collection does include things that are otherwise impossible to find in Portland (at prices that don't seem to imply that getting them here was hard work). You'll find a little bit of everything, from jeans and cocktail dresses to coats and cashmere scarves. Warning: Just try to leave without buying some luxurious bedding from Kerry Cassill.

MAP 1: 410 SW 13th Ave., 503/223-1998, www.odessaportland.com; Mon.-Sat. 11am-7pm

Northwest and the Pearl District

Map 2

ACCESSORIES AND JEWELRY
★ GILT

If you are in the market for a unique engagement ring or one-of-a-kind piece of jewelry, Gilt is likely to have something you can't live without. The cozy boutique has an immense selection of vintage and antique jewelry, mostly purchased from estate sales. Many of the rings here hail from the 1880s to the 1940s, and each piece has a story. Find a wedding set that belonged to high school sweethearts married for 60 years, or try on a cocktail ring that adorned a flapper's finger.

Gilt also has a selection of new, locally made jewelry and accessories, like delicate droplet earrings from Brunet, bright colored lockets, and mixed media statement pieces.

MAP 2: 720 NW 23rd Ave., 503/226-0629, www.giltjewelry.com; Mon.-Sat. 11:30am-6pm, Sun. noon-5pm

3 MONKEYS

If a burlesque dancer, a fashion designer, and a costume designer shared an apartment, it might look a little like 3 Monkeys. The shop is a colorful extravaganza of hats, handbags, masks, bow ties, costume jewelry, candles,

Top: Pioneer Place Mall. **Bottom:** Frances May.

flasks, and more tiaras than a beauty pageant. They also carry a number of quirky gift ideas and cool wall art. The store looks small from the outside, but be sure to explore both levels and maybe pick up a unicorn or chicken mask for your next costume party.

MAP 2: 803 NW 23rd Pl., 503/222-5160; daily 11am-7pm

BATH AND BEAUTY
BLUSH BEAUTY BAR

This adorable little boutique in the Alphabet District promotes the idea of shopping local and still carries a fairly extensive selection of top-of-the-line cosmetics and skin-care products (from brands like Nars, Bare Escentuals, Lorac, and Mario Badescu). The prices are not inflated, as you might suspect they would be in this neighborhood, and the staff is knowledgeable. Book a makeover and a team member will teach you all the tricks you need and walk you through the products. It costs $30-75 depending on whether you want a 30-, 60-, or 90-minute lesson, and the cost can be redeemed in products. They also offer threading, waxing and facials.

MAP 2: 513 NW 23rd Ave., 503/227-3390, www.blushbeautybar247.com; Mon.-Sat. 10am-7pm, Sun. 11am-6pm

KIEHL'S

Kiehl's is a Portland favorite for its apothecary-style line of lotions, cleansers, shampoos, shaving creams, and lip balms made with natural ingredients. This is a great spot for men because the Kiehl's line has a simple, no-nonsense approach to skin care with results that far exceed that sticky bar of soap melting into the soap dish. The lab coat-clad employees are always friendly and more than happy to send you away with a handful of free samples.

If you don't want to deal with parking in the congested Alphabet District, just call ahead; they'll be happy to bring your purchases right to your car.

MAP 2: 712 NW 23rd Ave., 503/223-7676, www.kiehls.com; Mon.-Sat. 10am-7pm, Sun. noon-6pm

LUSH COSMETICS

It's hard to miss Lush when you can smell it from a block away. This bath and body shop is loaded with handmade bath bombs, body butters, creams, soaps, shampoos, and lotions. If you are new to the line, explore the bath bombs first. They're a fragrant and luxurious treat to use in a hotel bath or carry home as gifts. While Lush isn't a Portland-based company, the ideology certainly fits with the Portland dogma, since all the products are fresh, ecofriendly, and never tested on animals.

The sales team can be quite helpful (sometimes overly so) in aiding you in finding the products that will best suit your needs. Don't be afraid to tell them that you just want to explore and will ask if you have questions.

MAP 2: 708 NW 23rd Ave., 503/228-5874, www.lush.com; Mon.-Sat. 10am-8pm, Sun. 11am-7pm

CHILDREN'S STORES

HANNA ANDERSSON

When you want high-quality clothes that are extremely durable, this is the place. While many think this company—which specializes in cotton togs in a rainbow of colors—is a Swedish business, it was founded right here in Portland. Every button, stitch, zipper, and swath of fabric undergoes rigorous eco-testing to guard against chemicals and harsh radicals. Hanna stocks soft and comfy sweaters, leggings, sweatpants, and dresses (with some matching mommy-and-me outfits) in styles and colors designed to last through generations of hand-me-downs.

MAP 2: 327 NW 10th Ave., 503/321-5275, www.hannaandersson.com; Mon.-Fri. 10am-6pm, Sat. 10am-5pm, Sun. 11am-5pm

GOURMET TREATS

ELEPHANTS DELICATESSEN

For Elephants, the word "delicatessen" doesn't even begin to cover it. It is part grocery, with an amazing array of cured meats, fine cheeses, olives, capers, anchovies, pickles, gourmet chocolates, and handcrafted caramels, but it is also a popular lunchtime spot, catering company, and happy hour bar. It's a perfect place to stop and grab the makings for a simple gourmet picnic before you head out to Washington Park. Or check out the website and preorder a basket with a perfectly paired bottle of Northwest wine.

MAP 2: 115 NW 22nd Ave., 503/299-6304, www.elephantsdeli.com; Mon.-Sat. 7am-8:30pm, Sun. 9:30am-6:30pm

PEARL SPECIALTY MARKET & SPIRITS

Oregon's liquor laws can be pretty persnickety. You can't purchase hard alcohol in grocery stores, and the liquor stores close early and are often closed on Sunday. What's more, if you want to make a truly artisan-style cocktail with fancy bitters or gourmet olives, that usually means several stops. Pearl Specialty Market & Spirits was given special permission by the Oregon Liquor Control Commission to be open seven days a week and maintain longer hours, as well as the right to sell things like chocolate, crackers, olives, cheese, caviar, cigars, and champagne. Pearl Specialty also has an unbelievable selection of—get this—luxury water, in pretty, reusable decanters and Swarovski crystal-encrusted bottles.

MAP 2: 900 NW Lovejoy St., #140, 503/477-8604, www.pearlspecialty.com; Mon.-Sat. 9am-10pm, Sun. noon-8pm

SMITH TEAMAKERS

Before his death in 2015, Steven Smith was sort of the big daddy of tea in the Pacific Northwest. Dubbed the "All-Star Alchemist of Top-Shelf Tea" by the *Wall Street Journal,* Smith definitely did his part to change how tea was made in this area and far beyond. After launching both Stash Teas and Tazo into success, the cofounder then moved on to create Steven Smith Teamakers, a lovingly refined company that is arguably some of his best

Top: 3 Monkeys. **Bottom:** Smith Teamakers.

work. In this former blacksmith's shop, you can smell, sample, and imbibe the small batch, artisanal teas; and you can also meet the teamakers who are happy to tell you the stories behind the teas and their creator.

MAP 2: 1626 NW Thurman St., 503/719-8752, www.smithtea.com; Mon.-Fri. 9am-5pm, Sat. 11am-5pm

MEN'S CLOTHING
LIZARD LOUNGE

Lizard Lounge is a local hangout, especially during First Thursdays, when they have live music, free beer or wine, and art showings. If you miss the monthly event, it's still a great place to grab some free Stumptown Coffee, play some Ping Pong, or make use of the free Wi-Fi or iMac station while you browse through stylish, laid-back, and earth-conscious clothes. As it should be with any great lounge, the staff is friendly, stylish, and accommodating, and chances are, they know something about every piece or designer in the shop. Lizard Lounge stocks a bunch of Horny Toad apparel and its high-end, Portland-based, ecofriendly line, Nau. The clothing can be a little pricey, so check for sales or be prepared to pay a little more for something durable and guilt-free.

MAP 2: 1323 NW Irving St., 503/416-7476, www.lizardloungepdx.com; Mon.-Sat. 10am-7pm, Sun. 11am-7pm

UPPER PLAYGROUND

Upper Playground is a hybrid between an urban-chic clothes source (selling T-shirts, hoodies, and hats) and an art gallery. Street and graffiti art adorns the walls, and there's a full-blown gallery in the back. This place has screen-printed shirts by metro artists Alex Pardee, David Choe, and Jeremy Fish. It has Portland-themed shirts, which make great gifts for people who want a little piece of Portland with more character than your average tourist-trap buy.

If you don't mind a crowd, stop by on First Thursday. You can shop, sip beer or wine, check out the newest art in the gallery, and listen to a DJ spin some tunes.

MAP 2: 23 NW 5th Ave., 503/548-4835, www.upperplayground.com; Mon.-Sat. 11am-8pm, Sun. noon-6pm

PET SUPPLIES
LEXIDOG BOUTIQUE AND SOCIAL CLUB

At LexiDog Boutique and Social Club the standards are upped because they believe that every dog deserves to be spoiled. They host play groups, birthday parties, and "Yappy Hours" when dogs and humans can mingle and drink wine (or water) while nibbling on snacks. The boutique has everything you could possibly want to pamper your pet, like comfy beds, bowls, and homemade treats that look good enough for human consumption. It also has rainwear, cozy hoodies, jeweled collars, tutus, and leather jackets. The shop caters to all sizes and breeds, but it's the small dogs that definitely have their day in this Pearl District shop.

MAP 2: 416 NW 10th Ave., 503/243-6200, www.lexidog.com; Mon.-Fri. 10am-6pm, Sat. 9am-6pm, Sun. 10am-4pm

URBAN FAUNA

For the pet owner interested in unique items and accessories, Urban Fauna is the place to go. This store specializes in difficult-to-find, high-quality items from around the world. Urban Fauna offers obedience classes that can turn excessively energetic and unruly dogs into upright citizens, and there are also doggy day care and grooming services for pet owners on the go. It stocks chew-friendly toys, comfortable leashes, and cozy beds, as well as a good selection of high-quality food. Products in this store go way beyond man's best friend and cater to the needs of cats, birds, fish, and reptiles as well.

MAP 2: 235 NW Park Ave., 503/223-4602, www.urbanfauna.com; Mon.-Fri. 10am-7pm, Sat. 9am-6pm, Sun. noon-5 pm

SHOES

ZELDA'S SHOE BAR

In 2009 Zelda's Shoe Bar merged with the adjacent high-end clothing store, Elizabeth Street. In the smaller Zelda's space, there is some apparel, like French Connection blouses and ultra-versatile Butter by Nadia dresses, but the collection does not quite compare to that of Elizabeth Street. No one is complaining, however, because the shoes are what keep the serious collectors and curious onlookers coming back. You can tell that they take their work seriously by the display. Each shoe is treated like a piece of art. If you are a sucker for well-made heels, boots, flats, and sandals that err on the practical side, Zelda's is a good place to get your fix.

MAP 2: 633 NW 23rd Ave., 503/226-0363, www.zeldaspdx.com; Mon.-Sat. 10am-6pm, Sun. noon-5pm

SHOPPING DISTRICTS

NW 23RD AND NW 21ST AVENUES

Block-for-block, this district is Portland's prime shopping area. The Alphabet District is packed from A to Z (actually, from B to T is more accurate) with unique boutiques and a few high-end chain stores. Begin at West Burnside Avenue, where you will find Cost Plus World Market and Elephants Delicatessen. Stroll past Urban Outfitters, Restoration Hardware, and Pottery Barn to NW Glisan, where the street really kicks into gear. Try to hit one side and then double back to catch the other side before you head a few blocks over to NW 21st Avenue.

MAP 2: NW 23rd Ave. and NW 21st Ave. between W. Burnside and NW Thurman St.

High-end boutiques, sophisticated salons, and fashionable cafés mix to make these streets infinitely charismatic, particularly during the monthly First Thursday art walk. This is where you will find a number of Portland's hottest boutiques, like Moule, Mabel & Zora, and Hanna Andersson. It's also the home of the iconic Powell's City of Books and the retail chain Anthropologie.

Shop for shoes at Imelda's and Louie's or explore the art and street fashion of Lizard Lounge. Don't worry if you get overwhelmed; you can rest as often as you like in one of the many cafés or martini lounges.

MAP 2: Bounded by the Willamette River to the north, W. Burnside to The Pearl

WOMEN'S CLOTHING

LUCY ACTIVEWEAR

Launched in 1999, this Portland-based company specializes in cutting-edge women's athletic wear. It's a great place to check out if you are looking for some yoga basics or bright, colorful alternatives to your usual gym attire. The company was started by former Nike executive Sue Levin with the intention of creating active gear for women that has a sense of style and a fit that is both flattering and comfortable. Stop by on "Fitness Fridays," when you can meet fitness professionals who offer training advice and hold short classes.

MAP 2: 1015 NW Couch St., 503/226-0220, www.lucy.com; Mon.-Sat. 10am-7pm, Sun. 11am-6pm

MABEL & ZORA

This sweet little Doris Day-themed boutique is owned by husband and wife team Cory and Tiffany Bean, a pair that knows quite a bit about style. They stock a number of pretty, feminine, and retro-edged brands like Tulle, Sweet Pea, Trina Turk, Joe's Jeans, French Connection, Michael Stars, and Hanky Panky. They also have locally produced, handmade garments, jewelry, and accessories from some of Portland's favorite designers. Everything here seems to have a lot of perk and personality, from the apparel and the darling luggage sets to the staff behind the counter.

If nothing else, stop by to meet the owners and their staff. They are not only exuberant and helpful, they are pretty fun as well.

MAP 2: 748 NW 11th Ave., 503/241-5696, www.mabelandzora.com; Mon.-Sat. 11am-7pm, Sun. noon-5pm

MOULE

This bright boutique in the Pearl District is a bit of an odd duck. The selection is quirky, but there's a spectacular collection of women's clothing, including owner Rachel Gorenstein's pretty and polished line, Rachel Mara. Gorenstein's elegant designs have been featured on *Sex and the City* and in magazines such as *Lucky* and *InStyle*—and it's not surprising, since her slinky dresses and soft silhouettes fit quite well alongside top lines like Michelle Mason, Rag & Bone, and Habitual.

The shop has oddities as well, like men's clothes, *Playboy* collector books, baby clothes that sometimes tip the edge of appropriateness, and kitschy housewares. For all the randomness, the store makes browsing fairly easy with clean lines, pretty decor, and well-spaced racks.

MAP 2: 1225 NW Everett St., 503/227-8530, www.moulestores.com; daily 11am-7pm

OH BABY!

This is where good girls go to be naughty and naughty girls go to be even naughtier. The award-winning lingerie boutique is filled to the bedposts with lingerie in sizes 32A to 42G for all shapes and tastes. At the center of the shop, you will find a queen-size bed strewn with pretty panties in satin and lace. The girls who work here are experts at fitting and can no doubt put you in a bra that will make you wonder how you ever got along without it. They specialize in bridal lingerie and corsets, which you are welcome to try on in the private fitting room outfitted with floor pillows and enough room for an audience of one. If you're a little out of your element amid all the ribbons and lace, the staff will help you pick out something fabulous that would make a perfect bridal shower or bachelorette gift, or just a self-indulgent treat.

MAP 2: 722 NW 23rd Ave., 503/274-4190, www.ohbabylingerieshops.com; Mon.-Sat. 11am-7pm, Sun. noon-5pm

REI

If you are unaccustomed to the Northwest weather, or if you plan to explore the Oregon wilderness while you're here, take a trip by this Pacific Coast-based retailer. The gear and apparel are high quality and designed and sold by people with an expertise and passion for outdoor recreation. Shopping here can be especially invigorating for women who may have felt overlooked or simply nonplussed about the bland athletic-wear options at other retailers.

MAP 2: 1405 NW Johnson St., 503/221-1938, www.rei.com; Mon.-Sat. 10am-9pm, Sun. 10am-7pm

Northeast

Map 3

ACCESSORIES AND JEWELRY

REDUX

Walk into Redux and you are likely to feel like you've just stepped into a candy dish. From every wall and hook hang some of the most fascinating pieces, many repurposed from other items like typewriters, PBR cans, or bicycle chains. Owner Tamara Goldsmith stocks jewelry designed by many local folks and has artwork on display by great local artists. Ladies, grab a pair of delicate earrings made from real leaves or a set of leather cuffs made from a recycled belt. For guys, check out the quirky silk ties from Cyberoptix or some laser engraved, natural wood cufflinks from designer Frances Orna. Everything is unique, and the prices at Redux are remarkably affordable for such distinctive pieces.

MAP 3: 811 E. Burnside St., 503/231-7336, www.reduxpdx.com; Mon.-Sat. 11am-7pm, Sun. 11am-5pm

BOOKS AND MUSIC
IN OTHER WORDS

This mash-up of bookstore and community center is the kind of place where you feel smarter just by walking in. In Other Words is the only surviving nonprofit women's bookstore in the entire country, and it seems fueled almost entirely by passion. Besides offering a comprehensive collection of books, magazines, and zines that embrace feminist and queer studies, erotica, sexuality, transgender studies, and spirituality, the store also hosts community events such as yoga classes, networking meetings, children's playgroups, feminist film nights, and a fun event called Awkward Open Mic, a no-holds-barred chance at the microphone every third Saturday.

MAP 3: 8 NE Killingsworth St., 503/232-6003, www.inotherwords.org; Tues.-Sat. 10am-7pm

THINGS FROM ANOTHER WORLD

Things from Another World is the retail baby of local comic book giant Dark Horse, so TFAW (as it is affectionately called) has comics in spades, especially graphic novels. But what sets it apart is that TFAW focuses on toys, T-shirts, and other nerdy oddities. You will find games like Pathfinder, Warhammer, and Munchkin, as well as game supplies like boards and dice. If you are looking for a collectible statue, this is the place to stop. It has arguably the largest array of collectible figures in town—some of them quite spectacular and large.

MAP 3: 2916 NE Broadway, 503/284-4693, www.tfaw.com; Mon.-Sat. 11am-7pm, Sun. 11am-6pm

TITLE WAVE BOOKSTORE

Housed in an old Spanish Renaissance revival-style library building, this little book lover's dream is, not coincidentally, run by the Multnomah County Library. Overstock of books, CDs, audiobooks, and magazines from the county's libraries are sent here to be sold at astonishingly low prices. Hardbacks and novels are often go for $2 or less. And many items, like magazines and children's books are less than $1. The store is operated entirely by volunteers, and all the proceeds go to benefit the Multnomah County Libraries. The selection is hit-or-miss. Since the store is filled with cast-offs and overstock, you may not have luck finding something specific, but you are very likely to find something you didn't know you were looking for. They do not keep an inventory of the books available, so be prepared to peruse at length.

MAP 3: 216 NE Knott St., 503/988-5021, www.multcolib.org/library-location/title-wave-used-bookstore; Mon.-Tues. 10am-4pm, Wed.-Sat. 10am-6pm

TURN! TURN! TURN!

Like a great song mash-up, Turn! Turn! Turn! mixes the best parts of having a little boutique shop into one overall experience. Here, you will find nostalgia, atmosphere, personality, and beer—well, and records, of course. Turn! has a nice collection of rare and vintage country, kitschy 1960s and 1970s rock as well as some oddball LPs that have probably been collecting dust in someone's basement. In fact, the basement vibe extends throughout the shop from the old concert posters on the wall to the listening station complete with chairs that look like they were rescued from an old barbershop. There are books to read and/or buy, vintage clothes to peruse, and a menu with local beers, cider, wine, and sandwiches. The shop hosts regular trivia nights as well as live music and comedy. Turn! replaced the former Record Room, which also boasted vintage LPs and pints. New owner, Scott Derr wanted to make sure he created an atmosphere to showcase his love of vinyl, but also keeps customers coming back.

MAP 3: 8 NE Killingsworth St., 503/284-6019, www.turnturnturnpdx.com; Tues.-Thurs. 4pm-11pm, Fri.-Sat. 3pm-midnight, Sun. 3pm-11pm

CHILDREN'S STORES

BELLA STELLA

This little store has everything you could want in terms of brand-name and locally made clothing, organic slings and accessories, and imaginative toys. It's a fun place to shop for boys if you are tired of fire trucks, action heroes, and bugs. Bella Stella is both a resale and traditional retail store, so you can find new and used merchandise that is hip, bohemian, and affordable. Check out the ecofriendly marriage between cloth and disposable diapers, G-Diapers, or explore the extensive collection of carriers.

MAP 3: 2751 NE Broadway, 503/284-4636, www.bellastellababy.com; Mon.-Thurs. 10am-5pm, Fri.-Sat. 10am-6pm, Sun. 11am-5pm

GRASSHOPPER

Nestled in the midst of artsy Alberta Street, Grasshopper has a nice selection of organic and American-made clothes, funky rain boots, diaper bags, and bibs. It offers has a unique collection of playthings that are nontoxic and not found on the shelves of any big-box store. The carefully selected amusing and colorful toys, games, and books are both stimulating to the imagination and wildly collectible.

The all-female staff is very sweet and willing to help you find that special something for a gift—and will even gift-wrap it for free.

MAP 3: 1816 NE Alberta St., 503/335-3131, www.grasshopperstore.com; Sun.-Mon. 10am-5pm, Tues.-Fri. 10am-6pm, Sat. 9:30am-6pm

GREEN BEAN BOOKS

When schoolteacher Jennifer Green looked at the plethora of beloved children's books she had collected over the years, she didn't pack them up and haul them off to Goodwill. She opened a bookstore specializing in new and used children's books in English and a multitude of other languages. Exploring all the nooks and crannies of this charming Alberta Street shop can be a lot of fun, especially when you discover the custom-made vending machines. One dispenses finger puppets (made by the owner); another offers temporary tattoos. An old gumball machine hands out pom-pom pets, and what looks suspiciously like an old sanitary napkin dispenser is now an "Instant Disguise Machine" that distributes fake beards and mustaches for a quarter.

MAP 3: 1600 NE Alberta St., 503/954-2354; Mon.-Sat. 11am-6pm, Sun. 10am-5pm

POLLIWOG

This whimsical shop stocks the sort of baby clothes that make almost anyone wish they had a little girl to dress up. The clothes can be a little pricey, but it's worth it if you want to find something unique. Send the kids to play in the back corner while you check out the Glug tees' cute urban chic designs. Service can be a bit aloof sometimes, but this edgier-than-Gap store is full of fun children's clothing, like bright baby hats, striped PJs, and appliquéd onesies, as well as slings, wonderful wooden toys, and shoes.

MAP 3: 234 NE 28th Ave., 503/236-3903, www.polliwogportland.com; Mon.-Sat. 10am-6pm, Sun. 11am-5pm

CLOTHING
WELL SUITED

If you are in need of a suit but don't have the money to shell out for the usual designer store prices, Well Suited may be for you. The unassuming storefront hides a remarkable selection of high-end suits by designer labels like Prada, Hugo Boss, and Armani—as well as some beach-style shirts and basic business-casual wear. Since the store is a consignment shop, you can find a great suit for about 50-80 percent of what you might pay anywhere else.

If you spot the perfect suit but it doesn't fit quite right (or you already own a suit that needs tailoring), have it tailored right on the spot. The in-store tailor is one of the best in town, and his prices are quite reasonable.

MAP 3: 2401 NE Broadway, 503/284-5939, www.wellsuitedpdx.com; Tues.-Sat. 11am-6pm

THE PENCIL TEST

It's no secret that most women are wearing the wrong size bra. Our bodies fluctuate with the seasons, life changes, and age, so it is hard to keep up on proper fitting. It doesn't help that shopping for bras can be so daunting, confusing, and at times embarrassing. The Pencil Test (named for the informal test developed by Ann Landers to determine whether or not a woman could go braless in public) is a place that aims to fix that by providing

It's Easy to Be Green *and* Chic!

According to *Popular Science,* Portland is ranked number one as the greenest city in the world. Half of its power comes from renewable sources; more than a quarter of the workforce commutes by bike, mass transit, or carpool; and recycling is done as a matter of principle, and not as an ecological statement. More and more businesses are following suit by remodeling their buildings or altering their practices and products to embrace the green standard.

Little ones can learn from the start how to leave a smaller carbon footprint at **Polliwog** (234 NE 28th Ave., 503/236-3903, www.polliwog-portland.com). Polliwog is chock-full of organic clothing and environmentally conscious items from the likes of Under the Nile, Egg, and Imps and Elves. It also carries luxuriously smooth bamboo clothing by Kicky Pants, David Fussenegger recycled cotton blankets, nontoxic Natursutten natural rubber pacifiers, and Made in Oregon Earnest Efforts rattles, which are composed of reclaimed wood (don't worry—they're safe).

Similarly, **Pie Footwear** (2916 NE Alberta St., 503/288-1999, www.piefootwear.net) is saving the earth one step at a time with its smart and stylish shoes that are socially responsible to boot. The store is vegan-friendly and stocks ecoconscious socks, hats, and bags.

If you are looking to relax but don't want to fret about the impact your pampering might have on the environment, check out **Blooming Moon Wellness Spa** (2050 NW Lovejoy St., 503/222-2391, www. bloomingmoonspa.com). The spa uses only all-natural products that are never tested on animals, adheres to a recycling and sustainable energy plan, and encourages employees and guests to bike or take the streetcar to the spa. Book a Sore Muscle Relief package (foot bath, acupuncture, and massage) and you just might need to call a taxi to get you home.

Speaking of home, **Tropical Salvage** (2233 NW New York St, 503/236-6155, www.tropicalsalvage. com) makes some truly amazing furniture out of wood that was salvaged from demolition sites or pulled from landslides, lakes, and rivers. Craftspeople also take old, sometimes diseased wood culled from coffee plantations (or dredged up from centuries-old volcanic eruptions), clean it, cut it, kiln-dry it, and then turn it into some pretty impressive cabinets, tables, beds, dressers, and chairs. Local places like **ECOpdx** (2289 N. Interstate Ave., 503/287-8181, www.ecopdx.com) and **Ten Thousand Villages** (914 NW Everett St., 503/231-8832, www.portlandvillages.com) sell this salvaged-wood furniture.

Finally, if you want to find some environmentally friendly gourmet treats, check out **Cork** (2901 NE Alberta St., 503/501-5028, www.corkwineshop.com), where the focus is on supporting sustainable producers by stocking certified organic and biodynamic wines. Look for the green signs describing products that are certified organic, biodynamic, salmon-safe, or Low Input Viticulture and Enology (LIVE) certified.

measurement to all their customers. They carry a number of larger cup sizes (read: closer to the middle of the alphabet) in styles that are not the beige, matronly ones buxom girls find in most places.

MAP 3: 2407 NE Alberta St., 971/266-8611; Tues.-Fri. 11am-6pm, Sat. 10am-6pm, Sun. 11am-5pm

POPINA SWIMWEAR

I know what you're thinking: a swimwear store in Portland? Yes, even if it rains nine months out of the year in these parts—or maybe because of it—we occasionally need to chuck the raincoat and head off to sunny Mexico or Hawaii. Heck, we'll settle for a dip in a nearby hot springs or even a friend's Jacuzzi. And if Portlanders need a swimsuit, they go looking for something with panache. Enter Pamela Levenson, a swimwear designer specializing in retro-styled suits. Try on one of the many in her shop just off of Alberta Street; if it doesn't fit perfectly, they will alter it for you at a surprisingly small cost. There is also a **Popina Boutique in the Pearl District** (318 NW 11th Ave., 503/243-7946). Both locations are free of florescent lighting and will offer you a free Kona beer while you are shopping.

MAP 3: 4831 NE 42nd Ave., 503/282-5159, www.popinaswimwear.com; Mon.-Wed. 11am-6pm, Thurs.-Sat. 11am-7pm, Sun. noon-5pm

GOURMET TREATS
FOSTER & DOBBS

If Foster & Dobbs were a class, it would be called Gourmet 101. It has all the classics of cheese, wine, chocolate, olives, and cured meats. If you are overwhelmed by the cheese selection, the staff can talk you through the flavor profiles, give you samples, and steer you to the one that's perfect for you. Foster & Dobbs also holds regular classes that allow budding foodies to learn such necessary tasks as how to taste wine, make pickles, bake bread, use gourmet salts, and recognize a good port.

MAP 3: 2518 NE 15th Ave., 503/284-1157, www.fosteranddobbs.com; Mon.-Sat. 10am-7pm, Sun. 8am-6pm

PET SUPPLIES
FUREVER PETS

Whether you are shopping for cats or dogs, you'll find a fun, whimsical selection of reasonably priced items. While most pet stores lean heavily on dog supplies, Furever Pets has the best selection of colors, toys, condos, and treats for kitties. Furever uses local products whenever possible, like the locally made catnip pillows, treats, and collars. Stop by the bakery counter at the front and pick out a handmade goodie for your dog, or check out the high-end handbags to carry around your small four-legged friend. The staff is quiet knowledgeable and loves pets. If you bring your dog with you, they will more than likely give it a treat. But don't worry; they will ask first.

MAP 3: 1902 NE Broadway, 503/282-4225, www.fureverpets.com; Mon.-Fri. 10am-8pm, Sat. 10am-7pm, Sun. 10am-6pm

SHOES

AMENITY SHOES

Established in 2005, Amenity Shoes is a locally owned and operated resource for comfy shoes that don't look like they came from your grandma and grandpa's closet. The owners have a background in art and shoe manufacturing, clearly evident from the selection. From colorful, embroidered flats to classy patent-leather T-strap sandals, they choose the kind of footwear that is cute, modern, and comfortable all at once. The stock of men's shoes is equally well balanced and modern, with brands like Sole, Kenneth Cole, and Fly London leading the pack.

MAP 3: 3430 NE 41st Ave., 503/282-4555, www.amenityshoes.com; Mon.-Sat. 10am-6pm, Sun. 11am-5pm

SHOPPING CENTERS

LLOYD CENTER

On the north side of the river, you'll find Lloyd Center, a three-level indoor mall centered around an ice skating rink. Major department stores here include Macy's and Sears, plus two major discount retailers (Marshall's and Ross) as well as popular outfitters like H&M, Aeropostale, Hot Topic, and Old Navy, a sprawling food court and a multiplex movie theater.

MAP 3: 2201 Lloyd Ctr., 503/282-2511, www.lloydcentermall.com; Mon.-Sat. 10am-9pm, Sun. 11am-6pm

SHOPPING DISTRICTS

ALBERTA ARTS DISTRICT

Sprinkled with galleries and artsy boutiques, Alberta Street is a perfect neighborhood when you want to find something unique and inspiring. Once a month, when the street hosts the Last Thursday art walk, these shops throw open their doors and invite guests to partake in special discounts, treats, and meet-and-greet opportunities with designers, artists, and special guests. Head over to Garnish, where local designer Erica Lurie displays her flattering feminine line, or paint a pot at Mimosa Studios.

It will take a bit of walking to find all the great boutiques along this 20-block spread, but the street is always alive and vibrant with activity. If you are not a fan of crowds, avoid Last Thursday altogether and come in the afternoon when things are decidedly less chaotic.

MAP 3: Alberta St. between NE 12th Ave. and NE 33rd Ave.

ARTS AND CRAFTS
MUSE ART & DESIGN

This independently owned art supply store on Hawthorne is well stocked with all the pastels, paints, brushes, paper, sketchbooks, and printing supplies you need to keep your inner muse satisfied. The hole-in-the-wall shop is a nice place to venture into and seek out inspiration, whether it's from blank canvases, colorful pots of ink, or one of the workshops in the "Muse Room." Stimulate your creative juices by checking out the "Word to Draw," a random word chosen daily by the staff. It's fun to mull over and then check out what other people have created around the theme.

The staff at Muse is pretty unassuming. In fact, if they assume anything it's that you will ask for help if you need it. Otherwise, they are likely to leave you to explore on your own.

MAP 4: 4224 SE Hawthorne Blvd., 503/231-8704, www.museartanddesign.com; Mon.-Fri. 9:30am-6:30pm, Sat.-Sun. 11am-6pm

SHOPS
SOUTHEAST

BOOKS AND MUSIC
CROSSROADS MUSIC

What sets Crossroads apart from the ever dwindling pack of local record shops is it really is an intersection of multiple music tastes. While at most places you will either get one fanatic's curated selection of what is hip, or a mish-mash of eclectic tastes from customer buy-offs, the selection here is comprised of the self maintained inventory of over 35 different sellers. Since each has his or her own space for inventory, you can expect to spend some time searching for just the treasure you are looking for. The staff will help you if you ask for it, but otherwise tend to adhere to the idea that most music aficionados would rather be left alone to dig.

MAP 4: 3130 SE Hawthorne Blvd., 503/232-1767, www.xro.com; Mon.-Thurs. 11am-6pm, Fri.-Sat. 11am-7pm, Sun. noon-6pm

EXCALIBUR BOOKS AND COMICS

Back in 1974, Peter Fagnant visited every newsstand between Portland and Salem, buying up every copy of a comic book featuring a new character named Howard the Duck. When he opened his comic book shop, Portlanders soon found out that it was the place to go when you need comics—be they obscure or current. That legacy continues today. It's the oldest comic books shop in town, but Excalibur Books and Comics is still a favorite stop for true collectors. Boxes upon boxes of back issues sprawl over the floor, and an ever-rotating wall of rare finds can include golden, silver, and modern age back issues. It's a library you can own. Just inside the door you'll see an artist's rendition of a duck pulling the magical sword from its stone. Forty years later Excalibur is still aware this is the house that duck built.

MAP 4: 2444 SE Hawthorne Blvd., 503/231-7351, www.excaliburcomics.net; Mon.-Thurs. 11am-8pm, Fri.-Sat. 10am-8pm, Sun. 11am-7pm

★ GUARDIAN GAMES

Tucked behind an Office Depot is a place where "play time" takes on a whole different meaning. It may not look like much from the outside, but Guardian Games is a one-stop shop for gamers of all walks of life. If you like a traditional board game, they have those aplenty, but the real delight is for those who believe gameplay should involve strategy, creativity, and just a little bit of storytelling. Owner Angel May is said to have played her first game of Dungeons and Dragons at age six and was hooked. Since then, she has sought out the best in all things gaming: video games, table top games, card games, and role-playing adventures. Even with over 5,000 square feet of gaming and retail space, there are surprises everywhere you look, like an impressive collection of out-of-print board games, card games, and book sets. The store hosts regular gaming nights, D&D camps, beer and pizza nights, and even houses an in-store bar.

MAP 4: 345 SE Taylor St., 503/238-4000, www.ggportland.com; Mon.-Sat. 10am-10pm, Sun. noon-10pm

JACKPOT RECORDS

This independently owned music store has two locations in Portland (the other is **downtown** at 203 SW 9th Ave.) and is popular among those seeking indie labels, rock, and metal. The jewel cases are kept behind the counter and CDs are filed with their inserts into plastic sleeves, the color of which denotes whether it is a new or used album. While the method irks some music store purists, who enjoy the "clack clack" of searching the bins, it means you will find a greater selection thanks to the added space, and it means you can check out the liner notes before you purchase the CD.

MAP 4: 3574 SE Hawthorne Blvd., 503/239-7561, www.jackpotrecords.com; Mon.-Thurs. 10am-7pm, Fri.-Sat. 10am-8pm, Sun. 11am-6pm

★ MUSIC MILLENNIUM

You know those bumper stickers appealing to everyone to "Keep Portland Weird"? It all started here. What began as a public awareness campaign to keep local businesses alive and boost independent thinking has become a mantra for the Rose City way of life. Music Millennium gets it, and it always has. This independent seller of used and new CDs, DVDs, and vinyl has been a staple since 1969, in part because of its impeccable knowledge and taste, but also because of the constantly evolving selection. Music Millennium holds regular in-store concerts and events and also sells advance tickets to shows at the Doug Fir Lounge.

MAP 4: 3158 E. Burnside St., 503/231-8926, www.musicmillennium.com; Mon.-Sat. 10am-10pm, Sun. 11am-9pm

Just two spaces down from Powell's Southeast location is an outpost devoted to books on home and gardening. The cookbook section is fun, well organized, extensive, and inspiring, especially given its proximity to the Pastaworks specialty market next door. This branch has a wide range of books on crafts like knitting, jewelry making, and woodworking, and often hosts readings from crafting experts and chefs.

This Powell's is also a great place to pick up trinkets and gifts. It has a marvelous collection of candles, garden tools, dishware, tablecloths, and art.

MAP 4: 3747 SE Hawthorne Blvd., 503/228-4651, www.powells.com; Mon.-Sat. 9am-9pm, Sun. 9am-8pm

CHILDREN'S STORES
COFFEE KIDS

This surprisingly well-stocked children's boutique has two locations in Portland (the other is in the North Portland neighborhood of **St. Johns**). But they are not serving up lattes, as the name might imply. The store is named for owner Shamaine Coffee, who wanted to open a children's store stocking clever, fun items that encourage playfulness and mindfulness. Over the years, she has amassed fantastic collection ecofriendly apparel, toys, games, and books. She has also developed as strong base of customers who continue to shop in her stores for diapers, glass baby bottles, and adorable teethers because of her moderate pricing. Check out the impossibly cute Chooze shoes and bags, or maybe pick up some Piggy Paint, a nontoxic nail polish that is safe for even the tiniest fingers and toes.

MAP 4: 3354 SE Division St., 503/719-4599, www.coffeekidspdx.com; Mon.-Sat. 10am-6pm, Sun. 11am-4pm

KIDS AT HEART

Kids at Heart is a locally owned shop that specializes in creative and educational toys and games. That means you won't find any mega-blasters or current movie merchandise here, but you will find adorable puppets, plush robots, sticker books, magical costumes, and science kits. The books room has new releases and old favorites for newborns and readers up to young adults. The store is a wee bit on the small side compared to some others in the region, but it seems to make up for its size in judicious selection and knowledgeable service.

MAP 4: 3445 SE Hawthorne Blvd., 503/231-2954, www.kidsathearttoys.com; Mon.-Sat. 10am-7pm, Sun. 10am-6pm

GIFTS AND HOME
CARGO

A longtime purveyor of imported artifacts and antiques, Cargo is a veritable treasure trove of trinkets, oddities, jewelry, furniture, decor, and more. This industrial Southeast warehouse is just a few shouting vendors away from being an Asian street market, with baubles and beads adorning statues, colorful displays, and teak furniture stacked high. Cargo specializes in garden statuary, folk art, religious memorabilia, carpets, vibrant glassware, and propaganda art, as well as antique and custom-designed furniture, all with a heavy emphasis on Asian designs. This place is huge and there is something eye-catching at every angle, so allow yourself time to get lost for a while.

MAP 4: 81 SE Yamhill St., 503/209-8349, www.cargoimportspdx.com; daily 11am-6pm

MEMENTO

Memento is filled with everything you could possibly want, but nothing you need. On every shelf and wall, you'll find tchotchkes, cards, posters, bags, housewares, wind-up toys, and more—much of it from Northwest designers and craftspeople. You may not need three different sizes of mirrored disco balls, but you will want them. The same goes for the Virgen de Guadalupe candles, the cardboard blimp, or avenging narwhal play set. This is a terrific spot to find a gift for someone back home as proof-positive that Portland is a very weird place.

MAP 4: 3707 SE Hawthorne Blvd., 503/235-1257, www.mementopdx.com; Sun.-Thurs. 10am-6pm, Fri.-Sat. 10am-7pm

NOUN: A PERSON'S PLACE FOR THINGS

It is easy to miss Noun, unless you are looking for cupcakes as well. This little Belmont boutique shares a space with popular Portland bakery Saint Cupcake. While the cupcakes alone are worth a visit, this shop with the clever name is a wonderfully curated mix of vintage and modern. The buyers for Noun search everywhere for their vintage pieces—estate sales, flea markets, auctions, and even occasionally a dumpster. Modern and locally made pieces are then selected to fit the mood with the other furnishings, art, antiques, and artists works.

MAP 4: 3300 SE Belmont St., 503/235-0078, www.shopnoun.com; Mon.-Sat. 10am-7pm, Sun. 10am-5pm

PRESENTS OF MIND

Presents of Mind has an eclectic mix of amazing locally made jewelry, bags, and clothes, along with hilarious gag gifts and stationery. It's a fun place to pick up a killer diaper bag or a onesie for the newborn in your life, or a retro apron for a bridal gift, or a yodeling pickle. You never know when you'll need a yodeling pickle, but you will. It also has pretty, elaborately handmade cards, specialty wrapping paper, and premade bows that make the presentation of the gift rival whatever might be inside.

MAP 4: 3633 SE Hawthorne Blvd., 503/230-7740, www.presentsofmind.tv; Sun.-Thurs. 10am-7pm, Fri.-Sat. 10am-8pm

EDELWEISS

If you have spent any amount of time in Germany, Edelweiss will feel all too familiar to you: the narrow aisles filled with jars of mustard, pickles, and sauerkraut; the candy aisle with European sweets; the brusque, impatient service. Every inch of this store is crammed with sweets, treats, and authentic delicacies, many of which are made on-site, imported, or produced locally in the traditional European style. What's more, it has one of the best collections of imported European beers and wines in town.

Be sure to grab a number as you walk in the door. It gets crowded and the wait can be maddeningly long, but the selection in the deli case makes it all worthwhile. If you are a meat lover, don't be surprised if you get a little dizzy at the sight of all their handmade sausages, house-smoked meats, and house-cured bacon.

MAP 4: 3119 SE 12th Ave., 503/238-4411, www.edelweissdeli.com; Mon.-Sat. 9am-6pm

FOOD FIGHT

This store is just one part of what is essentially a vegan strip mall. The veggie-centric grocery is next to Herbivore Clothing Company and Sweet Pea Bakery, both of which share a desire to encourage a life free from the unnecessary use of animal products. Vegans and vegetarians can find everything from vegan health and fitness items to the delicious (locally made) NoFishGoFish soups and grab-and-go vegan nachos. You can also find vegan household products, including shampoos, cleansers, and vegan cookbooks.

MAP 4: 1217 SE Stark St., 503/233-3910, www.foodfightgrocery.com; daily 10am-8pm

PASTAWORKS

For the denizens of Portland's Slow Food culture, a walk through Pastaworks is like food porn. Suddenly you are salivating, your pulse is racing, and you feel incredibly inspired to go home and cook something up. Maybe it's because of the freshly made goat cheese ravioli or the lemon fig balsamic vinegar. Or perhaps a gooey wedge of triple cream brie tips you over the edge as you consider pairing it with black truffle honey and pancetta. Whatever the source of your excitement, Pastaworks has it. It's not terribly cheap, but then again, the good stuff rarely is.

MAP 4: 3735 SE Hawthorne Blvd., 503/232-1010, www.pastaworks.com; Mon.-Sat. 9:30am-7pm, Sun. 10am-7pm

MEN'S CLOTHING

DUCHESS CLOTHIER

For stylish men in the market for something custom made, unique, and beautiful, Duchess Clothier is a must. When it comes to bespoke suits, no one does it better. Duchess takes inspiration from the dandy men of the past using influences from film, literature, and life. From a classic *Mad Men*-style gray suit to a colorful double-breasted ensemble, the options are unlimited. They even do costumes and have created custom designs for a number of famous clients like Nick Cave, Crispin Glover, Lance Bangs, and John Hodgeman.

MAP 4: 2505 SE 11th Ave., 503/281-6648, www.duchessclothier.com; Tues.-Sat. noon-5pm

SHOES
IMELDA'S AND LOUIE'S SHOES

Like moths to a flame, Portland shoe addicts keep coming back to Imelda's & Louie's for a fix. The styles here range from functional work shoes to date-night pumps and everything in between—with many pairs boasting buttery leathers or ecofriendly materials. This is a great source of shoes for both men and women. The shoes are expensive but well made, colorful, and beautifully designed. Sizes are sometimes limited due to space, but if you fall in love with something, don't fret. They are often able and more than happy to order a pair in your size.

MAP 4: 3426 SE Hawthorne Blvd., 503/233-7476, www.imeldasandlouies.com; Mon.-Fri. 10am-7pm, Sat. 10am-6pm, Sun. 11am-6pm

SHOPPING DISTRICTS
HAWTHORNE BOULEVARD AND BELMONT STREET

On SE Hawthorne Boulevard and SE Belmont Street, the vibe is laid-back and independent. This is the area where Portland's counterculture has put down its bohemian roots, opening up funky coffeehouses, indie music stores, and hip and inexpensive clothing stores. Weird isn't weird on these parallel streets (separated by five blocks); it's the standard. While Belmont appeals with its sweet charm and quiet devil-may-care attitude, Hawthorne is a bit more like San Francisco's Haight-Ashbury with its mash-up of hippies and hipsters.

MAP 4: SE Hawthorne Blvd. between SE 11th Ave. and 55th Ave., SE Belmont St. between SE 31st Ave. and 60th Ave.

WOMEN'S CLOTHING
★ BUFFALO EXCHANGE

Buffalo Exchange is a great spot to find one-of-a-kind pieces, locally made T-shirts and dresses, as well as secondhand high-end brands like Joe's Jeans, Rock & Republic, Anna Sui, BCBG, Betsey Johnson, and Nicole Miller. The store seems to cater to the young, hipster crowd of Portland, so you are likely to find odd vintage blouses, punky leather pieces, and earthy organic cotton dresses. While there is a second **Buffalo downtown** (1036 W. Burnside St.), the Hawthorne location is superior, if only because the racks are easier to navigate.

MAP 4: 1420 SE 37th Ave., 503/234-1302, www.buffaloexchange.com; daily 10am-9pm

HOUSE OF VINTAGE

House of Vintage is a collective of more than 55 independent dealers all sharing over 13,000 square feet. This place is an absolute maze, but also a wonderful cache of odds and ends. Give yourself plenty of time to explore; you could easily spend hours wandering from room to room trying not to miss anything. Keep looking and you may just find a vintage lunchbox tucked into a curio cabinet, a kitschy table set for dinner with cute melamine dishes, or a diaphanous slip hanging from a wrought-iron gate. All you have to do is wade through the seemingly endless stacks of clothing, accessories, shoes, memorabilia, housewares, music, furniture, and tchotchkes.

MAP 4: 3315 SE Hawthorne Blvd., 503/236-1991, www.houseofvintage.net; daily 11am-7pm

Sellwood and Moreland   Map 5

ACCESSORIES AND JEWELRY
★ SOCK DREAMS

If your sock drawer doesn't cause you to giggle, ooh and aah, or at least smile, you need to make a trip to Sock Dreams. A longtime cult favorite on the web, Sock Dreams opened its Southeast store in a little Victorian that seemed the perfect place to house the colorful collection of toe socks, striped socks, thigh highs, garters, leg warmers, tights, and more. The company's online warehouse, with its dizzying array of socks—a collection so big only the Internet could hold it—is housed off-site from the tiny shop.

MAP 5: 8005 SE 13th Ave., 503/234-0885, www.sock-dreams.com; daily 11am-6pm

BATH AND BEAUTY
CAMAMU

This tiny, natural care-focused soap shop has been creating hand-crafted bars for over a decade. Everything in store and online is made in small batches using no animal fats. With the exception of a couple of products (like the delightful Argan Milk and Honey Soap), everything is certified vegan. They even have a couple of bars designed specifically for dogs with natural anti-itch and flea-repellant ingredients. The shop is pretty laid-back (they occasionally close up early), but employees are usually able to answer a lot of questions, especially for those with sensitive skin—a specialty of the Camamu folks.

MAP 5: 1229 SE Nehalem St., 503/230-9260, www.camamusoap.com; Tues.-Sat. 10am-5:30pm, Sun. 11am-5pm

Cheap Tricks

Fortunately for Portlanders, there are a lot of bargain shopping outlets out there. Unlike in many cities, the idea of "thrift shopping" doesn't carry much of a stigma in PDX. Maybe it's our DIY spirit or maybe it's our devil-may-care attitude, but from clothing to furniture, books to building supplies, P-Towners love to save whenever they can. Call it "junking," "thrifting," or simply "smart shopping"; no matter what, there are ways to survive today's economy without losing your sense of style.

One of the weirdest spots to find some bargains is **City Liquidators** (830 SE 3rd Ave., 503/238-4477, www.cityliquidators.com). Affectionately called "City Licks," this retail spot nestled under the Morrison Bridge is home to some great deals on everything from dishtowels and candles to lava lamps and microfiber sectionals. The merchandise at City Liquidators is so wildly diverse, it's downright entertaining to simply walk through.

Goodwill Outlet (1750 SE Ochoco St., 503/254-4795, www.meetgoodwill.com) is simply referred to as "The Bins." This is bargain shopping at its most hard-core—it's the *Jackass* of thrifting. Rows and rows of plastic bins are positively heaped with items you can't even begin to imagine, all sold for no more than $1.99 per pound. (The more poundage you buy, the cheaper it gets.) There are both horror and glory stories about the items found while digging through the bins. On one trip, you might find a pair of True Religion jeans, a Prada clutch, a bag of cool vintage Bakelite bangles, and a retro neon diner-style clock. On another trip, you may find a used diaper. That said, it's wise to wear gloves while excavating your treasures (you'll be glad you did).

When it comes to clothing, there's no end to the vintage, thrift, and consignment stores, such as hipster favorites **Red Light Clothing Exchange** (3590 SE Hawthorne Blvd., 503/963-8888, www.redlightclothingexchange.com) and **Buffalo Exchange** (1420 SE 37th Ave., 503/234-1302, www.buffaloexchange.com), where they will take your clothing donations in exchange for cash or credit. They're pretty selective about the items that they pick, which means that their racks are filled with interesting, often one-of-a-kind pieces that are remarkably affordable.

CLOTHING
WELLS AND VERNE

Lovers of the gothic, steampunk, or neo-Victorian style of dress should make a point of stopping by this little Sellwood gem. Everything is high quality, which is nice because lovers of this genre are often forced make their own outfits or settle for cheap Hot Topic costume pieces. Among the multi-button pants and waistcoats, you will also find hats, ties, socks, and accessories (for both men and women). Furthermore, owner Panda Lang has found the perfect spot to open up her boutique. In addition to its proximity to the neighborhoods multiple antiques shops, the store itself has a quirky, creepy history; it was once the local undertaker.

MAP 5: 8315 SE 13th Ave., 503/893-4968, www.wellsandverne.com; Mon. and Wed.-Sun. noon-6pm

One of Portland's oldest vintage clothing stores, **Avalon** (410 SW Oak St., 503/224-7156) has been in business since the 1960s—although it's unclear what would qualify as vintage back then (what would a vintage store be without bell-bottoms?)—and there's a reason why they are still in business. Most vintage stores have a fantastic selection of women's wear, but Avalon also boasts a pretty impressive array of men's clothing. For guys who want to find unique vintage suits and ties, Avalon has them in spades.

Another place to find affordable one-of-a-kind style is **Ray's Ragtime** (1021 SW Morrison St., 503/226-2616, www.raysragtime.com). The shop can easily overwhelm, because sparkly gowns, vintage tees, shoes, and pillbox hats are literally spilling out of every corner. The downtown store is a destination for many Portland costumers; in fact, the wares at Ray's have been featured in major films, including *Mr. Holland's Opus* and *My Own Private Idaho*.

If you can't bear the idea of preworn fashions but really want to find those designer deals, check out **Nordstrom Rack** (401 SW Morrison St., 503/299-1815, www.nordstrom.com), the off-price version of Nordstrom, which carries items from the regular retail stores at 50-70 percent off the original prices. The Rack gets new merchandise daily and is a reliable spot to shop when you are looking for jeans, shoes, and formal wear in particular.

Finally, if you're looking to save a little on edible treats, venture over to the **Grocery Outlet** (4420 NE Hancock St., 877/170-289), www.groceryoutlet.com) in the Hollywood District. It has close-out prices on everything from basic supplies (like crackers, chocolates, cheese, and pasta) to quirky never-made-it-to-the-shelves items. It's a bit like the "Island of Misfit Toys," only for food. The real find in this store is the wine section, where most bottles are less than $10. It is not uncommon to find a delightful Spanish red for $3.99 that may be selling for $18.99 at a wine shop just down the street. However, if you are shopping for groceries, it's best to pay attention to the sell-by dates on the packaging. It's not uncommon to spot the occasional expired good.

SHOPPING DISTRICTS
SELLWOOD AND MORELAND

Originally a city of its own, the Sellwood-Moreland neighborhood was annexed back in the 1890s but still retains much of its nostalgic allure. From the nation's oldest operational amusement park, Oaks Park, to the collection of shops giving this neighborhood the nickname Antique Row, Sellwood-Moreland keeps a firm grip on the past. Some two dozen antiques and vintage stores populate **13th Avenue** in Sellwood, while West Moreland is home to a number of antiques malls.

MAP 5: Bounded by Highway 99 W and McLoughlin Blvd. to the north, the Portland city limit to the south, Highway 99 E to the east, and the Willamette River to the west

BOOKS AND MUSIC
BRIDGE CITY COMICS

Ask a comic book enthusiast what his or her favorite shop in town is and Bridge City is likely to rate at the top of the list. Bridge City is bright and open with wide, passable aisles and displays that allow you to see what you are looking for (even if you don't know you are looking for it). The staff is helpful, and never in a sneering, judgmental way. They actually seem happy to help you find whatever it is you are looking for. They have a great kids' section and a wall of new releases from major publishers and local small presses. They even have local, self-published comics. Also, they offer staff picks and recommendations based on previous things you may have read and liked.

MAP 6: 3725 N. Mississippi Ave., 503/282-5484, www.bridgecitycomics.com; Sun.-Thurs. 11am-7pm, Fri.-Sat. 11am-8pm

CD GAME EXCHANGE

CD Game Exchange has five locations around the Portland metro area and is a popular stop for collectors of DVDs, video games, LPs and, yes, even old VHS tapes. The shop pays out cash for used discs and equipment, and it is a common thing for Portlanders looking for a little extra cash to schlep a bag of games and movies here. They price things according to availability, interest, and quality, so it is not uncommon to find more than one copy of that special disc you are looking for. It is an especially great place to pick up DVD box sets of favorite TV shows or classic movies at a fraction of what they would cost online or new. It could also be a great place to cash in on that Buffy box set you have been holding on to for far too long.

If you are looking for something really obscure, employees can check the other stores for availability. If none of the stores have it, they can special order it for an extra fee.

MAP 6: 3719 N. Mississippi Ave., 503/287-0382, www.cdgameexchange.com; Mon.-Fri. 11am-8pm, Sat. 11am-7pm, Sun. noon-6pm

CHILDREN'S STORES
BLACK WAGON

This hip and stylish shop has had a presence online for over a decade, and the flagship store on Mississippi Avenue is an adorable representation of the sort of hip baby chic the company represents. The brick and mortar shop is full of fantastic, fashion-forward items for babies and toddlers as well as handcrafted toys, games, shoes, and a fine selection of books. This is where to shop if you want your kids to look like tiny celebrities. The boutique is well stocked with specific attention to locally made pieces and unique, clever designs.

MAP 6: 3964 N. Mississippi Ave., 503/916-0004, www.blackwagon.com; Mon.-Fri. 11am-7pm, Sat. 10am-7pm, Sun. 10am-5pm

Top: Black Wagon. **Bottom:** The Meadow.

SPIELWERK TOYS

The name of this store is German for "play work," implying that children have the very important job of playing. For that reason, the objects in this store are designed to engage, develop, and thrill. Instead of simply entertaining kids, the hand-carved, hand-painted, or hand-sewn toys are meant to promote positive brain activity. The store also hosts regular "WerkShops," where young ones can learn how to do imaginative things like build a fairy garden, paint silk scarves, or make their own hula hoops.

MAP 6: 3808 N. Williams Ave., 503/282-2233, www.spielwerktoys.com; Mon.-Sat. 10am-6pm, Sun. 10am-5pm

GOURMET TREATS
THE MEADOW

Salt takes on a whole new life at The Meadow, a boutique specializing in gourmet sea salts, with a fine selection of chocolate, hard-to-find wines, bitters, and edible flowers such as apple blossoms and hibiscus. Before you do anything else, buy some of the salted chocolates, which hit the salty, rich, and sweet trifecta. Then, sample some of the alderwood-smoked salt or the Maboroshi plum salt. Ask for some advice on how to use the Vietnamese Pearl *sel gris* (gray salt) or the *sel rose* (pink salt) curing salt, and you'll find that regular table salt is actually pretty harsh.

Before you leave, pick up a Himalayan salt plate, a pretty, translucent pink slab quarried straight from the Himalayan mountains that will revolutionize the way you cook.

MAP 6: 3731 N. Mississippi Ave., 503/228-4633, www.atthemeadow.com; daily 10am-7pm

MEN'S CLOTHING
ANIMAL TRAFFIC

Animal Traffic is a vintage shop that aims to capture the rugged, laid-back style of the American West. Boots, flannels, and denim are in abundance, but there are usually some fun pieces from the 1970s, '80s, and '90s as well. If you are looking for a Levi's jacket or some Pendleton wool pieces, this is a good place to check. They also carry new merchandise from Americana style brands like Jansport, Minnetonka, Wigwam, and Duluth.

MAP 6: 4000 N. Mississippi Ave., 503/249-4000, www.animaltrafficpdx.com; Mon.-Thurs. 11am-6pm, Fri.-Sat. 11am-7pm, Sun. 11am-6pm

SHOPPING DISTRICTS
MISSISSIPPI AVENUE

Mississippi Avenue is a six-block-long walkable stretch of North Portland that is home to a number of quirky, local boutiques, restaurants, and bars. One of Portland's youngest hot neighborhoods, it has undergone significant change in the last decade and now has a very youthful, hipster vibe.

MAP 6: North Mississippi Ave., from N Fremont Ave. to N. Skidmore St.

Hotels

Look for ★ to find
recommended hotels.

Highlights

★ **Best Place to Sip and Stay:** The oenophile darling **Hotel Vintage Portland** recently received a pricey makeover. Their wine-themed rooms are a favorite for travelers looking for the pleasures of Oregon vineyards (page 224).

★ **Best Place to Think Small: Caravan: A Tiny House Hotel** lets guests try their hand living small. No expansive suites or lobbies here. Each "hotel room" is a self-contained tiny house complete with kitchen, bathroom, electricity, and running water (page 227).

★ **Most Charming:** A pretty little Craftsman-style home, the friendly **Bluebird Guesthouse** offers an unfussy welcome (page 231).

★ **Best Hotel to Party All Night:** If Studio 54 were a hotel in Portland, it would be the **Jupiter Hotel,** a sleek and modern urban lodge where the parties often spill out into the courtyard (page 232).

★ **Best Place to Engage Your Supernatural Fantasies:** Whether you believe in ghosts or not, the **White Eagle Motel** has a dark past that is titillating and scandalous (page 232).

★ **Best Place Stay Chic, But Not Freak:** If the idea of dealing with downtown seems daunting, **Aloft** near their airport is a stylish alternative to the sometimes drab accommodations often found in the area. Rooms are modern, attractive, and just steps away from the MAX transit center, which can whisk you straight to city center (page 234).

The Starlight suite at Hotel Vintage Portland provides spectacular views of the city.

PRICE KEY

$ Less than $100 per night
$$ $100–200 per night
$$$ More than $200 per night

If the most important things you look for in a hotel are a place to crash and a place to keep your things, your options are pretty unlimited in Portland. Reliable chains surrounding the airport can be very affordable, particularly if you will be renting a car and don't mind navigating the freeways to get into town. Whether you prefer luxurious five-star accommodations, seek the intimacy of a bed-and-breakfast, or want to meet some locals through a couch-hopping network, Portland's got a spot for you to lay your head.

The hotel scene in Portland has all the momentum of a snowball rolling down a snow drifted hill. In the past five years there has been a significant spike in the demand for lodging both downtown and east of the river. The demand was met with a number of new hotels and major renovations, all geared toward providing a place for everyone and every taste.

Not surprisingly, the greatest concentration of hotels can be found downtown. After all, this is where most of Portland's public transportation system converges, where performing arts companies perform every night, and where much of the city's commercial business takes place. Plus, with Portland State University, Oregon Health and Sciences University, and Lewis and Clark College all in the Southwest sector of town, downtown hotels are a particularly hot commodity, especially for visiting families and prospective students. For that reason, you will find everything from inexpensive motor lodge-style places to residential inns and luxury suites.

The best choice is really a matter of preference. Portland is home to a large collection of boutique-style hotels that offer an alternative to the occasional homogeneity of large chain hotel groups, as well as a peek at

Previous: the lobby of Ace Hotel; The Sentinel.

Portland's distinctive personality. Whether you're an artist, a foodie, a wine lover, or a rock-and-roll enthusiast, chances are there's a hotel that will feel like home (only, you know, better).

The rates can vary a lot by season, with the months between May and October often considered the high season. If you are not limited to a particular time for traveling, April can be affordable and the coldest days of the year have usually passed. The same is true of October and November, when the weather is still fairly mild and the rates have dropped. December, January, and February are great times to take advantage of low rates and super-saver specials, but these months usually bring with them the most inclement weather.

With bed-and-breakfasts, you can almost always get the best rate by calling directly instead of booking online. For hotels, it's best to check online rates, which are often as much as half the regular rate, but be cautious because some hotels set aside their smaller or noisier rooms for online bookings. If you are concerned about it, call ahead.

Downtown   Map 1

ACE HOTEL $

Ace Hotel, edging downtown and the Pearl, has one of the most photographed lobbies in town. Whether for a fashion shoot, headshots, engagement photos, or an impromptu photo op with friends, the lobby reeks of coolness. Friendly and affordable, this art-meets-music hotel is especially popular with creative professionals and international travelers. The rooms are achingly hip—some come with turntables and vintage vinyl records! With enormous murals painted by hot local artists, vintage furniture, clawfoot tubs, flat-screen TVs, and custom-made Pendleton blankets, each room is unique. If you're a light sleeper, bring your earplugs or ask for a room away from the street.

MAP 1: 1022 SW Stark St., 503/228-2277, www.acehotel.com

THE BENSON HOTEL $$

Simon Benson, a Portland lumber baron, visionary, and philanthropist (and namesake for the Benson Bubblers drinking fountains), opened The Benson (then The New Oregon Hotel) in 1913. It was a grand spectacle with a French Second Empire glazed terra-cotta and brick exterior, arched lobby windows, and mansard roof with dormers. The interior was no less grand, with carved Circassian walnut from the forests of Imperial Russia. Over the years, this hotel has seen a number of renovations and expansions, but still maintains remarkable beauty and opulence. The hotel has played host to celebrities, sports figures, and politicians—and has bedded almost every U.S. president since Harry S. Truman.

MAP 1: 309 SW Broadway, 503/228-2000, www.bensonhotel.com

COURTYARD BY MARRIOTT PORTLAND CITY CENTER $$

Opened in May 2009, this 256-room Courtyard by Marriott enterprise was all too recently a vacated bank building. But after a major renovation, the new hotel is sleek, stylish, and designed to meet LEED gold certification. It's a Marriott with a distinctly Portland twist. All of the artwork in the hotel was created by local artists. Paintings of local scenes adorn the hallways and lobby, and each guest room features an original ceramic piece by graduates of the Oregon College of Art and Craft. The hotel offers the regular comforts one would expect of Marriott, like smoke-free rooms, wireless Internet, business services, complimentary lobby coffee, and valet parking.

MAP 1: 550 SW Oak St., 503/505-5000, www.marriott.com/pdxpc

CRYSTAL HOTEL $$

A McMenamin property, the Crystal Hotel has a varied past having housed everything from a tire shop to a raucous nightclub and bathhouse. These days, the triangular Crystal bears the distinct artistic signature of its owners. The hotel's walls are covered with vibrant murals of the most famous musical acts to play at the hotel's namesake Crystal Ballroom next door, and hand-painted headboards and art panels inspired by the same grace each of the 51 rooms. While most of the rooms are "European-style" (the bathroom is down the hall), there are nine king-bed rooms with private bathrooms. There is a subterranean saltwater soaking pool, a full-service restaurant, and a cozy music venue that hosts live bands, comedy shows, and post-show concerts.

MAP 1: 303 SW 12th Ave., 503/972-2670, www.mcmenamins.com/crystalhotel

EMBASSY SUITES PORTLAND DOWNTOWN $$

If you have been to an Embassy Suites before, this one is going to seem just a little bit different. It is housed in the historic 1912 Multnomah Hotel building, one of the largest and most magnificent of its time. In its heyday the Multnomah hosted U.S. presidents, a Romanian queen, Charles Lindberg—and even Elvis Presley in 1957. John Kennedy gave an impromptu speech here. The building was renovated in 1995 to operate as an Embassy Suites with upscale, all-suite guest rooms, complimentary cooked-to-order breakfasts, and afternoon manager's receptions with free alcoholic and nonalcoholic beverages and appetizers.

MAP 1: 319 SW Pine St., 503/279-9000, www.embassysuites.com

HEATHMAN HOTEL $$$

When it comes to luxury, the Heathman is really trying to corner the market. French press coffeepots and electric kettles in every room with Peet's coffee and loose-leaf teas? Complimentary L'Occitane products? MP3-compatible sound systems? Blackout drapes? A menu that lets you choose your own mattress, with options like the oh-so-European featherbed? This historic elegant hotel is popular for travelers looking to take in a little culture, especially since it is mere steps away from the Portland Center for the Performing Arts, the Portland Art Museum, and Arlene Schnitzer Concert Hall. It has received a lot of attention lately for its featured role in the *Fifty Shades of Grey* books.

MAP 1: 1001 SW Broadway, 503/241-4100, http://portland.heathmanhotel.com

HOTEL DELUXE $$$

If you have ever imagined yourself Bette Davis or Cary Grant, the Hotel deLuxe, at the edge of downtown, has got your number. The former Mallory Hotel, built in 1912, has been carefully restored but still evokes Hollywood's Golden Age. With richly detailed high ceilings, elegant columns, and crystal chandeliers, the hotel has a sophisticated elegance and romantic ambience. Each floor has a different theme based on Old Hollywood personalities, and the rooms come equipped with luxurious amenities and menus that allow you to select your own pillow and even order up a Torah over the Bible if you prefer.

MAP 1: 729 SW 15th Ave., 866/895-2094, www.hoteldeluxeportland.com

HOTEL LUCIA $$$

Throughout Hotel Lucia you will find Pulitzer Prize-winning photographer David Hume Kennerly's odd and intriguing work. This downtown boutique hotel has 127 smallish guest rooms, each smartly decorated and appointed with pillow-top mattresses, high-thread count duvets, pillow menus, plush robes, 24-hour room service, and Lather bath products. One signature amenities is the "Make it So Button," which promises to get you anything you desire whether it be a basic amenity or a grand wish. If you are traveling with a dog, you will find Lucia well equipped to host. The fourth floor is devoted to travelers with four-legged friends.

MAP 1: 400 SW Broadway, 503/225-1717, www.hotellucia.com

HOTEL MODERA $$

Hotel Modera offers a comfortable and modern place to stay for people visiting Portland State University wishing to be downtown but not smack-dab in the middle of it. The beds are have pillow-topped mattresses, nice linens, and a fur throw that almost makes the whole stay worthwhile. Be sure to use the Tarocco blood orange bath products; they smell so good, you'll wish they were edible. There's a business center as well as free Wi-Fi, which works well in the hotel's pretty courtyard. It doesn't have a gym on-site, but you can get complimentary passes to the nearby 24-Hour Fitness.

MAP 1: 515 SW Clay St., 503/484-1084, www.hotelmodera.com

HOTEL MONACO $$$

This artsy hotel can be a lot of fun if you like art, wine, or free stuff. Every evening there is a wine reception with paints and canvases (in case you get inspired). Send your shoes out for a complimentary shoeshine or you take advantage of the free bike rental to explore the city. Work out in the 24-hour

Top: lobby of the Ace Hotel. Bottom: Crystal Hotel.

gym or browse the free Internet all night, knowing the morning brings complimentary Starbucks coffee and tea service with free newspapers. If you bring your dog, it gets free spring water and treats, a bed to sleep in, and "Dispose-a-scoop" bags. Didn't bring your dog? That's okay, Monaco will lend you a goldfish to keep you company (for free).

MAP 1: 506 SW Washington St., 503/222-0001, www.monaco-portland.com

★ HOTEL VINTAGE PORTLAND ⊛⊛⊛

Wine lovers will feel right at home in this boutique hotel, which offers wine-themed accommodations in a majestic, 1894 downtown building that just received a $10 million makeover. In addition to the new look and some graffiti-themed cork art, the hotel now has a stylish game room (with billiards and shuffleboard) and a lobby bar appropriately named Bacchus for the Roman god of wine. Each of the 117 casual, yet chic rooms is named after an Oregon winery and the namesake wine partners host a complimentary wine hour at 5pm. Along with the new look comes a new commitment to being ecofriendly. If you decline housekeeping services during your stay, they will give you a voucher for Pazzo, the attached Italian eatery.

MAP 1: 422 SW Broadway, 503/228-1212, www.vintageplaza.com

THE MARK SPENCER HOTEL ⊛⊛

Central to a number of downtown arts organizations, the Mark Spencer bills itself as Portland's "Hotel to the Arts." In fact, it's the hotel that many visiting artists take up residence in while performing here. Rates are remarkably reasonable given the hotel's proximity to downtown and the Pearl District, and they also give you the opportunity to "bid your own price." Simply submit a proposed price and they will let you know if they can swing it. If they can't, they'll let you know when that rate might be available or will offer you the best price for the date you would like to come.

MAP 1: 409 SW 11th Ave., 503/224-3293, www.markspencer.com

THE NINES ⊛⊛⊛

When your car pulls up to The Nines, you may wonder if there has been a mistake. This 331-room luxury hotel occupies the top nine floors of the historic Meier & Frank Building, and Macy's (which purchased the building from Meier & Frank) fills the building's lower five levels. The word of the day at The Nines is "posh," and that goes from valet service to beds that seem to swallow you in a heap of European linens. Interior rooms overlook the atrium—interesting if you like to people-watch but otherwise rather ho-hum. Book an exterior room and for views of the city and Pioneer Courthouse Square.

MAP 1: 525 SW Morrison St., 877/229-9995, www.starwoodhotels.com

THE RIVERPLACE HOTEL ⊛⊛

The RiverPlace Hotel is especially suited for business travelers. There's a 24-hour business center with all the amenities. The rooms are packed with creature comforts, like 37-inch flat-screen TVs, in-room DVD and CD players, L'Occitane bath products, plush bathrobes, and a coffeemaker with Stumptown Coffee and Tazo tea. They come equipped with complimentary high-speed Internet, a spacious Craftsman-style work desk, and an ergonomic office chair for finishing those big reports. The hotel is right on the waterfront, which is a bit more peaceful than downtown and is a great place to jog before you head out to begin your day.

MAP 1: 1510 SW Harbor Way, 503/228-3233, www.riverplacehotel.com

THE SENTINEL $$$

This historic hotel—known as The Governor Hotel until 2014—was originally built in 1909 as the Seward Hotel, a "hotel of quiet elegance." With its ornate facade complete with art deco gargoyles and an interior that boasts Native American-inspired themes, rustic chandeliers, and rich wood textures, it certainly is elegant. The building was added to the National Register of Historic Places in 1985 and has served as the set for films including Madonna's *Body of Evidence* and *My Own Private Idaho*. The entire hotel recently underwent a major renovation.

MAP 1: 614 SW 11th Ave., 503/224-1236, www.sentinelhotel.com

Northwest and the Pearl District

Map 2

INN AT NORTHRUP STATION $$

This hotel looks unassuming from the outside, but inside it is not your average hotel. It seems designed by Willy Wonka, right down to giant glass jars filled with colorful candies adorning the lobby tables. The staff is friendly and energetic, and the entire place feels modern, fun, and trippy. The inn will provide free tickets for the Streetcar to downtown and further connections. This is an all-suite hotel, and most rooms come with a kitchen—though there are plenty of Alphabet District restaurants nearby. Continental breakfast is free and usually includes pastries, cereal, fruit, bagels, and Tillamook yogurt.

MAP 2: 2025 NW Northrup St., 503/224-0543, www.northrupstation.com

PORTLAND INTERNATIONAL GUESTHOUSE $

This sweet little guesthouse in the heart of the Alphabet District is a great place if you're looking to save money but don't want to be far from the bustling heart of the city. With five bed-and-breakfast-style private rooms sharing two full bathrooms, it is a popular place for families who want to stay together. Here you will find free wireless Internet; a sitting room with a fireplace; a kitchen area with free coffee, tea, juice, and cereals in the

Top: Hotel Vintage Portland. **Bottom:** The Sentinel.

morning; and Steven and Thomas, two of the nicest hosts in town, who live on-site and are regular travelers themselves.

MAP 2: 2185 NW Flanders St., 503/224-0500, www.pdxguesthouse.com

SILVER CLOUD INN $$

Although referred to as Silver Cloud Portland–Downtown, this hotel is at the brink of Northwest Portland—about two miles from downtown at the Alphabet District's industrial edge. If you're a light sleeper, ask for a room away from busy Vaughn Street; otherwise, the location is removed from the bustle of the city, yet easily accessible by freeway and about six blocks from the main shopping and dining areas of NW 23rd Avenue. It's an attractive and comfortable place. Silver Cloud has moderately spacious, clean rooms and mini-suites with free Wi-Fi, 42-inch plasma televisions, refrigerators, coffeemakers, and microwaves.

MAP 2: 2426 NW Vaughn St., 503/242-2400, www.silvercloud.com

Northeast
Map 3

★ CARAVAN: A TINY HOUSE HOTEL $

The tiny house movement is sweeping the world, and this 6 home hotel in the heart of the Alberta Arts district offers guests an opportunity to try out the tiny home lifestyle. The houses range from 100 to 200 square feet, each with its own layout and personality. Each is equipped with a small kitchen and bathroom all with electricity, running water, and plumbing, and the neighboring Radio Room provides room service. Adding to the overall charm, the homes are assembled around a shared campfire space, where guests can gather, roast marshmallows, and occasionally hear some live music.

MAP 3: 5009 NE 11th Ave., 503/288-5225, www.tinyhousehotel.com

DOUBLETREE BY HILTON HOTEL PORTLAND $$

The best thing about this Lloyd District hotel is its location (and the warm chocolate chip cookies at check-in). It's just across the street from Lloyd Center, with department stores, boutiques, and dining options. It is also right on the Red and Blue MAX lines, which means you can take the MAX directly from the airport or hop the train downtown, to the Rose Quarter, or to the Oregon Convention Center and never have to worry about parking. The rooms are, for the most part, spacious, clean, and comfortable, but book through an online discount website if you can because the difference in price can be astonishing.

MAP 3: 1000 NE Multnomah St., 503/281-6111, www.doubletree.com

Top: Inn at Northrup Station. **Bottom:** Caravan: A Tiny House Hotel.

EVERETT STREET GUESTHOUSE $

Everett Street Guesthouse is decked out in the style of a true Portlander—elegant, eclectic, and not the least bit pretentious. The Wellfleet Room, for two, and Sophie's Room, a single, are in the main house, or the studio cottage is separate and features a kitchenette, tiled shower, washer/dryer, television, wireless Internet, private patio garden, and deck. Breakfast can be added for $10 per person. Everett Street has a three-night minimum for the cottage and a two-night minimum the other rooms. The proprietors require a 50 percent deposit to book and prefer cash or personal checks.

MAP 3: 2306 NE Everett St., 503/230-0211, www.everettstreetguesthouse.com

HOTEL EASTLUND $$

Answering the call for some much needed lodging near the Oregon Convention Center is Hotel Eastlund. The former Red Lion received a $15 million remodel and bears no resemblance to its outdated former self. The new, swanky digs are colorful, modern, and full of amenities that cater to the convention crowd, like a 24-hour business center, posh meeting rooms, and a rooftop bar. The rooms are equally stylish and well-equipped with Keurig coffeemakers, free Wi-Fi, and electronic "do not disturb" technology.

MAP 3: 1021 NE Grand Ave., 503/235-2100, www.hoteleastlund.com

KENNEDY SCHOOL $

This elementary school, which was built in 1915, was saved from probable destruction when the McMenamin brothers decided to turn it into a fantastic hotel. Now the old classrooms have been stripped of their desks (but not their chalkboards) in exchange for comfy beds. Work out your kinks playing basketball or dodgeball in the gymnasium. Watch a movie in the old auditorium while sipping beer and noshing on pizza, or take a dip in the soaking pool. If you still feel guilty for nodding off, you can always send yourself to the Detention Bar for a little redemption.

MAP 3: 5736 NE 33rd Ave., 503/249-3983, www.kennedyschool.com

LION AND THE ROSE VICTORIAN BED & BREAKFAST INN $$

This breathtaking Queen Anne inn sits amid stately Victorian homes in Portland's historic Irvington District. Rooms have a distinctive, romantic flair, like the pretty, sun-drenched, turret-style sitting area in the Lavonna room. Each room has a private bathroom, with the exception of the Avandel, which has a dedicated bathroom and claw-foot soaking tub down the hall. The Lion and the Rose offers two-course breakfasts and light refreshments in the afternoon or evening. If you're traveling with family, you can opt for the Victorian Apartment, which sleeps up to six and has a kitchenette, dining table, bathroom, washer/dryer, wireless Internet, television, and an electric fireplace.

MAP 3: 1810 NE 15th Ave., 503/287-9245, www.lionrose.com

Stay Strange

At Caravan, you get a whole tiny house to yourself.

In a city that thrives on being unique, it is no surprise there are a number of oddball options where would-be-travelers can rest their heads. Cyclists passing through may want to check out **The Friendly Bike Guesthouse** (www.friendlybikeguesthouse.com), a hostel-style spot where cyclists are given access to a mechanic stand, bike tools, and secure bike storage. Or take a walk down memory lane at **Kennedy School** (www.mcmenamins.com), a 1915 schoolhouse turned hotel, restaurant, and bar. Guests sleep in converted classrooms where chalkboards still hang on the walls and imbibe in adult libations in the Detention Lounge.

If you want to skip the hotel, Portland boasts a number of tiny houses, backyard studios, converted trailers, and funky lofts available for rental. The tiny houses especially are experiencing a boom in popularity. Answering that call is **Caravan: A Tiny House Hotel** (www.tinyhousehotel.com), a gaggle of tiny houses that reside in a former vacant lot with a security fence, a communal fire pit, and a lot of charm.

If you want to soak while you stay, you have a lot of options, like the Kennedy School and its downtown sister, The Crystal Hotel. But one of the cutest in town is the **Kuza Garden Cottage** (www.vrbo.com/3752450), a 350-square-foot cabin tucked behind the popular Japanese pub and eatery Yakuza. The cabin is set amid a lushly landscaped Japanese garden with a beautifully rustic hot tub and cold plunge tub.

Alternatively, if you feel like getting a little bit dirty, you can rent out the six-bedroom **Urban Farm and Guesthouse,** a charming farmhouse with a piano, communal table, sprawling front porch, and bees in the backyard. The family that rents the house also teaches farming classes for those who wish to really dig into the soil and learn how to live more sustainably.

From September to mid-June, you can arrange to spend the night at the Oregon Zoo with their **ZooSnooze program** (www.oregonzoo.org). It is an opportunity usually seized by schoolchildren, but groups of adults can also make arrangements to bring their camping gear and spend the evening hours touring the zoo, listening to special keeper talks, and engaging in hands-on activities.

PORTLAND'S WHITE HOUSE [$$]

If you find yourself peeking around the corners to catch a glimpse of the president, don't be surprised. No, POTUS hasn't stayed here, but the mansion does bear more than a passing resemblance to the "official" White House. The grand portico and circular drive are just the beginning. The five guest rooms in the main house and the three in the adjoining Carriage House are lavishly and meticulously decorated, each one a grand affair with fabulous linens, along with four-poster beds or magnificent canopies. The proprietors go to painstaking lengths to ensure that your stay is superb, so if you like a hands-off approach, either mention it in advance or stay somewhere else.

MAP 3: 1914 NE 22nd Ave., 503/287-7131, www.portlandswhitehouse.com

Southeast

Map 4

★ BLUEBIRD GUESTHOUSE [$]

This quaint and pretty guesthouse has seven guest rooms, each named for a different author, though not theme decorated. The one exception is the Elliott Smith room, which is (not surprisingly) in the basement. Bluebird is in Southeast Portland, a healthy walk from the adorable Clinton Street neighborhood and Hawthorne District. The decor combines vintage charm with modern character, lending to the place a cozy, at-home feeling that seems miles away from hotel life. Guests are allowed access to the sizable kitchen and refrigerator, with the understanding that they are responsible for their own clean-up. Robes, towels, washcloths, soap, shampoo, and a hair dryer are all provided, and there is an iron and coin-op laundry machine in the basement.

MAP 4: 3517 SE Division St., 503/238-4333, www.bluebirdguesthouse.com

EVERMORE GUESTHOUSE [$$]

This beautiful bed-and-breakfast has five beautifully decorated suites and a studio apartment with a private entrance. Each of the rooms is equipped with its own heat and air-conditioning controls and private bathrooms with claw-foot tubs and showers. The house provides continental breakfast each morning (available when you are ready for it) with goodies like coffee, tea, juice, yogurt, and locally made pastries, bagels, and muffins. The house is also in close walking distance to a number of great cafés and restaurants.

MAP 4: 3868 SE Clinton St., 503/206-6509, www.evermoreguesthouse.com

HAWTHORNE HOSTEL [$]

If you prefer a bohemian approach, Hawthorne Hostel might be for you. It is actively involved in the community, with potluck brunches every Sunday and summertime open mics or "bike-in" movies in the backyard. The upkeep of the place varies depending on current staff, but everyone is friendly

and easygoing. A private room goes for $48-58 a night, or a shared dorm space is $19-28. Sheets are included, but you'll need to make your bed every day and strip it when you leave (it's a hostel, remember?), and towels are extra, so it's wise to bring your own. It should be noted that there's a housecat; if you are sensitive to pet fur, you may want to skip this one.
MAP 4: 3031 SE Hawthorne Blvd., 866/447-3031, www.portlandhostel.org

★ JUPITER HOTEL [$]
Oh, the Jupiter Hotel. This inner southeast hub of the late-night crowd is the irresistible black sheep of Portland accommodations. It's not always as perfect as your fantasies might make it, but it comes darn close. It should be noted that the Jupiter is best experienced as a place to avoid sleeping. Throw your door open and interact with the other guests, who are likely to be spilling out of their own rooms and partying between the hotel and the attached Doug Fir lounge. The decor here is modern and sleek, and the attitude is definitely no-frills fun. Those wanting to shake things up can take advantage of the Love & Lust package, which includes treats from Spartacus leathers, or enjoy VIP entrance to a concert at Doug Fir and two free drinks. Boozing all night and can't make it home? Jupiter has a special after-midnight check-in rate (subject to availability) where you can literally "get a room" for $59 plus tax.
MAP 4: 800 E. Burnside St., 503/230-9200, www.jupiterhotel.com

North Portland
Map 6

PALMS MOTOR HOTEL [$]
The Palms Motor Hotel is not exactly luxury accommodations, but if you appreciate even a little bit of kitsch, this little dive is calling your name. The neon sign, alive with monkeys and palm trees singing the praises of free HBO and Starz, is one of the most photographed signs in town. For all its tropical silliness, the Palms is a Portland icon. The motel is not all that bad, plus it's right on the MAX's Yellow Line, so access to the rest of the city is steps away. The lime green "honeymoon suite" with Jacuzzi is less than $100 a night—although booking it for your *actual* honeymoon might send you straight into annulment.
MAP 6: 3801 N. Interstate Ave., 503/287-5788, www.palmsmotel.com

★ WHITE EAGLE MOTEL [$]
The White Eagle is a McMenamin salvage job with the distinction of one of the most sordid and storied pasts in Portland history. The legend dates to the early 1900s, when the venue was commonly called "Bucket of Blood." Dock workers and railroad men would stop in for a little pool, cigars, poker, liquor, and, if they played their cards right, a turn in the brothel or opium den upstairs. The hotel now rents inexpensive rooms (about $40-60 a night)

Top: decorative detail at the Kennedy School. Bottom: Jupiter Hotel.

that are unapologetically modest—and occasionally haunted. It's a fun, cheap way to spend the night in Portland, and you can watch some pretty legendary rock music in the saloon downstairs.

MAP 6: 836 N. Russell St., 503/282-6810, www.mcmenamins.com/whiteeagle

Greater Portland

Map 7

★ ALOFT PORTLAND AIRPORT HOTEL $$

Aloft provides a clean, fun, and affordable stay near PDX that is miles away from your standard airport stay. Service is quite personable, and they seem perfectly equipped to give visitors who won't make it into the city a little taste of the downtown scene. Decor is modern and chic, with high-tech touches like free wired and wireless high-speed Internet access and a plug-and-play entertainment center to charge and play cell phones, laptops, and MP3 players on the 42-inch flat-screen television. Choose between a 285-square-foot king room with one big bed or a 315-square-foot room with two queens. The 24-hour fitness center is equipped with cardio and elliptical machines, plus free weights, exercise balls, and a splash pool. You can also visit re:mix, the in-house lounge, offering a giant TV wall for game watching, billiards, and other games.

MAP 7: 9920 NE Cascades Pkwy., 503/200-5678, www.starwoodhotels.com/alofthotels

RED LION HOTEL ON THE RIVER–JANTZEN BEACH $$

While decidedly removed from the core of Portland, the Red Lion Hotel on the River is right off of I-5 and equidistant between Portland and Vancouver, Washington. The hotel boasts a handful of amenities that make it worthwhile to avoid the cost and chaos of downtown, like private balconies (some of which have lovely views of the Columbia River), a seasonal pool and Jacuzzi, a fitness center, tennis courts, boat dock, free high-speed wireless Internet, complimentary parking, and on-call airport transportation.

MAP 7: 909 N. Hayden Island Dr., 503/283-4466, www.redlion.rdln.com

SHERATON PORTLAND AIRPORT HOTEL $$

If you want to stay close to the airport, you can't get much more convenient than the Sheraton. Besides being the nearest to the terminal, the hotel has a free shuttle that will run you to and from the airport, where you can pick up the MAX Red Line into town. The staff is accustomed to dealing with last-minute arrivals and changes, so they are usually quite friendly to weary travelers. There's an on-site restaurant with 24-hour room service, a pool, an exercise room, a Jacuzzi, and sauna. The rooms are clean, comfortable, well appointed, and relatively quiet considering the airport nearby.

MAP 7: 8235 NE Airport Way, 503/281-2500, www.sheratonportlandairport.com

Excursions

Look for ★ to find
recommended sights and activities.

Highlights

★ **Best Place to Get Your Squeak On:** At the **Tillamook Cheese Factory,** you can sample some of the finest cheddar in the nation, take a free tour, and purchase some of the infamous squeaky cheese (page 240).

★ **Best Place to Fly a Kite:** At **Cannon Beach,** a blustery day can turn into a whole lot of fun. The annual kite festival in April is a perfect time to test your flight skills (page 240).

★ **Best Place to Sing "Roll On, Columbia":** Woody Guthrie wrote his famous song about **Bonneville Dam.** The facility features a fish hatchery and ladder, which Pacific salmon and steelhead pass through on their journey upstream (page 245).

★ **Best Photo Op:** "Majestic" is perhaps the word most often applied to **Multnomah Falls,** a 620-foot waterfall that plummets from Larch Mountain (page 246).

★ **Best Place to Sip a Future Star:** Revolutionary **Carlton Winemakers Studio** houses 10 small artisan winemakers who share the ecofriendly space, equipment, and a talent for making phenomenal wines (page 256).

★ **Best Place to Catch Flight Fever:** From a replica of the first plane to the awesome heavy bombers of World War II and Howard Hughes's remarkable *Spruce Goose,* the **Evergreen Aviation and Space Museum** has it all (page 257).

★ **Best Place to Go Sledding in the Summer:** There's always a good patch of mountain to ride in the winter months, but in the summer **Mt. Hood Skibowl** has a 300-foot inner-tube course and a 500-foot zip line (page 261).

Bonneville Dam

One of the great things about Portland is its proximity to some of the Pacific Northwest's most spectacular landscapes. With the slopes of Mount Hood to the north and the majesty of the ocean to the west, Portlanders relish the fact that they are always about an hour away from something spectacularly different than wherever they are. The terrain surrounding Portland is so diverse, in fact, that each year there is a relay marathon that begins at Timberline Lodge on majestic Mount Hood and ends one day later in Seaside, Oregon. For visitors, the diversity of landscapes is a bonus as well; when everything is so conveniently close, there is no need to choose between a ski vacation, a trip to wine country, or a stay in the city.

The Columbia River Gorge, which begins approximately 20 minutes east of Portland and extends for more than 100 miles, is a lush, breathtaking country, with numerous waterfalls, scenic drives, and a plethora of outdoor activities—like hiking, biking, golf, white-water rafting, kayaking, and windsurfing.

Mount Hood, about 50 miles east/southeast of Portland, offers 4,600 acres of skiable terrain and more than 1,200 miles of hiking trails. About 75 miles to the west, you will find the magnificent Pacific Ocean and a flurry of quaint coastal towns with fun shops and fresh seafood.

A little closer to town (about 25 miles to the southwest) is Oregon wine country, where they grow, age, and bottle some of the best pinot noirs in the world.

Previous: autumn colors along Oregon's highways; Multnomah Falls.

Excursions from Portland

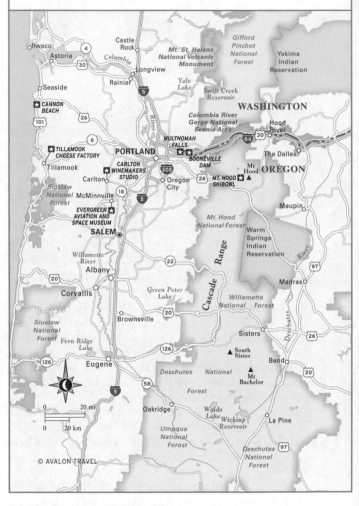

PLANNING YOUR TIME

Each of these excursions from Portland can be done in a day if you travel by car. Of course, if you have the time to linger for an overnight or weekend, the possibilities expand. Depending on which portion of the coast you visit, you can spend just a couple of hours driving or most of the day. Either way, for a trip to the Pacific, it is best to leave early in the day. Traffic to and from the coast and Oregon wine country can get particularly snarled on summer weekends, and both routes involve long stretches of scenic highway with few commercial areas. So be sure you make restroom stops when you can. You can easily visit most of the places you would like to see in wine country in one day, but the coast may be a little trickier. The roads between many of the coastal towns are scenic, but they are often winding, two-lane drives that don't provide for swiftness. It is best to decide which town you would like to visit and spend a day focused on that one.

Traffic to the east depends largely on the time of year. As the snow piles up on the mountain, more and more people head up to take part in the fun. Through much of the winter season (particularly Dec.-Feb.), tire chains are a must, even on vehicles with four-wheel drive.

The Oregon Coast

Oregon has more than 350 miles of coastline, much of it wild, jagged, and beautiful. The water remains fairly chilly (around 45-55°F in most places), and the coastal breeze means cooler climates, but the high basalt rock cliffs, long sandy beaches, and amazing tide pools make it a visitor's paradise.

Along much of the Oregon coastline, you can catch some serious whale-watching, as gray, humpback, and sperm whales migrate south toward Baja during their December pilgrimage from the chilly waters of Alaska. Prime season for whale-watching is between December and March, so coastal hotels with prime spots for viewing book up fast.

SIGHTS
Astoria
At the tip-top of the Oregon coastline, you'll find Astoria, a historic spot where Lewis and Clark spent the winter of 1805-1806, holed up at **Fort Clatsop** (92343 Fort Clatsop Rd., Astoria, 503/861-2471, ext. 214, www. nps.gov/lewi, summer daily 9am-6pm, after Labor Day daily 9am-5pm, $3 adults, free for children under 15), which still stands today. The visitors center at Fort Clatsop National Historical Park has an exhibit built in 1955 inspired by the expedition members' journals, as well as an interpretive center, gift shop, and orientation film. In summer months, the center also features ranger-led programs and re-enactors in the fort.

Fort Stevens (Fort Stevens State Park, Hammond, 503/861-1470, www. visitftstevens.com, daily generally 10am-6pm, free) is a former U.S. military installation that guarded the mouth of the Columbia River in the state of Oregon. The structure was built near the end of the Civil War and named for general and former Washington Territory governor Isaac Stevens. Nowadays, it is a popular campsite and day park with beach access to the famous *Peter Iredale* shipwreck, which ran aground in 1906 and is still visible today. . Nowadays, it is a popular campsite and day park with beach access to the famous *Peter Iredale* shipwreck, which ran aground in 1906 and is still visible today.

Astoria has a lot of history for such a small town. In fact, don't be surprised if you recognize a lot of the landscape as you walk through it. This has been the filming locale for movies like *Goonies, Overboard, Short Circuit, The Black Stallion, Kindergarten Cop, Free Willy, Free Willy 2, The Ring, The Ring Two,* and *Into the Wild.*

Both fishing and crabbing are popular sports in Astoria. **Astoria Fishing Charters** (503/440-0912, www.astoriafishing.com, $160 adults, $85 crabbing) provides guided trips for salmon, steelhead, sturgeon, and crab at reasonable prices.

Seaside

A little farther down the coast, Seaside is one of the most popular tourist destinations on the northern coast. It hosts annual events like the Miss Oregon contest, the Hood to Coast Relay After-Party, and Dorchester Conference, a convention of the Oregon Republican Party.

Just a short walk from Fort Clatsop National Monument is the **Seaside Aquarium** (200 N. Prom, Seaside, 503/738-6211, www.seasideaquarium. com, daily generally 9am-5pm, closing time varies seasonally, adults $8, children 6-13 $4, seniors $6.75, family $27, children 5 and under free with paid admission), where you can visit starfish, harbor seals, wolf eels, crabs, and other Pacific sea creatures. You can also find family-fun activities, like the carousel, arcades, miniature golf, bumper cars and boats, tilt-a-twirl, paddleboats, and canoes.

★ Tillamook Cheese Factory

If you love cheese, the only place you really need to go on your Oregon trip is the **Tillamook Cheese Factory** (4175 Hwy. 101 N., Tillamook, 503/815-1300, www.tillamookcheese.com, summer daily 8am-8pm, after Labor Day daily 8am-6pm, free) in Tillamook. You can tour the facility and find out how they make their world-class cheddar, plus—best of all—you can try endless samples of cheeses and 38 different kinds of ice cream. There is a store on-site for purchasing your favorites at prices that are far cheaper than online, and they even sell their famous "squeaky cheese"—the salty, fresh, and addictive cheddar curds that squeak when you bite into them.

The city of Tillamook is named for a Salish word that means "Land of Many Waters," and it's a popular coastal fishing area today. The seven rivers in Tillamook are abundant with coho salmon and wild steelhead salmon, and the Nestucca, Nehalem, and Tillamook Bays are perhaps the most popular crabbing and clamming areas in the entire Pacific Northwest. Fishing guides like **Lee Darby's Guide Service** (503/351-0547, www.leedarbysfishing.com, $180 full-day trip) can take you out into the churning waters of Tillamook Bay if you want to get your hands on a 30- to 100-pound sturgeon. If you just want to sightsee, charter boats such as **Garibaldi Charters** (503/322-0007, www.garibaldicharters.com, $40 for 2- to 3-hour tour) can take you out to whale-heavy waters for an up close and personal look.

★ Cannon Beach

Cannon Beach is a handsome coastal town famous for its four-mile-long kite-friendly beach, its galleries and specialty boutiques, and iconic **Haystack Rock,** which rises 235 feet out of the sand and is occasionally accessible by foot during low tide. The city acquired its name in 1846, when a cannon from the U.S. Navy schooner *Shark* washed ashore just north of Arch Cape. Two more appeared in February 2008, having been buried in the sand for about a century and a half. These artifacts and others are on display at the **Cannon Beach History Center and Museum** (1387 S. Spruce St., Cannon Beach, 503/436-9301, www.cbhistory.org, Wed.-Mon. 1pm-5pm, free). Late spring is a great time to visit, with the spectacular **Puffin Kite Festival** (www.surfsand.com) in April and the annual **Sandcastle Competition** (www.cannon-beach.net/sandcastle.html) in May or June, depending on the year.

Newport

It's a 2.5- to 3-hour drive from Portland, but if you head over to Newport, you can fill an entire day strolling in the pedestrian-friendly historic Nye Beach district or shopping along the boardwalk—and still sneak in some time on the beach.

The Oregon Coast Aquarium (2820 SE Ferry Slip Rd., Newport, 541/867-3474, www.aquarium.org, summer daily 9am-6pm, after Labor Day 10am-5pm, $19.95 adults, $17.95 seniors, $17.23 children 13-17, $12.95 for children 3-12, free for children under 3) is here. It's the home of more than 500 species of animals in both indoor and outdoor exhibits. Keiko (the whale of *Free Willy* fame) once lived here; when he left, his home was converted into Passages of the Deep, an exhibit that allows visitors to walk through acrylic tunnels surrounded by sharks, rays, and rockfish.

RESTAURANTS

Like sand in your shoes and windswept hair, **Mo's Clam Chowder** (www.moschowder.com, generally daily 11am-8pm, $6-10) is synonymous with a trip to the coast, and you can find locations in Cannon Beach, Lincoln City, and Newport. Since 1946, the company has served Mohava "Mo" Niemi's recipe of New England clam chowder, made with locally raised Yaquina Bay oysters.

A great place to dine in Cannon Beach is **The Wayfarer** (1190 Pacific Dr., Cannon Beach, 503/436-1108, www.wayfarer-restaurant.com, Sun.-Thurs. 8am-9pm, Fri.-Sat. 8am-10pm, $20-28), where you can find a superb omelet made with whatever is most fresh, like Dungeness crab, bay shrimp, or salmon—or maybe with Rogue Creamery blue cheese and local wild mushrooms.

In Seaside, you will find **Pig 'N Pancake** (323 Broadway St., Seaside, 503/738-7243, www.pignpancake.com, Sun.-Thurs. 6am-9pm, Fri.-Sat. 6am-10pm, $7-10), a rather iconic Northwest greasy spoon. It's been in operation in Seaside since 1961, and the franchise has since expanded to Lincoln City, Cannon Beach, Astoria, Newport, and Portland.

Also in Seaside, at **McKeown's Restaurant & Bar** (1 N. Holladay Dr.,

Top: Haystack Rock at Cannon Beach. **Bottom:** Fort Stevens State Park, Astoria.

Seaside, 503/738-5232, www.mckeownsrestaurant.com, Wed.-Fri. 11:30am-9pm, Sat.-Sun. 8am-9pm, $11-30), you can pick your crab fresh from the tank and pair it with some traditional clam chowder. The wine selection is decent and they even have some cute options for the kids like macaroni and cheese with an octopus shaped hot dog. For dessert, check out **Zinger's Ice Cream Parlor** (210 Broadway, Seaside, 503/738-3939, www.zingersicecream.com), where every flavor is made from scratch.

Newport has a number of local favorites, but **Café Mundo** (209 NW Coast Rd., Newport, 541/574-8134, www.cafemundo.us, Tues.-Thurs. 11am-10pm, Fri.-Sat. 11am-midnight, Sun. 10am-4pm, $10-15) tops the list for food, atmosphere, and overall creativity. The menu includes fantastic pastas, sandwiches, salads, and espresso drinks, as well as some great Northwest wines and beers.

For elegant dining, go to **Saffron Salmon** (859 SW Bay Blvd., Newport, 541/265-8921, www.saffronsalmon.com, Thurs.-Tues. 11:30am-2:15pm and 5pm-8:30pm, $20-28) on a public pier on the west end of Newport's Historic Bayfront. It makes good use out of its proximity to the best seafood in the Northwest by buying direct, which means the salmon you eat for dinner might have been swimming in the Pacific when you woke up.

HOTELS

In Astoria, the **Cannery Pier Hotel** (10 Basin St., Astoria, 888/325-4996, www.cannerypierhotel.com, $209-525), as the name might suggest, sits on what was once the site of the Union Fisherman's Cooperative Packing Company Cannery. In operation since mid-2005, this boutique hotel rests atop a pier some 600 feet into the river, offering breathtaking views of the passing ships and storms rolling through the mouth of the Columbia.

In Seaside, try the **Gilbert Inn** (341 Beach Dr., Seaside, 503/738-9770, www.gilbertinn.com, $109-229), a comfortable 10-room inn made cozy and romantic by classic Victorian decor. The inn is just one block from the beach and the popular promenade.

The Ocean Lodge (2864 Pacific St., Cannon Beach, 888/777-4047, www.theoceanlodge.com, $189-379) has spacious and comfortable rooms that have private oceanfront balconies with views of the sea and of Haystack Rock. The lodge is just a short drive from the shops and restaurants of downtown Cannon Beach and very close to great surf breaks as well as hiking and mountain bike trails.

Newport has a number of options, but at **Sylvia Beach Hotel** (267 NW Cliff Rd., Newport, 541/265-5428, www.sylviabeachhotel.com, $120-230), bookworms will feel right at home. There are no TVs, radios, or phones, but there are a number of books and reading nooks, and each room is decorated in the theme of a particular author, such as Edgar Allan Poe, J. K. Rowling, Amy Tan, J. R. R. Tolkien, and Dr. Seuss.

PRACTICALITIES

Information and Services

Before you go, check out **The Oregon Coast Visitors Association** (541/574-2679, http://visittheoregoncoast.com), where you can find advice on where to go and what to do, as well as links to the chamber of commerce and visitors association for each individual city along the coast.

Getting There and Around

From I-5, a number of routes will take you to the Oregon Coast. Most are two-lane highways that wind though vast acres of trees, hills, and valleys. To get to the northern part of the coast, you can take Highway 30 along the south banks of the Columbia River through St. Helens and continue on to Astoria.

Another popular route to the Pacific is Highway 26 (sometimes referred to in Portland as the Sunset Highway), which meanders west through Beaverton, Hillsboro, and Banks and continues on to Seaside. Both Highway 30 and Highway 26 connect with Highway 101, which runs north-south parallel to the coastline and passes through most of Oregon's coastal towns. Traffic can drag along Highway 101 on occasion, particularly as you pass through larger towns like Lincoln City. Heading south along 101 makes for a lovely drive with the Pacific Ocean at your constant right, but if you are planning on visiting an area along the central part of the coast, you might be better off finding a more direct route than this pretty but arguably less efficient one.

You can get to the central coast by traveling south down I-5 and heading onto Highway 99 (Portland Rd. East). From there, drive south toward Capitol Street and into downtown Salem. Follow the signs pointing out Highway 22/Ocean Beaches, which will lead you over the Willamette River and out of Salem. Stay on Highway 22 for approximately 25 miles until it intersects with Highway 18, then turn left onto 18 and continue west to the coast. Follow Highway 18 to the Highway 101 junction (about 25 miles), where you can turn south and get to Lincoln City, Depot Bay, and Newport.

Other routes to the coast will inevitably lead you through a series of small towns and blink-and-you-miss-them communities. Once you determine which area of the coast you would like to visit, map your own roundabout route or check with the town's visitors bureau for advice on how to get there.

The Columbia River Gorge

In about an hour or less from Portland, you can find yourself in the heart of the Columbia River Gorge, basking in the rugged natural beauty of the Columbia River, framed by sheer cliffs and majestic mountains. It's a beautiful drive, no matter how deep you get into it. Whether you are heading out to Hood River, stopping in Stevenson, Washington, or just checking out some historical landmarks, you will find plenty to do. There are countless outdoor adventures (like windsurfing, kiteboarding, rafting, mountain biking, and hiking) for those looking to get an adrenaline fix, but there are also a lot of places to kick back, sip a glass of wine, and enjoy the spectacular view for those who aren't.

SIGHTS

★ Bonneville Dam

If anything were going to harness the power of the Columbia River, it had to be the **Bonneville Dam** (70543 NE Herman Loop, 541/374-8344, www.nwp.usace.army.mil, daily 9am-5pm, free), which spans the river and provides the area with power. The first dam powerhouse opened in 1937 in the midst of the Great Depression. The creation of new jobs and the luxury of affordable hydroelectric power are part of what inspired folk singer Woody Guthrie to write the lines, "Thy power is turning our darkness to dawn. Roll on, Columbia, roll on." But, of course, the sheer command of the dam spoke volumes as well. Both the Oregon and Washington sides of the dam have a visitors center where you can catch a tugboat or barge passing through the locks, or watch salmon, sturgeon, and lamprey as they swim through the fish ladders on their way to spawn. While the visitors center is open year-round, the months between April and September are most abundant with fish.

Columbia Gorge Discovery Center

If you are marveling about the wild and mysterious beauty of the Columbia River Gorge, the best place to learn about how it was all created (spoilers—it involves raging floods, volcanoes, and massive landslides) is the **Columbia Gorge Discovery Center** (5000 Discovery Dr., The Dalles, 541/296-8600, www.gorgediscovery.org, daily 9am-5pm, $9 adults, $7 seniors, $5 children ages 6-16). This 48,200-square-foot center features exhibits, displays, and videos that bring the rich geological history of the gorge to life. You will also find an in-depth exhibit on the cargo carried along with Lewis and Clark and their Corps of Discovery, as well as Native American baskets and early American household furnishings and tools. Step outside and tour the 50-acre interpretive trail with a wheelchair-accessible paved path through cottonwoods, willows, cattails, and sedges. Follow the trail around the pond, which provides a home to turtles, ducks, and geese.

Crown Point and Vista House

You'll know you have arrived at the Columbia River Gorge when you see the unmistakable bluff that is Crown Point, a vantage formed by a 14-million-year-old lava flow that now offers a breathtaking view from 733 feet above the river. The **Vista House Visitors Center** (503/695-2230, www.vista-house.com, daily 9am-6pm, free), an octagonal stone structure, was built as a memorial to Oregon pioneers. Its observation deck provides panoramic views that stretch on for nearly 30 miles, as well as educational exhibits that relate the history of the area and the building.

Farther up the road, **Bridal Veil Falls State Park** (www.oregonstate-parks.org/park_149.php) on the Historic Columbia River Scenic Highway can be accessed off I-84 at exit 28. There are two fantastic hiking trails here, the lower of which bears the same name as the park and will take you down to the base of the eponymous falls. The hike is just under one mile round-trip and includes a number of switchbacks. The upper Overlook Trail can be accessed about 20 yards west of the Bridal Veil Falls trailhead. It is a relatively short half-mile loop that will take you to the famous geologic edifice known as the Pillars of Hercules, a stately pair of basalt towers. Both trails are alive with native flora like trillium, lupine, bead lily, and bleeding heart, all of which are native—but so is poison oak, so stick to the path.

Historic Columbia River Highway

The Historic Columbia River Highway is a 75-mile stretch of road that is significant in that it was the first planned scenic highway in the United States. While some sections of the original byway are no longer accessible by car, the stretch that runs from Troutdale to the Dalles provides about a 50-minute detour from the monotony of I-84. Designed to mimic the picturesque winding byways of Europe, the Historic Columbia River Highway takes full advantage of its natural charms, twisting past waterfalls, winding through tunnels, and wandering over bridges. To begin, take exit 17 off of I-84. The 24 westernmost miles of the highway begin in Troutdale and provide access to hiking trails and natural wonders, as well as Crown Point. The road from this point winds in figure eight loops through five miles of waterfalls, including majestic Multnomah Falls. The road here rejoins with I-84 until Mosier, where you can pick up the second leg of the historic highway at exit 74. This is where you will begin to see the drier regions of the Columbia Plateau and Hood River. Be sure to stop at the Rowena Crest vantage point before continuing on past the Columbia Gorge Discovery Center and Wasco County Historical Museum to the Dalles.

★ Multnomah Falls

There are seemingly more waterfalls in this region than you could count (and it varies by season and rainfall levels), but none is more grand than **Multnomah Falls** (50000 Historic Columbia River Hwy., Scenic Loop Dr., Bridal Veil, 503/695-2376, www.multnomahfallslodge.com, summer daily 8am-9pm, winter Mon.-Thurs. 10am-6pm, Fri. 10am-8pm, Sat. 8am-8pm,

Clockwise from top left: Multnomah Falls; the aptly named Vista House overlooking Columbia River Gorge; Columbia River Gorge.

Sun. 8am-6pm, free), which sprouts from an underground spring on Larch Mountain. The falls are a spectacular 620 feet tall, and broken into upper and lower courses. A trail from the Multnomah Falls Lodge leads to the trail system. The view alone is worth the trip, but the multiple trails that are accessible from the falls make it all the more exhilarating. You can pick up a free trail map in the visitors center and navigate your way along the Larch Mountain Trail to the historic Benson Arch Bridge. The footbridge was built in 1914, and it is a popular place for a photo op with the breathtaking falls as a backdrop. You can continue on from there to the top of the falls or hike all the way up Larch Mountain Trail, where the Cascade Mountains come into full spectacular view. The lodge is where you will find the visitors center as well as a gift shop and the historic Multnomah Falls Lodge restaurant.

Rooster Rock State Park

Along a beautiful stretch of the Columbia River is one of the largest swimming areas near Portland. **Rooster Rock** (Corbett exit off I-84, 503/695-2261 or 800/551-6949, www.oregonstateparks.org/park_175.php; daily 6am-6pm; $5 per day) also has the distinction of being the country's first officially designated clothing-optional beach. The beach is named for a column of basalt that rises from the Oregon side of the Columbia River Gorge in a natural obelisk; given the lax clothing rules and phallic nature of the rock, the park has acquired some rather unsavory nicknames over the years. Nonetheless, the area is beautiful and the area of the beach where nudity is allowed is completely separate and not visible from the clothing-required area of the large park. The non-nude area also has two disc golf courses, picnic shelters and tables, and a boat dock. The park is currently managed by Oregon Parks and Recreation and requires a day-use fee for entry.

Sightseeing Tours

If you really want to get the lay of the land, book a trip aboard the **Columbia Gorge Sternwheeler** (board at Marine Park at Cascade Locks, 503/224-3900, www.portlandspirit.com, June-Sept., $84 adults, $64 seniors and children) or the historic **Mt. Hood Railroad** (110 Railroad Ave., Hood River, 541/386-3556, www.mthoodrr.com, $15-82), both of which allow you to sit back and enjoy the scenery (and, of course, take lots of pictures). If you are looking for something a little more active, **Martin's Gorge Tours** (877/290-8687, www.martinsgorgetours.com, year-round, $49) will take you on a morning hike of one of the area's beautiful waterfalls—a different area for each day of the week. Weekday hikes range from easy to challenging and visit such sights as Ponytail Falls, Horsetail Falls, and the breathtaking Punchbowl Falls. Weekend hikes (which run July through February) take walkers past Latourell Falls, Bridal Veil Falls, and a picturesque overlook trail that offer some of the best views in the area.

Until you drive into some of the more populous towns like Hood River or Stevenson, Washington, your dining options are fairly limited to either home-style diner fare or romantic, elegant hideaways. If you aren't looking for anything fancy, swing by **Tad's Chicken and Dumplins** (1325 W. Historic Columbia River Hwy., Troutdale, 503/666-5337, www.tadschicdump.com, Mon.-Fri. 5pm-10pm and Sat.-Sun. 4pm-10pm, $13-20), located in Troutdale along the Historic Columbia River Highway. As the name implies, it has a special penchant for comfort food, particularly the eponymous dish; like any roadside diner worth its salt, it does a mean fried chicken, too.

Just a skip over the river into Stevenson, Washington, you will find a number of up-and-coming dining options, not the least of which is the **Cascade Room** (1131 SW Skamania Lodge Way, Stevenson, WA, 800/221-7117, www.skamania.com, Mon.-Thurs. 7am-2pm and 5pm-9pm, Fri.-Sat. 7am-2pm and 5pm-9:30pm, Sun. 9am-2pm and 5pm-9pm, $23-35), a fine dining restaurant housed in Skamania Lodge. Dinners boast such specialties as salmon, smoked pork loin, and roast prime rib of Washington beef, and breakfast and brunch are so good, even the oatmeal is worth writing home about.

For moderately priced burgers, sandwiches, beer, and wine, check out **Big River Grill** (192 SW 2nd St., Stevenson, WA, 509/427-4888, www.big-rivergrill.us, Mon.-Fri. 11:30am-9:30pm, Sat.-Sun. 8am-11am and 11:30am-9:30pm, $13-19), a popular spot with locals and passers-through that defines its cuisine as "High-End Roadhouse."

Also in Stevenson, a great spot to grab a microbrew and some grub is **Walking Man Brewing Company** (240 SW 1st St., Stevenson, WA, 509/427-5520, www.walkingmanbrewing.com, Wed.-Fri. 4pm-9pm, Sat. 3pm-9pm, Sun. 3pm-8pm, $10-15). The house-made beers really take center stage here (particularly the Belgian red ale), but the artisan-style pizza isn't bad at all.

If you are looking for seafood, **3 Rivers Grill** (601 Oak St., Hood River, 541/386-8883, www.3riversgrill.com, daily lunch and dinner, $12-24) has some of the best in the area. Located on Oak Street in Hood River, the place has a homey feel to it, with a deck area overlooking the river. In addition to some beautiful crab cakes, ceviche, and salmon dishes, it has an award-winning wine selection.

Another master of Northwest cuisine and seafood is **Celilo Restaurant and Bar** (16 Oak St., Hood River, 541/386-5710, www.celilorestaurant.com, daily 11:30am-3pm and 5pm-9:30pm, $14-24) in Hood River. They're about as committed to supporting all things local as the sun is to shining, and the result is simple, expertly crafted food. You will want to make a reservation for Celilo (pronounced "seh-LIE-low"), even if you have a small party, to ensure that you can take your time and that you will not have to sit at the bar.

Finally, as the evening winds down in Hood River, Brian's Pourhouse (606 Oak St., Hood River, 541/387-4344, www.brianspourhouse.com, daily 5pm-11pm, $15-22) is a great spot for a late dinner, or for drinks and appetizers. The small, Colonial-style, white clapboard restaurant has a basement bar that stays open just a wee bit later than many other places in town, and the atmosphere is relaxed and enjoyable.

FESTIVALS AND EVENTS
Portland Highland Games
It's not every day that you get to see bagpipes, kilts, and Scottish heavy games all in the same place—at least not on this side of the world. The Portland Highland Games (Mount Hood Community College, 26000 SE Stark St., Gresham, www.phga.org, $8-20, free for children under five) is hosted each year on the third Saturday in July by Mount Hood Community College. Somehow, it manages to bring the Scotsman out in everyone. But it's a lot of fun to don a kilt and slip into a series of bad Mike Myers impressions as you take in world-class Scottish athletic championships, highland dance competitions, traditional Scottish music, the Kilted Mile Race, genealogy workshops, children's activities, traditional wares, and, of course, beer and bangers.

RECREATION
Kayaking
The Columbia River is a favorite spot for lovers of water sports. The Kayak Shed (6 Oak St., 541/386-4286, www.kayakshed.com) in Hood River can hook you up with whatever gear you will need for a wild river adventure. If you are an inexperienced kayaker, Columbia Gorge Kayak School (541/806-4190, www.gorgekayaker.com) offers both group lessons and private instruction. Two-day weekender courses will run you about $225. For rafting, try Zoller's Outdoor Odysseys (800/366-2004, www.zooraft.com), which takes passengers on thrill rides down the rapids of the White Salmon (half-day trip, $65 per person) and Klickitat (full-day trip, $90 per person).

Windsurfing
Few sports are more popular in the Gorge than windsurfing. Hood River Waterplay (541/386-9463, www.hoodriverwaterplay.com) offers windsurfing and kiteboarding classes for all levels of experience, plus equipment rentals (starting at $39/day) and a thorough knowledge of the area—which makes them a great place to get wet, whether you are well versed or just starting out.

Fishing
For fishing, head to Laurance Lake, Drano Lake, Goose Lake, Lost Lake,

or the mouth of Eagle Creek, where you won't battle with the currents as you will in the Salmon, Deschutes, and Klickitat Rivers. Or book a guided excursion with **Columbia River Fishing Guides** (1087 Lewis River Rd., Ste. 206, 360/910-6630, www.columbiariverfishingguide.com, $200/day), based in Woodland, Washington. They will provide you with equipment, and they claim they can guarantee you will catch a sturgeon, steelhead, or salmon.

Hiking

Hiking options abound in the Gorge, especially since it provides access to the **Pacific Crest Trail** (PCT), which extends from the U.S. border with Canada all the way to Mexico. A good spot to access the PCT is the **Herman Creek Trailhead,** which provides a challenging but rewarding 16-mile hike up the Benson Plateau. Or, if you are looking for something a bit easier, try the **Latourell Falls Trailhead,** an easy two-mile hike past waterfalls, flowers, and streams. You can find detailed hiking plans and maps on **Portland Hiker's Field Guide** (www.portlandhikersfieldguide.org) to prepare you for your trip.

HOTELS

The Pacific Northwest has a number of lodgings built around its numerous hot springs, and **Bonneville Hot Springs Resort and Spa** (1252 E. Cascade Dr., North Bonneville, WA, 509/427-7767, www.bonnevilleresort.com, $189-499) is one of the most elegant, particularly if you're really looking to escape. Many rooms come equipped with their own private mineral-water hot tub, which overlooks the river canyon. The renowned 12,000-square-foot day spa has treatments that utilize those therapeutic waters that form when water descends through the planet's cracks and fissures, gets heated by the earth's core, and is forced back to the surface.

Collins Lake Resort (88149 E. Creek Ridge Rd., Government Camp, 888/422-4776, www.collinslakeresort.com, $169-369) also offers all the luxuries you'd expect from a top-notch resort; its spacious, well-appointed, and comfortable chalets—complete with views of magnificent Collins Lake—really make this a favorite vacation destination. They have a number of chalets and lodges available that are great for large groups or families.

Skamania Lodge (1131 SW Skamania Lodge Way, Stevenson, WA, 509/427-7700, www.skamania.com, $189-389) also makes use of its beautiful surroundings, sitting proudly on a hill with a commanding view of the river and surrounding hills. The lodge is elegant and peaceful, with grand stone fireplaces, high rustic ceilings, and enormous picture windows.

Adjacent to the historic Columbia Gorge Hotel, **Columbia Cliffs Villas** (3880 Westcliff Dr., Hood River, 866/912-8366, www.columbiacliffvillas. com, $169-895) offers a wide variety of accommodations in 28 privately owned condominiums that range from one to three bedrooms. The Villas are great for families because they come equipped with lockout doors, which allow the space to be reconfigured as needed.

For families or those traveling on a budget, **Vagabond Lodge** (4070 Westcliff Dr., Hood River, 877/386-2992, www.vagabondlodge.com, $75-190) has clean, simple, and affordable rooms, many of which have stunning views of the Columbia River. All of the rooms have cable TV, microwaves, and a small fridge.

PRACTICALITIES
Information and Services
The **Columbia River Gorge Visitors Association** (www.crgva.org) provides maps and information on events, dining, accommodations, and shopping. It also has a trip planner called *Gorge Guide* with beautiful photos of the area, historical information, and travel tips for regions all throughout the Gorge.

Getting There and Around
Word to the wise: You will very likely get distracted while driving through the Gorge. With so many viewpoints, historic landmarks, unexpected waterfalls, and surprising panoramas, it's natural to get a bit sidetracked, but that's half the fun. One of the best routes is the Historic Columbia River Highway (exit 17), the first planned scenic highway in the United States. The highway runs past waterfalls (including the majestic Multnomah Falls) and photo stops like Crown Point and the Vista House. You can rejoin I-84 at exit 35, where you can cross over the Bridge of the Gods to the Washington side or continue east to Hood River and access to Mount Hood.

If you are crossing the bridge (which was named for after a great Native American legend), you will need to pay a $1 toll. The bridge tollhouse is open 24 hours a day and serves as the emergency relay station for police departments on both sides of the river.

If you continue on to Hood River, which is about 45 minutes from Portland in good traffic, you can pick up the Mt. Hood Scenic Loop, a two-hour drive around the foot of Mount Hood over streams and through lush forests. From here, you can also drive the Fruit Loop, a collection of farms, orchards, vineyards, and wineries. There are easy-to-follow maps (which list Fruit Loop farms, attractions, and individual operating hours) available at the Hood River Visitors Center off exit 63 on I-84.

Oregon Wine Country

If you think the Portland metro area is scenic and green, you'll think Oregon wine country is exceptional. The vineyards of the Willamette Valley are situated between the Coast Range to the west and the Cascades to the east, nestled into a verdant landscape that is fragrant with spruce, fir, and pine.

The wine industry in Oregon is still remarkably young when you consider how much success it has had. It all began when David Lett of Eyrie Vineyards moved to the region in 1965 with some 3,000 clippings and grand intentions to make the most of the Willamette Valley's climate and latitude, which bear a striking resemblance to that of Burgundy, France, pinot noir's ancestral home. Undeterred by his California counterparts, who scoffed at the idea of producing wine in a region that was so cold and wet, Lett planted the first pinot noir grapes in the Northwest, thus sowing the seeds for Oregon's future as a heavyweight in the wine industry.

It wasn't until the late 1970s that people really started to turn their eyes toward what was happening here. Nowadays, the Willamette Valley alone has over 200 wineries and 12,000 acres of grapes, and in these places, artisan winemakers have put Oregon on the international wine map thanks to incomparable vintages and revolutionary practices. According to the Oregon Wine Board (www.oregonwine.org), there are 72 grape varieties grown throughout the state, but only 15 of those varieties make up 97 percent of the vineyards in Oregon. At the top of that list is pinot noir. In fact, this region has been recognized as one of the premier pinot noir–producing areas in the world—which comes as no surprise to the Lett family. Apparently, they knew it all along.

WINERIES

Sokol Blosser (5000 NE Sokol Blosser Ln., Dayton, 800/582-6668, www.sokolblosser.com) is a pioneer in Northwest wine. The Sokol Blosser clan has been a part of the Oregon wine fabric since its first planting in 1971. Years later, Sokol Blosser is still family-owned and going strong, receiving accolades for both their vintages and their commitment to sustainability. Their 72-acre estate vineyards are up in the Dundee Hills, which makes for a lovely picnic spot, and their tasting room is open 10am-4pm, with tours ($25) running every Saturday, and Sunday by reservation only.

The Four Graces (9605 NE Fox Farm Rd., Dundee, 800/245-2950, www.thefourgraces.com) is a much younger vineyard at the northern entrance to Dundee. When the Black family purchased its 110-acre spot of land in 2003, it was fulfilling a lifelong dream to have a family-owned wine estate.

Navigating Wine Country

The Willamette Valley has the perfect climate to grow pinot noir grapes.

As you travel along Highway 99 West, the first major wine town you will hit is Newberg, home to George Fox College. Great wineries here include **Adelsheim** (16800 NE Calkins Ln., Newberg, 503/538-3652, www.adelsheim. com, daily 11am-4pm), which recently added a tasting room to the 190-acre vineyard at the base of the Chehalem Mountains. At **Rex Hill Winery** (30835 N. Hwy. 99W, Newberg, 503/538-0666, www.rexhill.com, daily 10am-5pm), you'll find 17 acres of pinot noir grapes and one wee little row of well-attended muscat grapes.

Passing through Newberg, you can head west on Highway 240 to the quiet hamlets of Carlton, Yamhill, and Gaston, where you will find **Elk Cove Vineyards** (27751 NW Olson Rd., Gaston, 503/985-7760, www.elkcove.com, daily 10am-5pm). In 1974, Elk Cove became the first winery in the Yamhill-Carlton region to produce a commercial wine. This particular pocket of land is well protected by the Coastal Range, the Chehalem Mountains, and the Dundee Hills, which means slightly drier, more moderate growing conditions perfectly suited for cool-climate grapes like pinot noir.

Check out **Anne Amie** (6580 NE Mineral Springs Rd., Carlton, 503/864-2991, www.anneamie.com, daily 10am-5pm) or **WillaKenzie** (19143 NE Laughlin Rd., Yamhill, 503/662-3280, www.willakenzie.com, daily 11am-5pm) for fine examples of how pinot noir thrives in such climates. In addition to the tasting room, Anne Amie also offers a guided tour for $30 per person, which includes a reserve tasting and Oregon pinot noir glass. Tours are offered daily beginning at 11am, but you must call ahead to reserve a space.

Nowadays, people come from all around to sit in the historic farmhouse and sip extraordinary pinot noir, pinot gris, and pinot blanc. They are an enthusiastic and friendly bunch and more than willing to welcome you into their tasting room (daily 10am-5pm). You can also schedule a time to bring a group and meet one-on-one with the tasting room experts, who can explain how the happy trifecta of soil, climate, and topography, combined with meticulous winemaking, makes for outstanding wines.

About 10 miles west, in McMinnville, you will find **Eyrie Vineyards** (935 NE 10th Ave., McMinnville, 503/472-6315 or 888/440-4970, www.

This region is also home to **Carlton Winemakers Studio** (801 N. Scott St., Carlton, 503/852-6100, www.winemakersstudio.com, 10am-5pm), where 10 small-but-savvy vintners work in the same space, each producing some of the region's most remarkable wines.

If you stay on Highway 99 West as it passes through Newberg, you can head into the hills of Dundee. Here you can visit **Sokol Blosser** (5000 Sokol Blosser Ln., Dundee, 800/582-6668, www.sokolblosser.com, daily 10am-4pm), a long-time giant of the Oregon wine industry, and soak up the landscape in the picnic area. There are many vineyards in this area and a smattering of excellent restaurants, so it's a good place to stop and grab a bite to eat as you head toward Mc-Minnville, the largest city in Yamhill County and the cultural center of the valley.

In McMinnville, you will find **Eyrie Vineyards** (1015 NE 10th Ave., McMin-nville, 503/472-6315, www.eyrievineyards.com, Wed.-Sun. noon-5pm), which was founded by the man affectionately known as "Papa Pinot."

Here are a few other great wineries to check out:

- **Argyle:** 691 Hwy. 99W, Dundee, 888/427-4953, www.argylewinery.com, daily 11am-5pm

- **Bishop Creek:** 614 E. 1st St., Newberg, 503/487-6934, www.urbanwine-works.com, Wed.-Sun. 1pm-7pm

- **Chehalem:** 106 Center St., Newberg, 503/538-4700, www.chehalemwines.com, Thurs.-Mon. 11am-5pm

- **Dobbes Family Estate and Wine by Joe:** 240 SE 5th St., Dundee, 503/538-1141, www.dobbesfamilyestate.com, daily 11am-6pm

- **Domaine Drouhin:** 6750 Breyman Orchards Rd., Dayton, 503/864-2700, www.domainedrouhin.com, Wed.-Sun. 11am-4pm

- **Erath:** 9409 NE Worden Hill Rd., Dundee, 503/538-3318, www.erath.com, daily 11am-5pm

- **Torii Mor:** 18325 NE Fairview Dr., Dundee, 503/554-0105, www.toriimor-winery.com, daily 11am-5pm

eyrievineyards.com), which was founded by David Lett, who is affection-ately known as "Papa Pinot." Lett planted the first pinot noir grapes in the Northwest, thus sowing the seeds for Oregon's future as a heavyweight in the wine industry. In 1975, Eyrie Vineyards produced the first pinot noir to successfully vie for recognition alongside the long-recognized pinots of Burgundy, France. With that recognition came the acknowledgment of Oregon as the New World home for pinot noir. The Lett family is still at the helm of Eyrie, and they still produce some of the most respected wines in the region. You can visit their tasting room (Wed.-Sun. noon-5pm) and sample for $5 per person, which is refundable upon the purchase of two bottles of wine.

Finally, if you really want an inside peek, call ahead and book a tour with **Domaine Drouhin** (6750 NE Breyman Orchards Rd., Dayton, 503/864-2700, www.domainedrouhin.com, tours $30 per person). Winemaker Véronique Drouhin-Boss uses the Burgundy method, and she comes by it naturally. She is a fourth-generation winemaker who splits her time between Oregon and the other great wine region of the world, Beaune, Burgundy. The tour—a 60-minute walk through the vineyards and the four-story winery—is an exceptional peek into her process that culminates with comparative tastings between Oregon and Burgundy wines with water and cheese accompaniments.

Wine Tours

The best way to see wine country is to plan ahead, choose which places you want to see, and then map them out. Or, better yet, leave the driving to someone else and sign up for a tour with the likes of **Beautiful Willamette Tours** (877/868-7295, www.willamettetours.com, $100-175 per person), **EcoTours of Oregon** (888/868-7733, www.ecotours-of-oregon.com, $70-100 per person), or **Wine Tours Northwest** (800/359-1034, www.winetours-northwest.com, $139-350 per person). The benefit of opting for a tour is twofold: You do not have to designate your own driver, and you are often allowed to tour places that are otherwise closed off to the public.

★ Carlton Winemakers Studios

If you don't have enough time to tour a bunch of wineries, check out **Carlton Winemakers Studios** (801 N. Scott St., Carlton, 503/852-6100, www.winemakersstudio.com, daily 11am-5pm) where you can sample the wines of several up-and-coming winemakers. The studio is rather like a co-op, in that it allows as many as 10 vintners at a time to share one state-of-the-art, gravity-driven, energy-efficient facility. The concept is a revolutionary way to encourage artisan winemakers to produce ultra-premium wines, while still promoting an ecoconscious, cost-friendly approach. For the consumer, that approach means that the wines produced within the studio have both the pedigree and palate of high-end wines, with the intimacy and price of a mom-and-pop vintner. What's more, you need not be a connoisseur to appreciate their space, or even be certain of what you are looking for. The airy, modern, and sleek studio tasting room has most of its in-house vintages on hand for tasting, providing a rare opportunity to explore the diversity of the region.

SIGHTS

When you need a break from sipping wine, Yamhill County has other things to entertain you. Stop by **Red Ridge Farms** (5510 NE Breyman Orchards Rd., Dayton, 503/864-8502, Wed.-Sun. 9am-5pm, free), a family-owned herb and specialty plant nursery in Dayton. Nestled in the Red

Hills, the farm has more than 300 varieties of herbs and other culinary, medicinal, and landscaping plants, including more than 100 types of lavender. It makes for some really pretty scenery. You can call ahead and have them prepare a picnic for you, or simply wander through the fragrant gardens. While you are there, be sure to browse through the shop filled with handcrafted items and garden-inspired gifts.

★ Evergreen Aviation and Space Museum

The small town of McMinnville is home to the **Evergreen Aviation and Space Museum** (500 NE Captain Michael King Smith Way, McMinnville, 503/434-4180, www.sprucegoose.org, daily 9am-5pm, $26 adults, $24 seniors, $22 for ages 5-16, free for children under 5), the biggest air and space museum west of the Mississippi. It's home to Howard Hughes's H-4 Hercules, a heavy transport aircraft more commonly known as the *Spruce Goose*—a name that Hughes detested. The newest section of the museum, which opened in 2008, has interactive flight simulators that allow you to practice landing the space shuttle, docking a Gemini capsule, or landing the Lunar Excursion Module on the surface of the moon. You can also catch a flick at the 3-D IMAX theater, see a 32,000-pound meteorite, or simply marvel at the amazing collection of military and civilian aircraft, spacecraft, and memorabilia. The museum offers docent guided tours daily at 11am and 1:30pm.

RESTAURANTS

Nothing goes better with great wine than world-class dining, and this region has plenty of good spots to choose from. At the **Joel Palmer House** (600 Ferry St., Dayton, 503/864-2995, www.joelpalmerhouse.com, Tues.-Sat. 5pm-9pm, $29-37) the menu centers almost entirely around Northwest wild mushrooms. Once you have sampled the bounty of chanterelle, portobello, matsutake, and morel mushrooms, you will understand why. Try the Mushroom Madness menu, a prix-fixe meal ($75 per person) that includes six courses of fungus-y goodness.

Tina's Restaurant (760 N. Hwy. 99W, Dundee, 503/538-8880, www.tinasdundee.com, Tues.-Fri. 11:30am-2pm, daily 5pm-9pm, $22-30), on the other hand, is to wine what the Joel Palmer House is to mushrooms. Taking full advantage of the proximity to some of the best wineries in the business, it focuses on artisan producers from the Willamette Valley and typically has about 60 local wines on hand. Wines by the glass are usually about $10-12 and are served in small one-and-a-half-glass carafes. It's a nice touch because it allows you the opportunity to share and sample different wines with different courses. The quiet, 50-seat restaurant serves up rustic French and Northwest cuisine using whatever is locally grown and in season, but they are particularly known for their roasted duck.

In Newberg, check out the **Painted Lady** (201 S. College St., Newberg, 503/538-3850, www.thepaintedladyrestaurant.com, Wed.-Sun. 5pm-10pm, $60-100), a popular spot for elegant meals and special occasions. The restaurant, which is housed in an old Victorian home, was named for the movement that sought to restore and revitalize Victorian and Edwardian homes by painting them in three or more contrasting colors and highlighting their architectural beauty. Both the menu and the setting seem to embody that ideal of using simple flourishes to highlight what is already there. Dishes are unpretentious, pretty, and well prepared. There's a regular and a vegetarian menu each night, both of which feature a four-course, prix-fixe affair ($60 per person or $100 with wine pairings). In keeping with the elegance of the menu, the service at the Painted Lady is remarkably attentive as well, from offering a napkin to match your pants (thus preventing lint) to brushing the table between courses.

SHOPS

Shopping in and around McMinnville is also fun, and there are a number of great antiquing stops worth mentioning. **Lafayette Schoolhouse Antique Mall** (748 Highway 99W, Lafayette, 503/864-2720, www.myantiquemall. com, daily 10am-5pm) has more than 100 antique dealers housed in a 1912 schoolhouse and 1930s-era gymnasium. Also check out the **Downtown Historic District** and the **McMinnville Antique & Wine Gallery** (546 NE 3rd St., 503/474-9696, www.mcminnvilleantiqueandwine.com, Mon.-Sat. 11am-5pm), where you will find vintage jewelry, linens, home decor, art, kitchen accessories, and clothing—as well as wine tasting from a handful of small, artisan wineries. Also in McMinnville are galleries, restaurants, and independently owned boutiques and shops that specialize in handmade or locally produced items.

HOTELS

If anything is an indication that Oregon wine country is becoming a destination spot, it is the arrival of the region's first large-scale luxury hotel. Opened in 2009, **The Allison Inn and Spa** (2525 Allison Ln., Newberg, 877/294-2525, www.theallison.com, $315 and up) is set on 35 acres of wine country hillside and offers all of the amenities necessary for a lavish, romantic stay, such as plush robes, deep soaking tubs, and in-room fireplaces. With 85 guest rooms, including 12 junior suites, seven one-bedroom suites, and a two-bedroom grand suite, The Allison is the largest luxury inn in the area. It also boasts a 15,000-square-foot full-service spa and an 85-seat restaurant that serves Northwest cuisine, wine, and microbrews and provides 24-hour room service for guests.

If you enjoy a simpler bed-and-breakfast, you are in luck. Wine country is ripe with them. **Dundee Manor Bed and Breakfast** (8380 NE Worden Hill Rd., Dundee, 888/262-1133, www.dundeemanor.com, $250), an Edwardian home that sits on five sprawling, manicured acres, comes with a bit more luxury than the average bed-and-breakfast. Guests are treated to a full gourmet breakfast, in-suite snacks, complimentary beverages, fleece robes, fresh flowers, and nightly turn-down service.

In Carlton, **The R.R. Thompson House** (517 N. Kutch St., Carlton,

503/852-6236, www.rrthompsonhouse.com, $150-245) is a good bet. Built in 1936, this bed-and-breakfast features two suites with sitting areas and satellite HDTV, as well as three sunny rooms with private baths and whirlpool tubs. A bonus for the non-morning people: The breakfast room has multiple tables, just in case you are feeling under-caffeinated or antisocial.

Honeymooners and couples looking to get away may want to check out the **Black Walnut Inn** (9600 NE Worden Hill Rd., Dundee, 866/429-4114, www.blackwalnut-inn.com, $295-495), which has been building a reputation as a romance-inducing escape since 2004. Located along the back roads of Dundee, the inn boasts incomparable views of the valley from most of the well-appointed rooms and suites. All of the accommodations here are spacious, cozy, and plush, with decor reminiscent of an Italian villa. Breakfast is a real delight. You may choose from four items each day, all of which are hearty, delicious, and straight from local farms.

Hotel Oregon (310 NE Evans St., McMinnville, 888/472-8427, www.mcmenamins.com, $50-135) is a unique spot to dine or stay thanks to the enterprising McMenamin brothers, who are responsible for 53 properties in Oregon and Washington—including pubs, historic hotels, and movie houses. This particular hotel, which has been around since 1905, has European-style rooms for as little as $50 a night and suites with private bathrooms starting at $90. Hotel Oregon is known for its rooftop bar, which towers over old Main Street and offers a view of the Coastal Range and wine country.

PRACTICALITIES
Information and Services

Planning ahead for a trip to wine country is essential, because many wineries have limited hours and even more limited tour options. It's best to pick a few places and map out your day accordingly. A good resource for planning is the **Willamette Valley Visitors Association** (www.oregonwinecountry.org), a nonprofit group that provides travel and tourism information for the entire Willamette Valley region. In addition to having an online calendar of events, it has an interactive trip planner, a breakdown of area wineries, and descriptions of each of the area wine regions.

The **Willamette Valley Wineries Association** (www.willamettewines.com) is another good resource. It oversees more than 150 member wineries and tasting rooms in the valley and provides listings for recommended area restaurants and lodging options. The website also features a map and a link to request a detailed brochure. If you are planning ahead, check out the **Oregon Wine Board** (www.oregonwine.org), which provides extensive looks into the history and horticulture of Oregon wines, notes on sustainability and craftsmanship, and tourism resources. From the website, you can request a comprehensive packet that includes an overview brochure about the industry, maps, and vineyard listings from the Willamette Valley and all over Oregon. There's a small cost, but they will mail the packet to your home so that you can get a head start on mapping out your trip.

Getting There and Around

It's not a long stretch of road that separates Portland from the hub of Oregon's Willamette Valley wine region. To get there, take I-5 southbound until you reach exit 289 (Sherwood/Tualatin), or detour through the Champoeg State Heritage Area by continuing south to exit 282A. Follow the signs to Butteville, and from there to Newberg and Highway 99W. Traffic can slow to a crawl as you pass through each of the small cities along the route, particularly during rush hour, so try to avoid traveling that stretch in the early morning or late afternoon.

Getting around Oregon wine country can be a challenge, thanks to rolling hills, gravel roads, and sporadic signage. But there are plenty of maps and tours that can help you navigate. If you are driving yourself, appoint one person as the map checker, who can be on the lookout for driveways and landmarks.

Mount Hood

The Cascade Mountain Range is like no other mountain range in the country. The range is part of the greater Pacific Ring of Fire, which is home to 452 active and inactive volcanoes—where about 90 percent of the world's earthquakes occur. Portland and the Cascade Mountains surrounding it have not seen much volcanic activity since Mount St. Helens blew its top in 1980, but seismologists and scientists are never quick to forget what lurks beneath those luminous peaks and glaciers. Even Mount Hood, which at 11,245 feet is Oregon's tallest peak, is considered a not-quite-dormant volcano. But try telling that to the locals who trek to the mountain all year long to ski and snowboard the 4,600 skiable acres, hike the numerous trails that wind their way through 1,200 miles of forests and wilderness areas, and enjoy the region's pristine rivers and lakes.

RESTAURANTS
Government Camp

Mount Hood has a few little gems when it comes to dining, some of them upscale and some of them decidedly not. Government Camp, the community that serves as the gateway for most of the area ski resorts, is a favorite stop on the way to or from the slopes.

Ice Axe Grill (87304 E. Government Camp Loop, Government Camp, 503/272-0102, www.mthoodbrewing.com, daily 11:30am-9pm, $10-20) is a traditional pub that also happens to be the home of Mt. Hood Brewing Company. The menu consists of all the fare you would expect from any self-respecting pub, like burgers, sandwiches, salads, pizza, and beer-battered fish. But in a surprising turn from tradition, vegetarian dishes are also available.

Another popular pub is **The Ratskeller** (88335 E. Government Camp Loop, Government Camp, 503/272-3635, www.ratskellerpizzeria.com,

Mon.-Thurs. 2pm-10pm, Fri.-Sat. 11am-2am, $8-10), a casual joint that specializes in pizza. "The Rat," as it is affectionately called, has one side devoted to family dining and another side with a bar, where you will find billiards, live music, and karaoke.

The 24-hour family-style restaurant at **Huckleberry Inn** (88611 E. Government Camp Loop, Government Camp, 503/272-3325, www.huckleberry-inn.com, daily 24 hours, $8-10) is a great place to stop for breakfast or if you want to treat yourself to a little coffee and pie. The food is homey and hearty here, and for good reason. Stacks of huckleberry pancakes or heaping plates of steak and eggs are sure to fuel you up for a day in the snow.

Feel like dining at 6,000 feet? The views are spectacular from Timberline Lodge, and *Sunset* magazine has named the lodge's **Cascade Dining Room** (27500 E. Timberline Rd., 503/272-3104, www.timberlinelodge.com, daily 7:30am-10am, noon-2pm, and 6pm-8pm, $16-22) one of the top 10 mountaintop restaurants in the Pacific Northwest and Canada. The Farmers Market Brunch runs every day 11am-3pm and is practically worth the trip itself. Reservations are required for dinner, but breakfast and lunch are more casual and first-come, first-served.

Welches

In Welches, **Altitude** (68010 E. Fairway Ave., Welches, 503/622-2214, www.altituderestaurant.com, daily 5pm-9pm, $14-29) has classy but casual upscale dining in the ambient Resort at the Mountain. It focuses on food that embraces the Northwest bounty and offers one of the very few romantic anniversary or special occasion dining spots in the region.

The **Rendezvous Grill and Taproom** (67149 E. Hwy. 26, Welches, 503/622-6837, www.rendezvousgrill.net, daily 11:30am-9pm, $15-20) is perhaps a little less serious, but no less devoted to great food. It is particularly known for desserts but cooks a mean steak Oscar as well.

El Burro Loco (67211 E. Hwy. 26, Welches, 503/622-6780, www.burroloco.net, daily 11am-10pm, $8-15) is a bright cantina with inexpensive but tasty food, fresh cocktails, and an extensive collection of microbrews and tequila.

You will find other dining options nearby in the small communities of Brightwood, Rhododendron, and Zig Zag.

RECREATION
Downhill Skiing
★ MT. HOOD SKIBOWL

Mt. Hood Skibowl (87000 E. Hwy. 26, Government Camp, 503/272-3206, www.skibowl.com, Mon.-Tues. 3pm-10pm, Wed.-Thurs. 1pm-10pm, Fri. 9am-11pm, Sat. 8am-11pm, Sun. 8am-10pm) is one of three major ski resorts on Mount Hood, and America's largest night-skiing area. With the highest lift at 5,027 feet and the base lodge at 3,600 feet, it ranks lowest in elevation but still has some of the steepest terrain on the mountain, with vertical drops of 1,500 feet. There are no high-speed lifts at Skibowl, but

Top: Mount Hood. **Bottom:** Timberline Lodge.

that keeps things laid-back and the mountain from getting overly crowded. Avid skiers who travel with beginners will like the diversity of the mountain, from the simpler lower bowl to the upper bowls and backcountry areas for the more experienced. Skibowl is also the closest and least expensive ski destination to Portland, but what really sets this place apart is that it stays open year-round. When the snow and ice are still months away, Skibowl has an adventure park that offers warm-weather alternatives, such as an Alpine Slide, mountain bike park, hiking trails, disc and miniature golf, batting cages, bungee jumping, horseback riding, and zip-line trails.

TIMBERLINE LODGE

The beautiful **Timberline Lodge** (27500 E. Timberline Rd., Timberline Lodge, 503/272-3158, www.timberlinelodge.com, daily 9am-4pm, night skiing Fri.-Sat. 4pm-10pm) was the picturesque outdoor setting for the 1980 thriller *The Shining,* but don't worry: all those creepy things happened at a studio far away, and there is no such thing as room 237. Instead of scary ghosts, Timberline is famous for offering year-round resort skiing on the Palmer snowfield at 8,540 feet. Also, Still Creek Basin, Timberline's newest network of trails, has eight alpine trails and a lift-served snowshoe and cross-country skiing trail.

MOUNT HOOD MEADOWS

Finally, with its steep terrain and abundant snowfall, **Mount Hood Meadows** (14040 Hwy. 35, Mount Hood, 503/337-2222, www.skihood.com, Mon.-Tues. 9am-4pm, Wed.-Thurs. and Sun. 9am-9pm, Fri. Sat. 9am-10pm) is arguably one of the most popular resorts in Oregon. The 11 chairlifts at Meadows run on 100 percent wind power and provide access to the 2,150 acres of terrain on the southeast flank of Mount Hood. The Cascade Express lift will take you to the highest point at Meadows. At 7,300 feet, it is the access point to a handful of the 85 runs and the 1,700 vertical feet of terrain the resort has to offer.

Cross-Country Skiing

With the sprawling acreage of the Mount Hood National Forest on hand, there is some great cross-country skiing to be had. **Cooper Spur Mountain Resort** (10755 Cooper Spur Rd., Mount Hood Parkdale, 541/352-7803, www.cooperspur.com, Fri. 4pm-9pm, Sat. 9am-9pm, Sun. and holidays 9am-4pm) has four miles of groomed track and up to 14 miles of ungroomed trail nearby. Track fees are small and you will need a wilderness permit to explore the backcountry, but permits are free and accessible via self-service at the trailhead.

Hiking

Hiking and backpacking are popular pastimes in the Mount Hood area. **Timberline Trail** is one of the best challenging but beautiful hikes. Constructed in the 1930s by the Civilian Conservation Corps, the trail loops near Timberline Lodge and Mount Hood Meadows, but is otherwise surrounded by wilderness. The 40-plus-mile trail has a number of variations depending on where you start and what the season is, but the entire route takes about five or six days to complete. This and many other trails in the region present seasonal hazards that should be researched and prepared for, such as hypothermia, landslides, unstable terrain, and risk of drowning. **Portland Hikers** (www.portlandhikers.org) is a good resource for information on terrain, seasons, and safety tips.

Fishing

If you would like to take in some fishing, there's no better spot to head than **Lost Lake** (www.lostlakeresort.org). On the north side of the mountain, this is a place of quiet serenity where motorboats are never allowed. The best fishing is along the shores, where aquatic insects are most prevalent and the lake's population of rainbow trout and steelhead appear, trying to snatch a meal. There are no fees for using the lake or its surrounding forested areas, but a license is required for anglers over 14 years of age.

HOTELS

Accommodations abound up in the mountains, whether you are looking for a cozy cottage or a stately lodge. **Timberline Lodge** (27500 E. Timberline Rd., Government Camp, 503/272-3104, www.timberlinelodge.com, $110-290) is easily one of the most iconic lodgings in Government Camp. Rooms vary from positively dorm-like chalet rooms with bunk beds and bathrooms down the hall to lofty private suites that sleep as many as eight people.

Right next to the Ice Axe and Mt. Hood Brewing Company, **Best Western Mt. Hood Inn** (87450 E. Government Camp Loop, Government Camp, 503/272-3205, www.mthoodinn.com, $109-209) is an affordable way to avoid the big lodge but still be close to all the action. Resembling a hotel more than an inn, Mt. Hood Inn has three room types, from the basic deluxe room to the king spa room, which rents for as little as $129 a night. There's an indoor public Jacuzzi on-site as well, which is nice after you've been hitting the slopes all day.

If a bed-and-breakfast is more your style, check out the **Doublegate Inn** (26711 E. Welches Rd., Welches, 503/622-0629, www.doublegateinn.com, $139-169). Every detail has been labored over here and the refurbished inn is practically oozing with cozy vibes. The rooms are beautifully appointed, and the largest features a king-size canopy bed, writing desk, full-size sofa, and a two-person soaking tub.

Also in Welches, you will also find the beautiful and modern **Resort at the Mountain** (68010 E. Fairway Ave., Welches, 503/622-3151, www.theresort.com, $129-569), a premier golf, ski, and meeting resort where you can occasionally hear the bagpipes play as they herald the sunset. The resort was remodeled in 2008 and can now accommodate couples, families, outdoors enthusiasts, meetings, and event groups. It is, of course, popular for its proximity to the slopes, but it also has two restaurants, tennis courts, 27 holes of golf, a heated outdoor swimming pool, and a professional croquet court. Families can stay in the resort's enormous two- and three-bedroom villas, both with a full kitchen and dining room area, laundry facilities, private parking, and private decks. Standard rooms at the Resort at the Mountain can only be oxymoronically described as "basic luxury," with plush memory-foam mattresses, 42-inch plasma HDTVs, terrycloth robes, and environmentally friendly products.

PRACTICALITIES
Information and Services

You can find a wealth up-to-date information about road conditions, snowfall, and weather online. For tips on travel and recreation, check out **Mt. Hood Territory** (www.mthoodterritory.com), which has maps, calendars, and recommendations on everything from activities to lodging. If you plan to take in a little Mother Nature, **Mt. Hood National Forest Headquarters** (www.fs.fed.us/r6/mthood) can provide you with maps, conditions updates, and details on permits and passes. Be sure to check with the **Oregon Department of Transportation** (www.odot.state.or.us/roads) before hitting the road to see if traction devices will be required to make it to your destination. It's also a good idea to check with the **Northwest Weather and Avalanche Center** (www.nwac.us) to be sure that conditions are safe, particularly if you plan to venture into the less-groomed areas.

All of the major ski areas have a regularly updated snow report, which will advise you on ski conditions, snow depth, and snowfall, oftentimes providing live webcams of the lifts and slopes. You can visit the **Timberline website** (www.timberlinelodge.com) or call the snow line at 503/222-2211. The same goes for **Mount Hood Meadows** (503/227-7669, www.skihood.com) and **Skibowl** (503/222-2695, www.skibowl.com).

If you plan to hike or explore the backcountry, it's a good idea to rent a Mountain Locator Unit from one of the local mountaineering and outdoor shops or from **Mt. Hood Inn** (503/272-3205, www.mthoodinn.com). The device, which is exclusive to Hood, costs about $5 to rent and is worn on a sash across the chest. When activated, it sends out radio beacons to rescuers, giving them a better chance of finding you in the event of an emergency.

Getting There and Around

From Portland, take I-84 East as it passes through some of Oregon's most scenic natural wonders, like the Columbia River Gorge and Multnomah Falls. You can opt to take the Historic Columbia River Highway for a truly spectacular picturesque drive; it will reconnect with I-84 later on. Continue on I-84 to the town of Hood River, where you can visit pretty orchards and vineyards. Next, continue on to Oregon Route 35, where you will soon connect with Highway 26, which passes through Sandy and on to Government Camp.

If conditions are poor, you might be better off skipping the scenic highways and taking the road more traveled. From I-84 East, take exit 16 (Wood Village/SE 242nd) and turn right, through the city of Gresham. Stay on SE 242nd south, and turn left onto SE Burnside, which becomes Highway 26 and passes through the small town of Sandy before continuing on to the mountain.

Sno-park permits are required for vehicles almost everywhere, including at the resorts. They are sold through various **Oregon DMV offices** (www.oregon.gov/ODOT/DMV/vehicle/sno_park_permits.shtml) and by permit agents in resorts, sporting goods stores, and other retail outlets. It will cost you about $3 a day or $20 annually.

Background

The Setting

GEOGRAPHY

Situated approximately 110 miles from the Pacific Ocean, the city of Portland lies between the Cascade Mountain Range to the east and the Coastal Range to the west. The city, which is the largest in the state and one of the chief cities in the Pacific Northwest, is divided by the Willamette River, which flows into the Columbia River just to the north.

The land in the Willamette River Valley is agriculturally productive, and for that reason, it was the desired destination of many pioneers who set out on the Oregon Trail in the 1840s. Although Portland is not often regarded as part of the Willamette Valley basin, it is well within the defining mountain ranges. Much of the area's fertility can be credited to its past, when massive ice dams in the prehistoric Glacial Lake Missoula in Montana repeatedly ruptured, each time flooding through eastern Washington and down through the Columbia River Gorge. It is estimated that during that time, much of the Willamette Valley, including Portland, was under several hundred feet of water—so much that only the West Hills, Mount Tabor, and Mount Scott were visible.

As Portland was beginning to blossom, the logging industry dominated the economy, and around 1847, the city experienced a growth so major that developers decided that they needed more roads to encourage trade and to compete with the elder trading post upstream, Oregon City. Unfortunately, they discovered that as they cut down trees to make roads, the labor needed to remove the stumps was stiflingly inadequate, forcing work crews to leave the arboreal remains until workers could address them. To prevent wagon accidents and stumbling, locals began painting the stumps white for visibility, which aided pedestrians in traversing the notoriously muddy landscape and earned the city the nickname Stumptown.

Despite its distance from the waters of the Pacific, Portland has one of the busiest ports on the West Coast, as ocean shipments can reach the city by way of the Columbia and Willamette Rivers. There are also two interstate highways, several freight railways, and rail transit systems that serve the city, and numerous domestic airlines that fly through Portland International Airport.

By car, Portland is only 45 minutes from Salem, the state capital, 1.5 hours from the ski slopes of Mount Hood, two hours from the Pacific Ocean, and about 3.5 hours to Seattle, Washington, or the Great Basin high-desert plateau in Bend, Oregon. But even within the city limits, Mother Nature is rarely more than five minutes or five blocks away. There are a number of botanical gardens, rose gardens, and arboretums; Forest

Previous: dancers perform during Pica's T:BA Festival; the Aerial Tram.

Park, with its 5,000 acres of alder, fir, cottonwood, maple, and yew trees, is the largest wilderness park within a city in the United States.

CLIMATE

The weather in Portland is usually quite mild thanks to the White Mountains to the northwest, which keep snow from reaching the metro area and the temperatures moderate. Fog and rain showers are common, but contrary to popular belief, it doesn't rain all the time. In fact, Portland receives about half of its annual rainfall between November and February. All told, it rains about 36-42 inches per year, with December and January being the wettest months.

The summer months are often mild and pleasant, with temperatures that rarely top 90°F, a climate that often continues into the early months of fall. Winter begins late and usually extends into March, with one or two cold snaps that can last several days.

ANIMALS AND INSECTS

Of course, Oregon is the Beaver State, and while the state mascot is currently under environmental protection, you can still find the beaver in Pacific Northwest streams and rivers, along with its cousins, the muskrat and nutria. Within the city itself you're more likely to see squirrels, chipmunks, raccoons, opossums, frogs, skunks, and the occasional mouse, garter snake, rat, or bat. Step into the wilderness of one of the parks or wildlife refuges and you might see deer, rabbits, otters, turtles, or possibly even a cougar or coyote.

Portland is heaven for bird-watchers, and the city's numerous trees are populated by pigeons, blue jays, swallows, crows, hummingbirds, starlings, thrushes, warblers, woodpeckers, and wrens. When the weather is stormy at the coast, it's not uncommon for seagulls to come inland for a little respite, and when they get a little curious, it is not unusual for owls to set up residency in the rafters of a large building (such as the Oaks Amusement Park carousel) or home.

As far as pests and insects go, Portland is low on the radar. There are, of course, house flies, mosquitoes, honey bees, wasps, ladybugs, butterflies, and moths, all of which are small in comparison to the size they achieve in the southern and northeastern United States. Most of the spiders are harmless, and those that aren't (like the black widow) are extremely rare.

Symbols of the Oregon Spirit

- **Bird:** The medium-size blackbird with a distinctive yellow belly is known as the **western meadowlark,** a state symbol shared with Kansas, Nebraska, Wyoming, North Dakota, and Montana. Portland has its own symbolic bird, the **great blue heron,** which can be spotted in some of the wetlands and nature conservatories.

- **Animal:** The industrious **American beaver** is right at home in a state known for logging, but the semi-aquatic rodent is considered a pest in some parts of the world.

- **Flower:** The **Oregon grape** is an evergreen shrub that has pretty yellow flowers in late spring that form into clusters of purple berries that resemble grapes. They may look tasty, and the birds sure like them, but don't be tempted to try them yourself. While not poisonous, they are extremely tart. Portland's city flower is, of course, the **rose.**

- **Tree:** The hills and parks of Oregon are abundant with **Douglas firs,** the second-tallest conifer in the world (second only to redwoods). The tree commonly lives for 500 years and sometimes as long as 1,000.

- **Fish:** The **chinook salmon** is born in freshwater and may spend anywhere between one and eight years in the Pacific Ocean before returning to its birth waters to spawn. The fish was a highly valued part of Native American culture.

- **Rock:** Similar to geodes, **thunder eggs** are formed within rhyolitic lava flows. They look like plain Jane baseball-shaped rocks on the outside, but once split in half and polished, they reveal pretty layers of agate, jasper, and opal.

- **Nut:** In 2008, Oregon produced 34,000 tons of **hazelnuts.** These popular

History

LEWIS AND CLARK AND THE EARLY SETTLERS

As Meriwether Lewis and William Clark neared the Pacific Coast goal of their epic expedition across the United States, they were struck by the splendor of the region that would one day become Portland. But long before their journey would begin, Oregon was home to a number of Native American tribes. The mild climate and abundance of fish, game, and wildlife, coupled with the wealth of water sources—not the least of which are the Willamette River and the mighty Columbia—made the Willamette Valley a very rich area indeed. Native tribes such as the Multnomah and Clackamas based their entire economies and cultures upon the land and the water. Nearby Celilo Falls, for example, was a tribal fishing area on the Columbia River

nuts are not only quite tasty, they are also a superfood, rich in protein and unsaturated fat with significant amounts of thiamine, vitamin B6, and fiber.

- **Mushroom:** The delicious **Pacific golden chanterelle** is distinguished by its fluted martini glass shape, apricot smell, and mild peppery taste. They commonly grow under pine, beech, or birch trees and can be found from July until the first frosts.

- **Fruit:** Superior growing conditions in the Hood River Valley make it the top **pear** producer in the United States. The Anjou pear, in particular, thrives in the warm sunny days and crisp, cool nights.

- **Beverage:** The Oregon dairy industry contributes over $600 million to the state's economy, so it's no surprise that **milk** takes top honors in the beverage department, although there is a push right now to make beer the statewide drink.

- **Dance:** We all did it in gym class, do-si-do-ing with that awkward kid who had two left feet. But the **square dance** reflects on Oregon's pioneer heritage, and the friendly, spirited nature of it was deemed a part of the Oregon character.

- **Motto:** The Latin phrase *Alis Volat Propriis,* which means "She Flies with Her Own Wings," was adopted in 1854, was replaced about one hundred years later, and then readopted in 1967 to reflect the state's independent spirit. Portland has its own motto, **"The City That Works."**

- **Song:** The state song, *"Oregon, My Oregon,"* was written for a contest in 1920 by John Andrew Buchanan and Henry Bernard Murtagh. The first verse honors the early settlers and the pioneers of the Oregon Trail. The second praises the natural beauty of the land.

close to what is now the border between the Oregon and Washington. This area, called Wyam after the tribe that inhabited it, was a hub of activity for fishing and trading that Lewis and Clark called a "great emporium . . . where all the neighboring nations assemble," until the completion of the nearby Dalles Dam flooded the falls and the neighboring village.

PETTYGROVE AND LOVEJOY'S LEGENDARY COIN TOSS

Portland wouldn't be what it is today if not for the collective $0.26 of Asa Lovejoy and Francis Pettygrove. Back in 1843, a Tennessee pioneer named William Overton and a Massachusetts lawyer named Asa Lovejoy steered their canoe down the Willamette River from Fort Vancouver toward Oregon City and stopped on the banks of what was then known as The Clearing. Knowing that a city would have to be established near the convergence of the Willamette and Columbia Rivers, Overton was certain that establishing a claim on the land would be a lucrative endeavor. Sadly, he lacked the $0.25 required to file a land claim. Fortunately for Overton (and all the rest of us), Lovejoy made a deal with him. Lovejoy would pay the fee and in exchange share the 640-acre site with Overton. This suited Overton just fine and he set about building a homestead on what added up to about 16 blocks of land, but after a year, Overton decided to leave Oregon behind and depart for Texas. So, he sold his share of the claim to Pettygrove and the city as we know it began to evolve.

When the founders of this budding city discussed what to name it, however, they hit a snag. Pettygrove wanted to name the city after his hometown of Portland, Maine, and Lovejoy thought it only proper to name it after his home of Boston, Massachusetts. They agreed to flip a coin, and after heads came up two of the three times the penny was tossed, Pettygrove had won. The coin used in this legendary meeting has come to be known as "the Portland Penny" and is currently on display at the Oregon Historical Society.

PORTLAND'S NOT-SO-PRETTY PAST

As the city grew into a lively port town, so did the traffic of ne'er-do-wells. By the late 19th century, a constant influx of sailors, loggers, sheepherders, ranch hands, and vagabonds meant a growing need for saloons and boardinghouses. Sadly, even the most practical intentions soon fell victim to vice. Brothels and opium dens began to spring up all over town, and visiting them often led to robbery, kidnapping, or death. One notorious tradeswoman of the time was simply known as Sweet Mary. Mary cleverly avoided the usual legalities of owning a brothel by housing hers on a barge that floated to whichever quadrant of the city offered the least attention from the law. The police and vice squads couldn't do much about it since her placement on the river meant that she wasn't officially under anyone's jurisdiction.

It was during that time, however, that Portland's more notorious reputation developed, as it came to be known as the "Unheavenly City" or the "Forbidden City." Despite the fact that the United States Constitution had declared slavery illegal, countless intoxicated or naive men came to Portland only to be kidnapped or tricked into captivity and sold into slave labor on merchant ships.

Throughout much of downtown, particularly in Old Town, there is a maze of underground tunnels that were used to trap and transport unsuspecting souls to their doom. There was money in it for the sort of guy who was willing to swindle, drug, or beat his victims into submission—and no one was more notorious for it than Joseph "Bunco" Kelly. Legend has it that Bunco once swiped a wooden statue from a local cigar shop and sold it to a ship's captain as a drunken sailor. During Prohibition, bars that wanted to allow patrons to drink and gamble moved their operation to the tunnels, which provided some protection from the law, but only served to increase the possibility of capture.

Still to this day, there are hints of Portland's disreputable past, such as trap doors leading to bars, human-sized holding cells, mysterious artifacts, and rumors of ghosts inhabiting the underground tunnels, a veritable warren of deception and despair.

THE McMENAMIN KINGDOM

In addition to owning nearly 60 brewpubs, microbreweries, music venues, historic hotels, and theater pubs, Mike and Brian McMenamin are rather like historians. A number of their restaurants, pubs, and hotels are salvaged historical buildings that have colorful pasts as mortuaries, poor farms, vaudeville houses, churches, and elementary schools. The "McBrothers" have a reputation for breathing new life into buildings that would have otherwise met with a wrecking ball, while still holding on to the venues' original charms. Given the nature of their business, the brothers take history pretty seriously, and their kingdom (as they call it) employs a full-time historian to dig up and preserve stories, like that of a prostitute killed by her jealous lover at the White Eagle Motel, or that of the Zakojis, a family of Japanese immigrants who owned Hotel Louie long before it became a notorious bathhouse.

PORTLAND TODAY

Looking around Portland today, you can see that the city is changing, because somehow, the city never lost its pioneering roots or its desire to build or re-create something from nothing. Early efforts in city planning from some of the city's founders ensured that there would always be plenty of green space even in the most urbanized areas. That is why there are big parks, small parks, tree-lined streets, and rooftop gardens all over the city. Some of these spaces are meant for play and some for reflection, but all encompass that need to mix the Pacific Northwest love of nature with a need for growth and progress. Whether it's dogs scampering through the off-leash area of Overlook Park, kids splashing through the fountain at Jamison Square, or a performance of *King Lear* under the trees in Laurelhurst Park, these green spaces are valuable and well used.

The city has also seen quite a bit of urban development of late. In the 1980s, the Pearl District was little more than abandoned warehouses and railroad tracks. Today it's a bustling neighborhood full of world-class restaurants and more galleries than you can shake a paintbrush at. Mississippi Avenue was falling into disrepair before an influx of creative youthful energy turned it into an artsy, eco-focused, and affectionate community. The same can be said for the Alberta Arts District, but perhaps on a much grander scale. Spread throughout the city there are neighborhoods that, despite being interconnected, bear a personality and style all their own. In every district, there are funky, unique, and elegant shops, top-notch restaurants, and stylish bars. Getting to all those neighborhoods is a snap, since the transportation system has evolved along with the city—a little more each year, with the streetcar, light rail, and bus system providing yet more car-free access to the metro area. Since the transportation system was built around the idea of urban growth and city planning, it has thus far been a pretty happy marriage.

Cycling is hugely encouraged and supported throughout the city with bike lanes, paths, and parks that often lead to vantage points where, on a clear day, sparkling water and distant mountains are an awesome sight to behold.

The locals, for the most part, are very friendly and willing to point you toward the best cup of coffee, plate of fries, or hamburger in town, but their opinions are likely to vary as much as the weather. One thing is certain, however: Portlanders are all about self-expression, self-sufficiency, and the pursuit of the next best story. It might be about that amazing gnocchi from that shop down the street, the next project we are working on, or that artist we met while touring First Thursday. Every experience seems to be treated as if it is ripe with possibility. That is why chef-owned restaurants are so much more common than franchises and why you will find them around almost every corner. Almost all of them pride themselves on using local fresh ingredients and tailoring the menu to what's in season.

Government and Economy

GOVERNMENT

The city of Portland leans largely to the left of the political scale. In 2009, there were 341,962 registered voters and 206,412 of those were Democrats. The city as a whole tends to be fairly progressive, with the mayor, four city commissioners, and a city auditor at the helm. In fact, Portland's system of government is one of the few things it is not progressive about as a city. Of all the large cities in the United States, Portland has the last remaining commission form of government. Under the commission structure, the officials elected to represent Portland constitute the legislative body of the city and are, as a group, responsible for taxation, appropriations, ordinances, and other general functions. Each commissioner is assigned a responsibility to one aspect of municipal affairs, like public works, public affairs, or public safety. All city officials, including the mayor, are elected to serve four-year terms, with elections being spaced out every two years so as not to inadvertently fill a council with inexperienced members.

The mayor and city commissioners make up the city council, which carries out its duties in accordance with the laws of the state and the Portland City Code and Charter, and are primarily responsible for making laws that govern the city of Portland. And while the council is accountable for legislative policy and for keeping Portland running like a well-oiled machine, the auditor keeps the council in line with the system of checks and balances. Both city and state law allow Portlanders the right to initiate legislation through the proper processes or even to refer legislation that has passed through city council to a vote of the people.

ECONOMY

Early in its history, Portland's economy was largely dependent on the rivers that flowed through it. The Willamette and Columbia Rivers provided access to the Pacific Ocean, and their deep waters meant that the city was well placed to become a nucleus for logging, farming, and fishing. When the city was selected as the West Coast terminal for the U.S. mailing ship *The Petonia,* it seemed like the city was well on its way to becoming a major part of the nation's economy. But disaster struck in 1873, when a fire reduced 22 downtown blocks and parts of Chinatown to ashes. To add insult to injury, another fire had occurred just eight months earlier when anti-Chinese arsonists set ablaze three city blocks, with a loss estimated at about $2 million. Despite the devastation, the city began to rebuild, this time with only cast iron, brick, and stone. By the turn of the 20th century, the construction of the transcontinental railroad that linked Portland to the East Coast caused the population to swell to 90,000 people.

Today, the city's economy is quite different, and the technology and research industries are leading the pack. In fact, Intel, Providence Health Systems, and Oregon Health and Sciences University are the city's top employers, followed at a distance by Fred Meyer, the Kaiser Foundation, and Legacy Health System. Despite having significant layoffs in the early part of 2009, the health and tech industries continue to dominate the economy for the entire state and the Portland metro area in particular. Even within those fields there has long been a focus on utilizing sustainable practices whenever possible and devising eco-action plans when practices weren't readily available. For a long time, this focus on the environment gave Portlanders a reputation for being tree-hugging hippies, but now that the city is poised to become the leader in green technology and sustainable practices, things are looking even brighter. Cities all over the world are turning to Portland to find out how they can conserve energy and resources without diminishing their way of life.

In the late 2000s, former mayor Sam Adams and the city council made a push to develop a new economic strategy to brand Portland as the nation's most sustainable city; the city's residents followed in stride. The program included economic incentives and training for workers in targeted industries (health, technology, manufacturing), and set up Portland as a "city to watch" in the global green economy.

Top: Portland's City Hall. **Bottom:** the Willamette River

People and Culture

In 2011, the population of the state of Oregon was estimated at 3,970,239. Of those, about 19 percent lived in Multnomah County—the smallest of Oregon's 36 counties—which encompasses Portland, Gresham, Fairview, Troutdale, Wood Village, and portions of Lake Oswego. In the same year, Portland's population swelled to 619,360, marking a 6 percent increase in the past four years alone, a statistic that outpaced the national average for population growth.

The median age for Portland metro area residents is 35, with 46 percent of the population aged 15-44 and 14 percent of residents over 60. It has been said that Portland is "the whitest city in America," and while the statement is a bit hyperbolic, it is not far off. As of the latest census estimate, the city is about 76 percent Caucasian, 6.3 percent African American, 7.1 percent Asian or Pacific Islander, and 9.4 percent Hispanic.

Portland frequently makes the list of top cities to find single men in a number of online and print publications. This claim is often based less on demographics (which is almost evenly split between men and women), and more on Portland's status as a destination for the youthful creative class. More and more, people are coming to Portland to work and live life outside of the lines. Creative types like artists, chefs and even engineers and scientists have been lured by the city's tolerant, off-center way of life, and their presence has had a lasting effect on the economy, the lexicon, and the overall personality of the city. The city has long been called a "big small town" because it is easy to meet people and also quite easy to find solitude. People tend to be easygoing, helpful, and more focused on the success of the community than on individual success.

CHINATOWN

Chinese immigrants have been in Portland almost as long as the city founders, and most were brought here to build bridges, tunnels, and railroad beds, and to work in the mines, salmon canneries, and textile industries. The numbers in Portland continued to grow each year between 1850 and the early part of the 1880s despite the Chinese Exclusion Act, which was the first federal law to ever be passed banning an ethnic group from entry into the United States based on the fear that they would be an endangerment to the public. In 1885 and 1886, however, the population of Chinese immigrants mushroomed due to the expulsion of immigrants from Seattle, Tacoma, and Olympia in neighboring Washington. At the time, the Pacific Northwest was facing an economic downturn, and the Chinese were blamed for taking jobs away from Americans and driving the average wage down. Although the city of Portland had not yet chosen to expel the Chinese, the immigrants were forced from outer communities into what was essentially a ghetto, an area that was notorious for kidnappings (through the Shanghai Tunnels), opium dens, and brothels. While Chinatown had those less attractive qualities, the neighborhood also had a strong sense of community, with barbershops, grocery stores, schools, and restaurants.

Today, Chinatown residents and property owners are struggling to overcome the neighborhood's reputation as a haven for crime, homelessness, and drug abuse, and they are also struggling to maintain a sense of community. With proposed development that includes large-scale grocery stores and higher-end restaurants, the proponents of Chinatown are eager for the opportunity to clean up the streets but cautious about a development plan that might force out the very families and businesses that have maintained the spirit of Chinatown.

AFRICAN AMERICAN CULTURE

Ask most locals about the earliest recorded history of African American culture in Portland and you are likely to get a variety of answers. What most people don't realize is that there was an African American community that thrived as far back as the early 1900s, near the spot where Union Station still stands today. Job opportunities at the railroads stimulated a small population growth within Portland's African American community. People came from all over the United States, and particularly the South, as part of the Great Migration to work as Pullman porters, Red Caps, cooks, waiters, and shop laborers. The Portland Hotel, which was located at the present site of Pioneer Courthouse Square, was another big draw. More than 70 African American men were brought up from the Carolinas and Georgia to work in the hotel at service positions for what would become a major hub of the city's business and social activity.

Between 1850 and 1900, Portland's African American population increased from about a dozen to 775—not a staggering number, but enough to support two churches, a handful of businesses, and a newspaper. Along with those newcomers came a hardworking sense of spirit and a community alive with barbershops, restaurants, pool halls, haberdasheries, and hotels. On Sundays, the Golden West Hotel, which was owned by an African American man named W. D. Allen, became a gathering spot of sorts when services at the nearby Mt. Olivet Baptist and Bethel AME churches let out. Dressed in their Sunday best, people would congregate in the Chinese restaurant, Turkish bath, barbershop, gambling room, gymnasium, and ice cream parlor and share stories.

In the early part of the 1900s, the African American community faced less discrimination than it would come to see in later years. In 1906, African American people were allowed to vote and serve as jurors. African American children shared classrooms with Caucasian children, and both sat side-by-side in restaurants. In 1894, Charles Hardin became the first African American man to join the police force, and by 1915, he was the first African American man to be made sheriff's deputy. When work was scarce, many African American men began to explore the opportunity of owning a small business and in turn began to shop in and patronize only community-owned businesses as a means of economic survival. For many

Talk Like a Local

If there is one thing that will mark you as a tourist (a term sometimes even applied to people who have lived in Portland for several years), it's the mispronunciation of several key words and phrases. A Portlander may not correct you if you get their name wrong, but call the state "Oree-Gone" and you are likely to get an earful. Here are a few phrases and tips on how to speak like a native.

- **Aloha:** This suburb of Beaverton is just a few miles west of Portland and far from the Hawaiian islands. Unlike the island greeting, the name of this community is pronounced *ah-LO-wa*.

- **ART:** This is the acronym for Artists Repertory Theatre. However, if you say "art" when referring to the theater, everyone will know you are either a neophyte in the arts or that you aren't from around here. It's *A-R-T*.

- **Clackamas:** This is the name of a Native American tribe that once inhabited this area, and is now one of the major Oregon counties. It is pronounced *CLACK-uh-mas*.

- **Couch Street:** We're not talking about furniture. This street is named after John H. Couch, one of the city founders. It is pronounced *COOCH*, which rhymes with pooch.

- **Eugene:** The city to the south is referred to as *yoo-JEEN*, not *YOO-jeen*.

- **Glisan Street:** This street in Northwest and Northeast Portland was named for Dr. Rodney Glisan, a doctor for the U.S. Army in the 19th century. The good doctor's name was pronounced *GLISS-an*, but for reasons unbeknownst, the street name is pronounced *GLEE-san*.

- **Marquam:** It's a double-decker bridge in Portland named after Philip Marquam, a state legislator and Multnomah County judge. It's pronounced *MARK-um*.

- **Multnomah:** It's a county, a waterfall, and a Native American tribe, and pronounced *mult-NO-muh*.

- **OMSI:** The acronym for Oregon Museum of Science and Industry is treated like a word, *AHM-zee*, and almost never pronounced in full.

- **Oregon:** There are only two acceptable pronunciations: *OR-uh-gun* and *OR-ee-gun*—and the last one is pushing it.

- **Sauvie Island:** This pretty area about 10 miles northwest of Portland boasts a number of U-pick farms and a wildlife refuge, and is alternately referred to as *SAW-vee* or *SO-vee*.

- **Schuyler Street:** This Northeast Portland street can claim that it is loaded with beautiful historic homes, but it can't claim that it rhymes with "ruler." In fact, the street name is pronounced *SKY-ler*.

- **Tigard:** This suburb of Portland is not a buddy of Winnie-the-Pooh. It's pronounced *TIE-gard*.

- **Weidler:** The street in Northeast Portland is pronounced *WIDE-ler*.

- **Willamette:** This word comes up a lot. Whether you are referring to the river that divides the city, the alternative weekly newspaper, or a number of other things, it is pronounced *wil-LAM-met*.

years, it worked. By 1920, 8 percent of Portland's African American community owned or operated their own business, a statistic that was almost unheard of at the time.

But the tide began to turn as more European immigrants began to settle in Portland. Housing discrimination forced most African Americans to settle near the industrial area on the east side of the Broadway Bridge, where you will now find Memorial Coliseum and the Rose Quarter. The Great Depression, too, was devastating to the African American community. Within a year, most of the African American-owned businesses were forced to close their doors, including the Golden West Hotel. Jobs became even more difficult to come by, with racial tensions rising every day.

Today, little remains of the area that was once so alive with the city's first African American leaders. The Golden West Hotel still stands, but now serves as transitional housing for homeless, mentally ill individuals. The African American community is largely centered in the Albina area, which includes the Boise, Concordia, Eliot, Humboldt, Piedmont, Sabin, Vernon, King, Alberta, and Woodlawn neighborhoods. In many of those neighborhoods, the threat of gentrification has spurred conflict and conversation. The liberal-minded tendencies of Portlanders help a little, but even the best of intentions can have negative results. It's a bit of an uphill battle, but the city and organizations like the Urban League of Portland and National Association for the Advancement of Colored People (NAACP) are doing what they can to preserve the community and promote equality, and encourage a healthy rate of growth and development.

THE LGBT COMMUNITY

The city of Portland has long had an active gay community, and has one of the strongest feminist and lesbian communities in the United States. The history of the community dates back to World War II, when the city received countless traffic in and out of town from lonely soldiers, sailors, and war industry workers away from their families and friends. During that time, though the gay and lesbian community was still fairly closeted, the beer parlors, vaudeville houses, bars, and hotels were willing to look the other way while same-sex curiosities were explored and thrived. One such spot, the Music Hall, became a popular hangout for lesbians and was known to put on a pretty remarkable drag show. The club received a lot of attention when sin-busting mayor Dorothy McCullough Lee (1949–1953) attacked it most vociferously with liquor license queries and investigations. She did not succeed in shutting the venue down, but did manage to drive the drag act out of town.

At that time, there were gay rights organizations popping up all over the West Coast in major cities like Seattle and San Francisco, but Portland had no such movement toward encouraging pride and establishing rights. In spite of the community's lack of effort, however, gay men and lesbian women continued to flock to the more laissez-faire Portland after being chased out of other cities. In fact, the Portland police department tended to leave suspected gay hangouts alone. When Commissioner Stanley Earl wanted to shut down the Harbor Club in the late 1950s, it was the police who talked him out of it, suggesting that it was better to have homosexuals gathered in one place rather than scattered throughout the city.

Things reached a bit of a boiling point in 1964 when the papers began to run numerous headlines about "homosexual rings" that preyed upon children. Mayor Terry Schrunk was determined to crack down on bars that catered to gay men and lesbians, and formed the Committee for Decent Literature and Films to stop the production of publications that depicted homosexual activity. That summer, an *Oregon Journal* columnist stated to the police that the "unmentionables" were numerous in Portland, and that the number of gay and lesbian bars had inflated from three to ten. He assured the police that some local businessmen promised to take "vigilante action" against them in order to restore the civility of the city. Also that year, the Portland City Council asked the Oregon Liquor Control Commission (OLCC) to revoke the liquor licenses of all the city's suspected gay and lesbian bars. The licenses were revoked but quickly renewed when the OLCC admitted that the bars were operating within the law. After that, the city and the police department were largely unmotivated to continue pressuring the gay and lesbian venues. Throughout the tough periods in the 1960s, Portland still did not have much in the way of activism for the gay and lesbian community, but there was little need for it. Portland was essentially wide open.

The LGBT community in Portland these days is far more active, and the complacency about citywide or nationwide activism seems to have worn off. Organizations like the Portland Area Business Alliance, Basic Rights Oregon, Northwest Gender Alliance, and the Q Center are working overtime to ensure that the city stays "wide open," but smartly so. In 2008, the election of Mayor Sam Adams, the first openly gay mayor of a major American city, sparked a lot of attention and further confirmed Portland as a gay-friendly city.

But there are other reasons why the city is so attractive to the gay community. The city is socially conscious and progressive, with organizations that offer everything from financial to emotional support, HIV/AIDS education and assistance, and networking opportunities and social activities. Portland also offers domestic partnership registration. While Multnomah County made a decision in 2004 to allow such unions, it wasn't until the passage of the Oregon Family Fairness Act in 2007 and its subsequent signing by Governor Kulongoski that the domestic partnership system was made legal by the state of Oregon. Under that ruling, same-sex couples are now allowed to enjoy many of the things that they would have otherwise been denied, like hospital information, mortgage loans, and parental rights.

EDUCATION

Oregon students historically exceed national averages for math and verbal on their Scholastic Aptitude Test (SAT) scores. For dozens of years, Oregon

P-Town Catchphrases

There are so many nicknames for Portland, it's hard to keep track of them all. The city also has a number of catchphrases that are helpful to know so you don't get confused if someone asks you if you have seen "Big Pink."

- **Beervana:** With all the fantastic microbreweries and artisan beermakers in town, this designation makes sense. Portland is a beer lover's heaven.

- **The Benson Bubblers:** Those public drinking fountains you see on the street corners were named for philanthropist Simon Benson. And in case you were wondering, it is safe to drink from them. The water comes from the same municipal source as the rest of the city's drinking water and is not recycled back into the fountain.

- **Big Pink:** This term refers to the 43-story boxy pink building at SW 5th Avenue and Burnside Street.

- **Bridgetown:** Eleven bridges keep Portland cars, buses, bikes, and people moving.

- **Brewery Blocks:** The former site of the Blitz-Weinhard brewery, this Pearl District area is a five-block shopping and professional district that still houses a number of brewpubs.

- **The City of Roses:** The city comes by this nickname naturally. People figured out a long time ago that Portland has the ideal climate for growing roses. It wasn't long before the International Rose Test Garden was established and an annual festival was planned to celebrate this fact.

one of downtown's Benson Bubblers

- **Lake O:** This refers to Lake Oswego, an affluent suburb south of the city.

- **Little Beirut:** Portland has always been pretty blue, politically speaking, and when President George H. W. Bush visited the city in the early 1990s, he was met with so many protesters that he and his staff dubbed the city Little Beirut.

- **NoPo:** This term refers to North Portland. A number of other neighborhoods have tried to adopt this method of nicknaming (SoWa for the South Waterfront, FoPo for Foster-Powell), but NoPo is the only one that has really caught on.

- **PDX:** Yes, it is the airport code for the city, but it is also a well-recognized shorthand epithet.

- **Pill Hill:** This is Oregon Health and Sciences University, which looms above the city in Portland's west hills.

- **Pod:** A group of food carts, oftentimes occupying a whole city block.

- **Puddletown:** With 36-40 inches of rain per year, this name is self-explanatory.

- **Rip City:** Thank basketball announcer Bill Schonely for this nickname. The play-by-play man was known for his creative exclamations during the Trail Blazers games, and this one became a rallying cry for the team and eventually a city moniker.

- **The Schnitz:** Slang for the Arlene Schnitzer Concert Hall.

- **Snob Hill:** This term affectionately refers to Nob Hill, or the shopping districts on NW 21st and NW 23rd Avenues.

- **Stumptown:** This nickname was first meant as an insult when the forested landscape was rapidly stripped to make way for growth. The stumps were not cleared and became hazards when traveling through the mud or dark. Eventually, the stumps were painted white, which made for a scene that rather resembled a graveyard.

- **The Sunset Highway:** A lovely name for the road that jams up bumper-to-bumper during rush hour each weekday, otherwise known as Highway 26 West.

- **Zoobombers:** These daredevils take a weekly wild ride down the hills of Washington Park on kiddie bicycles that they carry with them on the MAX to the Oregon Zoo stop. It is not intended to be an aggressive act, and the Zoobombers are mostly regarded with bemusement. There's a sculpture on the corner of 13th and West Burnside where the participants stack their bikes with joyful abandon.

and Washington have held the top two positions among the 23 states that test at least 50 percent of their high school graduates. There are more than 600 schools and 21 districts within the Portland metro area, and a number of secular and religiously affiliated private schools at the primary, secondary, and high school levels.

The Portland metropolitan area is richly endowed with educational resources, including some of the best colleges in the nation. It is a bit of a chicken and egg question because it is hard to define which came first, the prevalence of smart, creative, and educated citizens, or the schools to entice them here. Whatever the cause, Portland boasts a number of colleges, universities, and trade schools.

Portland State University (PSU) is a public university in the heart of downtown and the fastest-growing school in the Oregon University System. At the outset, PSU was mainly a liberal arts college, but the university has since added doctorates in mathematics, biology, chemistry, computer science, applied psychology, engineering and technology management, mechanical engineering, and sociology. Since the university is located in an urban area, traditional college housing is fairly limited, but there are affordable apartments in the area. PSU is part of the Big Sky Conference and its mascot is the Viking. The Viking football team got a lot of attention when Jerry Glanville, who coached for 21 years in the NFL, became the 12th head coach in the history of the Portland State program.

In Southeast Portland, **Reed College** is a private, independent, liberal arts college known for its disproportionately high number of graduates who go one to earn their master's degree and/or PhD. The university has a distinct reputation for liberal, progressive, and anti-establishment leanings. In order to graduate, all students have to complete an intense year-long thesis project that will eventually become a part of the college's permanent research library. Upon completion of the senior thesis (which usually culminates in the form of a "thesis parade"), students must also pass an oral exam that focuses on their thesis but may also include questions about any course previously taken. The official mascot of Reed College is the Griffin, but the unofficial mascot is the legendary Doyle Owl, a roughly 280-pound concrete bird that has been continuously stolen and re-stolen since 1913.

Lewis and Clark College is a private, liberal arts school in Southwest Portland that offers degrees in arts and sciences, law, and education and counseling. The students who attend Lewis and Clark are often globally minded, environmentally conscious thinkers, so it was no surprise when the college became the first campus in the country to comply with the Kyoto Protocol's emission targets in 2003, and just two years later became the first private institution in Oregon to sign the Talloires Declaration, a 10-point action plan created in France for incorporating sustainability and environmental literacy in teaching, research, operations, and outreach at colleges and universities.

The **University of Portland** (UP) is a private Roman Catholic university located in North Portland. It is affiliated with the Congregation of Holy Cross and is a sister school to the University of Notre Dame. It is the only school in the state that offers a college of arts and sciences; a graduate school; and schools of business, education, engineering, and nursing in one location. The UP mascot is the Portland Pilot, and the women's soccer team received a lot of recognition when they won the 2002 and 2005 Division I NCAA Women's Soccer Championships.

Two other smaller, religiously affiliated colleges in the city seem to draw a lot of students to the city. **Concordia University** in Northeast Portland is a small Lutheran college with an enrollment that tops out at around 1,700 students each year. Though it is a private college, it is open to students of any faith who wish to pursue any of the 18 undergraduate majors. **Warner Pacific College** is a private liberal arts school in Southeast Portland that is affiliated with The Church of God and offers 19 majors, four areas of preprofessional study, and 25 minors for traditional students and adults seeking to further their education later in life.

Of course, given the city's love of art and food, it's no surprise that Portland has three colleges of art: **The Art Institute of Portland, Oregon College of Art and Craft,** and **Pacific Northwest College of Art.** A culinary school, **Western Culinary Institute,** is considered to be top-notch.

The city also happens to have a world-class teaching hospital and research center that draws in students, scientists, and patients from across the country and around the world. **Oregon Health and Sciences University** currently has five schools in medicine, nursing, dentistry, science and engineering, and pharmacy and is the only place in Oregon that grants doctoral degrees in medicine, nursing, and dentistry.

HEALTH CARE

The state of the health-care system in Portland is a hot-button issue, and for a while, Oregon had the fastest-growing rate of uninsured constituents in the nation. The downturn in the economy had some effect on that, and so did the influx of wealthy retirees and out-of-state transplants, who have driven a deeper wedge between the haves and the have nots. While there was and still is some animosity about the increased gentrification of older Portland neighborhoods and the accompanied increase in cost of living, locals and city officials are attempting creative solutions to ensure that all Portlanders are protected from the rising cost of medical care. Oregonians who do not have easy access to health care often visit boutique same-day medical clinics and pay out of pocket, utilize community services, or take advantage of the medical and dental schools at Oregon Health and Sciences University.

Portlanders love a good festival, particularly if it celebrates beer, bikes, music, or that favorite local pastime—devouring delicious treats. Late spring and early summer is festival season, when throughout the city, you can hear the twang of a band warming up, feel the hum of the parade passing by, and smell the waffle cones toasting. In fact, if you listen carefully, you'll hear the faint "shhhhhh" of a new keg being tapped.

But we're not exactly sitting on our thumbs through the winter waiting for the sun. With venues like the Oregon Convention Center, the Expo Center, and the Rose Quarter, Portland has plenty of places to celebrate the bounties of the region, no matter what time of year it is.

SPRING

CINCO DE MAYO FESTIVAL

The largest **Cinco de Mayo Festival** (Waterfront Park, www.cincodemayo.org; $8 adults, $4 seniors and children, free for children under 6) in North America heats up in the first days of May with all the colors, cuisine, arts, music, and folklore of Mexico—more specifically, Guadalajara, Portland's sister city. The four-day fiesta usually kicks off bright and early with a ribbon-cutting ceremony followed by a naturalization ceremony. After that, it's time to enjoy all manner of music, food, and entertainment and a magnificent fireworks display come nightfall. There's an interactive children's area, and Guadalajara artisans and jewelers demonstrate their crafts on-site and sell their wares.

FAUX FILM FESTIVAL

It's all about spoofs and satire at the annual **Faux Film Festival** (Hollywood Theatre, 4122 NE Sandy Blvd., www.fauxfilm.com; $7 per night) in March, where feature films and shorts from the United States, Canada, Russia, Belgium, Australia, Germany, Scotland, and the United Kingdom offer a much-needed humorous break from the daily grind. So what can you expect to see at the Hollywood Theatre during the festival? Counterfeit commercials, phony movie trailers, mockumentaries, and all manner of fake, phony, and funny stuff. The festival is basically a great big thumb in the eye of highbrow festivals like Sundance. It lasts three nights and culminates with an award show—where they hand out a bizarre mish-mash of cast-off bowling, little league, and karate trophies.

RED DRESS PARTY

What started out as a party in the basement of a North Portland home has blossomed into one of the most anticipated fundraising events to grace our city every April or May. Over the years, the annual **Red Dress Party** (various venues, www.reddresspdx.com; $75-150) has raised more than $87,000 for charities that work with youth, adults, and seniors living with HIV and AIDS. The event seeks to entertain party-goers with hosted food, beverages, red cocktails, fire spinners, and music. There's just one rule: Everyone—yes, everyone—must wear a red dress to get in.

SPRING BEER AND WINE FEST

More than 80 different beers and 25 wineries can be found at the **Spring Beer and Wine Fest** (Oregon Convention Center, 777 NE Martin Luther King Jr. Blvd., www.springbeerfest.com; $8), which turns the Oregon Convention Center into a mecca for brew connoisseurs and vino aficionados alike every March. A wide assortment of breweries—like Full Sail, Bridgeport, and Deschutes—serve up frosty mugs of their most popular hoppy concoctions, while wineries the likes of Cooper Ridge or Naked Winery will gladly pop a cork of their latest vintage for your imbibing pleasure. You will also find several local distilleries like Dry Fly and Big Bottom Whiskey offering samples of their spirits. Of course, there's food to sample as well, from barbecue to seafood—not to mention artisan cheeses, specialty chocolates, and chef's demonstrations. You must purchase souvenir beer or wine glasses and tokens to fill your glass with the beverage of your choice.

SUMMER

ART IN THE PEARL

Rounding out a Portland summer filled with as much inspiration and entertainment as can be packed into the warm months, **Art in the Pearl** (Northwest Park Blocks, between W. Burnside and NW Glisan at NW 8th Ave., www.artinthepearl.com; free) is a lovely gathering of artists, entertainers, and art lovers in the northwest Park Blocks on Labor Day weekend. Here, you can dance to world music, sample delicacies from around the globe, and check out the jury-selected work of 130 artists from across the United States and Canada. You can also work on building your art collection, as there are usually well over 100 artists showing and selling works ranging from jewelry to furniture at very reasonable prices.

THE BITE OF OREGON

In August, food lovers drop their triple cream brie and put away their reduction sauce to come out for **The Bite of Oregon** (Waterfront Park, www.biteoforegon.com; $5, free for children under 12), a festival that celebrates the bounty of fantastic restaurants, breweries, and wineries in the Northwest. Lots of great entertainment, celebrity chefs, and the annual Iron Chef Oregon competition make it worth the price of admission, but the real draw here is the plethora of food, wine, and beer. Plus, the event benefits the Special Olympics, so you're eating that deep-fried asparagus for a reason, right?

BRIDGE PEDAL

Even in bike-friendly Portland, it can be a pretty harrowing experience to navigate some city streets. Oh, the narrow bike paths, car doors swinging open, and missed signals! And that's just in the streets—never mind making your way across some of our many bridges. For one day in August, cyclists of all walks and all ages get a rare chance to ride freely over many of the bridges that span the Willamette River—including such forbidden territory as the Fremont and Marquam Bridges (which are basically freeways). **Bridge Petal** (citywide, www.providence.org/bridgepedal; $15-60, free for children under 12) is a popular event, and the city works hard to keep traffic moving in a reasonable fashion by shutting down only portions of the bridges to vehicles and only for short durations. A portion of the proceeds from the event goes to the Bicycle Transportation Alliance and to the Providence Hospital Heart and Vascular Institute.

OREGON BREWERS FESTIVAL

If there is anything we truly love in Portland, it's beer. It's no wonder, then, that we would host an entire festival in its honor every July. The annual **Oregon Brewers Festival** (Waterfront Park, www.oregonbrewfest.com; free) is regarded by many as one of the finest craft beer festivals you can find. In years past, more than 60,000 people have attended the event—and the numbers climb each year for beer lovers of all walks seeking a sampling of local favorites, new brews, and micros from all over the nation. Food is provided by local restaurants, and there's always live entertainment. Admission is usually free—unless, of course, you want to drink. A souvenir mug (required for tasting) will cost you $7, and you can buy as many $1 tokens as you'd like (but it will take about four to fill a mug).

PEDALPALOOZA BIKE FESTIVAL

Each June, the **Pedalpalooza Bike Festival** (citywide, www.shift2bikes. org; free) features an unbelievable lineup of events, ranging from family-friendly events (like a tricycle race or the Kidical Mass) to the adventuresome (like Unicycle Polo). There are even bike crawls that will take you on tours of pubs, vegan restaurants, or spoken-word joints. Or, if you really want to see a spectacle, check out Cirque du Cycling—part circus, part parade—which lights up Mississippi Avenue. Cirque du Cycling events in the past have included parades, races, biker performers, and even occasional impromptu naked rides.

PORTLAND PRIDE FESTIVAL

If you really want to see a party, head down to the waterfront in June and check out the **Portland Pride Festival** (Waterfront Park, www.pridenw.org; $7). The event is intended to encourage and celebrate the positive diversity of the lesbian, gay, bisexual, trans, and queer communities and allow an opportunity to gather together and celebrate with music, entertainment, food, demonstrations, and exhibits in Tom McCall Waterfront Park. The whole shebang lasts only one weekend and builds up to a fantastic and colorful parade through the streets of downtown on the last day of the event. If you miss that, however, there are other fun events around the city

The Rose Society

queen and princesses of the 2015 Portland Rose Festival Court

Portland's annual Rose Festival is quite the event. It's all thanks to the Rose Society, which was founded in 1888 by Georgiana Pittock, the flower-loving wife of *Uregonian* publisher Henry Pittock. But it started long before that, when in 1837, the first rose plant was brought to Oregon and presented to Anna Maria Pittman, the bride of missionary Jason Lee and the first European woman to be married, give birth, die, and be buried in Oregon. After much of the mission was destroyed by a fire years later, pioneer and legislator John Minto salvaged the rose and transported it to his home. The plant flourished in Portland's climate, and, thanks to Minto's willingness to share clippings, the city soon fell in love with the thorny beauty.

In an effort to teach and encourage amateur gardeners to plant and cultivate roses, a group of Portlanders decided to form a society, which would one day become the oldest of its kind in the United States. While the city's first rose show occurred in 1889—a tradition that is still practiced during the festival to this day—the first official Rose Festival didn't happen until 1907.

In the early days of its existence, a king, Rex Oregonus, was chosen to rule over the festival. His identity (masked by a gigantic beard) was kept secret until being revealed at an annual celebratory ball. In 1914, the king was replaced by a queen, a socialite chosen from Portland's elite. The tradition continued until 1930, when the city decided to let each of the area high schools choose a representative from their senior class to serve as a Rose Festival princess. One year later, the title came with a college scholarship. Nowadays, the princesses (sometimes called "ambassadors") are not chosen for their beauty and social status; instead, they must have a minimum grade-point average of 2.75 and demonstrate exemplary citizenship. As ambassadors for their schools and the city, they are evaluated for their character, communication skills, and presence.

during the festival and in the weeks before and after it. The Pride Glow Run, for instance, is a night race wherein participants are encouraged to adorn themselves with all manner of glow sticks and lights or, at the very least, wear something bright and outrageous. With mixers and parties and parades galore, the whole celebration is more fun than a barrel of sequins and a bottle of spray glue.

PORTLAND ROSE FESTIVAL

The big daddy event for Portland is the **Rose Festival** (Waterfront Park, www.rosefestival.org; $7, free for children under 7), held every year from the end of May through the first two weeks of June to celebrate the riches of the Pacific Northwest heritage and environment. It's all about bringing the city together, but also about extending a hand to communities across the world. The spectacular Grand Floral Parade, which is the centerpiece of the festival, is the second-largest floral parade in the nation and the biggest spectator event in the state of Oregon. But the festival has events that are worth checking out besides that. Kids are released from school early to march through the Hollywood District in the Junior Parade. After the sun goes down, the Starlight Parade, which winds through the streets of downtown, is always fun, and the party is always raging at Tom McCall Waterfront Park, with music, vaudeville acts, exhibits, acres of food, and Funtastic rides.

SAFEWAY WATERFRONT BLUES FESTIVAL

The **Safeway Waterfront Blues Festival** (Waterfront Park, www.waterfrontbluesfest.com; $10) is one of the largest blues festivals in the nation (second only to Chicago), attracting more than 120,000 blues lovers from all over the world. Fans show up to catch just a few of the 150 performances that happen on the festival's four stages in early July. Proceeds from the festival benefit the Oregon Food Bank, a nonprofit organization that provides food to low-income people in Oregon and southwest Washington. With such fantastic performances from such legends as Marcia Ball, Keb' Mo, and Isaac Hayes, the festival is able to raise around $500,000 and more than 80,000 pounds of food (by collecting donations of money and nonperishable foods at the gate). If the crowds are a bit much for you, consider taking one of the Blues Cruises on the Portland Spirit, which sails down the Willamette to Oregon City. On board, you'll be treated to live music and a no-host hors d'oeuvres buffet and full bar.

FALL
FASHIONXT

Portland has garnered quite a name for maintaining a high standard of ecofriendliness and creative design, and that attitude is creating a buzz in the fashion industry these days, too. In October, the annual **FASHIONxt** (pronounced "Fashion Next," citywide, http://fashionxt.net; $25-165) once again rolls out the runway. Designers from across the world unveil their upcoming spring and summer collections. For several years, FASHIONxt (formerly Portland Fashion Week) has been illuminating the Northwest style scene with a focus on lifestyle, technology, and innovation, and now, the world is paying attention—and not just to chuckle about a Northwest show that features only fleece and hiking boots. It's no wonder. It may have been laughable 10 years ago, but each year, more talented Portland designers emerge onto the scene. Portland-area designers have claimed the top prize on Lifetime's Project Runway four times and the winners and all-stars frequently showcase their work at this event. Attendees can choose from a variety of tickets ranging from a one-night soiree to a whole-week affair and from VIP seating to general admission.

H. P. LOVECRAFT FILM FESTIVAL

Twentieth century American author Howard Phillips (H. P.) Lovecraft has a name synonymous with blood-curdling screams, night terrors, and noisome monsters like "the green, sticky spawn of the stars." His stories dominated the literary scene with a new genre labeled "weird fiction," which encompassed horror, myth, and science fiction. In 1995, producer, author, and avid fan Andrew Migliore founded the H. P. Lovecraft Film Festival so that professional and amateur filmmakers could transport to the screen what Lovecraft had so brilliantly put on page. There's no better way to kick off the month of October than attending the **H. P. Lovecraft Film Festival** (Hollywood Theatre, 4122 NE Sandy Blvd., 503/281-4215, www.hplfilmfestival.com; $15-55), where goosebumps are a guarantee and horror is a form of art. The festival takes place at the historic Hollywood Theatre, lending a creep factor that is likely to make you believe that Cthulhu himself could crawl out of the balcony.

MUSICFEST NORTHWEST

What started as North by Northwest—a smaller, grungier version of Austin's annual South by Southwest Festival—has blossomed into a pretty exciting event. These days, the September festival, now called **MusicFest Northwest** (MFNW; citywide, www.musicfestnw.com; prices vary), is Portland's multiday extravaganza of rock music, and it brings in some pretty stellar acts from all over the nation. As interest begins to build around Portland as a music town, more and more big acts are adding their names to the roster, which gives fans a great opportunity to see them play in a more intimate setting. The festival also manages to give a platform to the lesser known, hardworking local musicians that keep Portland's music community feeling so alive. During the festival, acts perform on stages all across the city (like the Doug Fir, the Crystal Ballroom, and Mississippi Studios), giving attendees a glimpse of some of the best venues in town.

NORTHWEST FILMMAKERS' FESTIVAL

With so many eyes and cameras on the Northwest these days, it is not surprising that we need our own film festival just to behold a portion

Top: Oregon Brewers Festival. **Bottom:** aerial view of MusicFest Northwest.

of it. Since the 1970s, the **Northwest Filmmakers' Festival** (Whitsell Auditorium, 1219 SW Park Ave., www.nwfilm.org; prices vary) has presented feature-length, short, and documentary films showcasing Northwest talent. Typically, there are about 50 films shown over the course of a week in November, all of them made by artists from Alaska, Oregon, Washington, British Columbia, Montana, or Idaho. The festival is a showcase of what's on the minds of Northwest filmmakers, and an opportunity to seek inspiration and connections. The Northwest Film Center, which hosts the festival and is part of the Portland Art Museum, was established as a resource for media arts in the region. It offers a variety of film and video exhibitions in addition to education and information programs throughout the year and during the festival.

PICA'S T:BA FESTIVAL
Stimulate your senses all over the city at the Time-Based Art Festival (T:BA), an exploration of every form of contemporary art—including dance, music, new media, and visual. Unique to Portland, **Pica's T:BA Festival** (citywide, www.pica.org/tba; prices vary) provides a forum for contemporary as well as emerging artists from Portland and from around the world. With well over 100 workshops, installations, lectures, and performances, this 10-day festival in September is packed with opportunities to experience art as you have never seen it before. Since the festival happens all over the city, you can buy a pass that will allow you access to more than you can possibly see—or you can buy tickets to individual performances and events, available on the day of the show at the venues themselves.

PORTLAND LESBIAN & GAY FILM FESTIVAL
The **Portland Lesbian & Gay Film Festival** (Cinema 21, 616 NW 21st Ave., www.plgff.org; $10-100) has been around unofficially since the early 1990s, but officially began in 1997 when the first annual festival was launched. By the third year, things really started to take shape with sold-out screenings, world premieres, Oscar-winning features, and emotionally moving forums. Each year from late September to early October, the festival showcases feature, documentary, and short films from all over the world that are made by, about, or of interest to the LGBT community. Films are selected based on the quality of storytelling, uniqueness, and overall appeal. The festival now works through a partnership with Film Action Oregon.

REEL MUSIC
Reel Music (Whitsell Auditorium, 1219 SW Park Ave., www.nwfilm.org; $9 adults, $8 seniors and students), the Northwest Film Center's annual October celebration of music on film, is a cinematic love letter to music's most intriguing artists (both legendary and unknown). Not limited to any particular genre, the festival highlights jazz, rock, reggae, bluegrass, bossa nova, and indie rock. Featuring everything from vintage performance clips to new documentary and dramatic films, to cutting-edge music videos and

animation, it's an interesting way to explore the ways sounds and images play off each other to affect the human experience.

THE SWASHBUCKLER'S BALL

The **Swashbuckler's Ball** (Melody Ballroom, 615 SE Alder St., www.swash-bucklersball.com; $40) is an annual fundraising event in November that has come to be known as the "pirate prom." Pirates are a big thing in Portland, and while there are a number of events throughout the year that cause people to throw on a tricorn hat, this event is the biggest and most extravagant. Piratical bands come from all over the country to play for this event, which raises money for a different charitable organization each year. There are often two levels of entertainment to choose from, such as live bands and dancing in the main ballroom and burlesque shows and more intimate concerts in the cabaret lounge below.

WINTER

ANNUAL PORTLAND GOLF SHOW

Kicking off the annual Pacific Northwest golf season, the **Portland Golf Show** (Oregon Convention Center, 777 NE Martin Luther King Jr. Blvd., www.portlandgolfshow.com; $11 adults, $9 seniors, free for children under 12) gives enthusiasts a chance to get their swing into shape every February. You can try out the latest technology in clubs in the Green Demo Room, take the 50-foot putting challenge, get some free lessons from some of the area's top instructors, and shop the 5,000-square-foot clearance center, where you can replace all those balls you lost in a lake for a fraction of what you paid the first time. There's even a kiddie area where pint-sized golfers will receive a custom-made club and a mini lesson for free.

CHRISTMAS SHIP PARADE

The **Christmas Ship Parade** (citywide, www.christmasships.org; free) started back in 1954 when one guy with a sailboat decked the bow with lights and sailed the Willamette. Each year since then, the fleet has grown, and now it averages 55-60 boats between the Columbia and Willamette River fleets. The parade happens nightly for two weeks beginning in early December. The displays are elaborate and brightly lit, and can be seen from bank to bank on each river, which is a real treat for those dining, staying, or strolling riverside. Book well in advance if you want to witness this event from the warmth of a restaurant or hotel room. The skippers pay for their own fuel, decorations, and other expenses, so they welcome donations to keep the tradition going. The website provides a means for donations, plus gives an overview of hotels, restaurants, and viewing spots that offer a good vantage point.

FERTILE GROUND FESTIVAL

All right, so January in Portland isn't exactly a "showcase" month. Tourism is down, the skies are gray, and the weather is, at best, unpredictable. It's tempting to sulk about the house, but frankly, a whole month indoors is just not natural for most Portlanders. Thank goodness this city is full of creative folks who are not willing to give up on January. Thanks to them, the city suddenly has a reason get out of its collective pajamas and experience something truly original. In 2008, Portland launched its first citywide performing arts festival devoted entirely to new works. More than two years in the making, the **Fertile Ground Festival** (citywide, www.fertilegroundpdx.org; prices vary) is an ambitious 10-day event that unites more than a dozen performing arts groups to present a series of world premiere productions. Portland has always been a "fertile ground" for playwrights and premiere performances, so it's no surprise that so many companies are consistently able to develop their seasons around the idea of producing something new and groundbreaking during this event.

FESTIVAL OF LIGHTS AT THE GROTTO

For more than 20 years now, The Grotto, a 62-acre Catholic shrine and botanical garden, has hosted the **Festival of Lights** (8840 NE Skidmore St., 503/254-7371, www.thegrotto.org; $10 adults, $9 seniors, $5 children ages 3-12, free parking), which is open nightly from around Thanksgiving through December 30 (except for Christmas Day). The spectacle features 150 musical performances, more than 500,000 lights, petting zoos, puppet shows, carolers, family entertainment, and more. Local choirs perform at the Chapel of Mary, a remarkable cathedral constructed of rock quarried from a cliff; it's an awe-inspiring display of polished marble, magnificent statues, and beautiful murals, and the acoustics are said to rival some of Europe's finest cathedrals. During the festival, The Grotto is open nightly 5pm-9:30pm.

HOLIDAY ALE FESTIVAL

Who says you can't have a beer festival in December? The annual **Holiday Ale Festival** (Pioneer Courthouse Square, www.holidayale.com; $35) features some of the season's best craft beers (with names like Auld Nutcracker, Lumpa Coal, Ebenezer, and Sled Crasher). Held at Pioneer Courthouse Square, the event manages to get pretty heated, despite the chilly temperatures. A large, clear tent keeps patrons dry but allows views of the city. Beer lovers sample robust brews, listen to seasonal music, and warm themselves by the gas heaters that surround the city's enormous holiday tree. Admission includes a souvenir mug and 12 beer tickets. Don't miss the annual **Brewers Brunch** (tickets can be purchased on the website), where breakfast and local and imported beers not otherwise available at the festival are served.

PORTLAND INTERNATIONAL FILM FESTIVAL

Portland International Film Festival (PIFF; Whitsell Auditorium, 1219 SW Park Ave., www.nwfilm.org; prices vary) annually draws an audience of over 35,000, making it the biggest film event in Oregon. The festival

Top: Festival of Lights at The Grotto. **Bottom:** the Portland International Film Festival.

premieres over 100 international shorts and feature films to film-loving audiences each February and hosts visiting artists and talkback sessions throughout the one-week event. This is often a great place to catch foreign films that are creating an Oscar buzz, or check out Short Cuts, a program of experimental films presented by Cinema Project and the Northwest Film Center. In addition to films, there are also a number of parties and special events surrounding the festival, a full schedule of which can be found on the website.

PORTLAND JAZZ FESTIVAL

Held every February, the **Portland Jazz Festival** (citywide, www.pdxjazz. com, $15-130) showcases local talent, as well as widely known performers like Branford Marsalis, Esperanza Spalding, Bill Frisell, and Charlie Hunter. Spread out over various venues around the downtown area, the festival offers a unique look at both the future and history of jazz. It's not uncommon to see up-and-coming musicians take the stage with the legends who inspired them in the first place. Ticket prices for the headliners can run about $30-60, but there is something in it even for jazz fans on a budget. The festival always offers a number of free and low-priced music performances, jam sessions, films, lectures, and exhibits.

PORTLAND SEAFOOD & WINE FESTIVAL

While you are busy savoring all the bounties that the Northwest has to offer, you'll want to save some room for the **Portland Seafood & Wine Festival** (Oregon Convention Center, 777 NE Martin Luther King Jr. Blvd., www. pdxseafoodandwinefestival.com; $12 adults, $10 seniors and children, free for children under 5) in early February. Stop in at the Oregon Convention Center to taste some of the state's most savory seafood and most veritable vino, all while enjoying some local live music. Show up early and be one of the first 300 people through the door and you'll receive a commemorative wineglass to sip from all year long. Food prices range $2-15 and wine samplings start at $0.50.

PROVIDENCE FESTIVAL OF TREES

The **Providence Festival of Trees** (Oregon Convention Center, 777 NE Martin Luther King Jr. Blvd., www.providence.org/festivaloftrees; $6 adults, $5 seniors, $4 children, free for children under 3) is your opportunity to stroll through nearly 50 decorated trees on the last weekend of November, as well as wreaths and holiday vignettes created by the city's top designers, businesses, and volunteers. The festival lights up the season in style and raises funds to support critically needed health-care services at Providence Hospital. The public show features children's activities, including the adorable Teddy Bear Hospital and Santa's Workshop, live entertainment, model trains, gingerbread houses, and a holiday bookshop. Tickets can be purchased at the door, and there are often coupons on the festival website that will save you money at the gate.

If you are visiting Portland in December, and you happen to see a large gathering of people dressed like Santa, don't be alarmed. You are simply witness to one of the city's most mysterious and talked-about events: **Santacon** (citywide, www.portlandsantacon.com; free). Each December in Portland, revelers dress up as Santa and engage in a daylong pub crawl that takes them to several bars, a few parks, and the occasional stop for (relatively) innocent mischief. The event is so popular, it has spawned a number of copycat events. As such, the details of when and where the Santas meet is kept very much a secret until right before the event. Joining the crawl isn't hard if you do your research and make sure you are following the right event. While you are there, be sure to behave yourself in a manner befitting a true Portland Santa (don't be a jerk, bring cash, and above all, be nice to the city and your fellow Santas).

ZOOLIGHTS FESTIVAL

Every evening (except Christmas Eve and Christmas Day) from November 28 until December 28, the Oregon Zoo transforms into a holiday fairyland for its annual **ZooLights Festival** (Oregon Zoo, 4001 SW Canyon Rd., 503/226-1561, www.oregonzoo.org; $10 adults, $8.50 seniors, $7 children). It's a spectacular event for the entire family. Decorated with nearly a million lights, this winter wonderland is a more whimsical display than your traditional holiday light show, with swinging monkeys instead of snowmen, slithering snakes instead of nodding reindeer. Sip some cocoa from the Zoo Café or ride the special Christmas train, brightly decorated and aglow with lights, as it winds through the zoo.

Essentials

Getting There

AIR

Portland International Airport, which goes by the call sign PDX, is the number one airport in the state of Oregon. It has direct connections to major airport hubs throughout the United States, plus nonstop international flights to Canada, Japan, Mexico, and the Netherlands. While the airport does have service from some smaller airlines like JetBlue (www.jetblue.com) and Hawaiian Airlines (www.hawaiianair.com), PDX is a major hub for Alaska Airlines and Horizon Air (www.alaskaair.com), and serves as a maintenance facility for Horizon Air. The route between PDX and Seattle-Tacoma International Airport is considered the 19th busiest air route in the world, in terms of flights per week, thanks to a number of travelers who prefer to skip the sometimes slow I-5 crawl (otherwise known as "the slog").

PDX has won a number of awards for its accessibility, courtesy, security, and amenities. Most visitors are pleased with the number of shops, like Brookstone, Powell's Books, and Nike, where they can pick up last-minute supplies or gifts. Stores are not allowed to charge more than their off-site locations would charge, and as always in Oregon, everything is sales-tax free. There are great places to grab a bite to eat or a drink as well. Locals love to stop by Good Dog/Bad Dog, Gustav's Pub & Grill, Laurelwood Brewing Company, or Pizzacato, all of which are favorites in town as well.

Getting to and from the Airport

The pickup area for taxis, airport shuttles, parking shuttles, and towncars is located outside baggage claim in the center of the terminal's lower roadway. A few hotels offer complimentary shuttle service to and from the airport, but many are located prohibitively far from the center of the city. However, Portland's light rail system, MAX, picks up at the south end of the terminal, and you can ride straight into the heart of downtown for about $2.50 per person. There are plenty of cabs to hail if you prefer to take one in, but cabs are expensive in Portland and will run you about $30 and possibly as much as $70. A towncar service, like **Pacific Cascade** (888/869-6227, www.towncar.com), can be cheaper (about $35-60) if you arrange ahead of time. Just make sure you give them your flight number when you make the reservation so they can track any delays or cancellations.

Car Rental

All the major national car rental companies have outposts at PDX, so whatever your preference is, you can find it here. If you can wait until you get

---

Previous: a tour of the city in a pedicab; crossing the Hawthorne Bridge by bicycle.

into town, you can always set up an account with **Zipcar** (503/328-3539, www.zipcar.com) or **Car2go** (www.car2go.com). Both are popular services that stash cars all over the city for temporary usage. With Zipcar, you reserve the one nearest to you and return it to the same spot when you are done. With Car2go you are limited to Smart Fortwo cars, but you can park the car anywhere inside the Car2go home region (which is most of the city). With both companies, gas and insurance are included.

CAR

From Portland International Airport, head southwest on Airport Way to I-205 South and turn right onto the freeway. Follow I-205 to exit 21B to merge onto I-84 West and US 30 West to Portland.

If you are continuing to downtown Portland, take the I-5 exit on the left that leads to Salem and Beaverton, and keep right as you take the exit marked City Center. Follow the signs to merge onto the Morrison Bridge and into downtown Portland.

TRAIN

Portland's historic **Union Station** (800 NW 6th Ave., 503/273-4865, www.amtrak.com) is served by three Amtrak passenger trains, including three daily departures between Seattle and Portland as well as daily service to Vancouver, British Columbia. The *Amtrak Cascades* travels along the pretty countryside of the Pacific Northwest and British Columbia and offers reclining seats; laptop computer outlets; bicycle, ski, and snowboard racks; and regional food, local wine, and microbrews from the Bistro car.

Amtrak's *Coast Starlight* operates daily, connecting Los Angeles, San Francisco, Portland, and Seattle. This train has both a coach section (with optional at-seat meal service) and sleeping cars, as well as an Arcade Room with a selection of arcade-style video games.

Amtrak's *Empire Builder* takes you through the Lewis and Clark Wilderness, beginning in Portland and heading east to Chicago. Stops along the way include Spokane, Whitefish, Glacier National Park, Minot, Minneapolis, and Milwaukee.

BUS

The **Greyhound bus terminal** (550 NW 6th Ave., 503/243-2361, www.greyhound.com) is next to the Amtrak station at the edge of Old Town. Greyhound offers connecting services all over the United States for reasonable rates, and often combines with Amtrak to reach destinations otherwise unreachable by train. The station is one of many along the I-5 corridor that connects Bellingham, Seattle, Salem, Eugene, and much of California. There are also select affiliate routes that can get you just about anywhere in the United States.

Travelers can also take the Bolt Bus, a sort of young, hip brother of Greyhound that offers super low rates (sometimes less than $20) between Portland and such cities as Eugene, Bellingham and Seattle in Washington, and Vancouver, British Columbia.

Getting Around

Portland is often thought of as a very European city. People here like to walk, bike, and utilize the various systems of public transportation available. In fact, the city as a whole encourages it. Many venues along the MAX or streetcar lines offer discounts to patrons who show their TriMet ticket. Neighborhoods that are particularly bike-heavy (like Mississippi Avenue, Alberta Street, Belmont Street, and Hawthorne Street) are equipped with plenty of bike lanes and places to park and lock up your bike. Most Portland neighborhoods are extremely walkable and have wide, pedestrian-friendly sidewalks with easily recognizable, wheelchair-accessible crosswalks.

The public transportation system in Portland is known for being just about as easy to use and reliable as a system can get. It's a safe, dependable way to get around on the weekdays, but becomes a little more complicated on weekends and holidays as it all but stops running after 2am. So, if you are planning on staying out past last call, be prepared to take a cab or walk. For areas that are particularly congested when it comes to parking (like the Pearl District or NW 23rd), it is best to bike there or ditch your car in a **Smart Park** (www.portlandonline.com/smartpark) lot and use the MAX or streetcar.

PUBLIC TRANSPORTATION
TriMet Buses
Nearly all of the **TriMet buses** and some of the **C-TRAN buses** (a system that serves Vancouver, Battleground, Hazel Dell, Camas, and Washougal, Washington) congregate at the transit mall on 5th and 6th Avenues downtown. Buses stop every three to five blocks, with one bus stop location per block. Northbound buses travel along 6th Avenue and southbound buses travel along 5th Avenue. Each bus stop is assigned a Stop ID number, which will be posted on the bus stop sign or on the schedule in the stop's bus shelter. You can use **TriMet's Transit Tracker system** (503/238-7433) by entering the Stop ID number when you call or by texting it to 27299. The system will tell you exactly how long it will be before the next bus arrives.

MAX
Portland is particularly proud of its **Metro Area Express,** or **MAX,** system. TriMet and the city of Portland worked to integrate transportation

needs with land use planning to give the city a longer-term model for urban growth, energy resources, and environmental concerns. For this reason, MAX is a popular, affordable, and efficient way to get from place to place in the metro area. The Red Line runs about 25 miles from the Beaverton Transit Center to the Portland International Airport. The Blue Line begins at the Hatfield Government Center in Hillsboro and runs about 33 miles, well into Gresham. The Yellow Line, which is currently the shortest, runs about seven miles from the Portland Expo Center to SW 10th Avenue downtown. The Green Line, runs from Clackamas Town Center to Portland State University, and the Orange Line, which opened in September 2015, travels from Portland State through inner Southeast to Milwaukie.

The Streetcar

The **Portland Streetcar** (www.portlandstreetcar.org) is a little more lightweight than the MAX line but essentially serves the same purpose, which is to connect the various quadrants of town and encourage people to take public transportation instead of cars. Unlike MAX, the streetcar runs with the traffic and must obey signals, so it is obliged to cover shorter distances than its big brother. The streetcar (which arrives about every 12-15 minutes) runs from Legacy Emmanuel Hospital in NW Portland to SW Lowell and Bond at the South Waterfront District and the base of the OHSU Aerial Tram. The streetcar will not automatically stop at every stop, as the MAX does. To indicate your desire to stop, push the yellow strip or the stop button to let the operator know. The fare for the streetcar is the same as MAX or TriMet, and you can use your TriMet ticket or transfer as proof of payment. If you wish to purchase a ticket for the streetcar, you can do so at the fare box on board.

Portland Aerial Tram

The **Portland Aerial Tram** (www.portlandtram.org), a $57 million project that opened in February 2007, can accommodate up to 78 passengers on each of the Swiss-made silver cabins. When the weather is clear, the view is spectacular, offering a vista that includes Mount Hood, Mount St. Helens, the Willamette River, and the city's downtown skyline. The tram takes about three minutes to travel 3,300 feet up to Oregon Health and Sciences University (OHSU) at the top of Marquam Hill, a rise of 500 feet in elevation. OHSU footed much of the bill for the construction of the tram, which has served as a valuable link between the main campus on the hill and the new Center for Health & Healing at South Waterfront.

You must purchase a round-trip ticket to ride, which will cost you $4.50 (children under six and bicycles ride free). The ticket machine will not take dollar bills, but it will take quarters and credit or debit cards.

TAXIS
Broadway Cab and Radio Cab
Broadway Cab (503/227-1234, www.broadwaycab.com) and **Radio Cab**
(503/227-1212, www.radiocab.net) have been neck and neck for decades
in Portland, and very little has changed now except that Broadway (in the
iconic yellow cab) has added six Toyota hybrids to their fleet of more than
200 cars. It is part of their long-term goal to replace all their cars with vehicles that use sustainable or alternative fuels.

Radio Cab has been driving Portlanders around since 1946, and it is still
one of the most popular numbers dialed after last call. If you are planning
at least 24 hours in advance, you can book your trip online. Radio Cab (the
black and white tuxedo cabs) has a state-of-the-art system for dispatching,
so the response can be pretty quick. Ask your dispatcher for an estimate
when you call. As with all the cab companies in Portland, it is best to book
a taxi ahead if you are on a schedule.

Uber and Lyft
The use of these app-based ride hailing programs was fairly controver-
sial when it first was introduced to the city. For a while, city officials even
deemed it illegal because it could not be regulated in the same way that
commercial cabs could. Since then, trial agreements have been made, and
now you can hail a ride from your smartphone for prices that do occasionally give cabs a run for their money. Many locals like to use these programs
because the people driving are artists, performers, or just underemployed
locals looking to supplement their income.

PDX Pedicab
If you happen to be downtown or in the Pearl District, **PDX Pedicab**
(503/839-5174, www.pdxpedicab.com) may just be your best (and most fun)
way to get around. This bike-powered, rickshaw-style vehicle can transport
two or three people comfortably (they have canopies and lap blankets) and
quickly. You can hail one if you happen to see an empty one, or call dis-
patch to have one sent. They operate Monday-Friday 10am-midnight and
Friday-Saturday 10am-3am. The drivers are fun, knowledgeable, safe, and
oftentimes able to tell you a lot about the city. If you're feeling adventurous,
you can also book a pedicab tour of Old Town, where you will be given a
recorded audio history of the city's most scandalous section.

DRIVING
Driving in Portland can be a bit confusing at first, and it's simpler if you
look at a map before you drive so that you can navigate the many one-way
streets and sudden on-ramps to bridges and freeways. There is no need to

panic. For one thing, even if you get lost, you are still likely to be only a few minutes away from your destination, and if you accidentally land yourself on a bridge or freeway, it is still pretty simple to take the nearest exit and follow the signs back to where you were.

One notable frustration is that once you are in downtown Portland, it is nearly impossible (and often illegal) to make a left turn. To avoid the frustration of going too far and having to backtrack, turn right a few streets early and C-turn yourself back in the right direction.

If you are heading into Southeast Portland and have to pass through or near Ladd's Addition, here's hoping you packed a lunch, because you may be there for a while. This neighborhood is notoriously confusing, so again, consult a map before you drive. Seeing the grid of the area from overhead can make the crazy turns and broken-up streets more navigable.

BIKING AND WALKING

Portlanders love to bike and walk, which may come as a surprise considering the fickle weather in the Pacific Northwest. Even in the winter, cycling remains one of the top methods for locals to commute from place to place. For that reason, the streets (and drivers) tend to be respectful of cyclists and pedestrians.

Downtown, the blocks are approximately half the size of a normal city block, with public art, fountains, and parks scattered throughout the urban areas. In the Pearl District and Northwest, the streets are numbered in one direction (ascending order from the waterfront) and run alphabetically in the other direction using the names of famous Portland historical figures, like Couch, Davis, Everett, Flanders, and so on. Burnside Avenue divides Portland by the north and south, the Willamette River divides the city by the east and west.

Portland has arguably the nation's most progressive support system for bike transportation, thanks to the wide, clearly marked bike lanes on most major commuter routes, municipal bike racks, and access to most bridges. TriMet has created space for bikes to be taken on the MAX trains, and buses are equipped with bike racks on the front, which makes traveling long distances on a bike that much more feasible.

If you prefer to explore on foot, you can pick up a walking map at most downtown hotels, at the **Travel Portland Visitor Information Center** in Pioneer Courthouse Square (701 SW 6th Ave. at Morrison St., www.travelportland.com), and at **Powell's City of Books** (1005 W. Burnside St., www.powells.com). Cyclists will find the **Bicycle Transportation Alliance** (www.bta4bikes.org) and **Bike Portland** (www.bikeportland.org) to be good resources for bike routes, repair shops, and bike-related events.

Top: the Red Line MAX in downtown. Bottom: Even the animals travel by bike in Portland.

All of Portland's buses and MAX trains are equipped with lifts, ramps, and accessible seating. The seating near the entrances of both the bus and MAX is reserved as priority seating for seniors and people with disabilities. Both the MAX and the streetcar have a ramp that extends out for easier boarding, and the buses have either a boarding ramp or power lift. Seniors and passengers with disabilities may qualify for the "Honored Citizen" rate of $1 for a two-hour ticket.

Conduct and Customs

UMBRELLAS

The quickest way to mark yourself as a tourist is to pop open an umbrella when it rains. For native Portlanders, a hooded jacket is all you need to ride out the inconsistent weather. Given that the average rainfall in a year is about 36 inches, it may seem like madness not to rely on an umbrella, but there's method in it. For one thing, the rain is often accompanied by a good deal of wind, and an umbrella doesn't fare well in such circumstances. Also, the weather changes so often that you may only need protection from the rain for a few moments before a sun break passes through. Finally, when you have a cell phone in one hand, a latte in the other, and laptop bag on your shoulder, an umbrella just becomes cumbersome.

SHOPPING BAGS

As a means of keeping the city even more environmentally minded, city officials have banned the use of plastic shopping bags within city limits. The ban includes all grocery stores, retailers, and restaurants. Stores can still provide you with a recycled or reusable bag (usually for a fee), but the best thing to do is bring your own bag and consolidate purchases whenever possible. You can buy a reusable bag at all grocery stores, at **Powell's City of Books** (www.powells.com), and a number of other stores all over the city.

DRINKING SUSTAINABLY

Portlanders love their coffee. While a cup or two of Stumptown a day is not a bad thing, cups, lids, and coffee sleeves add up to a lot of trash—even if it is all made from recycled materials. So bring a travel mug with you and you'll end up fitting right in with the locals. What's more, some places give you a discount on your cup of joe if you bring your own container.

The same is true for bottled water. The tap water in the city comes from the Bull Run Reservoir, one of the purest drinking-water sources in the world. Go ahead and fill up your Nalgene or stainless-steel water bottle right from the tap. Cover your bottle with stickers and people will assume you have lived here all your life.

PUMPING GAS

Oregon and New Jersey are the only two states where self-serve gas is banned. You will not be allowed to pump your own gas, even if you have been doing it your whole life and you are in a hurry. If you try to do so, you could get smacked with a pretty hefty fine. The Oregon law has been amended to allow motorcyclists to pump their own gas, but an attendant must still be there to remove the nozzle and replace it when the fueling is finished.

STRIP CLUBS

Thanks to a liberal free-speech clause in the state constitution and several rulings by the state Supreme Court, Oregon strip clubs and other sex-oriented businesses are practically untouchable. Portland has more strip clubs per capita than anywhere else in the world (including Las Vegas), or at least it did until the tiny town of Springfield, Oregon, opened its seventh club—knocking Portland off the top seat. Inside the 50-plus Portland clubs, pretty much any kind of no-contact nude performance is allowed; with the sheer number of strip clubs in town, that means you can see a vast array of sizes, styles, ages, and shapes.

While in some cities, the industry is treated as something that gets whispered about, Portland tends to be rather unabashed and unapologetic about it. The clubs that are most popular are the ones that embrace the Portland ideal of self-expression and individuality. In these clubs, the dancers are not likely to look like models out of a gentlemen's magazine, but will instead be tattooed and pierced, and might be wearing tube socks instead of fishnets.

TIPPING

While always a hotly debated issue, tipping is customary in Portland. For services such as haircuts, manicures, pedicures, and massages, 15-20 percent is acceptable, or 25 percent if there were extra services or special attention given. Ten percent or less is appropriate if the services are poor.

Servers in Portland make minimum wage but pay taxes on their tips and must oftentimes share them at the end of the night with kitchen staff, busers, and dishwashers. About 20 percent is standard, or 15 percent if the service is underwhelming. Anything less than that can be construed as insulting, particularly if it is not accompanied by an explanation to the management or the server.

SMOKING
Smoke-Free in 2009

It was a big battle that finally ended on January 1, 2009, when all Portland bars and restaurants went smoke-free. Some places were relieved by the ban; others were angry and are still a bit sensitive about it. Some places saw it as an opportunity to expand, remodel, or make changes to accommodate both their smoking and nonsmoking customers. Until such accommodations can be made, it is not uncommon to see a gaggle of smokers huddled outside their favorite bar.

Where You Can Still Smoke

You can smoke 10 feet or more away from any building, which means most sidewalks, parks, and the waterfront are places where it is okay to light up. One notable exception, however, is Pioneer Courthouse Square. Smoking is not allowed on that entire block, and you will be asked to put it out or leave if you don't comply.

As far as bars go, there are still places that have smoke-friendly patios and decks, but they are likely to be crowded with displaced smokers. Several bars have expansive patios with outdoor heaters, fire pits, and covered seating. More than 50 restaurants and bars in the metro area have heated patios for smoking. If you want an updated list or details on the venues, check out the **Bar Fly** website (www.barflymag.com), which offers reviews and roundups of the bar scene.

CITY HOURS

While Portland might seem to be the antithesis of New York, the city isn't exactly sleeping when the sun goes down. If you intend to do some boutique shopping, you'll want to get it done early since most shops close around 6pm or 7pm. Shopping malls and department stores stay open only until 9pm, except during holidays, and most music stores and bookstores stay open until at least 10pm or 11pm. Bars and restaurants are usually bustling around this time, however, because Portlanders tend to be more interested in spending time together and sharing good food than they are with working. The prime dinner hour is 7-8pm, but for particularly popular places, it is not uncommon to see a line forming when the venue opens around 5pm. For most venues, things stay busy until about an hour before last call, particularly on the weekends. Around 2am, it's time to go home or head to an all-night diner like the **Doug Fir Lounge** (830 E. Burnside St., 503/231-9663, www.dougfirlounge.com) or **The Roxy** (1121 SW Stark St., 503/223-9160).

Travel Tips

TRAVELING WITH CHILDREN

Portland is a great city for children, and the locals tend to take their kids everywhere they go, from gallery openings to dinners at four-star restaurants. If you would like to take your child along on one of the many art walks in the city, skip First Thursday in the Pearl, which caters more to the over-21 crowd and focuses more on the appreciation of art than it does on frivolity. Instead, opt for Last Thursday on Alberta, where the art tends to spill out onto the street, along with tall-bike riders, performers, stilt walkers, and impromptu parades.

The city is also chock-full of things to do with children that won't bore parents out of their skulls—like the **Oregon Museum of Science and Industry** (www.omsi.edu), the **Oregon Zoo** (www.oregonzoo.org), and the **World Forestry Center** (www.worldforestrycenter.org), which is more fun than the name implies. While you are here, check out **Metro Parent** (www.metro-parent.com) for an updated calendar of family events and tips on what the hottest kid-friendly places are.

SENIOR TRAVELERS

Portland is becoming a particularly popular place for people to retire because it offers the excitement and variety of city life but still retains a sense of small-town charm and security. Seniors also enjoy Portland because the streets, parks, buses, and trains make the city very navigable, which in turn encourages a healthy, active lifestyle that places very little demand on the individual.

TriMet tickets are only $1 for those 65 or older (with proof of age); a two-week unlimited pass goes for $13.50. Many of the local theaters and movie houses offer discounted rates and midweek matinees for seniors.

GAY AND LESBIAN TRAVELERS

Portland has a vibrant and active lesbian/gay/bisexual/transgender (LGBT) community and, in fact, has one of the most active lesbian communities in the United States. *Just Out* (www.justout.com) is the city's free weekly newspaper devoted to the LGBT community, and it is a great resource for what's happening and where.

In mid-June, Portland celebrates the community with its annual Pride Festival, wherein people from all walks gather along the waterfront for food, drinks, entertainment, and one of the city's most colorful parades (second only to the Grand Floral Parade during the Rose Festival). All told, a number of festivals, arts organizations, and performance groups are particularly popular among the LGBT community. Along with Film Action Oregon, the Portland Lesbian & Gay Film Festival produces an annual showcase of feature, documentary, and short films that are made by, about, or for people in the LGBT community. Another big event, the annual **Red Dress Party** (www.reddresspdx.com), draws thousands of revelers (all of whom are required to wear a red dress) to party all night as a fundraiser for programs that support gay youth, as well as people living with HIV/AIDS and other serious diseases.

There is very little of Portland that is not gay-friendly, and while you won't find a nightlife scene that rivals that of New York or San Francisco, there are plenty of hot spots for lesbians and gay men, whether you prefer to dance all night or share a quiet, romantic meal. A good resource is the Gay Yellow Pages (www.pdxgayyellowpages.com), which catalogs gay-owned or gay-friendly restaurants, bars, businesses, and services.

TRAVELERS WITH DISABILITIES

Particularly in the former industrial areas, like Old Town and the Pearl District, Portland has not always been the most accessible city, but things are improving at a rapid pace. The TriMet system is very accessible, with seating, ramps, and lifts on all of the buses and MAX trains; braille signage at all MAX stations; and ticket machines with both audio and visual instructions. TriMet also has a special service called LIFT (503/802-8000), which offers prearranged public transportation service for people who are unable to use buses or MAX due to a disability or disabling health condition. The cost is comparable to that of the regular transit fares.

One way to know if a place is accessible before you go is to check Where's Lulu (www.whereslulu.com), a free online database where Portlanders can rate and review places based on their services and accessibility. If you want to know whether or not Bagdad Theater & Pub has wheelchair-friendly tables (they do), you can find out using the search engine. The website also filters for criteria such as whether nearby public transit options exist, whether braille signs are present, and whether aisles and hallways are wide and easy to pass through.

TRAVELING WITH PETS

Portland is a tremendously dog-friendly town. Many downtown hotels, like Hotel Monaco (www.www.monaco-portland.com) and Hotel Vintage Plaza (www.vintageplaza.com) have in-house pet-relations managers (dogs) and will accommodate your pet at no additional charge. Along with your regular accommodations, some will even provide food bowls, pet beds, water, treats, and toys for use during your stay, but you can go all out and book a pooch pampering package that includes massage and keepsake gifts.

Want to take your buddy out for a bite to eat? Portland has pet-friendly restaurants in spades. Lucky Labrador Brew Pub (915 SE Hawthorne Blvd., 503/236-3555, www.luckylab.com) is a P-Town favorite for beer drinkers who hate to leave their dog at home; so is the Tin Shed Garden Café (1438 NE Alberta St., 503/288-6966, www.tinshedgardencafe.com), where they'll not only welcome your dog, they'll serve him too. The special doggy menu includes (among other things) Kibbles-n-Bacon Bits, a blend of rice and free-range hamburger, for about $5. Or, if you are strolling through the Pearl District, you can stop by Cupcake Jones (307 NW 10th Ave., 503/222-4404, www.cupcakejones.net) and pick up a doggy cupcake. Pups (and cats!) love the sweet treats, made fresh daily by owners Lisa Watson and Peter Shanky using oats, nuts, and bananas.

Paws on PDX

Traveling with your pooch is easier than you think. Walk down the sidewalk of any Portland neighborhood and one thing is certain: Portlanders love their dogs. Dogs have been unofficially welcomed at restaurant patios and sidewalk cafés for years, but lately, some establishments are taking the needs of their canine customers very seriously.

Come summertime in the Park Blocks and the Pearl District, you will find welcoming bowls of water set near entryways and sidewalk cafés. Frequenters of the Saturday Portland Farmers Market and Portland State University dog owners also appreciate **Shemanski Fountain** (between SW Salmon and Main), a triangular sandstone structure that features three small drinking basins, placed low so that passing dogs can quench their thirst.

If you ask most dog owners about their favorite dog-friendly establishments, chances are, the **Lucky Labrador Brew Pub** (915 SE Hawthorne Blvd., 503/517-4352, www.luckylab.com) is at the top of the list. With three area locations, the Lucky Lab caters to dog owners' desires to enjoy a pint on the covered patio while spending time with their favorite pooch. Or, you can sip some coffee, wine, or beer at the café inside **Sniff Hotel** (1828 NW Raleigh St., 503/208-2366, www.sniffdoghotel.com), which offers free doggy day care five days a week during their happy hour.

Other restaurants, have special items on their menu like in-house baked cookies and cupcakes just for pooches. **Tin Shed Garden Café** (1438 NE Alberta, 503/288-6966, www.tinshedgardencafe.com) offers a special doggie menu with whimsical items made to order for your best friend.

When the dogs need to stretch their legs, there are plenty of parks for them to run and mingle with other dogs. Some of the most popular off-leash areas are in **Gabriel Park** (SW 45th and Vermont), **Normandale Park** (NE 57th and Halsey), and **Chimney Park** (9360 N. Columbia Blvd.). According to Portland Parks & Recreation, however, there are areas for off-leash playtime in 32 Portland parks.

When it's time to check in, numerous hotels will roll out the welcome mat for your four-legged friend. **Hotel deLuxe** (729 SW 15th Ave., 503/219-2094, www.hoteldeluxeportland.com) charges a small fee per day but stocks your room with food and water bowls, a pet bed, a squeaky toy, a bag of treats, and clean-up baggies. Upon check-in, you will also find a personalized note, addressed to your pooch, that outlines the hotel pet policy, offers up a list of things to do that are pet-friendly nearby, and best of all, includes a pet-focused room service menu.

Wherever you go, there are many options for bringing your pooch out to play, especially in the warmer months when many restaurants have open patios.

Dogs get special treatment at The Sentinel.

Whether you are looking for relaxation, refreshment, or sport, there are a number of places to please both the two-legged and four-legged Portlander. The elegant **Benson Hotel** (309 SW Broadway, 503/228-2000, www.bensonhotel. com) offers a roof overhead for dogs of any size for no extra fee. Call ahead to book, and make sure you advise them that you will be bringing your pet. Your dog will be accommodated with a foam pet bed, collapsible water dish, squeaky toy, and a rawhide chew bone upon arrival. At **The Sentinel** (614 SW 11th Ave., 503/224-1236, www.sentinelhotel.com), your pet will be greeted with a bed and goodie bag and you will even receive a comprehensive list of pet resources for things you might actually need while visiting, like groomers, dog walkers, veterinarians, and even some crazy-out-there things like pet acupuncturists and psychics.

Finally, the two hotels that probably get the most attention for being pet-friendly are **Hotel Vintage Plaza** (422 SW Broadway, 800/263-2305, www. vintageplaza.com) and **Hotel Monaco** (506 SW Washington St., 503/222-0001, www.monaco-portland.com), both Kimpton hotels. Dogs are treated like royalty to the extent you allow (and are willing to pay for). You will be greeted with complimentary amenities, such as treats, food bowls, water, a mat, a bed, and clean-up bags; you can also set up dog-walking service, pet massage, veterinary services, and grooming.

HOSPITALS AND PHARMACIES

Portland is home to **Oregon Health and Sciences University** (OHSU), which has been recognized several times over by *U.S. News and World Report* as one of the best hospitals in the world and is considered one of the top research and teaching facilities in the United States. OHSU is the place where Gleevec, an anti-cancer medication, was discovered and developed.

This is also the home of **Doernbecher Children's Hospital,** which provides the region's widest range of children's health-care services, serves as the primary center for OHSU pediatric programs, and boasts a kids-only emergency room with a specialized pediatric staff. OHSU and Doernbecher reside in Portland's west hills (affectionately known as Pill Hill) and are easily accessible by car, bus, or aerial tram.

Other notable hospitals in the area are **Legacy Health System** (www.legacyhealth.org) and **Providence** (www.providence.org), both of which have a number of hospitals and clinics around the Portland metro area.

If you have a pet emergency, there's no better place to take your pet than **DoveLewis** (www.dovelewis.org), a clinic that employs board-certified critical care specialists who provide emergency care, observation, and treatment. The clinic is fully equipped and staffed to provide state-of-the-art intensive care medicine around the clock.

You can pick up prescriptions at a number of grocery stores, such as **Safeway** (www.safeway.com) and **Fred Meyer** (www.fredmeyer.com), as well as at drugstores like **Rite Aid** (www.riteaid.com) and **Walgreens** (www.walgreens.com).

EMERGENCY SERVICES

In the case of an emergency, you can reach a dispatcher for police, fire and rescue, and paramedic services by dialing **911** from any phone. To reach the Portland Police Department's nonemergency line, call 503/823-3333.

CRIME AND HARASSMENT

Thanks to the number of walkable streets in Portland, it is relatively safe to be out, even at night, so long as you keep alert and stay in areas where people are congregating.

Of course, every city has crime, but for the most part Portland's rate is relatively low and seems to be centered in outer Northeast, Southeast, and North Portland (close to the airport and Vancouver, Washington). With the growth of neighborhoods like Mississippi Avenue and the area surrounding the Wonder Ballroom on NE Russell Street, crime has largely been pushed out by the bustling crowds.

In the heart of downtown and on a number of the well-trafficked streets, you will find a lot of homeless people, but they are generally nonconfrontational. If you feel you're in danger, call 911. If you find someone to be of

who are very good at dealing with public drunkenness, disorderly behavior, and aggressive street youth.

Information and Services

MAPS AND TOURIST INFORMATION

The best place to find maps and get information on what's happening in and around Portland is at the **Travel Portland Visitor Information Center** (701 SW 6th Ave. at Morrison St., 503/275-8355, www.travelportland.com) in the center of downtown at Pioneer Courthouse Square. In addition to having a comprehensive calendar of local events, the center offers brochures, maps, and itinerary-planning assistance.

COMMUNICATION AND MEDIA
Phones and Area Codes

All land lines in Portland should have either a 503 or 971 area code. You must use all 10 digits in order to place a call.

While the number of payphones in the city has dramatically decreased with the advent of the cell phone boom, there are still a few located in prominent public spots, like in shopping centers and on some street corners. The cost of making a local call is $0.50, and you can call any of the Portland metro area cities (Tigard, Tualatin, Beaverton, etc.) without paying long distance fees.

Internet Services

Thanks to the **Personal Telco Project's initiative** (www.personaltelco. net) to provide free Internet access to the city, virtually all of downtown Portland has free Wi-Fi access. You can check the Personal Telco page or **WiFi PDX** (www.wifipdx.com) to find where the hotspots are. Pioneer Courthouse Square is a great spot to pick up free access, and, if you don't mind sitting on a bench or the steps, there are a number of places where you can grab a seat. Another hotspot is in the South Park Blocks, where you can hunker down in the shade or grab a bench. You can always find access at one of the many local coffee shops and at some of the chain coffee stores.

Mail and Messenger Services

Most downtown hotels offer mail services, but if you need a post office, you can find branches **downtown** (1505 SW 6th Ave.), in the **Pearl District** (715 NW Hoyt St.), and in **Northeast Portland** (815 NE Schuyler St.), just to name a few.

If you need courier service, you have a number of options. **Magpie Messenger Collective** (www.magpiemessenger.com) can deliver anywhere in the greater Portland area for $5-40, depending on distance and

10 Great Wi-Fi Coffeehouses

- **Albina Press:** On the north side of town, Albina Press (4637 N. Albina Ave., 503/282-5214) is a popular spot to grab a cup of Stumptown Coffee. The café is always bustling with energy, but there are some cozy couches available if you can catch one. Albina is also pretty laptop-friendly, since they have an abundance of outlets.

- **Case Study Coffee:** There are three locations for Case Study around Portland. The downtown spot (802 SW 10th Ave., www.casestudycoffee.com) has comfortable workspaces and free Wi-Fi (although, you do have to use your email address to log in). The coffee is great here and the flavors are made in-house. Try the toasted hazelnut or the bourbon caramel.

- **Coffeehouse Northwest:** This quiet little place with the unassuming name (1951 W. Burnside St., 503/248-2133, www.coffeehousenorthwest.com) has some of the best coffee and hot chocolate around. There are a couple of larger tables for gathering, but mostly, the place is lined with small tables and outlets, perfect for plugging in and getting down to business.

- **Costello's Travel Caffe:** This European-style coffeehouse (2222 NE Broadway St., 503/287-0270, www.costellostravelcaffe.com) has the distinct feel of the sort of café and *konditorei* it is patterned after. There are a number of heavy wooden tables and chairs, and the space is pretty open and accommodating. The Caffe Umbira coffee is good, but the food is even better. Quiche, soups, sandwiches, and pastries are homemade and fresh. Their scones are some of the best in the city.

- **Courier Coffee:** This quiet little place (923 SW Oak St., 503/545-6444, www.couriercoffeeroasters.com) with its hand-drawn signs and menus has some of the best and most thoughtfully served coffee in town. It's a small place and seating is limited, but they have free Wi-Fi. There is usually music spinning from the record player at the bar and monthly rotating art.

- **Fresh Pot:** There are two Fresh Pots in town, but the Mississippi Avenue café (4001 N. Mississippi Ave., 503/284-8928, www.thefreshpot.com) holds some truly undeniable charm. It was the set of the 2007 film *Feast of Love,* which captured the coffee shop's welcoming vibe.

- **Red Square Cafe:** A legit Internet café, Red Square (4505 SE Belmont St., 503/51-5700, www.redsquarecafe.com) is popular among gamers. Bring your

urgency. **Rose City Delivery Service** (www.rosecitymessengersvc.com) is another great option. It is a family-owned local business that hires the highest number of women of any company of its kind. The employees are friendly, well informed, and prompt.

Newspapers and Periodicals

The Oregonian (www.oregonlive.com) is Portland's oldest daily newspaper and the largest paper in Oregon and the Pacific Northwest in terms of circulation. *The Oregonian* publishes a weekly Arts and Entertainment guide on Friday. It can be found on newsstands and the web.

Portland Monthly (www.portlandmonthlymag.com) is the city's

Sip a cappuccino while surfing the web at Stumptown Coffee.

laptop or use one of their six in-house computers while enjoying coffee, tea, soda, or beer. They also offer a full menu of bagels, sandwiches, and snacks.

- **Stumptown Coffee:** A number of venues call themselves Stumptown, and even more places serve this signature roast, but the downtown Stumptown Coffee Roasters (128 SW 3rd Ave., 503/295-6144, www.stumptowncoffee. com) is the perfect fit if you are someone who works best while a cacophony of noise surrounds you. There are a number of tables where you can sip some perfectly brewed Hairbender blend.

- **Townshend's Alberta Street Teahouse:** If coffee is not on the menu for you, but you still need to caffeinate and update your Facebook, head over to Townshend's (2223 NE Alberta St., 503/445-6699, www.townshendstea.com). The wall of tea is both pretty to look at and wonderfully fragrant, and the whole place is outfitted with comfortable couches and overstuffed chairs, as well as tables and chairs for more serious working.

- **Urban Grind:** There are two locations for Urban Grind. The Northeast Portland location (2214 NE Oregon St., 503/546-0649, www.urbangrindcoffee. com) is shockingly spacious, with ample seating and lots of natural light. It also has a separate kids' room accessible through a small door that has been painted like the trunk of a tree.

full-color, glossy magazine, which covers the arts, fashion, entertainment, and dining. It particularly caters to the mid- to upper-class demographic of the city. It is available on newsstands and online.

Portland Tribune (www.portlandtribune.com) is a free weekly publication published each Thursday and distributed in green boxes on street corners scattered around town. The paper is best known for its coverage of local high school, college, and professional sports teams as well as some splashy coverage of local interest stories and the performing arts.

Willamette Week (www.wweek.com) is a free alternative weekly that can be picked up in the blue boxes on street corners and in coffee shops, bars, and restaurants all over the city. The content in print is also accessible online, along with expanded blogs by the writers and editors of the publication. It features reports on local news, politics, and culture with music previews, performing arts reviews, and gallery write-ups. It has a strong liberal bent, with touches of sarcasm and sharp humor.

The *Portland Mercury* (www.portlandmercury.com) has many similarities to *Willamette Week* in terms of coverage, distribution, and political leanings. The *Mercury* tends to push the envelope a little further and occasionally adopts a sillier, more mocking tone than its sharp-tongued competitor. You can find the *Mercury* online and in white boxes that are oftentimes placed alongside the blue boxes of the *Willamette Week*.

Just Out (www.justout.com) is Portland's life and culture biweekly newspaper serving the LGBT community. It has a small web presence and distributes in a number of bars, restaurants, and coffeehouses, as well in as free distribution boxes all over the city. *Just Out* often has news stories and opinion pieces related to current events as they affect the demographic, as well as profiles of prominent Pacific Northwest people who are living within the LGBT community.

El Hispanic News (www.elhispanicnews.com) is the oldest Hispanic publication in the Pacific Northwest, providing national, international, and local news and opinions, along with its sister publication, *más,* which features local, national, and international talent, culture news, reviews, and events.

The *Skanner* (www.theskanner.com) is a newspaper that is published in Portland and Seattle for the African American community, focusing on news, entertainment, business, and sports. You can find a free copy of the newspaper at a number of newsstands and coffeehouses around town, or read it online. Similarly, the *Asian Reporter* (www.asianreporter.com) is a free weekly paper that includes international, regional, and local Asian news. It too is available for free from newsstands and street boxes, or you can go to the website to download a PDF copy.

Finally, *Exotic* (http://xmag.com) is a free, monthly, full-color glossy magazine. It focuses for the most part on sexual, musical, and pop culture subjects, and primarily serves Portland's booming sex industry. It contains occasionally explicit articles on local tattoo artists, exotic dancers, and sex workers; industry-related stories; and advertising that focuses on adult businesses, nightclubs, and music. *Exotic* is available at most strip clubs, some nightclubs, and a few select street boxes around town.

Radio and Television
TALK RADIO

Portlanders are big fans of National Public Radio's Oregon station, **OPB** (91.5 FM). One of the popular local shows is LiveWire!, a one-hour radio variety show recorded in front of a live audience that includes witty speakers, musical performances, and readings. It is essentially Oregon's version of Prairie Home Companion, and it airs weekly at 7pm.

For talk radio, there's locally owned **KBOO** (90.7 FM), a volunteer-powered, noncommercial, listener-sponsored, full-strength community radio that emphasizes cultural awareness and the arts. On the AM dial, there's **KEX** (1190 AM), a news radio station that airs a number of syndicated shows from the likes of Rush Limbaugh, Dr. Laura Schlessinger, Mike Huckabee, and Dave Ramsey. **KXL Radio** (750 AM) airs the syndicated shows of Bill O'Reilly, Michael Savage, Brian Berger, and Bob Brinker, as well as the locally produced, nationally syndicated show by talk host Lars Larson. **KPAM** (860 AM) is another popular talk radio program that has garnered awards for breaking news coverage, traffic reporting, sports, and overall excellence. KPAM has a decidedly conservative propensity and airs popular programs like that of Sean Hannity and local right-wing commentator Victoria Taft. Another noteworthy station is **KPOJ** (620 AM), which was the first Air America affiliate to be owned by Clear Channel Communications. It features non-Air America syndicated host Ed Schultz. Through Schultz, KPOJ was the first station to call its format "progressive talk," a tag that is often used to describe that particular type of liberal-leaning program. Finally, if you're looking for sports, turn to **KXTG** (95.5 FM), an all-sports radio station owned by Paul Allen, who also owns the Portland Trail Blazers.

MUSIC STATIONS

For classic rock, Portlanders turn to **KGON** (92.3 FM). For a mix of modern and classic rock, go to **KUFO** (101.1 FM), where you will find shock jocks on Wednesdays and head-banging music all day. For alternative rock, the favorite is **KNRK** (94.7 FM), which plays a lot of local musicians, in addition to indie rock and favorites from the 1990s. You can find top 40 hits on **KKRZ** (100.3) and on **The Buzz** (105.1 FM). You'll find acoustic rock, pop, blues, and folk on **KINK** (101.9 FM). There's soul, blues, and rap on **KXJM** (107.5), soft rock on **KKCW** (103.1 FM), and oldies on **KLTH** (106.7 FM). For country music, turn to **KUPL** (98.7 FM) and **KWJJ** (95.5 FM); for classical music, you can turn to **KQAC** (89.9 FM), as well as a number of the aforementioned talk radio stations.

TELEVISION STATIONS

- KATU 2 (ABC)
- KOIN 6 (CBS)
- KGW 8 (NBC)
- KOPB-TV 10 Oregon Public Broadcasting (PBS)
- KPTV 12 (FOX)
- KPXG 22 (ION)
- KRCW-TV 32 (The CW)
- KUNP-LP 47 (Univision)

Resources

Suggested Reading

HISTORY AND GENERAL INFORMATION

Barrett, Alexander. *This Is Portland: The City You've Heard You Should Like.*
Portland: Microcosm, 2013. Written by a Vermont transplant to the City of
Roses, This Is Portland is a commentary on getting to know the oddity that is
P-Town. The affectionately critical Barrett explains why you will find so many
bars with tater tots. He tells readers whether or not it really rains all the time
and explains what the deal is with all of the beer, beards, bikes, tattoos, strip
clubs, and yard chickens. Regarding the rain, he writes, "Portland is full of cool
people. Raincoats are not cool. How do cool people stay cool in the rain? They
get really wet, that's how."

Boehmer, Gabriel. *City of Readers: A Book Lover's Guide to Portland.* Portland:
Tall Grass Press, 2007. *City of Readers* is a "literary umbrella" that encompasses
all things loved and adored by Portland's literati, such as bookstores, libraries,
landmarks, lectures, authors, and titles. A self-proclaimed bookworm who got
married at Central Library in downtown Portland, Boehmer has compiled a
comprehensive directory of the city's bookstores and provides excellent chap-
ters on the authors and titles that have defined the city and the best places to
find solitude among many (in other words, great places to read). Borrowing its
title from the city's monolithic bookseller, Powell's City of Books, the guide
is a love letter to a city where book lovers can read with relish and share with
enthusiasm.

Granton, Shawn, and Nate Beaty. *The Zinester's Guide to Portland: A Low/No
Budget Guide to Visiting and Living in Portland, Oregon.* Portland: Microcosm,
2014. This locally produced biannual book targets anyone who is looking to
experience Portland on the cheap or discover those sometimes hidden gems
and hard-to-find happenings. It offers a glimpse into the city's history and
local lore, offering up a guide to low- to no-cost bars, bookstores, coffeehouses,
restaurants, record stores, video stores, thrift stores, performing arts spaces,
and more. Their way is not simply to tell you where you should go but why you
want to and give you the story behind the story whenever possible. The book
is illustrated with fantastic line drawings of P-Town landmarks as depicted by
the authors and some other notable local artists. The book is broken down by

Johns, Kenton, and Sellwood, and also includes a section that will help
the reader navigate the city's bus system and bike culture with aplomb.

Lansing, Jewel. *Portland: People, Politics, and Power, 1851-2001.* Corvallis:
Oregon State University Press, 2005. This ambitious work covers more
than 150 years of Portland's political and economical past, from the days
when the excessive logging of a new city in the Pacific Northwest earned
it the nickname Stumptown to the 21st century and the bustling, progressive city that we know today (but still occasionally call Stumptown).
Lansing served as an elected city auditor, so she knows all too well how
the city government works. Lansing's well-researched and lively book
gives an insightful account of the mayors of our past, from ambitious
Hugh O'Bryant, the city's first mayor, to the savvy and persuasive Vera
Katz. Lansing highlights the political, business, and cultural forces that
have shaped the city—once a hotbed of corruption and vice—into the
cultural metropolis we know today.

Shomler, Steven. *Portland Beer Stories.* Mount Pleasant: Arcadia Publishing, 2015. Portland is a haven for beer lovers, and the men and women
who have put the city and the state of Oregon on the map for making
some of the world's best beer have some interesting stories. Using his
intimate connection to the industry, Shomler takes readers behind the
scenes of the process with anecdotes about everything from how popular
breweries got started to the life of a beer delivery driver. Shomler is a
radio host and organizer for the Spring Beer and Wine Festival, who also
wrote a book that gets into the heads of some of Portland's smallest, most
popular businesses, the food carts. It is, not surprisingly, titled Portland
Food Cart Stories.

Stanford, Phil. *Portland Confidential: Sex, Crime, and Corruption in the
Rose City.* Portland: Westwinds Press, 2004. It's no secret that Portland
has a few skeletons in its historical closet, and this account of the city's
colorful past takes you right into the dark and mysterious heart of it all.
Written by former *Portland Tribune* columnist Phil Stanford, the book
shows us the Portland of bygone days when prostitution, gambling, and
drug running were de rigueur. By the 1950s, underworld kingpin James
"Big Jim" Elkins was ruling over the city's vice industry, and just happened to have most of the police force and the local political movers
and shakers on his payroll. Loaded with photographs and newspaper
clippings of the time, Stanford's book seeks to expose our dirtiest little
secrets and show its readers the landmarks that still stand where it all
went down.

Meloy, Colin. *Wildwood*. New York: Balzar + Bray, 2011. Decemberists front man Colin Meloy has long been known for his creative lyrics and storytelling songs. When Meloy set out to write a novel, he took those same skills and turned his eyes to dark passages of Portland's own Forest Park. He created a whole series of novels about the wonders found within those trees and the city of Portland plays a strong role in the books.

Palahniuk, Chuck. *Fugitives and Refugees: A Walk in Portland, Oregon.* New York: Crown Publishing, 2011. This book from the author of the best-selling novel *Fight Club* is part travelogue and part memoir as the author reveals some of the city's most interesting (and sometimes terribly unattractive) landmarks, historical moments, and bits of culture. Go behind the doors of sex clubs; learn about the annual rampage of Santas; find out where you can mingle with the dead; and discover the not-so-secret location of Palahniuk's tonsils.

Sampsell, Kevin. *Portland Noir.* New York: Akashic Noir, 2009. A series of short stories from some of the Pacific Northwest's most exceptional writers, *Portland Noir* takes the reader through the underbelly of the Rose City, with stops at the Shanghai Tunnels, Powell's City of Books, Pirate's Cove, Voodoo Doughnut, and many other all-too-familiar places for local readers. This book is a dirty, pretty depiction of the weird, wonderful world otherwise known as the City of Roses. With funny anecdotes of petty mischief, haunting tales of tragedy, and mysterious stories of violence, it's a deliciously dark read.

Vlautin, Willy. *Lean on Pete.* New York: Harper Perennial, 2010. This heartbreaking and beautiful novel from Portland musician and author Willy Vlautin is about a 15-year-old boy who lives and works at a run-down horse racing track in Portland. After he befriends a beat-up old horse named Lean on Pete, the story takes on the rich, mysterious, multilayered tone that made Vlautin such a popular writer and lyricist among his peers.

INFORMATION AND EVENTS

City of Portland
www.portlandonline.com
This is the official website for the city of Portland, with links to information on current city and state politics, top news stories, and visitor information. Here you will find maps, calendars, and facts about public transportation, city planning, and city services.

Eventful
www.eventful.com/portland
Eventful enables its community of users to discover, promote, share, and create events such as concerts, markets, store openings, political rallies, fundraisers, sporting events, readings, and more.

Geek Portland
www.geekportland.com
This up-to-date and reliable calendar has the dish on all geek-related events happening in and around Portland, from trivia nights to shows and from book signings to burlesque.

Oregon Beat
www.oregonbeat.com
Oregon Beat is a weekly calendar with links to exhibits, lectures, festivals, sporting events, tours, performing arts events, gallery showings, and special food and wine affairs.

PDX Pipeline
www.pdxpipeline.com
PDX Pipeline is a word-of-mouth-fueled website that has up-to-date listings for concerts, festivals, fundraisers, restaurant events, and gallery showings. It does regular promotions through social media and provides links to a number of the city's most popular venues.

Travel Portland
www.travelportland.org
Travel Portland is the city's official visitors association and has a comprehensive website with an events calendar, resources, special offers, historical accounts, and in-depth profiles on what makes the city great. You can also visit the association in person at **Pioneer Courthouse Square** (503/275-8355), where you can pick up the annual *Travel Portland* magazine, an insider's guide to the city.

NEWS

The Oregonian
www.oregonlive.com

Portland's oldest newspaper is online with extensive "real-time" news coverage and in-depth reports on sports, entertainment, and local culture.

Portland Mercury
www.portlandmercury.com

One of Portland's most popular weekly sources for the dish on news, music, art, theater, fashion, and food has an active web presence with the particular tongue-in-cheek style we have come to expect.

Portland Monthly
www.portlandmonthlymag.com

This monthly full-color glossy lifestyle magazine focuses on news and general interests. On the website, you can catch the first few paragraphs of the articles from the most current issue and find comprehensive listings on restaurants, theaters, shops, and galleries.

Portland Tribune
www.portlandtribune.com

The *Tribune* is best known for its coverage of issues local to Portland and the state of Oregon, as well as its extensive coverage of local high school, college, and professional sports teams, with concentration on the NBA, Pac-10, Big Sky Conference, and West Coast Conference.

Willamette Week
www.wweek.com

Much like the *Portland Mercury,* the *Willamette Week* provides savvy, sometimes sardonic coverage of local news, politics, and culture. The website provides extended coverage of the articles that appear in print and offers updated stories, reviews, listings, calendars, and classifieds.

HISTORY

Kicka** Oregon History
www.orhistory.com

This website is young, hip, and not at all afraid to be a bit brash in its telling of history. It posts regular podcasts and even has frequent events like history-based pub crawls, lectures, and film contests.

Lewis and Clark Trail
www.lewisandclarktrail.com

This comprehensive website details the historic trip that explorers Meriwether Lewis and William Clark made from Pennsylvania to the Pacific Ocean. You can read quotes from their journals about their first glimpse of Portland and see what remains of their stay in this area.

www.ohs.org

The Oregon Historical Society (which is also a museum) has studies on its website that offer insight into the history of Portland and the state of Oregon, like the Oregon History Project, which explores the history of the state through the perspectives of the people who helped shape it, and Timeweb, an interactive timeline that uses over 800 records from the society's archival collection to tell the story of Oregon.

Portland History

www.pdxhistory.com

Portland History is a scrapbook of the past, with vintage postcards and pictures of the city from the earliest days, when pioneers began to make their homes here. You can find pictures of Portland's streetcars of the 1870s, when they were powered by horse, and a number of hotels that were open at the turn of the 20th century that are still in operation today.

NOTEWORTHY BLOGS

Art Scatter

www.artscatter.com

This blog is an assemblage of articles, essays, and musings about art, storytelling, the performing arts, and life around Portland. The entries come from some of the most educated and innovative minds in the industry, and while it occasionally dips into sessions of navel-gazing, it is still quite a beautiful read.

Beervana

www.beervana.blogspot.com

Beervana (a mash-up of "beer" and "nirvana" and sometimes a nickname for Portland) is a blog devoted to all things beer in Portland and the entire state of Oregon. It's a good resource for information on breweries, bottles, and festivals in a state where beer is taken quite seriously.

Bike Portland

www.bikeportland.org

Bike Portland is an independent, daily news source for Portland's many bike enthusiasts. In addition to posting regular articles about new business, bike-related events, and thought-provoking ideas about a life on wheels, Bike Portland provides the most up-to-date bike-related news, including updates about the accidents that occasionally happen.

Culturephile

www.portlandmonthlymag.com/blogs/culturephile

Lisa Randon spent five years running the **Ultra PDX blog** (www.ultra-pdx.com), which showcased art, fashion, music, performance, visual arts, and dance; as the associate editor of *Portland Spaces* magazine, Randon has the pedigree to be called an expert in the field. In August 2009, she started Culturephile, which "chronicles the vibrant world of Portland arts, its movers and makers," and the site is already proving to be a very viable voice on the scene.

Dave Knows: Portland
www.portland.daveknows.org

A native Portlander and lover of beer, soccer, basketball, books, pinball, and other such things, Dave maintains a blog that is especially helpful for information on Portland sports (such as Timbers soccer and the Trail Blazers) and any festival that involves beer.

Extra MSG
www.extramsg.com

Nick Zukin of foodie favorite extramsg.com posts ultra-detailed reports about the meals he eats at the city's most popular diners, taquerías, *pho* joints, sandwich shops, and more. He is particularly known for highlighting those hole-in-the-wall places that have the kind of food people would swim through shark-infested waters to have.

Food Carts Portland
www.foodcartsportland.com

This blog is a virtual guidebook on where to find the best food carts and what to eat once you get there. The blog is easily navigated with categories by cuisine type and specific locations, and it provides frequently updated listings of carts with a map to guide you.

Geek in the City
www.geekinthecity.com

Self-proclaimed geek Aaron Duran rants about all things geeky, dweeby, nerdy, and cool, such as games, comics, movies, music, and pop culture. His website features a geek-centric calendar with links to comic book releases, movie premieres, game nights, and shows. Duran is a freelance writer and media producer who is a regular guest on various Portland radio programs.

Our PDX
www.ourpdx.com

This roundup-style blog acts as a conduit to many of the other great writers in town, with links to the reviews, inside stories, and insights that are helping shape the city. The bloggers read everything they can, click the mouse, pluck out the gems, and put them on their site, thereby saving you the trouble of culling through 100 blogs to find the good stuff. They also offer up their own opinions, insights, and pointers whenever possible.

www.pdxplate.com

This gastronomical adventure of a site is both knowledgeable and well traveled around this fair city. It was gutsy enough to compile a list of 100 things that are must-eats for Portland, and it regularly puts together useful lists on topics such as great late-night dining, recession-proof drinking, and eating local.

PDX Sucks

www.pdxsucks.com

This parody website is meant to call up the days when Portland was just a big small town, with "Rants from the Tree-Hugging, Birkenstock-Wearing, Dope-Smoking, Red-Headed Sustainable Stepchild of the Pacific Northwest." The site has regular podcasts with interesting Northwest people and write-ups about what's happening around town.

Portland Food and Drink

www.portlandfoodanddrink.com

This restaurant review site was born out of a frustration that many venues were receiving overly glowing and not entirely honest reviews. The site rates restaurants on a star system after visiting no fewer than three times. It also has a menu section, where you can view the menus of more than 100 restaurants and bars.

Silicon Florist

www.siliconflorist.com

This blog highlights the websites and startups in the Portland area that might otherwise be missed amid the mighty giants of the Silicon Forest (thus the references to flowers, not trees). Founder Rick Turoczy enthusiastically gives readers news and events straight out of the city's blossoming tech scene.

Urban Honking

www.urbanhonking.com

Urban Honking is a Portland-based hub of more than 80 active bloggers who post articles about everything from writing and visual art to music to movies. UrHo (as it is affectionately called) began as a web magazine and then exploded as its web presence and readership grew. The site now hosts an annual competition, The Ultimate Blogger, which is inspired by reality TV contests, wherein participants engage in challenges and then post the results in their individual blogs.

Nightlife Index

Hotels Index

Photo Credits

Title page photo: a rose in the International Test Garden in Washington Park © Travel Portland; page 2 (top left) © Jamie Francis/Travel Portland, (top right) © Jamie Francis/Travel Portland, (bottom) © Torsten Kjellstrand/Travel Portland; page 18 (top left) © Travel Oregon, (top right) © Bobkeenan | Dreamstime.com, (bottom) © Groovysoup | Dreamstime.com; page 19 © Tracy Fox/123rf.com; page 20 © Lan Su Chinese Garden; page 22 © David Reamer/Travel Portland; page 23 © Tracy Fox/123rf.com; page 24 © Oregon Zoo/Julie Cudahy; page 26 © Jamie Francis/Travel Portland; page 27 (top) © Torsten Kjellstrand/Travel Portland/permission granted by Georgia Gerber/Randy Hudson/www.georgiagerber.com, (bottom) © Debbie Orlean/123rf.com; page 28 © Leesniderphotoimages | Dreamstime.com; page 33 (top) © Jpldesigns | Dreamstime.com, (bottom) © Travel Portland; page 36 (top) © Jamie Francis/Travel Portland, (bottom) © Jamie Francis/Travel Portland; page 39 (top) © Jamie Francis/Travel Portland, (bottom) © Torsten Kjellstrand/Travel Portland; page 42 (top) © Jamie Francis/Travel Portland, (bottom) © Robert Crum/123rf.com; page 45 (top) © Jit Pin Lim/123rf.com, (bottom) © Travel Oregon; page 48 (top) © Travel Oregon, (bottom) © Jnevitt | Dreamstime.com; page 51 © Oregon Zoo/Michael Durham; page 52 (top) © Travel Portland, (bottom) © Jamie Francis/Travel Portland; page 54 (top) © Carly Diaz/Blue Star Doughnuts, (bottom) © Jamie Francis/Travel Portland; page 59 (top) © John Valls/ Imperial, (bottom) © Red Star Tavern; page 61 (top) © Travel Portland, (bottom) © Basil Childers/Mother's Bistro; page 64 (top) © Dina Avila/Blue Star Doughnuts, (bottom) © Torsten Kjellstrand/Travel Portland; page 67 © Salt and Straw; page 69 (top) © David Reamer/Travel Portland, (bottom) © Nader Khouri/Pazzo Ristorante; page 71 (top) © Torsten Kjellstrand/Travel Portland, (bottom) © Jamie Francis/Travel Portland; page 76 (top) © Cupcake Jones/Amy Vining Photography, (bottom) © Salt and Straw, page 93 © Jamie Francis/Travel Portland; page 95 (top) © Carly Diaz/ Travel Portland, (bottom) © Jamie Francis/Travel Portland; page 110 (top) © Travel Portland, (bottom) © Oliver7perez | Dreamstime.com; page 112 © Travel Portland; page 115 (top) © Travel Portland, (bottom) © Lincoln Barbour/Ground Kontrol; page 125 (top) © Travel Oregon, (bottom) © Torsten Kjellstrand/ Travel Portland; page 136 (top) © World Forestry Center, (bottom) © Tarina Westlund/Portland Cello Project; page 138 © OMSI; page 141 (top) © Tracy Fox/123rf.com, (bottom) © Appalachianviews | Dreamstime.com; page 143 (top) © Owen Carey/Artists Repertory Theater, (bottom) © Patrick Weisample/Portland Center Stage; page 147 © Rob Finch/Travel Portland; page 155 (top) © Jamie Francis/Travel Portland, (bottom) © Torsten Kjellstrand/Travel Portland); page 160 (top) © Travel Portland, (bottom) © Travel Oregon; page 162 © Bill Zingraf; page 168 © Travel Portland; page 173 (top) © Jit Pin Lim/123rf.com, (bottom) © Jit Pin Lim/123rf.com; page 181 (top) © Jamie Francis/Travel Portland, (bottom) © Jamie Francis/Travel Portland; page 182© Jamie Francis/Travel Portland; page 188 (top) © Hollyanna McCollom, (bottom) © Jamie Francis/Travel Portland; page 191 (top) © Torsten Kjellstrand/ Travel Portland, (bottom) © Travel Portland; page 194 (top) © Jamie Francis/ Travel Portland, (bottom) © Travel Portland; page 215 (top) © Rob Finch/Travel Portland, (bottom) © Travel Portland; page 217 (top) © Torsten Kjellstrand/ Travel Portland, (bottom) © Sentinel Hotel; page 218 © David Lewis Phelps/ Hotel Vintage Portland; page 223 (top) © Hollyanna McCollom, (bottom) © Travel Oregon; page 226 (top) © Hotel Vintage Portland, (bottom) © Sentinel Hotel; page 228 (top) © Travel Portland, (bottom) © Jeffery Freeman/Caravan;

Also Available

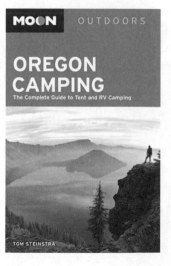

MAP SYMBOLS

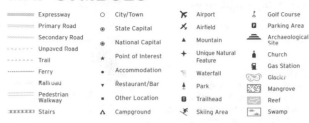

Expressway	○ City/Town	✈ Airport	⛳ Golf Course
Primary Road	◉ State Capital	✗ Airfield	🅿 Parking Area
Secondary Road	◉ National Capital	▲ Mountain	Archaeological Site
Unpaved Road	★ Point of Interest	✛ Unique Natural Feature	Church
Trail	• Accommodation		Gas Station
Ferry	▼ Restaurant/Bar	Waterfall	Glacier
Railroad	▼ Restaurant/Bar	♣ Park	Mangrove
Pedestrian Walkway	■ Other Location	Trailhead	Reef
Stairs	▲ Campground	Skiing Area	Swamp

CONVERSION TABLES

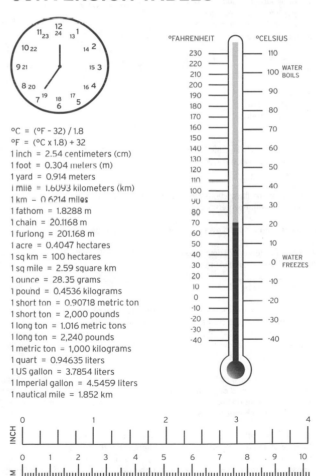

$°C = (°F - 32) / 1.8$

$°F = (°C \times 1.8) + 32$

1 inch = 2.54 centimeters (cm)
1 foot = 0.304 meters (m)
1 yard = 0.914 meters
1 mile = 1.6093 kilometers (km)
1 km = 0.6214 miles
1 fathom = 1.8288 m
1 chain = 20.1168 m
1 furlong = 201.168 m
1 acre = 0.4047 hectares
1 sq km = 100 hectares
1 sq mile = 2.59 square km
1 ounce = 28.35 grams
1 pound = 0.4536 kilograms
1 short ton = 0.90718 metric ton
1 short ton = 2,000 pounds
1 long ton = 1.016 metric tons
1 long ton = 2,240 pounds
1 metric ton = 1,000 kilograms
1 quart = 0.94635 liters
1 US gallon = 3.7854 liters
1 Imperial gallon = 4.5459 liters
1 nautical mile = 1.852 km

MOON PORTLAND
Avalon Travel
An imprint of Perseus Books
A Hachette Book Group company
1700 Fourth Street
Berkeley, CA 94710, USA
www.moon.com

Editor: Erin Raber
Series Manager: Erin Raber
Copy Editor: Ashley Benning
Graphics Coordinator: Elizabeth Jang
Production Coordinator: Elizabeth Jang
Cover Design: Faceout Studios, Charles Brock
Interior Design: Domini Dragoone
Moon Logo: Tim McGrath
Map Editor: Albert Angulo
Cartographer: Brian Shotwell
Proofreader: Rachel Feldman
Indexer: Greg Jewett

ISBN-13: 978-1-63121-278-9
ISSN: 2153-3741

Printing History
1st Edition — 2010
3rd Edition — April 2016
5 4 3 2